As Far As Ever the Puffin Flew

To Gordon + Your dear wife who I hope will stay with us at Emmsclave!!

As Far As Ever the Puffin Flew

Frank Petrie

With All Best Wishes
Frank Petrie

VANTAGE PRESS
New York

FIRST EDITION

Copyright © 1997 by Frank Petrie

Published by Vantage Press, Inc.
516 West 34th Street, New York, New York 10001

Manufactured in the United States of America
ISBN: 0-533-11922-7

Library of Congress Catalog Card No.: 96-90155

0 9 8 7 6 5 4 3 2 1

To my grandchildren,
Derek, Kate, Heather, Bruce, Brian, Craig,
Leanne, and Scott

Contents

Preface

When I grew up in Newfoundland, the only contact with the outside world for the majority of Newfoundlanders who lived in the numerous outports along Newfoundland's six thousand miles of rugged coastline was by boat. In contrast to travel by boat, people would watch with envy the ease with which the common puffin could flit over water and headland to distant bays. There was a saying that any traveller who visited such distant bays or places beyond had gone "as far as ever the puffin flew."

I went as far as ever the puffin flew. In over forty years in the public service of Canada, in the Secretariat of the General Agreement on Tariffs and Trade (GATT), as president of the Canadian Exporters Association, with International Trade Panels and Boards, and briefly with the Australian government, I traveled to some eighty or ninety countries. As interesting as my travels around the world were, of greater interest were my meetings with people who made things happen. Of equal interest were the trade and economic developments I became involved in at home and abroad as a direct participant or a close observer.

My work brought me into contact with many of the people who helped shape the world's postwar international trade and economic system. I also met many who knowingly or unknowingly stood in the way of the development of closer international economic relationships! Many of the players who had the greatest impact were relatively unknown to the general public. Others were names that were on almost every lip. Amongst the relatively unknown were people like Joe Maggio of Italy, Harry Reed of Rhodesia, Constant Shih of China, Jean Royer of France, Paul Luyten of the EEC, and Maurice Schwarzmann, Bob Latimer, and Rodney Grey of Canada. Amongst the well-known were people such as Premier Chou En-lai and Chairman Deng Xiaoping of China, the shah of Iran and his last ministry, President Mugabe of Zimbabwe and his first ministry, Fidel Castro of Cuba, General Stroessner of Paraguay, Kings Faiysal and Khalid of Saudi Arabia, Prime Minister Indira Gandhi of India, and President Marcos and his wife of the Philippines. Still others were very well known only in the international circles in which they worked, people such as Sir Eric Wyndham White (the first and most influential director general of GATT); Sheikh Yamani, the oil minister of Saudi Arabia (who was involved in the great rise in oil prices in the 1970s); Jake Warren of Canada (who was deputy minister, ambassador, high commissioner and chairman of GATT); and the many involved in Southern Africa's struggles for independence and against apartheid. My work also brought me into close contact with our own Canadian prime ministers, particularly Prime Ministers Pearson, Trudeau, and Clark. I got to know personally almost all of the ministers associated with economic and international affairs in the governments of the sixties, seventies, and eighties.

This account of the trade and economic events of the years since the fifties is not meant to be a trade and economic history of the period. It is rather a relatively minor player's recollections and thoughts on people and events that played a role in developing the global economy that is encompassing us today. Any number of my colleagues could write more authoritatively on many of the individuals and events mentioned. Some colleagues were in positions at home or abroad from which they were able to observe in depth the peoples and events that I gloss over. They must forgive me if my own recollections and views appear shallow and not as informed as their own.

One thing that I am certain of is that few of the well-known foreign characters whom I met and spent time with would, if they are still living, recall ever meeting me. I was but one of the hundreds of officials who crossed their paths during their time in international affairs. This record of my reflecting moments with them and my involvement in the matters that concerned them might serve to give some small insight into the trade and economic developments of our time. My hope is that those who are now involved in international trade and economic affairs will safeguard and build on the crude beginnings of international cooperation that our generation launched during the second half of the twentieth century.

As Far As Ever the Puffin Flew

Chapter One
Newfoundland Beginnings

In the early 1940s, a British Shakespearean actor performed in my hometown of Grand Falls in central Newfoundland. This complete stranger, unknowingly, had a tremendous influence on me. His influence was to help "chart my life's course," as they say in Newfoundland.

I don't remember his name. I didn't meet him or speak to him. I didn't even attend his performance. Like most of my teenage peers, I had little love for Shakespeare. I do remember hearing that many of those who did attend considered him to be the finest in the field. It amazed me that anyone could come to that conclusion. To the best of my knowledge, he was the only "outside" Shakespearean actor to perform in central Newfoundland. Anyway, it was not his ability as an actor or an orator that had any impact on me; it was his well-informed views about lands and peoples far from our island of Newfoundland that captivated me.

The Englishman's performance was on the stage of our town hall. It was one of the annual community concerts that were held in small towns throughout the Canadian maritime provinces and Newfoundland. My parents were very much involved, so it came as no surprise to me when they arrived home with the actor and a few local "patrons of the arts" for a small reception. I sat quietly in an adjoining room listening as the actor held forth on all things Shakespearean. It was far from my favourite subject matter, but my interest was suddenly aroused when he stated that one of the areas of the world where Shakespeare was best appreciated was in the distant native states of India. He was not referring to the British India we had learnt about in our history and geography books but to those British-protected states that were barely within the British sphere of influence. I was as surprised as my parents and their guests at the actor's claim! It was difficult for us to accept that these non-British, very foreign maharajas and their courts could have a great understanding of and love for Shakespeare!

As was usual in Newfoundland, the subject of conversation soon

1

turned to weather and climate. Everybody was asking where of all the places in the world the actor had travelled was the ideal climate in which to live. This was a natural question for anyone who had survived the long northern winters and so-called Newfoundland springs. The Englishman's response silenced everyone. It made a great impression on me! The actor ranged over several desirable areas, east, west, and, most of all, south of our world in Grand Falls. In the end he focused on two locations that he felt enjoyed the almost perfect climate and quality of life. Both were in Australia.

He described in detail the northeast coast of the state of New South Wales where it borders on the more tropical state of Queensland. Here, between the Pacific Ocean and Australia's Great Dividing Range, was an area sufficiently far from the muggy heat of Brisbane in the north and the Antarctic winds that sometimes invaded southern parts of eastern Australia. In this coastal or near-coastal region were a number of small towns where our actor had performed. Here, he claimed, was as perfect a climate as one could hope to find.

The second region he described was a relatively small area at the southwest tip of the state of Western Australia, not far from the beautiful state capital of Perth. To the east and north, the country changed radically to plains and then to desert, but in this small corner of Western Australia was also a climate and quality of life close to perfect.

I had from early childhood been very interested in Australia. I had read everything I could get my hands on relating to the country. I had studied our own encyclopedia and the encyclopedic accounts in our small Grand Falls library. I wrote to "pen pals" in Australia. I spoke to Newfoundland sailor friends in the Royal Navy who had been there. I was steeped in fact and fiction on the country. While the Englishman was talking about Western Australia, I recalled that the supposed landfall of Jonathan Swift's Gulliver in Lilliput was given as southwest of Van Dieman's Land, latitude 30 degrees 2 minutes south, not far from the area being described!

When the reception ended and the actor left, I was certain that I would someday visit the places he spoke about. Little did I realise then that I would spend years in Australia, and I would, as an official of both the Australian and Canadian governments and in the company of my Australian wife, visit the areas so enticingly described that winter evening so long ago in Newfoundland.

My journey to Australia would have to wait a decade or so. I had a lot of growing up to do. I realised that I had to do that right there in Newfoundland. I had no difficulty accepting this, for I loved Newfoundland and I believed then, as I do now, that it was a great place for a young boy in the 1940s. Any boy attracted to the outdoor life of woods, pond, and stream had to enjoy Newfoundland.

One-third of the area inside the coastline of Newfoundland is fresh water, so we had the best of trout and salmon fishing. Grand Falls is surrounded by thousands of square miles of wilderness, so we had the uncluttered environment for a wonderful outdoor life. I spent many days and nights, summer and winter, up in the woods with my father, grandfather, and school friends. We built cabins, set rabbit snares along miles of trails, fished through the ice in winter and in the countless ponds and streams in the spring and summer. We went moose hunting in the fall.

I had four school friends who, from kindergarten days, shared my love for the outdoors. Fred Morgan, Vince Eveleigh, John Mercer, Wilbert Budgell, and I spent most weekends in the woods during our high school years. We usually went on Friday after school, returning home at church time on Sunday. At the age of thirteen or fourteen, we built a cabin on an island. The island was in a stream behind our local "mountain," Redcliff, about five miles from town. When you left the town you were already in the woods, for there were no farms or other evidence of civilisation until you reached the small village of Badger some twenty miles away. We dragged a sled or harnessed Fred's dog in the winter. In summer or fall we rode our bicycles or walked.

We cut and barked the logs for our cabin. These we interlocked, so we had no need for nails. We gathered moss that we stuffed between the logs. We lugged in a tarpaulin to cover our roof. With the warmth provided by our pot-bellied stove we were snug in any weather. We had many wonderful nights "away from it all." We caught and cooked trout and rabbits and worked like beavers on our "crown-owned" property. While most fishing was done in the orthodox way with rod and line, I do remember the five of us stretched out on our stomachs and shooting trout with .22 rifles as they made their way from our stream to a pond. The trout had to cross a very shallow stretch of flowing water and in doing so exposed their fins and backs for about twenty feet of the stream. I believe it must have been the concussion from the bullets that brought us success because rarely did we see any wound where we actually hit them.

We feared little in the woods. Newfoundland had to be amongst the safest areas as far as confrontation with wildlife was concerned. There were

3

no wolves, snakes, porcupines, skunks, or other such bothersome creatures. We did have many bears and we were leery of them. While we saw many signs and sometimes sighted bears in the distance, we never had unfriendly encounters. The only thing that really sent chills running up and down our spines were "the French drums." At night we would fall asleep listening to the wind in the high conifers that surrounded our cabin. This sound we knew as "the French drums." I guess the centuries of wars between the French and English, which had a particularly bad impact on Newfoundland settlers, left a lasting, unrealistic fear in Newfoundlanders of French attack after such threats had long gone.

Newfoundland had a long and cruel history of settlement. It was long in that it was one of the first parts of North America frequented by Europeans. They exploited Newfoundland's rich fishing grounds for over five hundred years. It was cruel because it was not until the early 1800s that settlement was legally permitted. Every possible action was taken by the "mother" country to discourage settlement. Those who did settle stayed hidden in the many bays and coves that are found along Newfoundland's ten thousand kilometres, or six thousand miles, of coastline. Even today you can round a headland in any of Newfoundland's great bays and find a small "outport" hidden from the outside world.

The Viking sites on Newfoundland's northern tip give proof to early European discovery and temporary settlement over a thousand years ago. It was not until John Cabot, sailing out of Bristol, "discovered" Newfoundland in 1497 that a continuing link developed between the island and Western Europe. Just thirty years after Cabot's visit, a Capt. John Rut entered the harbour of St. John's on August 3, 1527. He found "eleven sail of Norman, Breton, and Portuguese barks all a fishing." This would suggest that non-English fishermen had been frequenting Newfoundland waters before Cabot's "discovery."

Some fifty years later, Sir Humphry Gilbert, half brother of Sir Walter Raleigh, was given the first charter for colonisation in the New World by Queen Elizabeth. He laid the cornerstone for the British Empire when he took possession of Newfoundland for England in 1583. On arrival in St. John's harbour on August 5, he found thirty-four vessels engaged in fishing and only half of them English. The rest were from France, Portugal, and Spain.

By the end of the 1500s, unorganised and unrecognised English-speaking settlers were living permanently in coves along Newfoundland's east

4

coast. They were mostly from Devon, Dorset, Somerset, and Cornwall. Until 1610, the island was a kind of no-man's-land ruled only in a rough way by men from southwest England.

For the next hundred years, the captain of the first English vessel to reach a harbour at the beginning of the summer was to be "the Admiral" of the harbour with supreme authority for the fishing season. With few exceptions, these men were disastrous for the local inhabitants. They were first and foremost in the employ of the fish merchants of the west of England. These merchants were those most opposed to settlement on the island. English mercantilism regarded Newfoundland, not as a colony or a plantation, but as a base for mother country enterprise.

To support this situation the English authorities introduced the infamous Star Chamber Laws, which made life a misery for would-be settlers. Amongst a host of restrictive measures, these laws required that fishermen must live at least seven miles from the shore where they made their living. At the same time, the Royal Navy was determined to maintain the fishing fleet in Newfoundland as a training ground for seamen. Settlement would diminish the numbers immediately available to the navy in time of war. The result was illegal, hidden settlement, which brought isolation and untold hardship. It did, however, preserve Elizabethan English in many parts of Newfoundland that sets much of Newfoundland's speech apart from all other on the mainland of North America.

Newfoundland settlers had not only to contend with an unfriendly mother country, they were continually harassed by the French. From their garrisoned base at Placentia, on Newfoundland's southeast coast, the French made repeated raids on the undefended English settlements. St. John's was destroyed in 1696 and again in 1697. On one occasion the French captured all of the known English settlements, except for a small island off the village of Carbonear where the villagers took refuge. On another occasion, at St. John's, the male inhabitants and defenders were slaughtered by Indians allied with the French, and the women and children were put aboard English fishing vessels and sent off to England. Pierre D'Iberville, who is a hero in French-speaking parts of Canada, was considered a villain in Newfoundland; at Petty Harbour, he and his men killed thirty-six settlers. There is much in Canadian history books about the expulsion of the Acadians by the British, but little is said of the terrible treatment of Newfoundland settlers at the hands of the French.

I was born in Corner Brook, on Newfoundland's west coast, on

December 9, 1929. I was the first of the family to be born in a hospital; my mother had been a nurse at Corner Brook Hospital and had insisted on it. My father and grandfather Petrie were born at Petrie's Point, just a few miles down the Bay of Islands from Corner Brook. Petrie's Point, Petrie's Crossing, and the village of Petrie's were all named after my great-grand-father, who settled on the best point of land in the bay in the mid-1800s. He came to Newfoundland from Sligo, Ireland, by way of the Bay de Chaleur in New Brunswick. My great-grandfather was in the herring and lumber business and I understand did well until several ships were lost without insurance.

I did a little research on the Petrie family in the summer of 1970 when returning from a posting in Switzerland. My wife, Peggy, and I, with our four children, made a brief visit to Dublin, Ireland. I took the two oldest children, Janine and Chris, to Sligo by train, while Peggy remained in Dublin with Julie and Jennifer.

Sligo is a beautiful county, but our stay was so short that we were only able to do a quick walking tour of the town of Sligo while seeking information on the family. People referred us to several villages in the county where there were Petries but told us there were no longer Petries in the town. We were advised to search the cemetery around the local Presby-terian church. We searched in vain but did locate an overgrown and collapsing Petrie grave site in a cemetery a mile or so from the town. While we were not sure that these were graves of direct family, the dates and Christian names indicated such.

There must be many grave sites throughout the surrounding country-side, since the Petries, who were of Scottish origin, were in the area for some two hundred years. The first Irish Petrie in the Sligo area had migrated in the 1700s from Scotland (Aberdeen and Kincardine) and settled on the borders of Mayo and Sligo near the mouth of the river Moy. Family history has it that after the Petries were well established, a terrible tragedy took place during a family picnic on Sligo Bay, when many people drowned.

My great-grandfather chose well when he settled on Petrie's Point. It was one of the most beautiful spots in the lovely Bay of Islands. A picture of some of his land appears on a 1923 Newfoundland postage stamp. The point, for many years, accommodated the golf course for the town of Corner Brook. Nine fairways meandered through huge oak trees that had been brought from Ireland and planted by my great-grandfather. It was a terrible disappointment for me when my grandfather and his brother Jack sold the property for the construction of a fish plant. It was later resold to house oil tanks. The result was the complete destruction of the oaks and the golf course and the downgrading of a most beautiful area to an oil depot.

My grandmother Petrie was a Soper, of English descent. Her father had been lighthouse keeper at Cape Saint Francis on the northern tip of the Avalon peninsula. My mother's family, Harris, was from the south coast around Burgeo, where the names Guy and Rose also featured in the family. My grandfather Harris, who lived in Port aux Basques, was a carpenter-fisherman. He must have been a good carpenter, for in his younger days he did fine carpentry on the cable-laying steamships as they laid their cables on the floor of the Atlantic between Newfoundland and Britain.

While Corner Brook was my place of birth, Grand Falls was really my hometown. Both were "pulp and paper" towns and, as such, were new towns. They were the first major departures in Newfoundland from the traditional way of life in the fisheries. Both were modern towns, built for the sole purpose of supplying newsprint to Britain's newspaper publishers. Corner Brook quickly became more diversified industrially and eventually grew to become Newfoundland's second city. Grand Falls, in my day, was strictly a one-industry town and has pretty well remained such.

In Grand Falls, the Anglo Newfoundland Development Company owned and operated the mill and the town. A company train delivered paper on a company-owned line to the company-built port of Botwood. Here it was placed aboard company-owned ships for export. Grand Falls was well planned and well run, by the company! There were few complaints from the residents, since all properties were granted on a ninety-nine-year lease, with only a token rent imposed of two cents a year. These payments had to be made and receipts given to ensure that nobody could clam squatters' rights.

Virtually all of the government-owned (or "Crown") land around Grand Falls and well beyond was leased to the company for cutting pulpwood. This provided good employment for fishermen off-season. The wood was pulled along winter roads and piled on river banks for feeding into the rivers in the spring when the thawing waters would rush the logs to the mill at Grand Falls. There was no reforestation. The regrowth of cutover areas was left to nature.

Life in Grand Falls in those days had many positive aspects. The company paved the streets, built many of the public buildings, supported and subsidised the formation of sport and social clubs. They encouraged the formation of very successful drama and glee clubs. In the years between the two world wars, Grand Falls probably had more performing singers and actors per capita than any town of its size on the mainland. Gordon Pinsent (whose brother Haig was in my class at school) wasn't the only good actor to come out of Grand Falls!

There were, however, negative aspects. It was most disturbing for me that Newfoundlanders not of the main British stream, such as Chinese, Jews, and Syrians (which was the word used for all people from the Arab Middle East), were not permitted residency in the town. These people had to live "across the tracks" outside the company's jurisdiction. Since they were often the entrepreneurs of the population, the impetus was provided for the growth of the town of Windsor. Windsor quickly outpaced Grand Falls as a commercial centre.

It was difficult at the time to question this blatant discrimination. Unfortunately, it was very widely accepted that this was the way things were. My parents had very strong views on the subject. My mother told me that the discrimination was in line with the views of the people who ran the company, such as Lord Rothemere, who controlled the company's policies on such matters. My mother, an avid reader, claimed that she had read that Lord Rothemere had some very fascist views. Indeed there were many in Britain who would have agreed with her. My father went out of his way to include in his circle of friends people who were forced to live and work across the tracks. I knew that he always enjoyed being with them because he shared their views as entrepreneurs.

In retrospect, I suppose that the company's discriminatory attitude was little different from the attitudes common at the time throughout the English-speaking world and Europe. The European was on a pedestal, high above all others. This was not only the case in Rothemere's Britain, but in Australia, with its White Australia policy; in South Africa, with its apartheid (although it was not yet official); and in the United States, where all men were created equal but certainly not treated so. Even in our own Newfoundland, while Chinese men were admitted as immigrants in very small numbers, their wives were not!

Despite all its shortcomings, life in Grand Falls, in both summer and winter, was a joy for me. Christmas during high school and university years was exactly what Christmas cards portrayed: sleigh rides, carol singing, skating for miles on well-frozen ponds, sliding, and good times with family, neighbours, and friends.

The long summer evenings were times for playing or watching baseball. This was very popular in the 1930s and 1940s in Newfoundland. My father was a star player. One of my first recollections was when I was five or so and my father was playing one of his last games. He hit the winning home run in an important championship game and carried me from the field on his shoulders, allowing me to share the applause he received from the admiring crowd for driving in the winner.

About eight miles west of Grand Falls was a beautiful stream called Leech's Brook. Up the stream were some of our favourite swimming holes. We seldom stopped at the first pool, preferring to climb farther up the brook to where there were a series of falls. Below each of these, the falling water had created wonderful swimming spots. The best of all was the last of the falls, which plunged into what we knew as "the bathtub." The perpetually falling water had worn the rock below into the shape of a smooth bathtub in which you could recline and be showered by water so clean you could drink it as you bathed. Many years later I took my children to experience the bathtub. They enjoyed it as much as I had as a child. A devastating forest fire raged through the area in the 1980s, and since then I could never bring myself to return to this favourite childhood haunt.

With relatively few cars in Grand Falls in the 1940s, everybody walked, and on a summer's evening the roads would be crowded. You knew everybody and they all greeted you. A favourite walk was the mile or two road to the railway station (now Windsor) to meet the train when it stopped on its 550-mile struggle from St. John's to Port aux Basques and return. It was not only the exercise and social contact that prompted people to walk to the station. The Overland Limited, as we knew it, or the "Bullet," as the mainlanders and Americans mockingly referred to it, delivered the weekly liquor supply to central Newfoundland. Since there was no liquor store, people would order their two bottles (restricted to two by the government) from St. John's, and the order would arrive by train. It had to be personally picked up by the customer. Little wonder an outsider once remarked to me, after witnessing from the train the crowd at the station that surely here must be a city of fifty thousand! In fact the population was around seven thousand.

It was rum that generally made the trip by train; a Newfoundland-bottled dark Demmerara rum that everyone called "screech." It sold for about two dollars a bottle. When the American troops were in Newfoundland during the Second World War, they used to refer to it as "block and tackle," in that, "you took a drink, walked a block, and tackled the first person you

9

met." It was said that screech originated when Newfoundland schooners delivered salt cod to the British West Indies and British Guiana and brought back barrelled rum. The rum was required to be delivered to the Board of Liquor Control. The board management would look around their warehouse, and if there was other liquor, such as gin or sherry that was not moving, they would add it to the rum. The result would make you "screech." Word went around if there was a good batch, and it disappeared quickly. If a batch was considered inferior, it was left for the mainlanders and the Americans to clear out the stock.

It was not just the liquor delivery that made the train such an important part of life. The train was really our lifeline. It was the only way for us to get to any major centre east or west, for our road system only ran about twenty miles in either direction. Everybody poked fun at the train, but everybody seemed to love it. It was narrow gauge, notoriously slow, and always off-schedule. My father travelled frequently to Corner Brook and St. John's. He would ask "Central," the local telephone operator, to phone him when the train was in Badger (eighteen miles west) if he was travelling east, or when it was in Bishop's Falls (ten miles east) if he was travelling west. Central never failed to stir anyone going on a trip and consequently was the recipient of many boxes at Christmas!

One Christmas holiday, when I was about fifteen, I took the train to Corner Brook to visit with friends. On the way back, we ran into a snow storm that only those who have experienced a real northern winter could visualise. The struggling train charged through snow drifts, sometimes taking several runs before breaking through. Finally, just east of Kitty's Brook, it came to a standstill. We were in a "cut" where the snow on both sides towered above the train. We were at the western approaches to the Topsails, which were mountainous barrens between Corner Brook and Grand Falls. We settled in for what was to be a three-day wait, until the storm abated and the snow ploughs got through from the eastern side.

Everybody seemed to accept the situation without fuss. We entertained ourselves as best we could with cards, singing, reading, and dozing. Some of us who carried skates got off the train and chopped steps up the bank of the cut and went skating on windswept ponds. This really amused a group of British sailors who were on the train. There were two passenger cars filled with them. They were being transferred from a ship in Corner Brook to one in St. John's. They would beg us for our skates and, to the amusement of all, would waddle around in their mostly vain attempts to master the art of skating.

For the first day it was meals as usual in the dining car, but after that, food was rationed and served free of charge. The train crew established contact with the outside world by tapping the telephone line that ran along the railway. My father took advantage of this contact to get in touch with the conductor. He asked him to give me five dollars if I was short of money, saying he would repay him when the train arrived in Grand Falls. The conductor approached me and asked if my name was Petrie and whether I was in need of money. I needed money, but pride dictated that I decline this offer from a complete stranger. So I went hungry until the train went on free rations.

When the ploughs finally got through to us and cleared our way over the Topsails, we continued our journey to Grand Falls. My grandfather was at the station to meet me. He may have been glad to see me, but he certainly didn't show it! He just lectured me on the foolhardiness of crossing the Topsails in the dead of winter without my snowshoes. He said that with snowshoes, I could have walked back the several miles to Kitty's Brook rather than sit for three days on a train "in the middle of nowhere."

My mind was continuously on travel to far-away places. The only place that I knew that had regular contact with the outside world was our little seaport of Botwood. The newsprint from Grand Falls and the lead and zinc from the mine in Buchans were exported around the world from Botwood. Even in those early days I realised the importance of exports because everybody I knew depended on exports for their living.

I liked to go to Botwood and watch the ships with their foreign crews loading newsprint and minerals and unloading sulphur and equipment for the Grand Falls mill. I often got aboard the ships with my father and his friend Jack Arklie. Jack held a senior position with the paper company's shipping department. I used to haunt him from a very early age to get me a job on one of the company's boats. He always found very logical and legitimate reasons why I couldn't be taken on, without ever mentioning my tender age.

My family kept a summer place near Botwood, at Northern Arm. The first place I remember was at Evans Point. This was a beautiful pebbled and sandy point jutting out into the bay several miles across the water from the town of Botwood. It was at Evans Point that I first came face to face with the fact of man's mortality. The owner and oldest resident we knew was "grandfather" Evans. He had cut and sawed the wood for his own coffin. The finished product was stored on the rafters of an old barn nest to our summer place. There was also an old truck in the barn. I doubt if the truck had been on a road in a decade. All the kids around liked to sneak into the barn and "drive" the truck. I was an almost daily "driver," but deep down, I believe it was grandfather Evans' coffin rather than the truck that really fascinated me. I remember that our little Presbyterian church in Grand Falls used to have their Sunday school picnics at Evans Point. Between the games, races, and other events, I would take my classmates over to see the old truck—and the coffin! While the little church and its Sunday school had a great influence on me, I think that it was grandfather Evans' coffin that really first caused me to think seriously about things spiritual!

Across the bay, at Botwood, were the "flying boats." These were the days when trans-Atlantic flights used water for takeoff and landing. Botwood, located in what was virtually a land-locked bay where aircraft could arrive and depart in any direction, was the chosen arrival and departure point in North America. We spent hours watching these "clippers" and marvelled that one could breakfast in England and have dinner in Newfoundland. Towards the dying days of the flying boats, just before Gander and Goose Bay took over as land bases, we had a visit to Botwood by Winston Churchill.

Further out the bay from Botwood were the icebergs. Perhaps one of the things that distinguished us in Newfoundland from folk elsewhere in North America was our regular household use of icebergs. I remember icebergs trapped in the inlets of Notre Dame Bay as high as a ten-story building. This was, of course, fresh-water ice, coming from the Arctic glaciers. The bergs were caught in the Labrador current and brought down to Newfoundland waters where they met the Gulf Stream and melted. However, not all the bergs reached the Gulf Stream. Many were grounded in the bays and coves of northeastern Newfoundland. All of the ice we used for refrigeration was from these grounded icebergs. Fishermen from out the bay sold the ice in Grand Falls. We would store a summer's supply beneath a huge sawdust pile in the shade of a shed in the backyard. We used this ice not only in our ice chests but in our summer drinks. It was excellent for drinks, since it was so compressed after tens of thousands of years of pressure in the glacier that it sparkled and gave off an effervescence as it melted.

On fishing trips out the bay during June and July, I always feared these icebergs. They were nine-tenths under water with only the peak, always large, protruding above the sea. I knew that with the summer sun and warm air, they were continuously foundering and changing form and place in the bay. I recall one large berg not far from my sister Janet's home in Lewisporte. I was fishing with my brother-in-law, Ross Tait, and my nephew, Roy. We decided to land on the berg to collect ice for our drinks. The air temperature was about twenty-four degrees Celsius, or seventy-six degrees Fahrenheit, and the sea was as smooth as glass. The berg was grounded and obviously in very deep water, for the portion above the water was as high as a five-storey building.

As we approached the berg, I could see twenty or thirty feet below us a tongue of green-blue ice extending some hundred feet out towards the open sea. My concern was that if the extended underwater shelf should break, the berg had to change its equilibrium and plunge or roll. It took all of the courage I could muster to leave the boat and join Ross and Roy on that berg. I felt that at any moment I could be like those poor souls who were left floundering in the freezing water when the Titanic hit such an iceberg only a few hundred miles from where we were. Ross and Roy were fearless. I hid my fear and joined them in chopping ice. I soon relaxed, and the three of us, stripped to the waist, stretched out on the ice in the bright, warm sunlight for an hour or so, as if we were on a Florida beach. It was difficult then to realise that in a few short weeks this great mass would disappear into the sea.

Newfoundlanders must have a preoccupation with ice. When we were in our midteens, we liked to venture out in winter and spring on the frozen bay at Northern Arm. This was very dangerous, particularly in spring, when the ice could quickly turn black and, under pressure from tides and current, break up and disappear almost overnight. In winter it was usually thick and safe once you got over the shoreline, which was generally piled with broken ice thrown up by the tides and winds. Our favourite pastime was to get clear of the shore onto smooth ice, each of us with two empty condensed milk cans, a blanket, and some twine. We would jam our feet into the cans in a way that would allow us to slide along the ice. We would tie the four corners of the blanket to our wrists and ankles. The wind would do the rest.

We would sail down the bay, blown along for miles towards the open sea. When we felt we were probably flirting with the ice-edge, we would collapse our blanket-sails and fall to the ice. After sliding for twenty yards or so, we would come to a stop, kick off the cans (which would blow away towards England), and labouriously make our way back towards shore. We never told our mothers about this favourite pastime.

The Newfoundland Regiment was one of the first all-volunteer regiments in the British army in which all officers had risen through the ranks. The regiment had been in existence since the War of 1812, when members fought against the Americans in the field and aboard British ships on the Great Lakes. During the War of 1812, the regiment, with a group of allied Indians, participated in the capture of Detroit. When I mention this to American friends, they invariably say we should have kept it.

During the First World War, some fourteen hundred men of the regiment were killed. The terrible day for the island was July 1, 1916. This was the first day of the Battle of the Somme. The regiment was one of the first to go into action. There were over eight hundred Newfoundland casualties that day. The first day of July has since been Memorial Day in Newfoundland. It is noteworthy that the Newfoundland Regiment was the only North American regiment to fight at Gallipoli, alongside the Australians and New Zealanders!

In the Second World War there were two Newfoundland regiments in the British Eighth Army, and they fought in North Africa, Sicily, and Italy. In the war at sea, Newfoundlanders were generally in the Royal Navy, and the British tried to make it a practice to spread them around on as many ships as possible. The result was that whenever a Royal Navy ship went down, there were often Newfoundlanders lost, but there was no great number from any one action. There was a Newfoundland Fighter (Mosquito) Squadron in the Royal Air Force, and many Newfoundlanders served in other British and Commonwealth squadrons. Newfoundland lost over two hundred airmen.

On the home front, Newfoundland was very close to the war at sea. German submarines were very active around its shores, and there were instances of ships being sunk right inside Newfoundland harbours. A submarine torpedoed two ore-laden ships sitting in the stream at Bell Island in Conception Bay. The sinking that caused the greatest shock was that of the *Caribou,* the ferry-steamer that ran between Port aux Basques and North Sydney, Nova Scotia. About twenty miles off Port aux Basques, the *Caribou* was torpedoed and went down with some one hundred and fifty passengers and crew. Most of the crew were from Port aux Basques, which was my mother's home. She was there at the time because of the death of her grandmother Guy. My mother's brother, Sandy, had an interest in photography, and since there was no photographer in the community, Sandy was pressed into photographing, for identification purposes, the bodies that had been pulled from the sea. Among those drowned was a cousin of my mother.

All the "paper" boats that carried newsprint from Botwood to England were lost. I remember well the *Geraldine Mary* and the *Rothemere,* for I had been aboard both and had met many members of the crew. There was also a German ship that had been captured in port at Botwood when war was declared. This ship had been loading ore concentrates. It sailed under the British flag only to be sunk shortly afterwards. I recall watching the captured German seamen behind wire at Botwood, playing soccer.

The most memorable sight of the war for me was when I visited St. John's on one of my annual visits to see the eye specialist. There was a large ship in the harbour with a hole right through its hull. Motor boats were chugging to and fro through the ship. How it ever reached port was a wonder. Close to the torpedoed ship was a captured German submarine. Perhaps all my fears and prejudices influenced me, but I recall this submarine was the most sinister looking ship I had ever seen!

Close to home, at Botwood, we were provided with a garrison of Canadian troops to protect the sea base. In the early years of the war, the troops were from proud and famous regiments, such as the Black Watch and the Winnipeg Rifles. These regiments would make names for them-selves overseas. Later in the war, we had the conscript regiments. These were not popular with the locals, whose men were all volunteers serving on active duty, many without home leave since the beginning of the war.

We had a home guard, made up mainly of First World War veterans and those not physically fit to serve in the active forces. I was too young for even the home guard, but I was taken on as a "casualty." I had a sign that I placed around my neck when the alarm went off. I would run to my designated spot on High Street and sit to await rescue. "Rescued" I always was, and taken to the back of the town hall, where the local first-aid ladies would put on splints and otherwise tend to my "wounds."

Grand Falls was at the time blacked-out. This meant that we had to have window blinds to prevent any display of light. One winter evening it had been arranged that the Canadian troops at Botwood, in an exercise with our home guard, would "invade the town." They arrived ahead of the agreed time and, to the disgust of all the residents, captured the town. In late afternoon, I happened to glance out our front window to see twenty or thirty soldiers dressed in white, skiing down our street. They took all our home guard "prisoners."

Grand Falls was very hospitable to the mainland soldiers. Every weekend, many hundreds of soldiers from the bases at Botwood and Gander would assemble in front of the town hall, to be billeted in private homes. My family took three each weekend for most of the war years.

One of the most interesting times for me during the war was when my father brought in from the mainland three hundred baby pigs. He was the Canada Packers representative in central Newfoundland and was much involved with supplying the troops at Botwood with meat, fruit, and vegetables. He visited the Botwood base every few days and always left more than a little disgusted at the great waste of food that was dumped daily from the base kitchens.

He made arrangements with the cooks to have the slops collected each day. He hired a couple of men to deliver them to an area he had fenced in on Crown land behind Botwood, where he had installed the pigs. He saw the pigs only on several occasions, generally when I pestered him to take me to see them. He had them all sold for fall delivery (live) before they arrived in Newfoundland. Joey Smallwood, who in 1949 was to take Newfoundland into Canada and become the first provincial premier, raised pigs in the same way in Gander as my father did in Botwood.

My father was one of the few employees of Canada Packers to be on commission. Central Newfoundland did not warrant a full Canada Packers branch, yet it was too promising to ignore. My father knew every account in the area, so Canada Packers agreed to have him market their Maple Leaf products on commission. I don't believe they realised what they were doing. My father made many Canada Packers products household words in Newfoundland. He sold more Maple Leaf bologna in Newfoundland than Canada Packers sold in the rest of Canada. It was a good, inexpensive source of protein and jokingly became known as "Newfoundland steak." It was said that my father's sales of bologna kept the Prince Edward Island plant in production.

Being on commission, and not a regular employee of Canada Packers, allowed my father to pursue many outside business ventures. He went into a business in Botwood that proved to be a great success. He was travelling the twenty miles from Grand Falls to Botwood on the paper company's train and chatting with Jack Arklie and the conductor, Pete Boone. As they came into Botwood, my father inquired about a hall they were passing, which had been recently vacated. Jack and Pete, who were both from Botwood, learned that it could be acquired for a modest sum. So the three of them set up Botwood's first movie theatre. It was an immediate financial success. My father and Jack Arklie later built a regular theatre in central Botwood that gave them a good return until the advent of television. Jack claimed that the theatre paid my way through university on the mainland!

The salmon was king in the numerous rivers on the island. I really enjoyed salmon fishing. I didn't realise it then but we were most privileged to have some of the best salmon fishing in the world "on our doorstep." My father and grandfather Petrie were acknowledged to be amongst the best fishermen. My father was not only good, he was lucky. I saw him hook a salmon on the back-cast when fishing from a canoe below the Big Falls on the Upper Humber. He went about his fishing with intelligence. He would cable friends near the mouth of the Gander River and ask them to let him know when the commercial fishermen took the first salmon from their nets. We would then take a freight train from Grand Falls to Glenwood and go down the river by canoe to Petrie's Rock (named after my grandfather) and cast until we hooked our first salmon of the season.

I remember my first salmon. I was eight years old and had already received as Christmas or birthday presents my greenheart half-pound salmon rod and a supply of prized salmon flies: Thunder and Lightnings, Silver Doctors, Jock Scots, Silver Greys, and Black Doses. These were wet flies; they sank just below the surface as you stood in the river in your waders and guided the fly over the deep, dark salmon pool, waiting for the water to explode when the salmon, fresh from the Atlantic, "rose" to take the fly. My father was standing next to me. I was used to casting for trout, so I did as I was told when my father said, "Cast across that ripple on the side of the pool over there!"

As soon as the fly hit the surface, the water seethed with the silver flash of a twelve-pound salmon. I didn't hook it, so I readied to cast again when my father yelled, "No, my son, leave him alone for a minute, and cast over there to the left of the pool."

I did, and there was another explosion. My father then left me and waded away towards another pool, nodding towards the ripple where the first salmon rose. Within three or four minutes I hooked it. I had the best half-hour of my short life playing that fish until I was able to drag it onto a sandbar. I took the twelve-pounder home to my mother. She knew I was "hooked."

My "sea travels" started at the end of a salmon fishing trip. I was fishing with my father and a family friend, Ned Pond, from Botwood. We were at Indian Falls on the Indian River a few miles from the beautiful village of Springdale. I was not yet ten years old. I had been pestering my parents about allowing me to go to sea. I suppose that all Newfoundland boys grow up with a love (and respect) for the sea. It was after all the only "open road" we knew to far away places. It had been my first really successful weekend of salmon fishing. The three of us had landed sixty salmon. I had landed five or six. We put all back into the stream except for the few we ate or salted to take home. On that Sunday afternoon we struck our tent and, covered with fly dope and camp smoke, we set out for the return trip home. We were to be driven from the falls to Springdale. From there we were to take a motor boat to Halls Bay, where we had left our car.

The drive to Springdale was in the only car in Springdale, an open roadster. It was owned, I believe, by the Inder family. Old "Skipper" Inder was the fish warden at the falls. As we came over the hill that led down to Springdale, we saw the coastal steamer, the *Northern Ranger,* that plied the north coast fishing villages. My father dug me in the ribs and said, "My son, here's your chance to go to sea." He was serious. I suspect that he believed that the trip that would take us round Cape St. John in the open North Atlantic would forever cure me of my longing for a life at sea.

We drove straight to the wharf, and my father led me aboard and up to the bridge. I wasn't at all surprised that he knew the captain, for I was sure that he knew everybody in Newfoundland. He had a few words with the captain. Suddenly, I was booked, alone, for an afternoon and overnight passage around Cape St. John to La Scie and a return to Springdale. My father would spend the night with a business friend by the name of Warr.

I was delighted. I was shown to my cabin (where it was suggested I wash off the fly dope and camp smoke before I came up on deck!). The ship sailed within ten minutes of my boarding. It was the beginning of one of those long summer evenings, and the sea was calm. I really enjoyed our calls at the many outports whose names were most familiar to me as we headed "down north," as we say in Newfoundland. We tied up at places such as Nippers Harbour, Shoe Cove, and Tilt Cove and joined the locals ashore on the big event of their day, the arrival of their contact with the outside world.

I was determined to stay up to experience the rounding of Cape St. John, which was a household name for me, linked with the annual seal hunt

18

and the voyages of our fishermen to Labrador. I slept through the time it took to round the cape, going and returning. This was most likely why I didn't get seasick and cured of my love for the sea.

Newfoundland outports were in those days very isolated. Roads were few, and generally the only contact with the outside world was by boat. I remember hearing of one fellow from Nippers Harbour who made his first trip to Halls Bay and from there by truck on the "woods" road, fifty kilometres to Badger. Here he saw his first train. When he returned home, he was asked to described what he saw. He said, "The only way I can describe it is to say that if that train came side-on it would sweep the country!"

Only once when I was growing up did I have a run-in with the law. It was the summer the war ended, and I was getting ready to go to university on the mainland. My parents had gone to the mainland, leaving the car. I thought it was a good time to get my driving license. The only problem was that you had to be seventeen and I was sixteen and a half. The seven or eight police constables in Grand Falls, members of the Newfoundland Constabulary, were all known to me personally. Constable Avery was on duty when I walked into the station. He filled out the form of routine questions, noting my name and address, the fact that I was a British subject, and that I was seventeen years of age. The latter certainly wasn't right but I made no attempt to correct his wrong assumption. He took me on the usual drive around Circular Road, and on return to his office, he handed me my license.

With my new license in my wallet, I drove to see my friend Boyd Cohen. Boyd and I had talked for months about getting our licenses. He decided to follow my example and call on Constable Avery. The trouble for Boyd, however, was that he was only fifteen. Nevertheless, he passed the test.

A few nights later, the chief constable was playing cards with Maxine Stone's father. Maxine, who was in my class at school, asked the chief if she could get her license. He told her that she was too young and must be patient for six months or so. She responded that Franklin Petrie was her age and he had his license, and Boyd Cohen was only fifteen and he got his. Next morning Constable Avery was at my door, asking, "Franklin, how old are you?"

I said, "I'm sixteen, going on seventeen, Constable Avery."

He said, "Sorry about this, Franklin, but I have to ask for your license and give you a summons to appear in court."

19

He left, saying he was on his way to see Boyd. As soon as he was out of sight, I phoned Boyd, even though I knew that the operator, Central, would probably be listening and our problem would be known all over town within minutes. In the short time it took the constable to reach Boyd's home, we agreed that the game was up, and we must do or say nothing that might get Constable Avery in trouble.

With a summons to court and my parents away, I went to see my favourite relative, Uncle Harry Baird. Uncle Harry was my paternal grandmother's brother-in-law. He was a Scot. He had come to Newfoundland as a very young man and had served in the Newfoundland Regiment during the First World War as a lieutenant, being one of the few officers to survive.

I said, "Uncle Harry, I'm in trouble." I told him the whole story.

He said, "Franklin, you are sixteen and a half; one might argue that you are already seventeen!" Uncle Harry went on, saying, "Some insurance companies claim that when you are born, you are already nine months old."

This sounded pretty good to me. I raced off to see Boyd and to tell him about Uncle Harry's argument. In no way could Boyd add nine months to his age and come anywhere near seventeen. Boyd decided to rest his defence on telling the truth. He would explain that he was going on a driving trip with aged members of his family and he simply wanted to do the decent thing and share the driving.

A few days later, we were in court. I had Uncle Harry with me. Boyd for some reason was alone. When our turn came, Constable Avery called, "Franklin Petrie and Boyd Cohen."

The magistrate first addressed me, asking for an explanation why I had misled Constable Avery about my age. I said, "Your Honour, I didn't mislead Constable Avery; I am sixteen and one-half years old, and according to some insurance companies, when you are born, you are nine months old."

The magistrate, who I am sure had heard every argument in the book and a few others, simply said, "That's interesting." He then turned to Boyd and said, "Boyd, what reason do you give for misleading Constable Avery?"

Boyd replied, "Your Honour, my family is going on a holiday to Canada and the United States, and they are getting old, so I wanted to help by sharing the driving."

The magistrate turned to me and said, "Interesting point you make, Franklin, about this nine-month business." (Uncle Harry beamed!) "I'll give you a slight benefit of the doubt and fine you ten dollars." He turned to Boyd and said, "Boyd, it was your intention to drive in three countries with a license obtained illegally, so I fine you twenty-five dollars." Uncle Harry paid my ten dollars and had to lend Boyd five dollars because he only had twenty.

As we left the courtroom, Constable Avery turned to me and said, "Franklin, drop in after your birthday at Christmas, when you return from university, and I'll give you back your license."

One thing that I loved in Newfoundland was the ability of people to laugh at themselves. I'm sure that most of the good Newfie jokes (comparable to Polish jokes in the United States and Irish jokes in Australia) originated on the island. We had our own private ones about the mainlanders whom we considered to be a little too serious! We used to say that the definition of a mainlander was someone who died at twenty but was not buried until eighty. We considered the Americans nice, friendly people but awfully ill-informed about anything beyond their borders. An article in the *New York Herald Tribune* in 1929 said it all. Concerning some missing aviators, it was stated, "There is still a chance that the Farman monoplane has landed in some desolate spot in Newfoundland or Halifax, where they may be lost for weeks without anybody knowing about it."

Our Newfoundland papers carried some beauties. As an example, "After the ceremony the bridal party left for their future home in a motor boat; in spite of a stormy night, an enjoyable time was spent." It was also reported, "The witness identified the pants which the prisoner wore in court this mornings as the property of Mrs. B." Another paper related, "The funeral procession reformed and went to Belvedere, where they were interred." It wasn't only the papers that committed such bloopers. *Who's Who in Newfoundland* ran an account of the loss of a steamer with all hands: "The body of Mrs. X, a passenger, was found floating on the water; it is assumed that her boilers blew up."

We used to joke that North America was an island off the west coast of Newfoundland. I soon got to know first-hand how enormous and diverse that "island" was. I was fifteen before I set foot on the mainland in 1945. Canada was then a Canada without Newfoundland. My parents, with another couple, had taken me with them on a driving trip to "Canada and the United States." Gasoline was no longer rationed and the world was getting ready for peace-time travel. We put our car on the train for Port aux Basques, for there was still no highway across the island. At Port aux Basques, the car was shipped by boat with us to North Sydney, Nova Scotia.

Here we had to switch our driving from the left-hand side of the road to the right.

I don't recall too much about that particular trip, but I do remember that our habit of driving on the left got us into trouble in Montreal. We entered the wrong side (the left side) of the bridge across the St. Lawrence into Montreal. One can imagine the fuss and embarrassment as we had to back across the bridge with seemingly every car in Montreal honking at us and every driver pointing with ridicule at our Newfoundland license plates. We also had trouble in Niagara Falls, New York, where the immigration people had difficulty believing that our license plates were genuine. I must admit that the plates did look a little less than professional that year. They had been stamped and painted without much skill by the prisoners at His Majesty's Penitentiary in St. John's.

I was only sixteen when I went off to the mainland to university. I went first to Mount Allison University in Sackville, New Brunswick, and later to Dalhousie in Halifax, Nova Scotia. The universities were getting their first big wave of ex-servicemen. I must have been the youngest and certainly most naive student at Mount Allison. One can imagine my mixture of pride, shock and concern when I was elected president of the largest incoming freshman class in the history of the university with over four hundred students!

There was little glory in the presidency. I spent an inordinate amount of time organising work parties of freshmen to clean the gymnasium and other recreational rooms after dances and other functions. These were paid jobs and were in great demand by students wanting to earn extra income. I had many "friends" looking to be selected. It was, however, a lot of work and responsibility supervising and paying the workers.

I was taking economics and commerce, but most of the friends I made seemed to have been in medicine and dentistry. Many were from the Commonwealth Caribbean. One of my new friends, Dan Ramesar, who is now a dentist in Trinidad, came home with me for Christmas. The following Christmas, a number of other students from Grand Falls joined me in inviting West Indian friends for the holiday season. Grand Falls played host for a number of Christmas holidays to five or six boys from Trinidad. They were well received and they couldn't have been better guests. The entire town opened their arms to them. One can imagine the thrill for these fellows, who were born and bred in the tropics, of going on sleigh rides, travelling on snowshoes for miles in the northern forest, and cutting Christmas trees that within a few hours they themselves decorated.

I was very proud of the fact that never did we have a suggestion of racial discrimination; I had explained to the boys that Newfoundlanders were ninety-nine percent of British origin, with a little infusion from other European countries. Consequently, a dark face (they were East Indian) was bound to attract some attention and stares. They all told me that their dark faces served as beacons in that they were singled out for special treatment as honoured guests. Dan continued to visit Newfoundland to stay with my parents after I had moved to Dalhousie.

I was at Dalhousie University when Newfoundland joined Canada as Canada's tenth province. It was All Fools' Day, 1949. Many of the New-foundlanders on campus, including myself, wore black arm bands and black ties. We were "in deep mourning" for the loss of what little independence Newfoundland had. A dozen or so of my "Canadian" fellow-students and a professor took me to the pub at the Lord Nelson Hotel and shouted the beer in my honour. I hardly showed my appreciation when a few hours later, I helped fellow Newfoundlanders lower the Canadian flag at the university to half-mast!

It was a very emotional time for Newfoundlanders. Without a doubt, confederation with Canada had to be economically good for Newfoundland; but about forty-eight percent of voters had opposed it. Many held the view that independence with economic union with the United States would be preferable. Pro-American feeling was widespread. Tens of thousands of Newfoundlanders (including two of my mother's brothers) had migrated to the "Boston states" for work during the depression. During the war and afterwards, some twenty-five thousand Newfoundland women married American servicemen, so most of us had relations in the United States. However, I feel that most anticonfederate votes were cast for emotional and nationalistic reasons.

I was nineteen and too young to vote, but I did drive a car for the anticonfederates, taking people to the polls. At the time, little did I realise that I would spend much of my life working for Canada!

Joey Smallwood was the hero of the day. Certainly most of the credit for Newfoundland's entry into Canada had to go to him, although my family tended to refer to it in the early years as "blame" rather than "credit." The Petrie family had a bit of a feud going with Joey, dating from the 1920s. At that time Joey was a member of the British Labour Party. He walked the railway line across the island, setting up unions and otherwise championing the cause of labour. While in Grand Falls, Joey stayed at my grandmother's boarding house. According to my parents, he left without paying, allegedly with the attitude that the Petries could afford to cover the bill as a contribution to the betterment of the Newfoundland worker!

Joey was on a nightly newscast in which he was known as "the barrel man." In real life, the barrel man was the fellow in the barrel, high on the mast of the schooner, ever on the lookout for seals, whales, drift ice, or whatever. The barrel man alone knew what was going on around the area. After the news report, Joey would tell greatly exaggerated tales of Newfoundland; his became a household name throughout the island and on the coast of Labrador. For my family and many others, his name was synonymous with "teller of tall (untrue) tales." It was little wonder that when Joey announced that he would form and lead the Liberal party in Newfoundland, my family all became Conservatives!

The entry of Newfoundland into Canada spelled the end of Newfoundland's separate currency and postage stamps, although both became legal for use throughout Canada. Newfoundland had twenty-cent pieces; the closest coin in size in Canada was the twenty-five-cent piece. Newfoundland students departing for university on the mainland would carry all the twenty-cent pieces they could accumulate. In Halifax, for weeks after our arrival at Dalhousie, the city would be awash with twenty-cent pieces. They were readily, if unknowingly, accepted by the locals as quarters. This, in a small way, we felt, got back at the mainlanders for those terrible "Newfie" jokes they told.

University years were enjoyable, and I trust rewarding, but I knew that I was not cut out for an academic life. I looked upon my degree, not so much as an academic achievement, but more as a diving board into the pool of life. I felt strongly that a degree, while important, was no substitute for real-life experience. I was certainly influenced by the attitude prevailing in Newfoundland at the time, that experience was the best teacher.

Chapter Two
Down Mexico Way

Following university, it was my intention to return to Newfoundland to join my father's business, which had expanded to embrace wholesale and import agencies. Before doing so, I decided to take one fling at seeing something of North America. In the summer of 1950, I set out with an American friend, Randy Erdman, for a hitchhiking and working summer in the southern United States. Randy was a Sigma Chi fraternity brother. He was from Virginia, and we made his home our first destination.

We hitchhiked down the eastern seaboard to the Gulf of Mexico. We would stop whenever we could at universities to scrounge a meal, a shower, and a bed from our Sigma Chi fraternity brothers. They welcomed us warmly for a night or two, and we always made it a point to move on before our welcome wore out.

In Austin, Texas, our money ran out! After a few days of the usual hospitality, at the University of Texas, we knew that we had to get a job and pay our way. With some difficulty, we got jobs cleaning apartments. We did this for a week, when we learnt that there was considerable work available on ranches just outside Austin.

We took jobs sticking fences, with excellent money and bunkhouse and grub thrown in. Randy and I took turns digging holes with an auger and carting poles by wheelbarrow and sticking them in the ground. After a month of this, being unable to spend our money, we had accumulated a considerable sum. We decided we would retire and head back north, but not before having a look at nearby Mexico.

We hiked down to Brownsville and crossed the border into Matamores. It was my first experience of things truly foreign, and I was fascinated. They discouraged hitchhiking in Mexico, so we took a bus to Monterey, where we planned to spend a few days savouring Mexico. Fortunately, within an hour of our arrival, we dropped in for a beer at the very un-Mexican Pennsylvania Bar.

There we met an American theological student called Gene, who was leaving within the hour for Saltillo, fifty miles away in the mountains, where he was going to study Spanish at summer school. He was Roman Catholic and was struggling to make up his mind whether or not to go into the priesthood. His alternative was to marry his girlfriend back home in Boston. She was Jewish, so he felt he needed to get away from the seminary and his girlfriend to settle matters in his mind.

I never learnt what his decision was, but on that evening, he had the good sense to talk us into joining him at summer school. He convinced us that we could pay for our tuition and live for six weeks in Saltillo on the money we would spend in a few days in Monterey. He was right!

Half an hour later, the three of us were on a bus for the mountains. Saltillo was in those days a sleepy and very typical Mexican country town. Its only claims to fame were that it was the capital of the state of Coahuila and it had a well-known summer school, La Escuela Interamericana. Saltillo lay on the northern edge of the great central plateau at an elevation of exactly one mile above sea level. It had a cool, dry, and healthful climate. Few Americans realise that from 1824 to 1836, Saltillo was the capital of a vast province that included what is now Texas and other areas of the American southwest.

Randy and I followed Gene to a hotel, where we rented a three-bed, rooftop room for the equivalent of one dollar each a day. The next morning we registered at the school for a very reasonable amount. The school provided lectures in the morning and made available private tutors for the afternoon. We paid the tutors, who were university students, the equivalent of fifty cents a day. They generally stayed with us all evening. The three fellows assigned to us could not speak English. They became good friends for the time we were there. They knew the town and the countryside and provided a link to the local community that would have been impossible had we been on our own.

In Saltillo they had the traditional "promenade," where the single young men and women would congregate at the city plaza each evening and walk. The boys would walk in one direction, the girls in the other, around the plaza. The girls generally had their duenas, or guardians, close behind them, but they were permitted to accept an invitation from an admirer to walk with him around the plaza. At the appointed time, the girls would be collected by their duenas and escorted home.

I had my first real experience with horseback riding near Saltillo. Gene claimed to be an accomplished rider and pressed the other five of us to go for an outing in the nearby mountains. We took a bus to a ranch where we found ourselves six horses. We set out feeling very much like cowboys heading into the mountains and the unknown. The horses knew every inch of the trail, which was just as well, because in places you could look down several hundred feet just inches from where the horses placed their hoofs. I left all decisions to my horse, interfering as little as possible with the course he took and the slow plodding speed at which he took it. After an hour or so, Gene decided that his horse was too docile, but he figured that mine looked as if it could be prodded into real action. He asked me if I would exchange horses. I agreed, for I wanted the most docile animal available. I saw Gene gallop away at breakneck speed and come flying off and tumble down an embankment. Fortunately he had no broken bones; his pride more than his body was hurt. It was then that I learned that my Mexican tutor friends had arranged for me to have the bucking bronco because I had told them that I had never been on a horse. I haven't been on one since!

The six weeks at the school passed all too quickly. Despite the reasonable cost of living, our money had pretty well run out by the time classes ended. Randy decided to make his way north, but Gene and I wanted to see Mexico City. Between us we had only enough money for one-way third-class train tickets. I had a source of funds, but I had difficulty getting at it. At Dalhousie University I had been consul, or president, of the Sigma Chi fraternity chapter, and in that capacity I was expected to attend, in Ohio, a conference of chapters from across North America. If I turned up in Ohio, there would be a cheque for several hundred dollars awaiting me for travel and living expenses. The problem was how to get there. Gene felt we should head for Mexico City, where he had a group of friends who he was sure would finance my way north by bus. They were holed up in an inexpensive hotel, six to a room, and didn't have sufficient funds to pay the bill. If I undertook to send back some of the funds from Ohio, he felt sure they would all scrape together enough to get me north!

We went to the Saltillo railway station and purchased one-way third-class tickets. It was several hours before the train was due, so we decided not to hang around the station. This proved to be a mistake, for when we returned an hour before the train was to arrive, there were many hundreds of people, fifteen or twenty deep, around the area where the third-class carriages were to stop. When the train arrived, there was truly a mob scene. We didn't get within twenty feet of the train before it pulled out with people

27

hanging on to every possible toehold. I guess our northern upbringing didn't allow us to push and shove as the Mexican men did in order to claw their way onto the train.

We adapted quickly; we were determined to push aside our manners and definitely board the next train that was due three hours later. We did, but it was quite a struggle. When the train pulled out, I had but one foot on a bottom step, one hand clutching my pack, and the other wrapped around an iron railing. A woman tried desperately to dislodge me from my foothold, but I hung on for dear life. As the train gathered speed, the woman let go and jumped to the ground.

I never did get inside the carriage. I travelled the twenty or so hours on the steps or on the platform between the cars. I didn't see Gene again until we reached San Luis Portosi, about halfway to Mexico City. Although I had to stand the entire journey, the trip was enjoyable and certainly most interesting.

Once the Mexicans knew that they were securely aboard, they resumed their usual friendly manner. They offered around food and tequila, and you had the feeling of being caught up in an impromptu party. Some of the women held babies and some carried chickens; one carried a small pig. I assumed that the chickens and the pig would become dinner whenever they arrived at their destination. We were packed together so tightly that you could sleep without fear of falling. Your conversation was, for hours, confined to those whose faces were only inches from yours. These were farm folk, and their accents were not those you heard around the school in Saltillo. I learnt that the reason for their travel in such large numbers was a major religious festival in San Luis Portosi. This was great news for me, for I felt that as soon as they got off, I would find Gene and we would make the rest of the trip in the comfort of the carriage. How wrong I was.

When we pulled into San Luis Portosi, I was horror-struck to see the same mob scene on the railway platform that we had in Saltillo. People were twenty deep along the side of the carriages. Those who had completed their pilgrimage were now about to board the train for their return trip home in southern Mexico. There was utter chaos as those on the train struggled to get off and those on the platform fought to get on. I felt that I was the only one on the train who wanted to stay on. I was swept off with the outgoing mob and then had to struggle to get caught up with the incoming tide of human bodies. Again I won a foothold on the carriage steps. It took me a few hours to win back a space on the platform between the cars. I was pleased to see Gene within hailing distance. I yelled to him that I really hoped he would become a priest and do something to make these pilgrimages a little more civilised!

In Mexico City we found Gene's friends. Although the six of them were jammed into one room, they offered to make space for us. They undoubtedly looked upon us as their means of financial rescue. Gene worked out a deal with them. They would give me a couple of days to see Mexico City, and then they would pool their remaining funds and buy me a bus ticket to my Sigma Chi conference in Ohio. The condition was that I wire them back money from Ohio sufficient to pay the hotel bill. My quick calculation was that the money due to me would be more than adequate to cover the hotel bill plus enough to get me back to Dalhousie in Halifax. I agreed, as did our new roommates.

After a quick tour of Mexico City, some of the fellows accompanied me to the bus station and stood over me as I purchased the bus ticket with their money. They gave me two dollars for food for the seven days it would take to reach Ohio.

The bus ride to Nuevo Laredo on the United States border was not the best. The bus was crowded to overflowing with men going north to work. All of them had the disgusting habit of continually spitting in the corridor. I was sure I would end up with tuberculosis or something worse and that they would all be completely dehydrated by the time we arrived at the border. How they would ever clean out the bus, I couldn't imagine.

I walked across the border, and as soon as I emerged from customs, a lady stopped her car and kindly offered to drive me to the bus station on the American side. I felt terribly embarrassed, for I hadn't had a shower since leaving Mexico City two days earlier and my white shirt was soiled and almost yellow in colour. I accepted her kindness and, within a few hours, was off on the five-day ride to Ohio.

The trip was uneventful and I slept a lot. The bus would stop every few hours at rest and food spots, and my two dollars were soon gone. I learnt that if I sat next to elderly people and didn't join them to go into the restaurant when we stopped, they would invariably enquire why I wasn't eating. I would tell them frankly that I was broke. They always insisted on treating me to a snack. I felt a little guilty about this and tried to make it up to them by carrying their bags or otherwise being of assistance when they arrived at their destination.

In Ohio, I collected and cashed my cheque, had a good meal, laundered my few clothes, and bought a ticket to Nova Scotia. I pocketed twenty dollars and sent the rest to Gene in Mexico. I had a note from him shortly after I arrived in Halifax telling me that they had paid the hotel bill and were all going their separate ways. I still wonder whether he made the priesthood.

At the Ohio Sigma Chi convention, I attended many of the meetings, but I had to forgo the social functions, since I didn't have the proper clothes, not even a tie! I left as early as I reasonably could for Canada, thus ending "my first trip abroad."

Chapter Three
Eastward Bound

I started my working life in Corner Brook, Newfoundland, in a company partly owned by my father. He held "sole" agencies for products, which meant that he was, under contract, the sole importer onto the island and sole distributor of the products concerned in Newfoundland, or a designated area of the island. My father would approach manufacturers and processors in Toronto and Montreal who had popular selling brands but no distribution network in Newfoundland. He would undertake to sell their products on commission. He and his partners could claim to know every account on the island. After confederation with Canada in 1949, their business grew considerably, since many mainland firms had no presence in Newfoundland. I was to learn the ropes at the company's offices and warehouses in Corner Brook.

I did not take well to the office work I was assigned. My relationship with the manager was the problem. He was my father's partner and treated me, not as an employee, but as "one of the family." I did the payroll and couldn't help noting that the two lowest salaries were those of the manager's brother and myself. When I raised this with the manager, he replied in anger that neither of us had much need for money and as "family" we should willingly make a contribution, through lower pay, to the family firm.

I loved living in Corner Brook but realised that I could not last long at the job I was doing. I began to think of my childhood dreams of going to Australia. I was told by a friend, Jess Skinner, who had been in the Royal Navy and who had married an Australian during the war, that there was work galore in Australia.

I wrote letters to the Australian immigration authorities in Canberra, and while I was at it, to the New Zealand authorities in Wellington. I received a polite, "Come and we will help you as best we can," response from New Zealand. I received from Australia an enthusiastic reply informing me that there were several hundred thousand positions open in the country and they were seeking immigrants to fill them! They suggested that with my degree and particular interests, I might wish to consider working for the Australian government in Canberra. I jumped at this, and after further, more focused correspondence, the Australian authorities told me that they could all but guarantee me a position in Canberra, subject to an interview when I arrived in Sydney. I would also have to pass a security check and have my Dalhousie University degree recognised by the University of Sydney.

At first I told only my mother of my plans. She knew I was unhappy with the office situation in Corner Brook, so she didn't discourage me at all. She influenced me tremendously when she told me that she felt I was destined for work in the international field and perhaps my decision to go to Australia would set me in that direction.

I resigned my job, sold the few stocks I had purchased, emptied my small bank account, and with a few hundred dollars extra that my mother slipped to me, I bought passage to Australia. I was to sail from St. John's to Liverpool, England, on the S.S. *Newfoundland*. The fare to England was one hundred and fifty dollars, and the voyage would take six days. I was to have a week in London and then take the Peninsula and Orient (P&O) liner *Himalaya* from London to Sydney. The cost was eighty pounds sterling for the thirty-three days it would take to reach Sydney. This would leave me with a nest egg of three hundred dollars for Australia.

My father was disappointed but quickly accepted my decision. After farewells galore, I took the train to St. John's and went straight to the ship. My Uncle Harry Baird came aboard to bid me farewell. Uncle Harry, always a favourite uncle, was even higher on my list since my Grand Falls court appearance! I don't recall what he was doing in St. John's, for he lived in Grand Falls, but to my slight embarrassment, he brought on board two dozen fresh eggs and several pairs of lady's silk stockings. He handed the eggs to the steward, instructing him to put them in the ship's refrigerator. The steward was to give a dozen back to me when we arrived in Liverpool, and to keep a dozen for his trouble. I was to give both the eggs and stockings to Uncle Harry's relatives in London. Both eggs and silk stockings were in short supply in postwar Britain.

The S.S. *Newfoundland* and her sister ship, the S.S. *Nova Scotia,* were Furness Line ships that sailed back and forth between Boston, Halifax, St. John's, and Liverpool. They didn't provide the fastest crossing, but they probably provided the cheapest. There were a lot of British war brides and young Americans taking advantage of this relatively inexpensive way of getting to England. When I boarded the ship, almost all of the passengers were ashore for a look around St. John's.

The ship was by no means a large ocean liner, but it was a comfortable, well-run ship in the British tradition, with good, solid meals, including kippers for breakfast! It was not crowded, it still being March and very early in the season. I had a four-berth cabin to myself. I enjoyed meeting and talking with my fellow passengers, who were mainly from the United States and Britain.

We sailed from St. John's late in the evening, and next morning we were already in the Gulf Stream a few hundred miles east of Newfoundland. The sea was calm and the air temperature was around fifteen degrees Celsius, or sixty degrees Fahrenheit. I played my first deck quoits and shuffleboard and readily adapted to life aboard a British passenger ship. I enjoyed reading on deck under a blanket, sipping morning and afternoon tea, and dressing in the evening for dinner. At night there were dances, films, and games for the passengers. It certainly was for me an enjoyable six days, and it passed all too quickly.

I caught my first sight of the Old World when we spotted Land's End and sailed up the Bristol Channel to Liverpool. My Trinidad friend, Dan Ramesar, was on the dock to greet me. Dan was doing dentistry in Liverpool. We had a good, but short, time together, for I was quickly shuffled onto the boat train for the trip to London.

My cousin, Noble "Speed" Baird, Uncle Harry's son, had been a Mosquito fighter pilot in the Newfoundland Squadron of the Royal Air Force during the Second World War and had spent the war years flying out of England. He persuaded me to stay at the Regent Palace in central London. It had been his favourite hotel when on leave. My stay there was in the early 1950s, long before the skyrocketing lodging and meal prices we now associate with London. I found that my Canadian dollars went a long way. From my vantage point at the Regent Palace, I was able to roam around central London, where there was so much to see. I spent almost a week touring the historic city, where every landmark seemed to be familiar to me. I had an evening with Uncle Harry's relatives when I delivered the eggs and silk stockings.

I departed for Australia on the first day of April. I took the boat train down to Tilbury and boarded the *Himalaya,* which was to be my home for the next thirty-three days. She was the newest and biggest of the P&O fleet.

33

Her crew was made up of British officers and Goanese seamen and stewards. At the time, Goa, in southern India, was still a Portuguese colony. Each time the ship docked in Bombay, the entire Goanese crew would change. The list of crewmen available was much longer than the jobs available. Consequently, the Goanese crew did their best to ensure that they would remain on the list and went out of their way to please. Tough, to be sure, but effective in maintaining the smooth running of the ship and the provision of superb service.

Most of the ship's passengers were young and middle-aged British migrants heading for a new life in Australia. They had each paid ten pounds for the Australian government's subsidised fare. I enquired whether I could qualify for such a favourable rate and was told that Australia and Canada, both being immigrant-recipient countries, had a gentleman's agreement not to entice away each other's residents!

The ship was not air-conditioned, so I got to know first hand the origin of the word "posh." Seasoned travellers from Britain to India always demanded a cabin away from the sunny side of the ship. They chose the port (or north) side on the way to India, and the starboard (or north) side going home to Britain. This was known as "portside out and starboard home," or "P.O.S.H." These letters were placed beside the names of passengers so favourably treated!

I shared a four-berth cabin with a very dour Scot, a very pleasant Englishman, and a Yugoslav. The Scot was not unpleasant but wouldn't say a word unless compelled by circumstances to do so. The Yugoslav had spent twenty years in Australia but spoke little English. I didn't realise that he wasn't a new immigrant until I saw his Australian passport one morning as we were all preparing to go ashore at one of the ports. I said, "Oh, you are an Australian?" He answered with one of the few English expressions I heard him use, "Yes, my bloody oath!"

After crossing the Bay of Biscay and entering the Mediterranean through the Straits of Gibraltar, we had very temperate or tropical seas all the way to Western Australia. If the transatlantic voyage was good, this one was superb. There were numerous passengers of my age; we joined for dances and other ship-run entertainment in the evenings and deck sports and swimming during the day. Every few days we called at some exotic port, and a group of us would band together to go ashore to take in the sights.

In Port Said, at the northern end of the Suez Canal, I allowed myself to be talked into a shoe-shine. I was horrified when the shoe-shine boy shouted, "I wish someone would start a riot so the British soldiers would come back; they are good for the business." This was the time of the Anglo-French confrontation with Egypt over the Suez Canal and the city was off-limits for British troops. The only British soldiers in evidence were those who stood alone on sentry duty along the canal, with nothing but sand dunes and desert behind them. They must have gazed longingly at the British ocean liners, pouring out their bright lights and music as they passed in the night, filled with their compatriots headed for the "good life" in Australia.

We were warned by the ship's company that while in Port Said, and in Port Suez at the southern end of the canal, we must keep our portholes locked. Some of the locals in their "bum boats" made it a practice to extend long poles through the portholes and hook out bedclothes, pillows, or anything else that might attach itself to the poles.

In Port Said, while having a drink on deck with friends after the day ashore, we were visited by one of the roving local "businessmen." He made us an offer that was almost impossible to refuse. It was a genuine diamond ring for only five pounds! To prove that the article was genuine, our salesman grabbed my glass and gouged a deep mark in it from top to bottom. He then "nervously" hid the diamond in a handkerchief. I asked him to show us the other ring in his handkerchief, which he probably got from a Cracker Jacks box and which he intended to leave with us for the five pounds. If looks could kill, I was dead! I was thankful for the company of my friends. He gathered up his wares and, looking hurt and disgusted, moved off to another table of people who, he undoubtedly hoped, would be a more friendly and trusting group.

Chapter Four
East of Suez

We sailed into Aden on the southeast corner of the Arabian peninsula. If the Red Sea area could be described as hot, Aden was even hotter, and terribly dry. We were told that they hadn't had rain for six years. Anybody of that age was in for a great surprise when rain eventually did come. As we pulled into port, the surrounding landscape compared to the popular image of the moon. There wasn't a tree or blade of grass in sight, just a rock-bound coast destitute of vegetation as far as the eye could see. The ship anchored in midstream, and passengers and cargo were ferried to and from the shore on lighters that plied their route every few minutes for the ten or twelve hours we were in port.

Aden is now part of the Yemeni Republic and has turned its back on its traditional life as a trading centre and become a socialist republic. At the time of my first visit, it was an important coaling and fueling station for the British navy and the commercial ships that travelled the Suez-Red Sea route from Europe to the Orient. Until the closing of the Suez Canal by the British-French invasion in 1967, Aden was one of the busiest bunkering ports in the world. In coal-bunkering days, it was nicknamed by seamen the "coalhole of the East." British interest in Aden dated from Napoleon's conquest of Egypt, an event that was regarded as a menace to Britain's communications with India.

A group of us went ashore and visited what was said to be the Queen of Sheba's wells. We saw no sign of water. We visited a golf course on the Royal Air Force base, where personnel were playing golf on packed sand. The only difference between the "fairways" and the "greens" was that the latter were packed a little harder. We also visited an oasis on the border with Yemen, where we saw our first trees. Here we watched with a mixture of fascination and disgust, blindfolded donkeys going around in circles for hours attached to a wheel, which, in turning, created the energy to grind grain. We mixed with caravans and camel trains that were arriving from, and leaving for, Saudi Arabia and the eastern Mediterranean countries to the north. It was incredible to stand there and consider that this form of commerce and transportation had changed little in appearance and purpose in thousands of years.

Aden was a free port, so I did some shopping. I managed to haggle the price of two "Made in USA" dress shirts down to one dollar each. I was sure that this was my best buy ever; they were in their original packaging and were marked as being my exact size. When later, far out at sea, I tried them on, the cuffs came almost up to my elbows and the shirttails fell below the bottom of my shorts. My friends, who really enjoyed my being taken, said they must be "seconds." I would say "thirds!" I left them on a deck chair when we were later docked in Bombay, and thankfully they disappeared.

I had been told by a Newfoundland sailor who had served with the Royal Navy in the Aden Gulf area, that the island of Socotra, en route from Aden to Bombay, was "heaven on earth." I sat on deck with binoculars for the entire time it took to pass along its eighty-five-mile coast, and I failed to see any "heaven." It was as desolate as Aden. I could see that there were in a few places, palm-lined beaches, but heaven must have been on the other side of the island, or my friend must have been comparing this with the most barren parts of Newfoundland's coast!

In Bombay, we landed on the steps of the Gateway to India, an imposing structure that had been built on the occasion of the visit of King George V to India. I had become friendly aboard ship with an Indian who had just completed his studies in Britain. He insisted that, with several English friends, I visit his home in Bombay and join his family for dinner. I felt a little guilty that he would spend but a few hours with his wife and children and then have five of us interrupt his homecoming. However, we did, and I very much enjoyed my first experience dining Indian style with an Indian family.

I had had many Indian meals aboard ship, where they were offered daily by the Goanese staff. On the ship, you ate English style, with fork and knife, but at my friend's house the curry was stronger and we had to eat with one hand and *chapatis*. The food was eaten with the fingers of the right hand only, for it was considered impolite to use the "unclean" left hand to touch food. I'm sure that our hosts were attempting to serve us as genuine an Indian meal as possible. Like many of their Western-educated compatriots in the major Indian cities, they would have adopted the European custom of serving food on dinner plates instead of chapatis, and would normally have eaten with dessert spoon and fork.

Our Indian host arranged for a car to take us around Bombay. His kindness and hospitality impressed us. We were shown the usual sights but also a few not on the routine "Cook's tour." Most impressive, in a rather gloomy way, was the Five Towers of Silence, where the Parsi dead were placed for "removal" by vultures. The sky was black with these creatures. It was all very fascinating, yet more than a little revolting for us, whose contact with the dead was generally only in funeral homes. We were used to seeing the departed after they had been embalmed, dressed in their finest, surrounded by satin and lace, and made to look their best for the last viewing. Another sight that we found pathetic was that of hundreds of prostitutes waving at us from their windows and verandas; they were in such contrast to the ordinary Indian women, who, whether rich or poor, carried themselves with great poise.

One could not visit Bombay, or indeed India, without being shocked by what would appear to us to be hopeless poverty. It was a very different world for those of us raised in the West, where most people have elbowroom and, even in the worst of times, enough to eat. Not so in this country of teeming and diverse millions, many of whom belonged to castes "untouchable" by others. Conditions appeared to us to be so poor and chaotic as to defy solution. The most terrible demonstrations of this were the beggars on the streets. We had all seen beggars before, but not accompanied by children purposely maimed to make them irresistible to would-be donors!

All of the squalor could not detract from the beauty of Bombay harbour. The entrance from the sea discloses a magnificent panorama framed by the western mountains. The side harbour was studded with islands and dotted with colourful sails of innumerable small crafts. Besides the expected freighters and liners that frequent every major port, there were hundreds of oceangoing dhows that had come down from Arabia.

We cruised down the west coast of India, bound for Ceylon (now Sri Lanka). For hundreds of miles, the sea was muddy, as if some giant river had directed its entire runoff towards us. As we approached Ceylon, the water cleared to the perfect blue-green one sees in the tropical resort advertisements.

Ceylon was not an advertised holiday destination in those days. The British were all but gone, and the locals looked to the passenger liners to fill some of the gap left by the free-spending military. It was a most beautiful island. Rich tropical vegetation bordered long, clean, sandy beaches that were pounded by surf from the thundering Indian Ocean, which rolled all the way from Africa.

Seven or eight of us went ashore and negotiated with two drivers to take us to Negumbo. This was a beautiful and virtually empty beach resort outside Colombo. We struck a deal for two pounds sterling per car return and set off for our destination. Once there the drivers guided us to the best area of the beach where there were no swimmers except ourselves. I was intrigued when two English girls who were with us did a quick change from street clothes to swimming suits while wrapped in towels. I spent the entire time in the surf wondering whether they would or could do the undressing and redressing in reverse after the swim! They did.

It was my first experience in tropical surf and I loved it! The only annoying thing was that from the moment we entered the water, our drivers stood on the beach yelling continuously that it was time to go. We finally gave in to their demands. On our return to the ship we were doubly annoyed when the drivers tried to extract more money from us than we had agreed to pay. We resisted but not without unpleasant and embarrassing moments when they sought to recruit the police and the ships officers to help them collect "fair" payment. The really unbelievable thing was that, later that evening, we ran into one of the drivers at the Galle Face Hotel and he insisted on buying us all a beer! I asked him as diplomatically as I could why he was so intent on being generous now, when earlier he tried in every way to extract an extra pound or two from us. He simply said that earlier, "it was business, but now it was a pleasure to have you as my guests."

We sailed late in the evening, and next morning we were already far out in the Indian Ocean. This ocean has to be the least known of the world's oceans. No Western country other than Australia borders on it. From Ceylon, or Sri Lanka, to the west coast of Australia is half as far again as from Newfoundland to Britain. Across its broadest expanse, from South Africa to Australia, the Indian Ocean is twice as wide as the North Atlantic.

The voyage across the Indian Ocean, while subjecting us almost continuously to a lot of rocking and rolling, had one thing going for it; it was in the latitudes we were sailing, tropical waters all the way. Unlike the North Atlantic, it seemed to be easier to tolerate high winds and rough seas when combined with warm temperatures. Further south, on the run from South Africa to Australia, were the old trade routes in the zone of latitude extending from forty to sixty degrees south. That zone of ocean is unique in that some ninety-five percent of surface of that zone, right around the world, is covered by sea. The absence of great land masses gives the winds a consistency that they lack in other parts of the world. The winds blow from the west in every season of the year, and mariners call the seas beyond the parallel of forty degrees south "the roaring forties."

Fortunately we were not in those latitudes. Nobody seemed to mind the relatively rough conditions. Perhaps we all had our sea legs by the time we left Colombo. My recollections are of seven days of delightfully warm, if breezy, tropical travel.

A day or so out of Colombo, we crossed the equator. For those of us who were crossing it for the first time, which was the vast majority, we had to meet King Neptune. We assembled poolside and subjected ourselves to a backward dunking by King Neptune from a chair precariously positioned on the diving board. There was also the greasy pole that stretched across the pool, where each of us was challenged to hold his or her position astride the pole while striking and being struck in a one-handed duel with partially filled leather water bags. Few survived for more than a few seconds, and even the victors invariably lost their balance and fell into the pool within a second of their victory. There was one contestant, a woman, who beat some ten challengers, all men. She was the undisputed champion of the afternoon, but I noticed later in the evening, at the Crossing of the Equator Ball, that nobody asked her to dance!

Chapter Five
The Sunburnt Land

A week out of Colombo we had our first sighting of Australia's sun-drenched coastline. Here truly was a land of sunshine and blue skies, a sunburnt land as large as the United States or Europe but with a population of just over half of Canada's. I was to learn over the next few decades that this was an immense country, of rugged beauty, with great scenic contrasts, from the tropical rain forests of the northeast to the arid deserts of the centre. If you were to stand on the summit of Ayers Rock in the dead heart of the continent (which I did years later), you would have to travel over a thousand kilometres in any direction to reach the sea.

Beautiful sandy beaches, like the one before us, ring almost all of Australia. We penetrated this ring to enter Fremantle, the port for Western Australia's capital of Perth. Perth is for Australia what Vancouver is for Canada. Here was the area described in such an enticing way as one of the best spots on earth by the Shakespearean actor on that wintry evening long ago in far-off Newfoundland. How right he was! And Perth is far-off! Perth is probably the most isolated city of its size in the world. Many would consider this in positive terms, but it is a fact of life for the million or so people who live there. Perth is as far from Adelaide in South Australia, which is Perth's closest neighbouring big city, as Vancouver is from Thunder Bay in Ontario. It is as far from Sydney on the east coast as Vancouver is from Montreal. The great difference is that between Vancouver and the Canadian East, there are large cities, such as Calgary, Edmonton and Winnipeg, as well as hundreds of square kilometres of rich prairie and well-watered forests. Perth, by contrast, is separated from the rest of populated Australia by thousands of square kilometres of desert and scrubland. There is no Seattle or Portland a short drive from Perth, as there is from Vancouver! As the capital of the state of Western Australia, it is the centre of a world in which the southwestern corner is fertile, well-watered, and has a wonderful climate year round. The northern and eastern parts of its domain are amongst the driest land on earth.

Perth is a beautiful, relaxed, and friendly city that could challenge any city in the world for quality of life. The Swan River and nearby ocean beaches provide opportunities for aquatic recreational activities second to none. I was impressed by the orderliness and cleanliness, perhaps this was because of having just visited the comparatively chaotic and dirty ports of the Far East. I was struck by the covered sidewalks throughout the city, where one could shop and walk for hours protected from the strong sun or the unexpected shower. (Was this the forerunner of today's malls?) I have returned to Perth many times since this first short visit, and my view hasn't changed; it is one of the most pleasant spots on earth!

Sydney was to be the final port of the voyage, but for many immigrants, Melbourne was to be home. Melbourne, capital of the state of Victoria, was founded as a free city fifty years after Sydney. While lacking Sydney's natural beauties of harbour and her many fine beaches, Melbourne is a well planned, well laid-out city and is probably more sedate and conservative than Sydney. Melbourne has been described by Billy Graham as one of the most moral cities he has ever seen, and by Ava Gardner, when she was there for the filming of Neville Shute's *On the Beach,* as a fine place to make a film about the end of the world! Both comments are of course extreme. Like any city of several million people, Melbourne can offer up whatever the visitor demands. The city is slightly smaller than Sydney and larger than Montreal or San Francisco.

Our ship stopped in Melbourne for three days. It was the port where all supplies were taken aboard for the return voyage to England and then back to Australia. Like the taking on of the Goanese crew in Bombay, in Melbourne, it was one-stop shopping as far as supplies were concerned. It was a great treat for those of us going on to Sydney to have three days ashore in Melbourne with the ship as our hotel.

Entering Sydney Harbour in the early morning with the sun appearing just over the horizon was a sight I shall never forget. Coming through the heads, except for the impressive city skyline in the background, the sight has changed little from that seen by those who arrived with the First Fleet. The heads were only a kilometre apart, thus giving the harbour the perfect security that originally attracted Phillip in his search for a site for a settlement. The total shoreline within the harbour stretches more than three hundred kilometres. Once through the heads, you catch sight of the Sydney

Harbour Bridge, the international symbol of Sydney. Today, another internationally known landmark joins it, the no less widely acclaimed Sydney Opera House.

Most world travellers can only compare Sydney Harbour, when it comes to real beauty, to the harbour of Rio de Janeiro. Years later I was to see and sail on the waters around Rio, and as beautiful as it is, I must come down on the side of Sydney!

Unfortunately most of us could not appreciate at that moment the splendour of Sydney Harbour. We were all too concerned with the uncertainties or responsibilities that were approaching us as quickly as the ship was approaching the dock. We pulled into our berth thirty-three days after leaving London. Shipboard friends made their farewells and separated. After a month of being lulled into worry-free life at sea, we all now felt abandoned and very much alone. Everyone traded addresses and promised to meet at such and such a beach at such and such a time. These were for the most part gestures, although a week or so later, I did meet, as arranged, an English family on Bondi Beach. When I arrived, they were virtually alone on the huge beach stretched out on the sand. Although it was winter in Sydney, they said it was warmer than summer at Brighton!

I had been invited to stay until I got settled with the Brent family. The Brents were the parents of Irene Skinner, the only Australian in Grand Falls. My friend, Jess Skinner, had met her in Australia during the war when he was with the Royal Navy. The Brents lived at Guildford, far out in the western suburbs. I took the suburban train with all my worldly goods and got my first introduction to Australian life, living for the next few weeks with this very hospitable family.

I spent a lot of time on the train going back and forth to downtown Sydney. I had a number of meetings with the immigration people and the Public Service Board. I found everyone genuinely helpful and trying hard to get me quickly settled into a job in Canberra with the federal government. I also visited the University of Sydney, where the registrar gave me a letter confirming that Dalhousie University was a member of the Association of Universities of the British Commonwealth and, accordingly, my degree would be recognised by the University of Sydney.

The only thing standing in my way for an immediate position in Canberra was my security clearance. On this I pressed the authorities almost daily, although I realised it would take at least a few weeks. During that time, I looked at the local job market as a matter of insurance in case the

Canberra position fell through. I could have had any number of positions if I had been prepared to commit myself to some degree of permanency. Out of curiosity I actually called on several would-be employers and found it great for the ego to be pressed to take a position; such was the shortage of labour in Australia at the time! I was particularly pressured by a car dealer, who told me that my American accent guaranteed me a successful future in the car-selling business!

In a few weeks, I received word from the Public Service Board that my security check was complete and that they could offer me a position in the Department of External Territories, working in the area of the economic development of Papua New Guinea, Norfolk Island, and Nauru. I readily accepted and went to their offices for my railway ticket and advance payment for the trip to Canberra. I had accommodation reserved for me in one of the many hostels that housed the quarter of the population of Canberra that was single. I was on my way to what was to be the start of a lifelong career in public service!

Chapter Six
The Capital in the Bush

Canberra today is a city of about a quarter of a million inhabitants. When I lived there in the early 1950s, it had a population of twenty-three thousand. It was said by its many detractors to be "the largest lighted paddock in the world." It was true that you could drive for miles along beautifully lighted streets without a building anywhere in sight! The city was being laid out strictly according to the plans of its designer, the American town-planner, Walter Burley-Griffin. He had been selected the winner of the international competition for a plan for Australia's federal capital, which was to be built virtually from scratch in the bush. When I arrived, there was more bush than city.

What is now the six-mile-long beautiful Canberra Lake, around whose twenty-four miles of shoreline are the impressive public buildings befitting a national capital, was in my day open grazing land. There were roads following the future shoreline but these made little sense for those of us who were there before the lake. To get from one point to another would take you five times the distance you would travel if you went straight through the fields that were destined to become the bottom of the lake.

Besides the "lighted paddock" description, Canberra had been described as a garden city, a planner's dream, and an exhibition grounds years before the exhibition opened! All descriptions were in a sense correct. Canberra was the result of an attempt to create a city where no economic, commercial, military, or other nonpolitical need existed.

Canberra is just over three hundred kilometres from Sydney and about twice that from Melbourne. It is set in beautiful surroundings, beneath hills and mountainous country covered with large eucalyptus trees. The Australian Capital Territory that surrounds Canberra is a separate political entity, like Washington's District of Columbia. With only a twenty-three-inch rainfall, the area would be considered dry by a Canadian, but the surrounding countryside made excellent sheep-grazing land and had the appearance

45

of a beautiful, if somewhat sunburnt, pastoral countryside. The Australian government has been intent on making Canberra one of the most beautiful of cities, a city of parks and innumerable planted trees, most of them of varieties seen nowhere else in Australia.

When I first arrived in Canberra, it consisted of several distinct and widely separated suburbs, each gravitating to its own commercial area. I was in Civic, which was eventually to be a central business district of the city. An officer from the Public Service Board kindly met me at the railway station and drove me to Reid House, which was a long, wooden, temporary hostel for single people. It was not unlike the temporary offices built during the war in Ottawa and other centres. As happened elsewhere, these temporary buildings were still around several decades after their intended life span.

The Civic commercial centre consisted of only one block of shops, a few restaurants, a police station, and a pub that was appropriately called the Civic. Drinkers and teetotallers alike would have found the Civic not very civil! The drinking laws at the time required six o'clock closing, and women were excluded from the men's stand-up bar. They were accommodated in a slightly more civilised, but not well-patronised, adjoining sit-down room, where ladies separately or with their male companions would be served. All the action was in the men's bar or just outside its doors on the sidewalk.

When government offices closed just a few minutes before five o'clock, there would be buses outside the offices to run nonstop to the various commercial centres, which were, of course, where the pubs were. The buses would be packed, and there would be a holiday or school-out air! Hundreds of thirsty civil servants would descend on the Civic and other pubs in other centres of the city. Only those who got there first had the dubious privilege of getting inside. The rest stood packed on the sidewalk near the door. They passed their change through scores of hands until it reached the bartender far inside the pub. In the other direction came the glasses of beer passed by the same hands over the scores of heads out to the sidewalk. Everybody on the inside had some feeling for everybody on the outside, for they knew that they could well be on the outside tomorrow.

Just before six the publican would shout, "Time, gentlemen, please," and twice as many coins would be passed into the pub and a continuous line of full glasses would be passed out. The glasses would be passed first to those far out on the sidewalk; then the intervening hands that had finished passing glasses would take their own. By the time the pub actually closed, everybody held two glasses. Like many of my colleagues, I was an occasional attendee at this ritual of the "six o'clock swill." I rarely got inside the pub, but I never heard of a single instance when either money or beer went astray!

When I arrived at the Department of External Territories, it was in the course of being renamed Department of Territories, because it was assuming responsibility for the Northern Territory of Australia as well as for Australia's offshore territories. I was introduced to everyone from the minister down. The minister was Paul Hasluck from Western Australia. He was later to become minister for External Affairs. I was introduced as being from Newfoundland, but he introduced me thereafter as being from "Saskatoon, Saskatchewan!" I think he liked the ring of it. However, since many Australians had a close association with our prairie provinces because of the thousands who trained there as flight crew under the Commonwealth Air Training Scheme during the war, I didn't object too strenuously. He did on one occasion introduce me as being from Nova Scotia, probably the only other province he could bring to mind. I do believe that by the end of my time in Canberra, he knew a little about the geography of Canada!

My two close "work mates" in Territories were as different as chalk and cheese. Fred Rose was my immediate superior. He was a renowned anthropologist and an expert on the aboriginal tribes of the Gulf of Carpentaria, particularly Groote Eylandt. Fred was subsequently to cause me a great deal of concern politically, but while working for and with him, I could not have asked for a better or more congenial boss. My immediate working companion was Rex Cross, with whom I shared an office. He became a close friend and my most reliable "adviser" on all things Australian. I made friends in other areas of the department. I single out one, Con Dawson, simply because he was eventually to play a role in orchestrating my future!

My boss, Fred Rose, was a communist. He made no attempt to hide it, particularly from Rex and me. Indeed he flaunted it. He was an Englishman, but obviously much more at home in Australia than he could ever be in England. His wife was from East Germany, and as future events confirmed, she supported, if not shared, his political views. Fred and his wife were always kind to me and, in my view at the time, were strange but very nice people. However, in spite of my naiveté and tolerance for different political views, I felt Fred was very wrong in his beliefs and constantly told him so. Rex was at the opposite end of the political spectrum from Fred. He was very supportive of the United States and its policies around the world and had no time or tolerance for communism.

Rex was an Australian navy veteran; Fred was a pacifist; so we had the ingredients for lively political discussions during morning and afternoon tea times. I always sided with Rex about things "left" and "right." For the first time in my life, I was forced to state my views and beliefs and found myself doing so unashamedly. Fred was fascinated that this young fellow from Newfoundland still had strong feelings for the values and ideals of the Western world, for the Christian religion, for the Commonwealth, the queen, and all the other underpinnings of that old fashioned world he had entirely rejected.

In a strange way, I felt he liked me because of my "dated" views and ideals. I guess other people had long ago given up even raising such matters with him. I was impressed that when Fred argued, using all the well-known communist clichés and rhetoric, he never once ridiculed me for my views. In spite of the great differences between us, Fred, Rex, and I got along wonderfully until Canberra learned one day that Fred had a closer relationship with the Soviet embassy than with his office colleagues; but this was much later.

In the meantime, Fred shared in the making of the tea. He brought a live baby crocodile back from a trip to the Northern Territory. He spent many evening hours with Rex and me, pouring over Australian stamps. He helped me set out a vegetable garden when I moved into a house, and assisted me with the important task undertaken by most Canberra residents of setting up a brew of beer.

While in Canberra, I had to renew my passport. I was travelling on a British (Newfoundland) passport that was considered Canadian until it expired, at which time it was to be exchanged gratis for a Canadian one. When I called at the Canadian High Commission on a Friday afternoon to collect my new passport, a group of people that I knew in the office performed a small informal ceremony. They pronounced that with my new passport I was now truly Canadian, so they presented me with a glass of Canadian rye and a pack of Canadian cigarettes; any excuse for a party.

Our small group in Territories was responsible for the department's work pertaining to the economic development of Papua New Guinea, Norfolk Island, and Nauru. This sounds very ambitious and more than a little presumptuous, given that we were only several people and the territory that was our main area of focus, Papua New Guinea, was one of the least known and least developed areas of the world. Our real job was to serve as the point of contact for the administrators in the territories and the government departments in Canberra, the private sector companies with current and potential interests in the area, and with academics and private individuals who were focusing on the territories.

In reality we had little to do with Nauru, a speck of an island in the Pacific, between Papua New Guinea and Hawaii. Nauru was covered with beds of phosphate rock derived from rich deposits of guano. Its phosphate-based economy gave the islanders a per-capita income amongst the highest in the world (currently more than twenty thousand dollars). The phosphate was expected to run out by the year 2000. With most of their island mined away, the people of Nauru would have to exist on their investment income and fishing and the food they could produce on the fifteen percent of the island that was at all suitable for agriculture.

"Our" other Pacific territory, Norfolk Island, also required little of our time. It was the home of a number of the descendants of the mutineers of H.M.S. *Bounty*. In 1856 the population of Pitcairn Island, where the mutineers had hidden after the burning of the *Bounty,* was transferred to Norfolk Island, where it was considered they could make a much better life. A number did return to Pitcairn, but many stayed. There was some added immigration from Australia and New Zealand in the late 1800s.

The two Pacific islands offered little challenge for the economic side of the Department of Territories. It was important to provide a continuing Australian presence in Nauru through the administrator, to nudge the island along its predestined course towards independence, for Nauru was a United Nations Trust Territory. It was the United Nations objective to give independence to all trusteeships and colonial territories. In the case of Norfolk Island, even the United Nations would have had to agree that the island had long been an integral part of Australia; it was a convict settlement from the time of the First Fleet in Sydney. The modest subsistence way of life of its population was well established. It was generally acknowledged that, except for tourism, there was little scope for further economic development without undue disruption of a generally contented island population.

Papua New Guinea was a different world from the two minute islands. Here was a huge territory, occupying the entire eastern half of the fourth largest island in the world. The northern portion had formerly been a German colonial territory, and the southern part British. To the west, the other half of the island was Dutch New Guinea, which was all that remained

49

of the great Dutch empire in the East Indies. The Netherlands had ceded to Indonesia all its East Indies territories except this one. This was now an area of bitter dispute between the Netherlands and Indonesia.

Australians were split between those who maintained that a line had to be drawn against Indonesian expansionism and those who felt that there was really no alternative to accommodating Indonesia. The hold-the-line group argued that the core of Indonesia (Java and Sumatra) had absolutely nothing in common with Netherlands New Guinea except that they were all former or current Dutch colonial territories. The New Guineans were as different from the Indonesians as they were from the Dutch.

I feel that the real concern of many Australians was that so soon after the Japanese threat, here was another Asian country pushing up to Australia's doorstep. Dutch administration would help contain the pressure; Dutch New Guinea would at least serve as a buffer between Australia and what some saw as a new expansionist power developing to the north. The proponents of this argument held that Australia should make the case in the United Nations and elsewhere that Dutch New Guinea should be united with their brethren in Papua New Guinea and the entire island brought along towards independence as a single entity.

The counterargument, which eventually prevailed, was that Australia had to accept that the Netherlands was finished as a colonial power. Indonesia was now a fact of life, and as Australia's closest neighbour, there was no sensible alternative to the development and maintenance of good relations. Australia itself would be under ever increasing pressure to grant Papua New Guinea early, and indeed premature, independence. This would be spurred on by the fact that the northern half of the territory, the former German portion, was a United Nations Trust Territory. The future independent Papua New Guinea should be left to worry about the Dutch portion of the island. In any event, Indonesia would have its hands full for years bringing together the disparate islands that stretched across three thousand miles of the Indian and Pacific Oceans. The addition of Dutch New Guinea would preoccupy them even more!

Dutch New Guinea, or West Irian, as the Indonesians renamed it, remained a matter of dispute between the Netherlands and Indonesia, and a matter of worry for the Australians, until its transfer to Indonesia in 1962.

The Department of Territories had to administer the largely unknown territory of Papua New Guinea under the eyes of the world. We had to present regular reports to the United Nations for the portion under United

Nations mandate. It was a mammoth task, given the difficulty of the terrain and the backwardness of the people, educationally, economically, and politically. Four-fifths of the people existed in a nonmonetarised self-sufficient economy.

One of the greatest problems was that there were over seven hundred different languages spoken by the three million people. About four hundred of the languages were related, but they showed considerable diversity and extreme grammatical complexity. The remaining three hundred were of doubtful or unknown affiliation. The number of speakers of each language varied generally from a few score to a few thousand, although Enga, numerically the largest, had over one hundred thousand speakers. As a consequence, English was the official language, although it was spoken by a small percentage of the population. About half spoke a Melanesian pidgin.

Rex Cross kept a huge map of Papua New Guinea on our office wall. From knowledge gained from many sources, including virtually every traveller, official, and missionary who visited the territory, Rex would note on this map, in the greatest detail, the languages spoken. He started the project well before my arrival. When I moved into the office I shared with him and where he displayed the map, it was a valuable source of reference for anybody going to the territory. We had a steady stream of academics, missionaries, and officials knocking at our door.

My work and also my social life couldn't have been better. For a young man in his early twenties, life in Canberra was exciting. A great part of the population was not only young but single. One of the peculiar and, I thought, civilised things about social life in the capital was that on almost every weekend there was a formal dance. These were not formal in the accepted sense of the word, but rather in that all dances were organised on the assumption that the men would be in black-tie and the ladies in evening gowns. I was thankful that I had brought my tuxedo with me. Before coming to Australia, I had not worn it more than a dozen times. Indeed, in my future career, I don't believe that I wore a dinner jacket as much as I did in Canberra. It was amusing at our weekend dances to see all the fellows around the kegs of beer in dinner jackets drawing beer for six pence a glass.

I made friends with three fellows outside the office: Erwin, a big, happy-go-lucky Hungarian; Frank, a former Czech diplomat who had defected; and Daryl Blaxland, an Australian from one of the best known families in the country. One of Daryl's forefathers was the famous Blaxland who, with Wentworth and Lawson, was the first European to discover the way through the Blue Mountains from the coastal plains to the inland.

Erwin and Frank, refugees from Eastern Europe, were very outspoken in their anticommunism. Erwin's views in particular were rather extreme and were well known throughout Canberra's large Eastern European community. I recall walking into the small dance club at Civic with Erwin and the band, which was made up entirely of East Europeans, striking up the communist song, "The International." The band members knew that the playing of this most sacred of communist pieces would send Erwin into a rage that would be as good as a floor show! It always was.

Erwin, Daryl, and I spent a lot of our free time together, but Erwin favoured the little night life we had in Canberra, whereas Daryl, who had a car, preferred drives and hikes in the country. He was brought up in the country and knew the area around Canberra well from his job as BP Oil representative for the Capital Territory and the nearby regions of New South Wales. I gravitated towards Daryl's country tours. We went to horse shows, rodeos, sheep dog trials, and explored the beautiful countryside that I would never have seen so thoroughly if it were not for Daryl's love for the land.

One area that fascinated me was Lake George to the east of Canberra. This was a several-mile-wide and ten-mile-long stretch of shallow water that had suddenly appeared fifty years earlier. At the time, the Australian Naval College at Duntroon had training exercises on the lake. A terrible tragedy had occurred shortly before my arrival; a large number of cadets had drowned when a sudden wind had whipped up the shallow waters. What fascinated me about the lake was that it had appeared and disappeared several times in the hundred and fifty years since European settlement. When I visited the area with Peggy and our daughter Julie in the 1980s, the lake was no longer there. Sheep were grazing where people used to go boating. Only at the extreme end of what used to be the lake bed was there any sign of water, and even there, it was little more than a swamp.

One winter afternoon on the bus from work, I noticed my friend Con Dawson sitting with a beautiful blue-eyed blonde. As we left the bus at the Civic area, Con called to me to join them for a stroll around the shops. He introduced me to Peggy Roberts! The spot where we met is now called (by coincidence) "Petrie Street"! Peggy and I were married on January 2, 1953. Daryl Blaxland was my best man, and his fiancée Hermina was Peggy's maid of honour.

It was the practice that as soon as you moved into Canberra, you registered for a government-built house. Peggy and I had both failed to do this, not anticipating anything as serious as marriage. We were, however, successful in renting a house in the nearby suburb of Turner. Our friends thought that four pounds a week was a bit much for us to pay for a house. I didn't agree, for it was well furnished and had all the appliances. We had two salaries; Peggy, with a degree in psychology, actually had an income that was a little higher than mine. I felt that about ten percent of our combined salaries was not an exorbitant amount to pay for a house.

We shared half a well-butchered lamb each week with a neighbour for ten shillings; every second week, we got the choice bits. You sure got tired of lamb, but the price was certainly right for your basic meat supply for the week!

I guess like all newlyweds, we had great fun setting up house. Peggy started her lifelong love of gardening. I got into vegetables and got to know the muscle soreness from splitting eucalyptus logs for the fireplace. We collected pine cones for our "Little Hero" shower heater, for although we had an automatic gas shower heater, it was much cheaper to use the Little Hero. A dozen large pine cones were sufficient for a shower, and two dozen would do for a bath. We would gather the cones during our walks in the pine-break that separated the suburb of Turner from Civic. In the pine-break you had to watch out for the Australian magpies that would often dive-bomb you as you wandered in areas where they nested. Financial necessity made us take the chance.

The summers were lovely in Canberra, but the winters could be cool at night. By late morning the temperatures would be comfortable, but after dark we could get frosts. It never snowed, for as soon as clouds arrived from the coast the temperatures would rise, giving us rain. We regularly used our fireplace. In order to keep the heat in the house, we placed long snakelike sand-filled bags at the bottom of the doors. The Australians loved their ventilation, and the house was well ventilated. This might be acceptable in the warmer coastal regions, but inland the vents created chilling drafts, so I covered them up.

From the time we first met, Peggy and I saw a lot of Daryl and Hermina. Peggy and Hermina loved the trips around the countryside as much as Daryl and I did. On one of our forays into the country we had lunch in a pub in a small settlement. The owner, a good friend of Daryl's, was of Chinese origin. He was third or fourth generation Australian, his forefathers having been drawn to the country by the gold rush. Peggy's maternal grandfather had also gone to the gold rush.

Meeting Daryl's Chinese-Australian friend stirred my curiosity about the "White Australia" policy, which was brought in originally against Asian immigration. The policy that was initiated by the new Commonwealth of Australia in 1901, reflected the long-standing sentiment of the various colonies that made up Australia. It remained fundamental Australian policy into the mid-twentieth century and, certainly at the time I worked there, was an accepted fact of life. Each Australian colony had passed restrictive legislation as early as the 1860s. In 1901 a federal act effectively ended non-European immigration. From the 1950s, the policy became less stringent and finally was abolished. A walk today down any urban street bears witness to the present liberal policy.

People who know little about Australia seem nevertheless to be aware of the rabbit problem. It really was a problem. Everywhere in the countryside were the rabbits and evidence of the destruction that came with them. Daryl, as a son of the land, considered them as we would consider rats. Whole hillsides around Canberra had been washed away when the heavy rains flowed down the burrows. According to Daryl, many a horse had to be destroyed after breaking a leg by stepping into a burrow. It was most probable that no country in the world has paid so heavily for the introduction of an alien species as Australia paid, and is paying, for the introduction of the rabbit.

It seems that the present Australian rabbit originated from a small shipment from England that arrived on the clipper ship *Lightning* in 1859. They were released near Geelong, Victoria. These rabbits gained a foothold within the vast belt of savannah woodland merging into the plains, where they found a favourable habitat. By 1880 the rabbit had crossed the Murray River and established itself in New South Wales in a remarkably short time. It was first sighted in Queensland, far to the north in 1886. The rabbits thus crossed and populated New South Wales at a rate of seventy miles a year. They entered Western Australia in 1907. Once the threat was appreciated, governments were stimulated to take action. Especially noteworthy because of the vast scale on which it was undertaken, was the erection of "rabbit fences." They failed, because it proved impractical to maintain such barriers at one hundred percent efficiency, which was necessary if they were to fulfill their role. By the end of the nineteenth century, rabbit fences of several thousand miles had been erected. Western Australia was particularly enthusiastic about fences, completing in 1907, after five years of work, a fence that ran from the south to the north coast of the continent, a distance of 1,139 miles!

The effect of the rabbit on the pastoral industry is incalculable. In areas of low rainfall, where sheep depend entirely on natural pasture, the extra load that the land had to carry because of the introduction of the rabbit led to virtual permanent degradation of vegetation and soil erosion and drift on a large scale. The eradication of rabbits on a property commonly resulted in a doubling of the carrying capacity of sheep, with a much greater ability to withstand droughts.

A large-scale demonstration of the effect of the easing of rabbit pressure on pastoral country occurred in 1953 when we were in Canberra. As a result of a highly effective epidemic of the introduced virus disease myxomatosis, they were decimated. To those who knew it well in previous years, the wide belt of sheep country, extending from northern New South Wales into the state of Victoria, appeared transformed. While some rabbits did build up an immunity to myxomatosis, it has had a major impact on checking and depleting what Australians really consider a terrible pest.

Our happy carefree days in Canberra were interrupted by the decision of my boss, Fred Rose, to leave for a holiday in East Germany with his wife and children. Peggy and I happened to be in Sydney on the day of their departure, so we boarded their ship and visited with them for an hour before the ship sailed. We never saw them again!

Stories were all over Canberra that Fred had been on the verge of arrest as a Soviet agent and was seeking asylum in East Germany. I'm not sure of the facts, but it appeared that he prepared the way for a university position in East Germany and actually returned for a while to a property on King Island, south of Melbourne. Whatever were the facts, it seemed that Fred did leave for East Germany intending never to return to Canberra. The situation blew wide open when, on April 3, 1954, an official of the Soviet embassy in Canberra, Vladimir Petrov, defected the Soviet service and sought and was granted political asylum in Australia. The train of events this set in motion led to a far-reaching enquiry into Soviet espionage in Australia, with extensive repercussions. Fred Rose, amongst many others, was named by Petrov.

I was understandably concerned that my name should not be associated with Fred's misguided actions. The Department of Territories could not have been more cooperative with me. They had the Australian security get in touch with Canada's, to ensure that there would be nothing in my file in either country that might trouble me in the future.

Peggy and I could have willingly stayed forever in Canberra, for we were supremely happy there. However, a number of developments, taken together, caused us to give serious thoughts to returning to Canada. Fred Rose's departure unsettled things at the office. Peggy had a whole new world beckoning her on the other side of the globe. My mother and father were understandably wanting to meet Peggy and were encouraging us to return. My father was pressing me again to enter the family business in Newfoundland. We had often discussed the possibility of one day settling in Canada, perhaps with a career in the Canadian government. We pushed all of these thoughts and considerations aside until, when several months into our marriage, we learnt that we were to become parents. This meant that a decision had to be taken; we either had to go well before the arrival of our baby or wait until the baby was old enough to face several weeks of going through the tropics, for in those days, there was no affordable cabin air-conditioning. We decided to take the leap and booked passage on the Lloyd Tristino Line from Sydney to Genoa.

Chapter Seven
Starboard Home

A departure by ship from Sydney used to be something very special. Perhaps it was that when you left Australia, you were generally going to the other side of the world, so farewells had to be taken seriously. The sadness of the moment of our sailing for all of Peggy's family and friends was tempered somewhat by the holiday atmosphere. After we boarded the ship and all visitors went ashore, everybody on ship and shore grasped colourful paper streamers, held on the other end by friends and loved ones. It appeared as if the ship was secured to the dock by a rainbow of paper and couldn't possibly depart. Peggy and I stood at the rail connected with her entire family and many friends by the ribbons until the inevitable moment when the ship pulled away from the dock and everybody on ship and shore gazed at the ends of their streamers dropping into the sea.

The ship, the *Oceania,* was a converted British aircraft carrier, but that was the only thing British about her. Being of Italian registry, she had an Italian crew. Peggy had made the trip to Europe before, when she had travelled with her mother by P&O. Thus our experience was only with British ships. By comparison we felt that life on this ship was more relaxed, but to the point of being a bit chaotic. The ship certainly wasn't well organised; the life-boat drill gave the impression that it was the first time the crew had tried it. There were many annoyances that we hadn't experienced on British ships. As a major annoyance, everybody gave top marks to the currency exchange rates that were so out of line that we suspected that the purser's office looked upon currency exchange as an important source of income with no regard to providing a service to the passengers.

In the middle of the Indian Ocean, we got living proof that Gresham's law, an economic law that holds that bad money drives good money out of circulation, is absolutely valid. The ship understandably operated in Italian lire. There was a small lira note that was scheduled to go out of circulation on a nationally designated day. The day happened to be when we were midway between Indonesia and Sri Lanka. We only learnt about this development a few days before while in port at Jakarta. The Indonesian traders knew about the proposed change and refused to accept the notes. For the next few days, you saw hardly any currency change hands except for the condemned notes. If you purchased anything aboard ship your change was always in a wad of these. People playing cards placed their bets with them. It was a big game throughout the ship not to get caught on the designated day with these notes. The ship's company were even more determined than the passengers to dump them. We unloaded all of ours and, like our fellow passengers, hoped that the purser's office would get caught with them all!

All was not bad about the *Oceania*. The meals were terrific, and excellent wine was served free of charge with the meals. The passengers were mostly young Australians heading for extended holidays in Europe. There was the usual ten percent or so of dissatisfied migrants going home, many of whom would return after discovering that by now "home" was really Australia.

After Melbourne and Perth, we called at Jakarta. The Indonesian capital had some of the earmarks of the corrupt and chaotic city that many Australians associated with the big new threat, Indonesia. I tended to look upon the difficulties we encountered as "teething" problems that a major new country had to face in the transitional years from a colonial possession to a nation. The first troubling thing was an announcement by the Indonesian authorities that all money had to be exchanged at a ridiculous official rate before going ashore. I got caught up in the scheming to get around what we all considered to be an attempt to undermine our purchasing power.

Everybody concentrated on how to get their pounds, dollars, and lire ashore so that we could get true value for our money. I hid five one-pound notes in my camera. While I was being searched, I passed the camera and other valuables to Peggy, and while she was searched, she passed them to me. I therefore could honestly say that I did not have any foreign currency on me while I was being searched. The amusing thing was that once ashore, things were so inexpensive that we had to smuggle a pound or two back onto the ship.

Jakarta was full of soldiers. While friendly, they liked to demonstrate their authority by continually demanding to see our passports. They were just lucky if they had them right-side up when they came to the photographs, for they were for the most part illiterate and, of course, had no knowledge of English. The tropical climate with high temperatures and oppressive humidity was so uncomfortable that Peggy had a fainting spell. It lasted only a few moments, but given her condition, we immediately cut short our visit ashore and headed back to the ship. When we were boarding the ship, we caught a glimpse of President Sukarno leaving the ship. I never did learn why the *Oceania* was being honoured by a visit from the president.

Going in and out of Jakarta, we sailed through the beautiful Sunda Strait between Java and Sumatra. The sea was like glass, disturbed only by the wake of our ship and the flying fish. We passed the island of Krakatoa, which I had heard about since early childhood. The calmness around us at that moment was in contrast to the world-shattering explosion here in 1883, when there was a phenomenal volcanic eruption.

The sound waves generated by the Krakatoa explosion travelled three thousand miles, being heard in Australia. Ash was propelled to a height of fifty miles. The surrounding region was plunged into darkness for days because of the ash. The fine dust drifted several times around the earth, causing spectacular sunsets throughout the following year. Tidal waves were recorded as far away as South America and Hawaii. The greatest wave reached one hundred and twenty feet and took thirty-six thousand lives in Java and Sumatra. Reestablishment of plant and animal life did not begin for five years. A shocking report was that with the arrival of the first humans to look over the wasteland came rats!

After calls at Colombo, Bombay, Aden, Port Suez, Port Said, and Naples, we arrived in Genoa. We spent several days touring the Rhine country of Germany, France, and Switzerland before continuing on to Paris and London. In London, we took a plane via Shannon, Ireland, to Gander, Newfoundland.

Peggy didn't know whether to be concerned or amused when, getting ready for the landing at Gander, she was asked by an American lady whether she was really getting off at this "God-forsaken place?" I'm sure that when the lady actually saw Peggy depart, she must have flown all the way to New York shaking her head in disbelief.

The first few days in Newfoundland must have been a traumatic time for Peggy. Despite my rather positive detailed descriptions of what she should expect, she had to face an environment completely different from Sydney or Canberra. I was thankful that it was still summer and the weather was warm. I had warned her that the road for the sixty miles from Gander to Grand Falls was unpaved. This didn't bother her, for she was absorbed and fascinated with the "Christmas trees" that lined the road all the way! When we had to cross the Exploits River, which was not yet bridged, she was flabbergasted that we had to pay ten dollars (the equivalent of five pounds Australian and rent for a week in Canberra) for a barge to take the car across.

I decided to try again to fit into business life in Newfoundland. I was to have several days in Grand Falls before reporting for work in St. John's with Canada Packers. The manager, Fred Blair, was a partner of my father in several businesses, and it was thought that the St. John's branch of Canada Packers, being the largest on the island, would be a good training ground for me in Newfoundland business.

Before leaving for St. John's, Peggy and I went fishing up in the woods. The salmon fishing was said to be still good, so we drove up the Halls Bay Line (a single lane, dirt road) and stayed overnight in a cabin of an old friend, the game warden of the region, Art Butt. Immediately on our arrival, Art took Peggy to the closest salmon pool and, on his second cast, hooked her a salmon. To his disbelief and mine, she refused to take the rod and land the salmon, being "afraid of losing it!"

Next morning we drove a few miles to a cabin that my father and friends had built on a three-mile-long lake that didn't even have a name. We fished for trout with considerable success. It was a delight to see Peggy pull them in. In the evening after a good meal of trout, we settled down for the night. Peggy was a little disconcerted when I stuck a rifle under the bunk. I told her it was in case of bears. That didn't exactly settle her. Nor was she settled next morning when we learned that the remaining trout I had rather foolishly left on the veranda, covered in moss, had disappeared. Peggy was convinced it had been a bear; I couldn't argue that it wasn't, because all other lovers of trout that I knew about in Newfoundland, such as weasels or lynx, would have left more of a mess.

I took the train alone to St. John's to start work and look for an apartment. It was only a matter of a few days until I found a couple of rooms and Peggy was able to join me. I had two good friends in St. John's; Fred Morgan, my childhood friend, who was now a senior bank official, and Bruce Woodland, who was with the Newfoundland Tourist Bureau. Their wives, Edna and Edith, respectively, were expecting about the same time as Peggy, so the six of us spent much of our spare time together preparing for the three big events. Our first child, Janine Claire, arrived on December

27, 1953. As far as we were concerned, she was the first and only baby ever born!

Business life in Newfoundland was certainly different. I was told by mainland colleagues in the office that Canada Packers had great problems operating in the way they were required to operate by Toronto. As in Toronto, customers in Newfoundland were expected to pay their bills weekly. If overdue by a few days, the customer received a reminder in the mail. Every few days thereafter, letters were sent that got nastier and nastier. A customer on the south coast of Newfoundland, having received several such letters, was said to have written back along the following lines:

"Dear Canada Packers, it's obvious, sir, that you people up there don't know how we people down here do business. At the end of each month, we only have so much money, so to be fair we put all the bills in a hat and draw them out until all our funds are exhausted. Now if you don't stop sending those nasty letters, we won't even put your bill in the hat!"

We were in St. John's for a year. We enjoyed life there but knew deep down that it was only temporary. Our social and intellectual lives were full, particularly with British theatre that had migrated to St. John's from Britain in the off-season, mostly for foreign exchange purposes, but also because St. John's provided a good audience for British theatre. I also had relations there; cousins Frances and Bob Innes were very kind to us, and we had many happy days with them at their summer place and aboard their boat at Long Pond. We did, however, have difficulty with the St. John's climate that undoubtedly was the worst in Newfoundland. Unlike the western parts of the island, St. John's didn't have a good winter; there was heavy snow one day and rain the next. There was no spring, and summers were cloudy and cool by central and western island standards.

I was at the time convinced that I should resume my life in the public service, preferably in some area of international affairs. The Canberra experience had developed in me a liking for dealing with issues in the international arena, and I felt that my future lay there rather than in the local Newfoundland business world, however lucrative that may promise to be. To get into any area of international affairs, I would have to head for Ottawa. Unfortunately, I was told by the federal people in St. John's that the annual examinations for the various professional categories in the Canadian Civil Service had already been held. I decided in any event to take my chances in Ottawa.

In late October 1954, we shipped our ageing English Prefect by ship

61

to Halifax and the three of us flew to the Nova Scotia capital. We stayed there only long enough for Peggy to see the ivy-covered walls of Dalhousie University and then headed to Ottawa through the magnificent fall colours of New Brunswick, Maine, New Hampshire, and Vermont. This was all new for Peggy, for the only trees that turned colour in Australia were the imported trees in Canberra that drew crowds from all over the country. The best of Australian colour couldn't begin to compare to the rainbow that flashed everywhere before us in the mountains of New England in the fall.

Chapter Eight
Ottawa

When we arrived in Ottawa, the fall was drawing to an end and winter was only a few weeks away. We found rooms, but as far as work in the government was concerned, I was told by the Civil Service Commission that there was nothing available. After telling me over and over that all the examinations had been written and there was nothing for me, they let slip the fact that they were recruiting clerks for the Army Pay Ledger Unit in National Defence. These positions were permanent but at the absolute bottom grade of the civil service. I officially applied for and was immediately accepted in a position as Clerk 2A. I can therefore claim that, unlike most of my friends in government, I started at the very bottom of the Canadian Civil Service.

I had nowhere to go but up. I studied all the vacancy notices and, on my second day, applied for a promotion to Clerk 2B. I had to write a competitive examination with two hundred others. I came second. Thereafter, I competed in virtually every competition offering a promotion until I was offered two seemingly good positions. One was an officer in training for dominion customs appraiser in National Revenue. The other was for an administrative officer in External Affairs. My good friend and university "fraternity brother," Andy MacKay, who was in External Affairs, advised me to take the position of dominion customs appraiser in-training. He argued that it would provide excellent training not only for Customs, but for a career in international trade or the trade advisory field. I took his advice.

On September 12, 1955, the day I joined National Revenue, we had our second child, Christopher (Chris). A year later, on September 28, 1956, Julianne (Julie) arrived. We had been thinking of buying a home for our expanding family. One evening just after Peggy and Chris arrived home from hospital to our Ottawa West apartment, I received a call from a long-time friend from university days, Graham Stymiest. I wondered how he knew I was in Ottawa until he revealed that he was with the Royal Canadian Mounted Police Security Service, and had just competed a security check on me. Graham and his wife, Margaret, had just put a down payment on a house in the new Alta Vista suburb of Elmvale Acres and persuaded us to have a look at the models.

We bought on a muddy two-rut trail. It is now Smyth Road, one of the main arteries in South Ottawa. In the spring, the service vehicles would drive down our backyards to avoid muddy Smyth Road. I backed my little English Prefect out of my driveway on one occasion, only to sink in the middle of Smyth Road. All the neighbours had to be summoned to lift me out of the quagmire. I sold the house a few years later when the road was declared a four-lane truck route.

Work in the old Connaught Building, across the street from the Chateau Laurier, was down to earth, interesting, and challenging. I was one of a dozen or so graduates who were being trained on the job to be dominion customs appraisers. These were positions that senior customs officers across the country sought. It was soon evident to me that those who made the grade were in great demand by other government departments and the private sector. My friend Andy MacKay had great foresight!

I was assigned to the Valuation Branch, specialising in determining the value for duty purposes of pharmaceuticals, chemicals, and miscellaneous products. Most of these products were imported in bulk or in an unfinished form requiring further processing and packaging, which challenged the normal procedures for establishing the value for duty.

My immediate supervisor was Murray Keam, who was a competent, congenial man and a good teacher. He never tried to hide his ambition to become one day the chief dominion customs appraiser, and everybody expected him to succeed. The most senior man we saw almost daily was assistant chief dominion customs appraiser Reg Hind, who was also a competent, pleasant, and very courteous man for whom I had the greatest respect. He told me, when I joined the department, that they had a standing order with the Civil Service Commission for economic and commerce graduates but received little cooperation. I very much resented that the Commission had allowed me to languish in a low paid, dead-end job in National Defence for many months when Customs was desperately seeking graduates; so works the bureaucracy! Reg Hind's superior, Lloyd Younger, the chief dominion customs appraiser, was for all of us just a little below God! I met him only rarely, and I must confess that while I was always impressed by whatever he said, what always took my attention were his spats, which he always wore.

We met daily with importers and foreign exporters and their representatives from the numerous consulting firms, frequently made up of former officers of the department. These former officers were, of course, as knowledgeable as we were about valuation law and practices. We were astonished, and often a little envious, when we learned about the fees and retainers they commanded. The imposition of regular customs duties on our often higher determined values would alone have been difficult enough for the Canadian importer or the foreign exporter. On top of this, there were generally dumping duties imposed if the goods were ruled to be of a class or kind made in Canada. Canada at the time had automatic dumping duties that had to be levied if the determined value was higher than the declared value, whether or not domestic industry was injured.

We were regularly required to visit the plants and offices of foreign exporters, which were for the most part in the United States. Other countries were covered by dominion customs appraisers attached to our embassies. Visits were necessary in order to obtain manufacturing costs and selling prices on which to base our determinations for value for duty purposes. Since I was not yet a dominion customs appraiser, I travelled armed with a document signed by our deputy minister stating that I was a "special investigator." This proved to be a powerful piece of paper. The document requested cooperation from the foreign exporter, noting that failure to do so could result in an arbitrary markup of the declared value. Only on one occasion did I meet complete resistance; this was from the management of a large multinational pharmaceutical company, who felt that the information I requested was too sensitive to release. I provided them with a letter from our deputy minister. This advised that all of their shipments of the goods in question to Canada would have a markup of fifty percent for regular duty and antidumping purposes until they complied with my request. They very quickly agreed to cooperate.

On one of my trips to New York, I was asked by the department to investigate the companies that were shipping buttons to Canada. Before delving into this, I had no idea that such an industry existed, let alone that there was a problem. The situation I was to look at started on Fifth Avenue in New York City, where the fashionable stores displayed their latest in ladies' dresses. As soon as the new dresses with their newly designed buttons appeared in the windows, copiers would be on the sidewalk sketching the button designs. The copies would be produced and put on the market within hours. They would sell well for a few days, and the manufacturer who first got his copies on the market would make a good return. The problem was that they usually overproduced and turned to the Canadian market to get rid of their surpluses. The Canadian industry had a man in New York who kept an eye on such developments. When shipments were made to Canada, he would assume that under Canadian law, they were being dumped. They generally were.

I "graduated" with my fellow trainees after a year with National Revenue and was named a dominion customs appraiser. Almost immediately, there were feelers out from Trade and Commerce and Finance, seeking indications of interest from most of us. I actually felt sorry for Customs that had put so much time and care into developing a useful officer, who when able to earn his keep, was enticed away by other departments. There were a number of competitions held to legitimise what had been arranged between the hiring departments and the candidates. One of our officers, a little more senior than our class of graduates, was invited to go through this procedure for a position in the International Trade Relations Branch of Trade and Commerce. I was attracted by the work of that office. It was suggested by a number of my colleagues that, although I couldn't win this particular competition, I should enter the competition to get to know and make an impression on the International Trade Relations people on the board. I allowed myself to be talked into competing. Our more senior colleague, as predicted, got the job. However, in a day or so, Maurice Schwarzmann, who was director of the branch, had somebody telephone and invite me to come to see him. I did and was asked if I would accept a transfer on the understanding that I would be considered for early promotion. I accepted and joined the International Trade Relations Branch of Trade and Commerce early in 1957.

Chapter Nine
Looking Outwards

Trade and Commerce was a very different world from Customs. The International Trade Relations Branch didn't have a protectionist in the group. I felt very much at home. Maurice Schwarzmann, the director, was a bright, well-informed individual on all matters pertaining to international trade relations. He was born in Spain and had been sent to England by his father for a British education. When war broke out and England was threatened, his father sent him to Canada. Once in Canada, Maurice joined the Canadian army and became an intelligence officer. In addition to his native Spanish, he was absolutely fluent in English, French, and German. After the war, he was granted Canadian citizenship, finished his studies, and moved into Trade and Commerce where he excelled in the trade negotiation field.

When I arrived, there were several people vying for the position of deputy to Maurice. Bob Latimer emerged the clear winner and quickly established himself as the undisputed leader under Schwarzmann in the trade policy field. Bob eventually rose to the top position and held it for years until his retirement when he was assistant deputy minister, Trade Policy in External Affairs. Bob was a former Royal Canadian Air Force fighter pilot and was fondly referred to by his colleagues as the "terrier," for although he was small in stature, he was mighty in performance. He could compete orally against the biggest and most senior opponents.

I had the good fortune of being assigned to the United Kingdom Division under Hattie Potter. Hattie was then probably the highest ranking woman and certainly one of the nicest persons in the department. She was acknowledged, even by the British Customs people, to be one of the greatest experts on the British tariff. In those days, prior to Britain joining the European Community, the British tariff was a complicated instrument. Few people in Britain and fewer in Canada had much knowledge about it. As a Commonwealth supplier, Canada had virtually duty free entry into the

British market. There were, however, Commonwealth content requirements and various "reefs and shoals" to be aware of to avoid being subjected to British customs duties. Hattie saw to it that Canadian exporters avoided such problems.

After several months in the International Trade Relations Branch, I asked one of the officers, Rex Nickson, who had been on the board that had recommended me for entrance into the department, why I had been successful. He said that the board had been intrigued by my response to the question about what I considered to be the main factors leading to the confederation of Newfoundland with Canada. I had said that there were two main factors; the Eaton's and Simpson's catalogues! I had maintained that all Newfoundland families had copies of the catalogues (some in their outhouses). They accepted Joey Smallwood's assurance that the prices in the catalogues for socks and such would be the prices Newfoundlanders would pay after confederation; there would be no more customs duties on shipments from Canada. I had mentioned that the elimination of customs duties had had a positive impact on Newfoundland, and it followed that cuts in tariffs around the world would have a positive impact on world trade. Sometimes it pays to be a little flippant and facetious.

The mission of the International Trade Relations Branch was to secure and maintain the best possible access for Canada's exports. The Branch kept abreast of treaties and agreements, both bilateral and multilateral, which governed Canada's trade relations with other countries. We maintained up-to-date information on tariff and nontariff barriers confronting Canadian exporters. This information was made available to exporters. As a consequence, there were many businessmen around for briefings and consultations daily. Our material was a major source of briefing for our international negotiators in their attempts to reduce barriers to our trade. Our officers were generally involved in these negotiations. In addition to geographic divisions, there were multilateral divisions that focused on multilateral trade negotiations, most importantly the General Agreement on Tariffs and Trade (GATT).

Our concerns were not limited to the barriers imposed against Canadian exports. We had to concern ourselves with the impact of Canadian measures, directly or indirectly, on the trade of our trading partners. In this regard, we had regular contact with the Department of Finance, which was the custodian of the Canadian tariff. Finance, consequently, also closely followed activities in GATT, and being responsible for the Canadian tariff, they held many of the "cards" that our negotiators needed to play in order to gain access for our exports through international negotiations. External Affairs had an Economic Division that also followed international trade developments. The strength of the Economic Division ebbed and flowed, depending on the strengths and weaknesses of individuals assigned to the division. The practice of External Affairs of having all officers rotational (between Ottawa and abroad) meant that people posted to the Economic Division, no matter how talented and informed, had to familiarise themselves with issues that the old hands in Finance and Trade and Commerce had been dealing with for years. Nevertheless, some of Canada's finest negotiators and best informed individuals on trade policy were products of External Affairs.

It was only ten years since the formation of GATT. Although there had been a few multilateral negotiations on tariffs as the major barriers to world trade, tariffs around the world remained high and continued to have an adverse impact on Canadian exports. At the same time, the Canadian market was surrounded by a very high tariff wall, and there was strong resistance on the part of many Canadian producers to having this protection reduced. Many of our manufacturing operations were branch plants of foreign companies enticed to locate in Canada by the high protective tariff and the Commonwealth preference system that gave them preferential tariff treatment in many Commonwealth countries over competing goods from the United States, Europe, and Japan.

It was clear to me, as to most of my colleagues, that action in the international trade field to improve the climate for Canadian exports would have to be centred in GATT. Despite all of its imperfections, GATT was the instrument that would develop and administer the multilateral trading rules to govern virtually all of world trade in the second half of the twentieth century. GATT would replace the restrictive and bilateral trade that held sway during the first half of the century. Bilateral trade had been conducted under a network of hundreds of separate agreements. These were laced with high discriminatory tariffs, quantitative import restrictions and other trade distorting measures. These prewar trade policies played havoc with what would have been any normal flow of trade, to the detriment of exporter and importer alike. Bilateral agreements would continue to be struck between many countries, but under the basic "Most Favoured Nation" (MFN) rule of GATT, the benefits given to one partner had to be given to all.

I like to think that I am one of the first to point out that the postwar multilateral trading system, of which GATT was the centrepiece, had its origins in Newfoundland. It was in Placentia Bay in southeast Newfoundland, aboard a United States warship in 1941, at the height of the Second World War, that President Roosevelt and Prime Minister Churchill signed the Atlantic Charter. The Charter, looking forward to the postwar world, envisaged the creation of a multilateral, liberal, and nondiscriminatory trade system. Immediately following the war, international negotiations took place within the United Nations framework on the organisations to be established to achieve the new world order.

The International Monetary Fund (IMF) and the International Bank for Reconstruction and Development (IBRD, or World Bank) were created at the Bretton Wood Conference in 1944. The IMF was to promote international monetary cooperation and exchange stability. The World Bank was to assist European economic recovery. When this role was taken over by the Marshall Plan, the Bank's focus shifted in 1949 to loans and technical assistance to promote the balanced growth of the less developed countries. The IMF and the World Bank were agreed to by all major nations and established with headquarters in Washington. The third key organisation, the International Trade Organisation, which was to contain a comprehensive set of rules for international trade, was not established, because of opposition in the United States Congress.

In 1947 a group of twenty-three of the world's leading trading nations, including the United States and Canada, met and adopted a version of the charter of the stalled International Trade Organisation. They called their new agreement the General Agreement on Tariffs and Trade (GATT). This was to be an interim agreement pending the establishment of the International Trade Organisation. In Geneva, Switzerland, in 1947, while the initial twenty-three countries were preparing the articles of GATT, they commenced negotiations on what was to be the start of the first major assault on customs tariffs. Each of the twenty-three countries had to enter into separate negotiations with each of the other countries, in the knowledge that any deal struck with one country would, under the newly established rules, have to be extended to all the others.

These Geneva negotiations in 1947 were to be only the first of eight rounds, involving more and more countries as others came to see the benefits to be achieved by acting together multilaterally. For the first time, the international trading community could see whittling away of bilateralism that so plagued the world before GATT. The real stability brought to world trade was the binding of the negotiated tariff rates against increase. This meant that except under exceptional circumstances and subject to cumbersome procedures, the rules of the various tariff negotiations were "bound" or "locked-in" against increase.

The GATT has pretty well rid the world of tariffs as a barrier to international commerce. The average tariff in the industrialised world when GATT was founded in 1947 was about 40%. The first two rounds of negotiations in 1947 (the Geneva round) and 1948 (the Annecy round) reduced these tariffs to an average of 25%. The Torquay round, starting in 1950, and a second Geneva round in 1956 resulted in reductions to about 18%. The Dillon round (1960–61) and the Kennedy round (1964–67) caused tariffs to fall on average to around 12%. The Tokyo round (1973–79) brought them below 10%. The recent Uruguay round brings them to below 5%, thus making tariffs, at least on average, no longer a major obstacle to trade amongst industrialised countries.

The tariff barriers against Canada's exports have been reduced to a degree that could not have been hoped for through one-on-one negotiations. The GATT has exerted greater restraint over the trade policies of Canada's trade partners than could have been negotiated by Canada alone. The same is certainly true for the developing countries that have little leverage in acting alone in bringing about lower barriers to their exports.

GATT has been said to have been the Cinderella of international organisations. This certainly was true insofar as budget and numbers of employees were concerned. GATT was, however, one of the most successful efforts ever undertaken in international cooperation. It was much more than a treaty or a set of rules for international trade. GATT was made up of "contracting parties," continually working together for the liberalisation of international trade in their own and in the common interest.

Half a century has now passed since the negotiation of GATT, and during all that period, it continued to be known as the Interim Agreement for the International Trade Organisation (ICITO). Following the most recent round of negotiations (the Uruguay round), the international trading community at last decided to establish a permanent World Trade Organisation (WTO). We can only hope that the new organisation can be as successful and beneficial to the world as has been GATT!

Chapter Ten
Geneva and GATT

In May 1959, I was thrown into the world of GATT in Geneva, Switzerland. My name had been put forward with some seventy others by GATT member governments as candidates for a few positions in the Trade Policy Division of the GATT Secretariat. I can't take much personal credit for the fact that I "beat out" most of the other candidates. I'm convinced that GATT wanted someone from an English-speaking trade ministry in one of the contracting parties that was not represented on the Secretariat. I was certainly given a boost by the fact that I was a Canadian and Canada was not represented, except for Peter Haight, who was born in Canada but was now very much of an international. I was also greatly supported by a personal appearance at the Secretariat on my behalf by Bob Latimer, my deputy director, during one of his official visits to Geneva. There were also persuasive letters to the Secretariat from my director, Maurice Schwarzmann. Both of these Canadians were well known and highly respected in the GATT Secretariat. Anyway, I won a position and went off to Geneva with a three-year leave of absence from the Canadian government.

Just before my departure I was summoned by my assistant deputy minister, Jake Warren, for a few last words of advice. Jake was a most dedicated public servant who believed strongly that Canada's full participation in GATT was crucial if we were to overcome our own trade problems. He believed just as strongly that Canada could, through GATT, help bring order to international trade for the benefit of all nations. He told me to remember that while at GATT, I would be an international civil servant and that I must work as hard for the international community as I would for Canada.

Our move to Geneva was in the days when sea travel was the norm, particularly when moving families and belongings to and from posts. My move was being paid for by the GATT Secretariat. They booked us on the *Saxonia* of the Cunard Line. Peggy and I sailed from Montreal with the three children: Janine, aged six; Chris, aged four; and Julie, aged three. We had our hands full, but all enjoyed the voyage and a few days of seeing the sights of Paris en route to Geneva.

Geneva in 1959 was a wonderful place in which to work and live. Located in the Rhone Valley, at the extreme southwest corner of the Lake of Geneva, we had the Jura Mountains just a few kilometres to the north and the Alps to the south. Access to the countryside, either within Switzerland or in the nearby French rural areas of the Jura or Savoie, was easy. The late autumns and early winters were dreadfully dreary with continuous overcast, but there was rarely snow, and it was only a few kilometres in any direction to any variety of sunny mountains and ski resorts. You could often look down on the Lake of Geneva covered in heavy cloud. However, spring started early and the summers were beautiful and long.

We found good accommodations in the village of Chambesy, about two kilometres from the United Nations' Palais des Nations and the GATT's Villa le Bocage. We were about a kilometre from the lake and the same distance from France. We registered Janine and Chris in the local Chambesy Swiss school and Julie in a kindergarten at the Chateau Banquet, where the Canadian Permanent Mission to the United Nations was located.

My entrance into the offices of GATT was a pretty sobering affair. I arrived at the Villa le Bocage just before the normal working hour, to be received by Mr. Becker at the door. Mr. Becker was a London Cockney, and he sounded like one when speaking either English or French. He was the doorman-cum-receptionist, and in due course, I came to realise that he was a man to get friendly with if you wanted to share the great knowledge he possessed of everything that went on in the Villa le Bocage.

Mr. Becker called Mr. Constant Shih, who was to be my immediate supervisor. Constant and his wife, Daisy, became our good friends, but for the moment, his duty was first to conduct me to the office of Mr. Jean Royer. Royer was the deputy director general, or number two, in the GATT Secretariat. He ran the Secretariat. I had been briefed before leaving Ottawa that Royer, a Frenchman, was a most competent but a very impersonal and authoritarian ruler of the Secretariat. What really worried me was that he was said to dislike Canadians.

Constant Shih led me to Mr. Royer's office. I was introduced to the man and experienced real panic when I offered my hand and he made no attempt to accept it. He never rose from his desk. He never looked me in the eye. He just kept on working, and I had to conclude that he had not heard

Mr. Shih's introduction. Suddenly he stated clearly in perfect English that he understood that I was a Canadian. Before I could confess that I was, he questioned whether, as a Canadian, I could ever be a true international. Could I swallow all those nationalistic things that set North America apart from all the great currents flowing in Europe and elsewhere aimed at establishing a new international economic order?

I don't believe that I was ever so angry, hurt, and frustrated as I was at that moment in Mr. Royer's office. The temptation to turn and walk out was almost overwhelming. With greater control than I can normally muster, I held back my feelings and mumbled something or other about having taken a serious decision to join GATT, and despite Mr. Royer's doubts, I thought that I could measure up to GATT's great standards and meet his expectations. Royer nodded and said no more, and I was ushered out of his office twice as quickly as I had been ushered in. I never got to look the man in the eye for some three years.

It was not until my final few months that I learned that he liked my work and I could talk to him in a relaxed way man-to-man. Nevertheless, even during the years I never got to talk to him, I had the greatest respect for him, particularly for his dedication to the objectives of GATT and the fine way he ran the Secretariat. He ran a truly tight ship. I learnt that others had been treated as I had been by Mr. Royer. He particularly gave the interpreters a hard time, continually correcting them at meetings at the Palais des Nations before all the delegates and officials. I knew all of these people and they were good, but they agreed that Mr. Royer's corrections were generally improvements on the language used by the experts.

My next meeting with a senior officer of the Secretariat was even worse than my dreaded meeting with Mr. Royer. I climbed the stairs with Constant Shih to where my own office was located but was rushed past the door and down the hall to the office of the director of the Trade Policy Division. This was Finn Gundelach, the Great Dane, as we were to refer to him. Gundelach was later to reach the exalted position of deputy director general and, even later, was to be appointed a commissioner (minister) of the European Community. At the time, however, he was to be my director. His welcome was in great contrast to what would happen in North America or Australia between a senior officer and a new employee. There was no "How do you do," or "Nice to see you," or even a "Please sit down." He simply directed me to sit, and said without any introductions that he understood that I could draft in the English language.

He summoned his secretary and, again without any introductions, handed me an official letter he had just received and ordered me to dictate a response to his secretary then and there! I was shocked but able to rally myself sufficiently to read the letter and dictate a response in front of him and a very embarrassed Constant Shih.

The secretary disappeared as soon as I had finished dictating. After four or five deadly silent minutes, she reappeared with the typed letter. Gundelach read it and signed it. He then broke the silence with the comment that he hoped I would overcome the fact that I was a Canadian and remember that here, I was an international civil servant and must fit into the work of an international secretariat. I really wondered who amongst my Canadian colleagues in Ottawa had caused such an anti-Canadian attitude amongst the senior people of the GATT Secretariat.

I was cast into action immediately in the work and life of the Secretariat. In contrast to the terrifying reception I had received from the senior people of the Secretariat, I found that Constant Shih and my fellow officers couldn't have been more friendly. Constant had been one of the originals in GATT, having been the Republic of China's representative at the original GATT meetings. His wife, Daisy, was the daughter of one of the last Nationalist Chinese ambassadors to the United States.

GATT's Villa le Bocage was well situated, with one of the most wonderful views in Geneva. Its spacious and beautifully treed grounds gave it almost complete seclusion from the outside world, with which GATT was so seriously involved. It was but a three-minute peaceful walk from the Palais des Nations, where all of our meetings took place in the great conference rooms of that mammoth building. My office was on the second floor of the two-storied villa, with a view of sloping fields uninterrupted except for magnificent trees for the couple of kilometres down to the lake. The view extended across the lake, where lovely countryside rose and disappeared into the snow-topped Alps. My office and those of my colleagues on either side had once been one large bedroom. It was said that Tolstoy wrote parts of his *War and Peace* while staying there. The Italian revolutionary, Garibaldi, was also said to have resided there. My colleagues used to say that the only difference now was that I slept there.

There were only some thirty officers in the Secretariat when I joined GATT. About two-thirds of these were interpreters, translators, and economic researchers. There were only about a dozen of us in the Trade Policy Division. While the work of the translators and researchers confined them pretty much to the villa, the Trade Policy people and interpreters were more "out front." They manned the committees, working parties, panels, and sessions of the contracting parties.

I was intrigued with the interpreters. They used to tell me that a good interpreter had to do three things at once. First, he or she had to deliver in another language that which had been said by a delegate twenty or thirty seconds before. Second, the interpreter had to translate in his mind that which had been said by the delegate ten to twenty seconds before. Third, he had to listen to what was being said at the moment. Some of these interpreters were extraordinary. I heard one translate into French football terms an American delegate's use of baseball terms, such as "striking a homer" or "catching a fly ball." I heard one translate an English-speaking delegate's reference to "once in a blue moon" into Spanish as "every time a bishop dies!" To have translated directly the English expression would have made it incomprehensible to a Spanish-speaking person.

Only once did I see one of my favourite interpreters stuck. The New Zealand representative (Doug Taylor, who later was to join the Secretariat) was very annoyed at the European Community representative. It was late at night, and we were in the midst of a tough discussion of the Community's Common Agricultural Policy that the New Zealanders and other agricultural exporters detested. With great frustration, Doug yelled, "Stone the bloody crows!"

The poor interpreter, who was translating into French, threw up his hands. He said in French, "The New Zealand delegate has made an untranslatable remark, not because it is vulgar or unrepeatable, but because it is a remark in the English language understood only by English-speaking people in the Southern Hemisphere." It was a good ending to a frustrating evening.

Within days of my arrival at the Secretariat, there were Balance of Payments consultations with the United Kingdom and New Zealand. With my experience on the United Kingdom desk in Ottawa, Constant felt that I should accompany him to the meeting and, under his tutelage, write the report. While Constant had to rework, rearrange, and rewrite much of my work, he was pleased with this first effort. At the New Zealand consultation, Constant had to do less reworking, rearranging, and rewriting. Thereafter, I did most of the Balance of Payments reports with less and less underpinning from Constant. However, I was always grateful that he was there if needed.

One might reasonably ask, what were Balance of Payments consultations? Under GATT, the customs tariff constituted the only legitimate means of protection and, in general, all other barriers had to be removed. But the GATT was long suffering. Most countries had, in addition to tariffs, quantitative import restrictions—that is, restrictive quotas for imports; goods in excess of the quotas were simply excluded from the market. These restrictions were only sanctioned by GATT (with a few exceptions) if a country had balance of payments problems as defined by GATT and the IMF.

Balance of Payments restrictions were at the time the meaningful barriers to international trade. All Western European countries; the Commonwealth overseas, developed countries of Australia, New Zealand, and South Africa; Japan; and all developing countries had elaborate systems for controlling imports. These systems were generally legally sanctioned by GATT and the IMF. For many years, only Canada and the United States were without restrictions imposed for balance of payments reasons.

These legitimate Balance of Payments restrictions rendered many negotiated tariff reductions virtually meaningless, since trade that otherwise would have flowed as a result of the reduction or elimination of tariffs, was stopped or hindered by the restrictions. For a nation to accept this terrible situation meant that it had to have faith in the future. The United States and Canada did have such faith. They believed that although world trade was laced with restrictions, this was a temporary situation that would disappear when countries emerged from their balance of payments nightmares and abolished their restrictive systems.

The Balance of Payments committee brought concrete results. It did not always bring about the complete removal of the restrictive systems, but it did cause them to be more transparent and manageable for the trader. Under pressure from the committee, countries moved gradually to negative lists of restrictions; that is, they were required to list all the items that were under control instead of the few that could be freely traded. This gave GATT a way of assessing progress in dismantling restrictions and of comparing one country's restrictive system with others. The committee's meetings with the British, French, and Germans were often "hot and heavy," and the reports and recommendations were often fought over until the early hours of the morning.

Any group has its characters. GATT, with few officers of the same nationality, had characters galore. One of my favourites was Joe Maggio, our Italian. Joe was born in New York, but his Italian parents returned to

Italy when Joe was a small baby. He was a graduate of British universities, and I would challenge anyone to tell that Joe was not an Englishman. His English was not only flawless, with an upper-class British accent, but he had a thorough knowledge of American, Canadian, Australian, and New Zealand English. My children were as fascinated as I was when Joe would take us all to the end of the runway at the Geneva airport, where he could spend hours with his latest radio receiving apparatus, listening to the pilots chitchatting in English with the control tower. Most of the aircraft were Swiss, and Joe said that they used a number of Australian pilots. He claimed that the Swiss air-traffic controllers had picked up an Australian accent!

Joe was not only proficient in Italian and English, he was absolutely fluent in French, Spanish, Russian, and German. While we were in Geneva, he learnt Japanese for a very good reason. Just months after I arrived in Geneva, in the autumn of 1959, Constant Shih, Joe, and I were included in the Secretariat group that had been selected to attend the Fifteenth Session of the Contracting Parties in Tokyo. Before our departure, Constant spent hours trying to convince Joe, a bachelor, that he should take advantage of the few months he would spend in Japan and find himself a Japanese wife. Constant told him that he was so set in his bachelor ways that no European woman would tolerate him. Joe didn't disagree. Constant claimed that there were numerous lovely Japanese ladies in their thirties who were considered beyond marrying years in Japan. I enjoyed and encouraged these chats that started as lighthearted conversations over morning coffee.

To our surprise, the more time we spent on the subject, the more serious Joe became, and he started to look at the possibility seriously. Joe approached the Japanese ambassador, who was a friend, and he agreed to ask the Japanese government to assist in finding Joe a wife. This would be done most discreetly, and any prospective bride would be "checked out" in every sense. By the time we arrived in Japan, they had already made their check with very positive results. Joe was introduced to a lovely Japanese lady who met all of Joe's criteria. He was impressed to the degree that it was arranged that she would go to Geneva and stay with a Swiss family and be courted by Joe until they both decided yes or no. The answer for both of them was yes, and Joe won himself a beautiful Japanese bride.

A few months after joining the Secretariat and already feeling very much the veteran, I was asked to take under my wing a new Japanese officer of about my age. We quickly became close friends, yet, following Japanese custom, for the three years we worked together, I was always "Mister" Petrie and he was always "Mister" Izeki. He had very little English when he arrived and used to call me Mr. "Pletely," having, like most Japanese when learning English, terrible trouble with the letters E, R, and L. Mr. Izeki followed me around everywhere I went. At meetings he listened carefully to the English language interpreters. I would drill him when we walked to and from meetings and during lunch hours. In a few months he mastered not only the usual Japanese troubles with English, but he began to hand me drafts of meetings. Since he was always at my elbow, the poor fellow learnt a lot of his English from me. Some Canadian delegates mentioned that he was getting a Newfoundland accent! Mr. Izeki wouldn't have minded that, because he wouldn't have known the difference.

One day I received a message during a particularly difficult and important meeting on agricultural protectionism that, following the meeting, I was to brief Sir Eric Wyndham White, the director general, on its outcome. Sir Eric rarely came to committee meetings, reserving himself for the sessions of the Contracting Parties. I sat most of the day worrying about what I was going to say to the great man. When the meeting ended, I headed straight for Sir Eric's office. Mr. Izeki was on my heels.

Sir Eric's first questions were related to the level of representation from the various countries on the committee. I told him that Mr. Brown represented the United States, Mr. Jones was there for the United Kingdom, and Mr. Martin was there for France. He asked, "Who was there for Australia?"

It had been the Australian Ambassador Corkery, whom we liked as an individual, but detested as a delegate, for he was often very nasty to members of the Secretariat. Before I could respond to Sir Eric's question, Mr. Izeki blurted out, "Sir, it was dat bugger, Corkery."

Sir Eric's pipe almost fell from his mouth! He rallied and almost smiling said, "Mr. Izeki, it is not very diplomatic to say that about one of our distinguished ambassadors."

Mr. Izeki simply said, "But, sir, that's what Mr. Petrie always calls him!"

79

Chapter Eleven
GATT Goes to Tokyo

In the autumn of 1959, GATT held its Fifteenth Session in Tokyo. This was the first of the annual GATT sessions to be held outside Europe, and the decision to go to Japan was not without great opposition. A number of national manufacturing associations in particular were opposed, feeling that Japan was attempting to improve its image by hosting the GATT meeting but had no intention of doing anything to change its trade practices that were seen as contrary to most of the principles of GATT. I was to encounter some of this opposition myself en route to the meeting.

The Japanese government was to pay all the costs to transport Secretariat members to Tokyo. They had chartered an Air France plane for the officers, English, French, and Spanish interpreters, translators, and secretarial staff who were to go. With Constant Shih and several others, I had to take a regular commercial flight to be there two weeks prior to the session to attend the Balance of Payments consultations that were also scheduled to take place in Tokyo. The Japanese gave me tickets from Geneva to Tokyo. I paid an extra fare to visit my in-laws in Australia.

I stayed overnight in Saigon, awaiting my connecting flight to Australia. The Republic of Vietnam had been established, and the city was crowded with refugees who had fled from the Communist north. The city still showed the terrible scars from the fighting that took place following the Second World War. We didn't appreciate then the additional destruction that Vietnam would suffer in the coming decades.

During my few days in Australia, my father-in-law drove me to Canberra. While in the capital, he told me that he would like me to meet a business friend who was involved in international trade. I didn't ask the nature of his friend's business, and to my horror, when we arrived at his office, I saw that he was the president of the Australian Manufacturers Association! When he heard of my position with the GATT Secretariat and that I was on my way to the Tokyo meetings, my father-in-law almost lost the man's friendship. I was subjected to a tirade of extreme views on the damage we were doing to international trade and manufacturing around the world by moving to legitimise Japanese unfair trading practices.

In the view of the Association, the GATT Secretariat's agreement to the Tokyo meetings was part of a Japanese plot to extend Japanese commercialism throughout the world, targeted especially at Australia. This struck me as a bit extreme. It did, however, demonstrate that the prewar image of Japan as an unfair trader would take a long time to disappear. The Japanese themselves had not been helpful in ridding themselves of the image. Japan had only recently joined the international trading community as a member of GATT and continued to maintain an import regime that caused even the most optimistic supporter of normal trade relations with Japan to have serious doubts and concerns.

I was in Tokyo for seven weeks. The first two were devoted to Balance of Payments meetings. We had the entire attention of the Japanese press focused on the consultations, particularly the one with Japan. As often happened in that country immediately after the war, there was absolutely no respect for confidentiality. The results of our first consultation with Japan and the second with Australia were leaked to the Japanese press!

One can imagine my surprise when I picked up my copy of the English version of the *Japan Times* from under my bedroom door the morning after I had drafted the reports and saw them reproduced on the front pages, taking the headlines and all! It mattered little that these were only the first drafts. The Japanese local staff who were "assisting" the Secretariat, had run off the required fifty copies for our purposes (all marked "Confidential") and then obligingly ran off a few for the press.

The Japanese delegation to the Balance of Payments Committee didn't take this too seriously. Obviously they expected the report to be leaked. The Australians on the other hand were livid! Their leader for the consultation, Ambassador Corkery (our "friend" from Geneva), wanted the consultation declared null and void. They were even more upset when the Japanese press coverage hit the Australian papers. In the end, good sense prevailed. It was realised that since the published reports were drafts, the final versions would be very different. The press would be so informed, and our security would be tightened to ensure that the final texts and future drafts would not get into the wrong hands. In the committee, when dealing with the final drafts, we all tried to introduce every possible legitimate change to make the reports different from the drafts published by the press. Thereafter we watched our Japanese "helpers" like hawks.

Goetz Leonhardt, a German colleague, shared an office with me in Tokyo. It was a converted hotel room in the old Imperial Hotel. This was the Frank Lloyd Wright building, one of the few major structures to survive the terrible earthquake in 1923. Goetz had joined the Secretariat on the same day I had. He came from a university teaching position in California. He told me that he was rather depressed about Jean Royer's view of him as an academic. Royer had made it clear to Goetz that he had little use for academics. Goetz was convinced there was little future for him in a Secretariat run by Royer. He was most relieved to learn that I also had been rated low on Mr. Royer's list, albeit for different reasons. Royer had a reason to dislike everybody.

After two weeks of the Balance of Payments Committee, the main body of the Secretariat arrived from Geneva on the Air France charter and the GATT session got underway. I was assigned with Goetz, Mr. Izeki, and Harry Reed to do the summary records of the session. This entailed doing a précis of the remarks of the delegates while they were speaking. I would be in for an hour with one of my colleagues, taking every second speaker. We would then be replaced by the other two while we reworked our notes and dictated the final text.

Our taskmaster for the summary records was Peter Haight. Peter was born in Toronto but had lived for years in South Africa and Geneva. He was a wonderful man, and in later years, when we were both in Australia, he became a close friend and golfing partner. At the time, however, he had the responsibility to put together a summary of the five-week session that would go into the records of GATT as the official record. The record of the discussion today had to be published tomorrow, so we were under very strict time constraints. If we had any more than three or four corrigenda requested by delegates in the course of week, we were on the carpet.

My favourite working companion was Harry Reed. We were close friends. He was a Rhodesian and had worked for the Federation of Rhodesia and Nyasaland before joining GATT. Fortunately, I was working with Harry on the memorable day when the Yugoslav ambassador made a speech committing his country to the Western trading system. Harry was taking the notes, and I was acting as his "cover." When the Yugoslav finished speaking, Harry and I stared at each other in disbelief. We hadn't understood a single word of the ambassador's speech. At Harry's desperate appeal, I rushed off to the French and Spanish interpreters' booths only to find that they had trouble believing that the Yugoslav had spoken in English! There had to be a report, yet nobody, and I mean nobody, in any of the official languages had understood a word of what the ambassador had said during this important moment, when his country was moving away from the Soviets towards the West.

Harry and I retreated to our back-room office without any notes. Harry poured us each a glass of wine and suggested that we relax and ask ourselves, "If we were from a Communist country that was getting rather friendly with the West, what sort of a speech would we deliver?" So together we concocted a speech that said all the good things about being a state trading country (none of which we believed), yet one dedicated to the Western-oriented trading system. We had it typed and took it to the Yugoslav ambassador. He was absolutely delighted! He couldn't wait for us to produce it in the summary records. The interpreters couldn't believe it when we came up with a text. Our text stands as the official GATT record of one of the first commitments of a Communist state-trading country to the market-oriented system of the Western world. What the Yugoslav representative actually said will always remain a mystery.

My Japanese colleague, Mr. Izeki, really rose to the occasion in Tokyo. Since he was the Secretariat's only Japanese, he was asked by virtually every Japanese government department to recommend "important" people from the Secretariat who might be entertained at dinner parties. Mr. Izeki always recommended the same five or six of his best friends (all being relatively junior). The Japanese Ministries of Agriculture, Finance, or whatever, never knew the difference. As a consequence, Mr. Izeki, Constant, Goetz Leonhardt, Harry Reed, and I were always in great demand by the Japanese for official entertainment. We went to so many of Tokyo's great restaurants (at Japanese expense) that we often found ourselves at the same ones several nights in a row. This was fine, except that the staff began to recognise us and call us by name: Frank-san, Constant-san, Harry-san, and the like. This was most confusing for our hosts.

The session in Tokyo was a regular annual GATT meeting of the Contracting Parties and not at all related to the Tokyo round of trade negotiations held a few years later. These annual sessions were not negotiating conferences. They dealt primarily with housekeeping matters, such as the setting up of working parties to deal with specific problems, the consideration of requests of waivers from GATT obligations, and the like.

The GATT sessions were, however, sometimes used to launch major new initiatives aimed at freeing up some aspect of international trade. The Tokyo session saw such an initiative when Sir Eric Wyndham White, the director general of GATT, proposed an Expansion of Trade Program, involving a three-pronged attack on remaining barriers to trade.

There was to be a focus on new approaches against tariffs and the beginning of work to document and tackle nontariff barriers, particularly those confronting trade in agricultural products and the exports of developing countries. Three committees were established, made up of some forty country representatives on each. Two of these committees, dealing with agriculture and the trade problems of developing countries, were to become the focus for much of my work over the next three years.

Sir Eric set the stage for this new Expansion of Trade Program by throwing out a challenge. He called on each country to draw up a list of what it considered to be the barriers facing its exports, naming the offending trading partner. First reactions were that such barriers were already well known and could be listed in minutes!

When we solicited and received from individual contracting parties the measures they claimed hampered their trade, we were bombarded with reports of some eight hundred and fifty specific impediments to trade. This was all very raw and unchallenged material, but it provided the grist for our future work. We were to have every contracting party "on the carpet" to explain why they maintained such measures that their trading partners claimed disrupted trade. The results of these consultations gave us a refined inventory of barriers such as could not have been anticipated at the Tokyo session, except possibly by the originator of the exercise, Sir Eric Wyndham White.

The Japanese must have considered the Tokyo session a success. One of their main reasons for inviting GATT to Tokyo had been to persuade the many countries that refused to recognise Japan as a full member of GATT to change their minds. (Article XXXV of GATT allowed individual countries to withhold recognition of a new entrant.) The Japanese had been successful in attracting most countries of the world to Tokyo, either as contracting parties or observers. A few did agree to accept Japan as a full member.

The meeting, GATT's first outside Europe, certainly did raise the image of Japan as a major player in international trade. It did at the same time confirm Japan as being one of the most restrictive markets in the world.

The Balance of Payments consultation with Japan and the many items on the session agenda on restrictive trade practices identified Japan as one of the main problem countries of international trade. Japan, while positioning itself as a great champion of freer trade, was, at the end of the session, a little more tarnished than it would have wished.

We left Tokyo for the return trip to Geneva just a few weeks before Christmas. We were all laden with silks for our wives, toys for our children, and cameras and projectors for ourselves. The homeward-bound trip was over the North Pole by Air France charter. As often happens with charter flights, this one was plagued with problems. We were delayed on take-off for hours. When we commenced the run down the runway, our real trouble started. Just before we reached the point of no return, the fire alarm sounded. Several hours later we made another attempt with the same unnerving result. After another few hours, we finally got off the ground. By now, everybody was referring to Air France as "Air Chance!"

We landed in Anchorage, Alaska. As we disembarked, I heard my name being paged and couldn't imagine who in this extremity of the world would have reason to call me. It was the Air France local representative, who, on reviewing our passports, noted that there was a Newfoundlander on board. The agent's name was Boone, from Notre Dame Bay, just north of Grand Falls, a family well known to mine.

We were eighteen hours in the air going over the North Pole to Europe. The flight was in total darkness except for about ten minutes, when we were all awakened to see a glimmer of light over the ice cap that told us it was about the shortest Arctic winter day. We were to refuel in Norway, but the airport was closed. We were diverted to Nice, France, because Geneva was closed. The pilot announced that he would make one approach to Geneva (which hadn't seen an aircraft for days). We all wanted to get home, but we didn't know whether to be pleased or concerned with the pilot's decision, particularly since we had lost confidence in Air Chance. We knew that on one side of our approach were the Alps and on the other side the Jura Mountains with the Saleve close to the flight path. Air Chance made it on that first approach!

Chapter Twelve
New Schisms in Geneva

It took only a few days to shake off the Tokyo session and Japan. Our families certainly helped the process. In Geneva, the focus quickly changed to coping with the monumental trade problems resulting from the development of the European Community. Our new Expansion of Trade Program, with its emphasis on tariffs, agriculture, and the trade of the developing countries, appeared to virtually everyone to have been written with a view to a concerted attack on the European community. The Community itself was convinced that all fingers were pointed in its direction. Perhaps the Community was excessively sensitive, and if so, they had good reason to be. All non-Community countries felt that the Common External Tariff of the Community, was the tariff "to get at." It was, after all, the average of the relatively low tariffs of countries like the Benelux and the historically high tariff of France, which resulted initially in an overall high tariff for the Community. Similarly, the Common Agricultural Policy was considered by overseas agricultural suppliers to be the ultimate in agricultural protectionism. As for developing countries, those not belonging to the former French and Belgian colonial empires that had preferential access saw the Community's measures against their exports as being straight discrimination and excessive protectionism.

I feel that Wyndham White, in putting forward his proposal for an Expansion of Trade Program, knew exactly what he was doing. Once the facts were all put on the table and the details of the inventory of barriers were on everybody's desk, the international community would quickly come to realise that the European Community, for all its sins, was not the only culprit. The extensive list of notified barriers against all countries would tell us that everybody, and not only the Community, had to bear the responsibility for the current problems facing international trade.

Wyndham White was well aware that Canada, Australia, New Zealand, and most other overseas countries maintained tariffs higher than those of the Community. The United States, with its widely embracing GATT agricultural waiver, which enabled it to legitimise its many restrictions against imports and its widespread subsidy programs, was to blame for much of the attitude adopted by others towards protecting their agricultural sector. (If the Americans can do it, why not us?) There were also deficiency payment systems in many countries that contributed to the mess.

Japan stood out as a shocking agricultural protectionist; as one Canadian involved in the trade put it, "The Japanese government pays its farmers three times the world price for rice, feeds its pigs at half price, and charges humans sixteen to twenty times what it charges the pigs." Discriminatory treatment of imports from the developing world was widespread. While the Community discriminated in favour of its former colonies, the developed Commonwealth countries discriminated in favour of Commonwealth suppliers. The European Community eventually overcame this problem by extending favourable treatment to all of its developing country accusers. The world community sought to deal with the issue by introducing a generalised system of tariff preferences for the developing world.

GATT stood on its head in attempts to accommodate the developing countries. There was a genuine Western desire in GATT (as in the IMF) to help but to insist that the developing countries accept some obligations and discipline in the exercise of their trade policies. In the end, the collective political pressures brought to bear by the developing countries gave birth to the United Conference on Trade and Development (UNCTAD). The creation of this organisation, centred in Geneva, initially had a negative impact on GATT and consequently on the continuing fight against protectionism. The more radical developing countries (and there were many) were not content to confine their attacks against the market-oriented trading system to the newly created UNCTAD. They were intent on debasing the GATT on every possible occasion. They saw to it that every statement or report by GATT excluded the developing countries from any obligations. The introduction of new articles by GATT (Part IV), in reality, extended to the developing countries a waiver from meaningful international obligations in the trade field.

Such was the disruption of the day-to-day work of GATT, that many developed countries were tempted to abandon GATT in favour of the Organisation for Economic Cooperation and Development (OECD). While the OECD had been used for negotiations between the industrialised countries on specific matters, such as export credits, it was never envisaged that it should involve itself in broad trade negotiations. Gradually most countries, observing the discord and irreconcilable differences of the various groups in UNCTAD, concluded that it could largely be ignored. They realised that, like it or not, UNCTAD was probably here to stay. Many of the resolutions adopted by UNCTAD, while they carried the United Nations banner, were often very radical, sometimes most unrealistic, and always pushed through with a great majority (for the developing countries indeed had a huge majority and were generally supported by the Communist bloc). The result was that more and more of the developed countries paid less and less attention to UNCTAD. GATT was encouraged to get on with its work and set in motion activity aimed at further rounds of trade negotiations. GATT remained largely the forum for action and market-oriented work in the trade field.

In the GATT Secretariat, not surprisingly, we were negative about the move to set up UNCTAD. We were fearful that it could, if not controlled, destroy the work that the international trading community had developed since the war. I was personally annoyed that all Western governments, including my own in Ottawa, while generally (but quietly) opposed to UNCTAD, paid lip service to the formation of the organisation and gave it financial support. I believe that UNCTAD made a mockery of serious international trade discussion and provided a soapbox for the more radical developing countries and the Eastern Europeans to criticise destructively our market-oriented international trading system. In later years I was to serve on numerous Canadian delegations to UNCTAD, and my negative views of the organisation were never to change.

Life as well as work in Geneva in the early 1960s was most enjoyable. Our family was comfortably housed in a small Swiss chalet in the village of Chambesy. It was an adequate family home, since we had little official entertainment expected of us. The garden was large and beautiful, with a small waterfall and fish pond. We had a very small children's swimming pool and a lovely Swiss playhouse. I followed Peggy in her keen interest in gardening, one of our great interests throughout our married life.

Our children certainly profited from the educational experience in Geneva, being immersed in the French language. Janine, aged six, and Chris, aged five, had started in the local Swiss school. Janine in a few months was fairly fluent. Chris was a bit resistant, and it wasn't until a few months later that it became apparent that, like Janine, he was on his way to fluency. I had a workman fixing the gas heater for the shower. When he finished, he attempted to explain something to me in French, but I could not fully grasp what he was saying. He gave up and departed, giving me a backward glance that told me he thought me something of an idiot. As soon as he went through the door, Chris said, "Dad, he said if you would clean the damn thing once in a while, it might work!"

Julie, aged three, was in a Swiss kindergarten and was soon at home in French. Her problem was that at the tender age of three she got her languages mixed up. She spoke English at home, French at school, and German with the neighbouring children. One day prior to setting out on a long drive I noticed she had wet pants and told her to go to the bathroom. She responded, "Nein, nein, I have fini," using three languages in one sentence. I feared the children were losing their fluency in English. We did nothing about this for a year or so until Janine one day asked her mother for her "apron blue," using the French construction. By this time, their French was good, so we felt we should move them into English, which we wanted as their first language. The International School, where we could enroll them, was inconveniently situated at the other end of the city, so we looked for alternatives. The result was the creation of the Geneva English School that we started with three or four other Commonwealth families. We rented a church hall, hired a well-qualified Scottish teacher, and started an early grade school with six or seven students. Chris learnt to read extremely well in a few weeks, if with a slight Scottish accent. It was a great success. When we lived in Geneva five years later, the school had grown to several hundred students.

In our Geneva years, we had wonderful family holidays. We spent all the time we could mountain walking, preferably above the tree line. On the Swiss side in particular, there were lovely, inexpensive hotels high in the Alps, away from the mainstream of tourists.

One of our most enjoyable was a midsummer hike high above Inter-laken. We stayed overnight in a hotel at the top of a cog railway. During the day it was crowded with tourists. When the last train departed around seven in the evening, the hotel was suddenly deserted and eerily quiet. Peggy and I, with the children, were almost alone with the skeleton staff, for most of the staff had departed by the last train with the tourists. With the closing of the railway for the day the lights went out. The children were delighted for they looked upon this as a great adventure. We ate dinner by candlelight and afterwards had to thread our way into the dark hotel with a lantern, up the stairs and though halls lined with stuffed animals and birds of the Alps.

We had a wonderful deadly quiet night. The silence was interrupted only by the occasional boom of avalanches cascading down from the surrounding peaks. I delighted in the fact that we were far removed from the action and civilisation in the distant valleys below. We breakfasted on the sunny terrace of the hotel, surrounded by the most magnificent panorama of snow-capped mountains whose sides plunged into beautiful river-laced green valleys. After breakfast we set off on our hike towards Grindelwald.

For several summer holidays, we took a chalet above the beautiful village of Grindelwald. Across the valley from our chalet was the four thousand-metre Eiger with its spectacular, yet frightening and infamous, North Face. It seemed that every serious climber in Europe wanted to tackle the North Face. Avalanches shot across the "face" at many angles. The locals named this dangerous area, on which the sun never shone and which had to be traversed if the North Face was to be conquered, the "White Spider." Many people had met their death trying to climb this dangerous precipice. Avalanches seemed to wait in ambush. One summer the villagers had a periscope trained on the body of a poor fellow who had been swept to his death. He dangled from a rope for some time before the best of Grindelwald's climbers could reach him and cut him down!

In winters, on several occasions we rented an old and wonderful chalet at Gstaad. This was owned by an American colleague in the GATT Secretariat, the widow of a wealthy Swiss. The chalet had a library of English books dated before 1850. I loved skiing, but when doing so at Gstaad, I looked forward to the sun going down so I could return to the chalet and bury myself before a roaring fire in that marvellous library.

We had a most happy development on November 2, 1960, when Jennifer arrived. She was born to "foreign" parents, and unlike English-speaking countries, Switzerland did not accept a birth in the country as a right to citizenship. They look to the nationality of the parents as the basis for citizenship. Thus Jennifer, with no say for herself, became a Canadian. Within weeks of Jennifer's birth, she was in the Alps. We took her with us on a short Christmas skiing holiday to Gstaad and our favourite mountain chalet. In the absence of a crib, she slept in a large drawer, which we put on the balcony in the sunshine during the day, and at night, on a table near our bed. The following summer, we took her to Spain with twenty litres of Swiss bottled water and a milk formula, and she didn't know she was out of Switzerland except for the Spanish sand she devoured while on the beach.

Our years in Geneva were certainly not all holidays. During the almost continuous GATT meetings, we were required to work night and day. Mr. Izeki and I worked together most of the time, and since the new agricultural committee held thorough consultations with each and every country in GATT on their agricultural policies and practices, we were very busy running the committee and writing and defending the reports. We generally would get together after the daily meetings at our house and work on our patio. When darkness approached, Peggy would bring out lamps and extensions, and we would often not finalise the fifteen- or twenty-page report until the early hours of the morning. We took turns getting up at the crack of dawn to get the text into the office for typing and reproduction in time for the morning meeting.

At the end of several weeks of such meetings, Mr. Izeki and I would be exhausted. We both liked, and found relaxing, an evening at the casino at Divonne, twenty kilometres away, in France. We would try to get there on the final evening of our meetings, after all the delegates had left. Our wives generally accompanied us, although they didn't entirely share our enthusiasm for the casino! We normally allowed ourselves fifty Swiss francs for the evening. On one occasion, Mr. Izeki quickly lost his allotted amount and joined me to "bring me luck." He did. I could do nothing wrong. Mr. Izeki would pocket my winnings, leaving me only with my original stake. When I finally lost my stake, he led me to the cashier. He took out of his pocket chips valued at about one thousand French francs (then worth about two hundred and fifty American dollars). He cashed the chips and pocketed the money. The next day at lunch hour, he drove me downtown, where at his suggestion, I bought a new suit with my winnings, so as Mr. Izeki put it, "The bugger casino won't get it back!"

Chapter Thirteen
Through the Iron Curtain

I didn't get to see much of Sir Eric Wyndham White, the director general of GATT, or to get to know him well personally, until I travelled with him on an official visit to Poland and Czechoslovakia. One evening in the spring of 1961, his assistant telephoned me to advise that Sir Eric "requested" that I be at the airport next morning to join him and his wife for a visit to the two GATT countries of Eastern Europe. Lady Tina was an American and was said to have been a bubble dancer and a small-part Hollywood actress when Sir Eric married her. It would certainly be an experience to see "Mr. International Trade" in action, so I was nervously delighted. I didn't know at the time, but there was one great difference between this and other trips on which he took junior officers. This time Sir Eric and Lady Tina had their small dog with them!

Our flight was with Polish Airlines from Geneva to Warsaw. We departed Geneva, but that day, we didn't reach Warsaw. Sir Eric and his wife (with the dog in her lap) sat in the front seats with their backs to the bulkhead, facing the rear of the plane. I sat immediately in front of them with all the official papers and bags. All went well until we approached the Polish border, when thunderstorms such as I had never experienced blocked our way. The pilot tried desperately to go over, under, and around the storms but to no avail. I could see an altimeter directly behind Sir Eric on the bulkhead, and it began to plunge. My stomach felt as if it remained on high. The dog suddenly leaped from Lady Tina's lap onto mine! Sir Eric and Tina looked grateful.

The plane about-turned and, unknown to us, headed for Prague, Czechoslovakia. Also unknown to us at the time, Prague refused to grant permission for us to land, claiming that the airport was closed because of the storm. The pilot attempted to land at a military base but again was refused entry. The desperate Polish crew headed back for Prague, determined to land even if the airport was closed. It was the most frightening approach in all my years flying. Hills raced by at our wing tips. The altimeter gyrated up and down, sometimes indicating that we were on the ground! The cabin crew sat on the floor in the aisle with sick passengers laid out around them. I held the dog and it held me. My stomach stayed with me until we hit the runway. Then, because of either sickness or relief, I had to reach for one of those all-too-small bags from the seat pocket beside me. These were in great demand. I do believe that the only ones who were not sick on the plane were Sir Eric, Lady Tina, the pilot, and the dog.

We didn't taxi far before we were stopped in the middle of the runway by a detachment of soldiers. They boarded the plane, and why they didn't immediately get sick with the stench of it all, I don't know. They kept us there in our misery, without fresh air, for about half an hour, until the "authorities" arrived. Before Sir Eric could suggest it, I approached the authorities and, finding somebody who spoke English, stated that Sir Eric was on an official visit to Poland and Czechoslovakia, and we would like immediately to get in touch with Czechoslovak Protocol. The man didn't understand. He had never heard of GATT, Sir Eric, or Protocol!

Eventually we were taken to the terminal, abandoning our Polish crew, far out on the runway, to explain why they had ignored the order not to land, as if that needed an explanation! By this time, Sir Eric was livid. As soon as we reached the empty terminal, I found a telephone and, after several frustrating attempts, succeeded in reaching Protocol. They couldn't believe they were to meet people at a closed airport. After lengthy explanations about who we were and why we were in Prague when we were not due for a week, they said they would consider sending someone to meet us. I suggested that Czechoslovakia's relationship with the Western trading world might be a little strained if they didn't send someone immediately. In the meantime, the authorities had arranged for the passengers to be taken to a downtown hotel.

Only those who have suffered through the difficulty of breaking from a group in a Communist country can appreciate the reaction when Sir Eric refused to go! He had me advise the authorities that he would await the arrival of Protocol. Sir Eric then turned his back on the crowd and walked towards the bar (which was closed), instructing me to follow him. Eventually the authorities gave up and departed for downtown, leaving one person to oversee us.

Sir Eric found a bartender and ordered drinks for the two of us, leaving Lady Tina to tend to the needs of the dog. A Protocol officer eventually turned up and invited us to accompany him. Sir Eric asked whether I had any small-denomination traveller's cheques. I did. He asked if I would pay the bill. I did. I had been warned that this was normal behaviour for the director general; like the queen, he never carried cash. My concern was that it was the sort of expense one couldn't put on an expense account. After that I made sure that the Czechs or Poles paid all of Sir Eric's bills.

We arrived in Warsaw to a beautiful day and a red-carpet welcome. There were several government ministers to greet us and familiar faces from the Polish Permanent Mission to the United Nations in Geneva. Some of the more junior Poles had been at the airport all night. The communications between Warsaw and Prague were so poor they had been unable to get any information from the Czechs on our whereabouts. They couldn't believe that we had run into a storm, since Warsaw had been in full sunshine all day.

We had two days of calls on ministers. The discussions centred on how Poland, as a state trading country, might fit into GATT. They had to give some assured access to the Polish market in order to be granted full Most Favoured Nation tariff status on their exports to the West. This was my first involvement in the difficult, if not impossible, task of fitting a Communist country in any meaningful way into the free-market trading system.

A Communist country has no meaningful system of custom tariffs. Some, in attempts to satisfy GATT countries, had introduced tariffs. It was considered ludicrous by Western countries to negotiate tariff concessions with a country that operated under a system where imported goods were not permitted to compete with domestic production. It was the Five-Year Plan that dictated whether there would be imports. These would only take place if domestic demand could not be met by domestic production (however inefficient) or by imports from a bilateral partner (usually another state trading country).

The Poles tended to trot out all the well-worn and regularly rejected offers that would allocate through quotas a portion of their market to GATT partners. This couldn't be taken seriously because a number of GATT countries were Communist (such as Czechoslovakia and Cuba) or state trading (such as India). Any Polish quota obligations could be met by state trading countries continuing with their existing practice of bilateral trading. Consequently, a number of Western countries refused to acknowledge Poland as a full GATT member and deprived it of Most Favoured Nation tariff status.

The Poles were wonderful hosts; they had so much to show. They were intent on having us see as much of Poland in a week as was humanly possible. We were provided with chauffeur-driven cars; Sir Eric, Lady Tina, and the dog (thankfully) were in the first with the Polish chargé d'affaires from Geneva. I was in the second with the number two in the Polish Geneva Mission (and with all the bags and papers).

After visits to the restored old city area of Warsaw, the Poles set out for Cracow (Krakow). A few minutes after we started, we stopped at the National Art Gallery, where a serious young man joined our group and travelled in "my" car, in front with the chauffeur. They both knew each other well, clearly having travelled together before. He was an "expert" on modern art, since it was well known that Sir Eric was a lover of this art form. On the outskirts of Warsaw, we stopped at a gallery that specialised in modern art, so Sir Eric was in his element. Our newly acquired expert shadowed Sir Eric, and they often seemed to be in deep conversation on various pieces on display.

When we completed our visit and returned to our cars, Sir Eric signalled that he wanted to have a word with me. He walked me away from the cars and told me quietly that our "art expert" was no expert. Indeed, he knew next to nothing about modern art, even less than I did. The Pole obviously had taken a quick course in the subject, but he would never be of the art world. Sir Eric said that beyond doubt, he was a security officer, detailed to watch over us and particularly to keep an eye on the accompanying Poles. From that moment on, Sir Eric always referred to him as "the spook." He directed that I be vigilant in my dealings with him and that I should speak to the other accompanying Poles only in English, because the spook's only foreign language was French. This instruction I welcomed because my spoken French was still far from the high standard displayed by the Poles. Thereafter, following every visit we made to a gallery, Sir Eric would mention to me that his first impressions of the spook were confirmed!

Cracow must be one of Europe's most historic and interesting cities. It had been the capital of Poland before Warsaw and remained the coronation city for years after Warsaw became the seat of government. There were said to be some fifty churches that had been declared national museums. I was particularly fascinated by two sites in Cracow, the main cathedral and Wawel Castle, which had a Canadian connection.

On the floor of the cathedral's altar there was half of a magnificent carpet, the other half having been cut off by the French and placed in a museum in Paris. On top of the cathedral, there continued, even in these Communist times, a practice that started seven hundred years ago when the Eastern hordes were at the gates of Cracow. The Tatars would have captured Cracow had not a watchman sounded his trumpet and awakened the city. As he blew his warning, a Tatar arrow hit him in the throat. The time of day has since been announced by a bugler on the tower blowing a tune that comes to an abrupt end on the very note that was played when the arrow penetrated the original bugler's throat.

At Wawel Castle, long the residence of the kings of Poland, one can see much of the national treasure that the Poles stored in bank vaults in Canada when the Germans overran Poland during the Second World War. After the war and the takeover of Poland by the Communists, there was much debate in Canada about whether or not to return the treasure. Canadian art experts realised that in the bank vaults the treasure could not be properly cared for, and they joined the Polish government in pleading for its return to Poland. Premier Maurice Duplessis of Quebec was the main opponent to the return of the treasure to "the communists." Good sense eventually prevailed, and one can now see beautiful ancient tapestries adorning the castle walls, fitting perfectly into the places for which they were made. Amongst the many items returned was the sword used for centuries in the coronation of Polish kings. I asked the Poles whether they were annoyed with Canada for its slowness in returning these cherished pieces. Their answer was that in their history they had been plundered and robbed by the Germans, Russians, Swedes, French, and many others; the only people who ever gave anything back were those who didn't steal anything from them, the Canadians.

After Cracow, we visited one of the most terrible of places, Auschwitz concentration camp. The German commandant of Auschwitz was executed in Warsaw in 1947 for the murder of four million persons, in this, the admittedly worst of German death camps. The killings were carried out on a scale that made it plain that the Nazi aim was the destruction of the Jewish people and the total subjugation of the Slavs. It was shocking to see buildings constructed for the sole purpose of housing gas chambers to exterminate human beings. Equally shocking were the grass-covered mounds built from the ashes taken from the incinerators, and the meticulously kept ledgers recording details of personal belongings such as combs and gold from the teeth of the victims. After this visit to Auschwitz and a later one to Dachau in Bavaria, I feel that everyone should visit these terrible sites to have it impressed on them just how really thin is the veneer of civilisation. Otherwise, it is difficult to accept that in our own time a supposedly civilised and advanced people could stoop to do such things to fellow human beings.

The great Polish hospitality and the sightseeing were all very enjoyable, but the moments I enjoyed most in Poland were the evening dinners with Sir Eric and our accompanying Polish hosts. Sir Eric launched detailed discussions that went on late into the night on all aspects of international economic and political affairs. He was dedicated to free enterprise and free trade and gave the Poles a hard time when they tried to justify any aspect of the Communist system. Most of the people we travelled with or met (except the spook) were involved in economic relations with the West and were generally pro-Western, although initially they were a little guarded in voicing their views. Sir Eric intellectually pushed them into corners and refused to let them escape with the usual communist rhetoric.

I was a bit surprised one evening when the Pole who shared my car, and whom I knew well from Geneva, voiced in private conversation with me very racist views about the Chinese. He felt no different about "the yellow peril" than did many threatened Westerners at the height of the war against Japan. Apparently, while the friendly relationship between the Communist countries of Europe and China ebbed and flowed, fear of China never changed. Perhaps it was the terrible history of the invasions by the "Mongol hordes" that affected their attitudes but there seemed to be a genuine fear of China. (In later travels throughout Eastern Europe and through Siberia, I found that many Communist officials were almost paranoid in their fear of the Chinese.) My Polish colleague was a Communist party member. I had never had much time for the Communists but I did at least give them a few marks for their brotherhood-of-man position. Discussions with him and later talks with other Communists had me erase even that one credit I had given them.

We ended our tour in Gdansk (the old Danzig) and in former Prussia where we visited the castles of the Teutonic knights. The entire trip was a tremendous introduction for a young Westerner to the vastly different world of the Communist east.

On leaving Poland, our next stop was to be Czechoslovakia. I spent several hours sending messages and making telephone calls to Prague in a futile attempt to learn about the arrangements they had made for our visit. In Warsaw, I visited the Czechoslovak embassy in an effort to move things

97

along, but it was of no help whatever in getting me in contact with Prague. When I reported on my failed efforts to Sir Eric, he instructed me to book flights immediately straight to Geneva. He relished the thought of the Czechoslovak authorities waiting in vain for us for hours at Prague airport. He said that after the shoddy way we had been treated on our forced landing in Prague on our way to Warsaw, it wouldn't hurt to have the Czech representatives in Geneva at our knees. So we flew straight home to Geneva. Next day the Czechoslovak ambassador was at Sir Eric's door with messages of great concern and apology from his government. I had the rest of the Czechoslovak Permanent Mission staff doing the same at my door!

Our three-year posting in Geneva came all too quickly to an end. The head of the Trade Policy Division of GATT, Finn Gundelach, offered me a more senior position if I would stay. Peggy and I were tempted but realised that, despite many positive things about life as internationals, there were serious downsides. To remain permanently with GATT would have meant resigning from the Canadian government. We feared that it would also have meant, in reality, that the children would have ended up without a country. We wanted the children to know and feel that they belonged somewhere, and we felt that Canada was that "somewhere."

There was certainly no way that the children would readily be accepted as Swiss. The Swiss made it all but impossible for a foreigner, even one born there, like Jennifer, to become a citizen. Unlike the New World, where immigrants and persons born in the country were readily accepted as citizens, this was generally not the case in Switzerland. We had a home in Ottawa to return to and my Department of Trade and Commerce was pressing me to return. Tom Burns, who would be my immediate supervisor, offered me a promotion and an "interesting" position in the department if I returned. We packed and headed home.

Chapter Fourteen
The Long Way Home

One of the benefits of working for an international organisation was the amount of leave one accumulated. While we had taken many short summer and winter holidays while in Switzerland, we had not taken home leave. I had sufficient leave due to me to allow us to go by ship to Canada via Australia. The GATT provided us with first-class air tickets to Ottawa. I asked whether I could put the money towards tourist-class sea fares to Vancouver via Australia. The response was that as long as we could provide receipts for travel to Canada that didn't exceed the allocated amount, they didn't care if we went via the moon. We booked passage on the P&O liner *Oransay* from London to Sydney and on the *Orsova* from Sydney to Vancouver.

With Janine and Chris, I drove to Antwerp to ship our small Volkswagen to Montreal. Peggy flew with Julie and Jennifer to London, where we all met at the Regent Palace Hotel. The children were fascinated with London, where the television was in English! They were surprised that the waiters, taxi drivers, and people in the stores all spoke English. They had been of the view that only Mom's and Dad's friends spoke English, that the rest of the world spoke French!

The Bay of Biscay lived up to its reputation for being a rough body of water. There was a howling gale, and on the first day out, virtually everybody was seasick. About the only one who wasn't was our Julie. She spent much of the crossing of the Bay on a rocking horse on the heaving deck of the children's play area. I had to watch over her as she rode her horse, and I felt none too good myself, thinking only of the Straits of Gibraltar and the more placid Mediterranean beyond.

We spent a day ashore at Gibraltar showing the children the monkeys that make their home on the famous Rock. We called at Naples, where we did the tour of the ruins of Pompeii, which we found so fascinating that we all vowed to visit them again someday. (We did.) After Port Said in Egypt

99

on the northern end of the Suez Canal, we had the great adventure of getting stuck in the sand in the middle of the canal. We were held fast for several hours, until the crew and canal authorities were able to get cables ashore and sufficiently fastened to allow our ship to winch itself free.

The children were captivated, but somewhat scared, by some of the surroundings in Aden and Bombay. In Aden it was getting dark when we returned to the ship, and the constant pressure of the beggars and vendors tended to unnerve them.

After a day ashore with the children in Singapore, Peggy and I felt ready for an evening alone, so we went ashore again for a good Chinese meal. The children initially welcomed the idea of being left alone in the care of the stewards, with permission to read and play games beyond their normal bedtime. The ship was to sail at midnight. At about ten o'clock, before we returned, the crew began to prepare the ship for departure. One of their first acts was to lift the tourist class gangway, asking all passengers to board through the forward first-class entrance. Unfortunately, the children could hear and see all of this activity through the porthole. They were convinced that their parents were being left behind. They had a tearful conference and decided they would stick with the ship and wait to be met by their grand-parents in Australia. We returned shortly afterwards to a scene of sobbing children with stewards trying to calm and reassure them. We felt very, very guilty.

Peggy's parents were the perfect hosts while we were in Sydney. They had rented for us a small flat in Manly and a car. Manly is one of the most beautiful and accessible areas of Sydney, being only a forty-minute ferry-boat ride from downtown. We were only a ten-minute walk from Manly's ocean beach, and from our flat we looked down on Manly's harbour beach, which was netted against sharks.

Our first port of call on the *Orsova* was Auckland, New Zealand. I shall never forget our evening departure from Auckland, when the band on the dock struck up the famous heartbreaking Maori love song, "Now is the Hour When We Must Say Good-bye." Every New Zealander on ship and shore was in tears as we pulled away and the thousands of coloured ribbons connecting the ship to the dock broke. New Zealanders will tell you that during the war the bands had to stop playing the song for departing troopships, because the familiar refrain would cause some of the boys to jump overboard and swim for shore.

Everybody loved Fiji. We were all impressed with the tall handsome

Fijians and their wonderful singing voices. Like many of the other South Sea islands, both British and French, the inhabitants had been converted to Christianity by the London Missionary Society, which was as strong on the old Methodist hymns, which the Fijians loved, as it was on Scripture. Our day in Honolulu was still at a time when Honolulu was for the most part an unspoiled South Sea port. We wandered around the relatively empty beaches and through the parklike gardens of the beautiful Royal Hawaiian Hotel, which is still there but now overshadowed and dwarfed by the concrete jungle of high-rise buildings.

Once ashore in Vancouver, we went straight to the airport, for I was due at work in Ottawa next day. Our round-the-world trip had eaten up much of our savings, but we looked upon it as money well spent. Normally one would have to wait for retirement to contemplate such a trip. We were able to do it while in our thirties and with all our children. It would have to be inexpensive cottage vacations around Ottawa for years!

When I checked with the Montreal shipping office about the Volkswagen "beetle" I shipped from Antwerp, they sheepishly advised that they had bad news and good news for me. The bad news was that the car had been shipped as deck cargo, and they had dropped the hatch cover of the ship on it while loading cargo at Hamburg. They said there were several items of good news. First, the car had arrived in Montreal. Second, the hatch cover had flattened the front and not the back of the car, where the engine was located. Third, they had taken the liberty of having it rebuilt. If I was not fully satisfied when I saw the car, they would discuss a financial settlement.

I took a late afternoon train to Montreal to look at the car. It looked and sounded as good as new. I went to Canadian customs, who told me that it was too late in the day to claim the car. They presented me with a slip (identical in size and colour to my newly acquired Quebec fishing license), telling me it authorised me to drive the car to Ottawa. Next morning I was to give it to the customs office in Ottawa and clear my car. The Ottawa customs people asked for my documentation, and I extracted from my wallet what I thought was the needed slip. The customs officer let out an oath about those "ding-a-lings" at headquarters who kept changing the forms. He retreated to consult with his superior. The superior in turn cursed headquarters and went to see the collector of customs. In a few minutes, all three emerged from the collector's office, emitting gales of laughter. They laughingly told me that I came very close to clearing a car through customs on my Quebec fishing license!

Chapter Fifteen
In the Years of Dief and Mike

Canada in the early summer of 1962, just months after our return from Geneva, was in the midst of an election. Prime Minister Diefenbaker was to see his big majority disappear, leaving him with a minority government. He was a great British Commonwealth man, and much effort had been directed by his government to increasing trade with Commonwealth countries. I had attended the Commonwealth Trade and Economic Conference in Montreal in 1958, and the prime minister had made it clear that the ever-increasing concentration of Canada's trade with the United States and the decline of our trade with the Commonwealth would have to be addressed. This was easier said than done. We were still in that postwar period, when all Commonwealth countries, while generally extending to Canada preferential tariff treatment, maintained quantitative import restrictions for balance of payments reasons. These were directed in particular against Canada and the United States. These restrictions generally nullified for Canada the value of the tariff preferences.

In spite of this sorry state, the Diefenbaker government made a number of valiant efforts to increase trade generally and with the Commonwealth particularly. Diefenbaker's trade minister, George Hees, mobilised the Trade Commissioner Service and gave it a very high profile in Ottawa and across Canada. The minister was well liked by the trade people who tended to overlook his often flamboyant and colourful behaviour that was not always backed up by substance. His most famous publicity stunt was when he was photographed with his feet on the desk with the soles facing the camera. Written on the soles were the letters, "YCDBSOYA," which stood for, "You Can't Do Business Sitting On Your Ass."

Britain's drift towards the European Economic Community caused Canada to make almost desperate moves to hang onto what we had, namely duty-free access to the British market. Clearly, if Britain was to succeed in its attempts to join the Community, it would have to adopt the Common

103

External Tariff of the Community as well as the hated Common Agricultural Policy. This would bring to an end free entry into Britain for Commonwealth products, including Canada's. In Ottawa, I was assigned to a small group under Maurice Schwarzmann, Bob Latimer, and Tom Burns, in the International Trade Relations Branch. My work was almost entirely on British-EEC negotiations.

We compiled a comprehensive inventory of Canadian trade interests in the British market. We attempted to assess how these interests might be adversely affected by the loss of free access should Britain embrace the Common tariff and agricultural policy of the Community. Where the applications of these measures were expected to bring an end to Canadian trade, we pressed the British to seek duty-free quotas or at least a very gradual introduction of the new barriers. In other cases, we pressed the British to pressure the Community to reduce their common tariff or moderate their agricultural policy, thus opening the larger European market to Canadian exports.

Unlike negotiations in GATT, where we often worked with the Americans, we could not look to them for support in these negotiations. They were dead against the Commonwealth preferential system. They only tolerated it because it was one of the conditions for the accession of the Commonwealth countries to GATT. Our attitude was that if the Americans, Europeans, Japanese, or other non-Commonwealth countries wished to see the tariff preferences ended, they would have to pay for their removal by granting tariff concessions to Canada in their own markets. Now it seemed that the preferential system was about to disappear without compensation. This would happen through the mere act of British accession to the European Community.

Our concerns about our access to the British market all but evaporated in January 1963, when French President Charles De Gaulle vetoed British entry into the Common Market. Britain would try again but would have to wait ten years, until 1973, before it would succeed. Some argued that De Gaulle achieved for us what we ourselves could not negotiate with the British. However, if the British-EEC negotiations taught us anything, it was that the United Kingdom was bent on abandoning the Commonwealth Tariff Preferential system that had been a pillar of Canadian trade policy for decades. As a country, we would have to prepare ourselves for great changes.

I had my first real introduction to "security" during my time on

British-EEC negotiations. I was called into the office one weekend to draft a reply to an important secret cable from London. Jake Warren, then our assistant deputy minister, was there. We were unable to gain access to the bar-locked security cabinet of one of the senior secretaries. In it was the needed material for our response to London. The secretary was away for the weekend. Jake calmly and methodically went through the various places in the office where a person might note the lock combination. It was a forbidden, but an unfortunately common, practice to record this number. He looked at the back of calendars, underneath desk pads, and in the front and back of dictionaries and reference books. Within minutes he found the numbers, expressed in dollars and cents, on the back of a title card on one of the filing cabinets. His only comment was, "Let this be a lesson to you, Frank Petrie, never write down a security combination number." I never have.

I worked fairly close to Jake Warren during much of his distinguished career. He became our deputy minister, and was one of the best. He was our ambassador to the United States and our high commissioner to the United Kingdom. I had most to do with him when he was the leader of many of our GATT delegations and the chairman of the Contracting Parties of GATT. Jake was a navy man. He had survived a terrible wartime experience. His ship was sunk in the North Atlantic and there were few survivors. He was picked out of the water with the frozen bodies of some of his shipmates and laid out with the other "dead" on deck. Somebody noticed a flicker of life, and he ended up in a St. John's hospital for "thawing." On GATT delegations, he was great to work with; he pitched in and helped on the most menial tasks. However, being ever the navy man, he insisted on the members of his delegation being properly dressed and always well presented. I remember one early morning after a late evening out with Jake, I was a little late getting up. I raced unshaven to our daily delegation meeting. Jake sent me off like a little boy to my room to shave before I could get involved in the meeting.

The General Election of April 8, 1963, brought about a change of government from a Conservative minority headed by Prime Mister Diefenbaker to a Liberal minority led by Prime Minister Pearson. With British-EEC negotiations no longer the high priority trade file, our work took on a much different focus. I was assigned to the International Organisations Division. (Wilfred Lavoie was the chief and I was the assistant chief of the division and David Knowles, the only other officer, claimed he was the lone Indian.) We followed developments in GATT, the Organisation for Economic Cooperation and Development (OECD), and the United Nations Conference on Trade and Development (UNCTAD).

The world trading community was again gearing up for another round of negotiations in GATT. These were to get underway in Geneva in 1964, to be known as the Kennedy round. They were so named because of the far-reaching authority the American administration obtained for their negotiators that was sufficient to set the stage for a new concerted attack on trade barriers. We were also getting more and more involved with the emerging UNCTAD, where our relationships with the developing countries were for the most part being relegated. Annoyed with the often disruptive tactics of some of the more militant developing countries in GATT, the Western countries were tending to breathe new life into the OECD. We were involved in this latter oganisation in working out arrangements on international financing, export subsidies, and certain industrial sectors.

I no sooner got settled in this interesting area of work when I was summoned to the deputy minister's office. Jake Warren was now our deputy minister. He had been approached by the assistant secretary to the Cabinet, Gerry Stoner, asking that Jake second an officer to the Privy Council Office to help service the economic committees of Cabinet. It was felt that someone familiar with GATT might be useful when issues arising from the new negotiations were referred to ministers.

Jake asked me whether I would like to go to the Privy Council Office for a few years. I responded, "That should be very interesting work, sir."

He was a little annoyed at what appeared to him to be my unenthusiastic response and shot back, "If it is only something of interest you want, you can get that on TV; this is a way to serve Canada in a manner offered to very few people." I gratefully took a secondment to the Privy Council Office.

Chapter Sixteen
Life on the Hill

I could claim to be the only person in Canada who knew during the working day when the prime minister went to the bathroom. His offices were immediately above mine and the piping from his washroom ran straight down to the Ottawa sewer system through my office. This was sometime before the gutting-out of the East Block of Parliament that removed the prime minister's pipes from my office and, indeed, removed the prime minister's office from that beautiful old historic building.

In the mid-sixties the Privy Council Office (PCO) was very small and was housed with the Prime Minister's Office (PMO) and External Affairs in the East Block. The PCO and the PMO worked together; the PCO, in much of its work, was practically an adjunct of the PMO. Before Prime Minister Pearson's time, the PCO had been mostly clerical in its operations, keeping records of Cabinet meetings and looking after Orders in Council. Under Prime Minister Pearson, committees of Cabinet increased in number and authority. Many of the decisions taken previously by full Cabinet were now left to the committees. It was in this field of Cabinet committee work that I was mostly involved.

Gordon Robertson was the secretary to the Cabinet and the clerk of the Privy Council and, as such, was the senior federal civil servant. He would brief the prime minister each and every morning about what was going on in Canada and the world. My immediate supervisor was Gerry Stoner, who was assistant secretary to the Cabinet on all economic matters. Gerry served as the secretary of the Cabinet committees on Finance and Economic Policy and on Trade and Resources. I served as Gerry's assistant secretary. The committee on Finance and Economics Policy was chaired by the Minister of Finance, who, for much of the time I was there, was Mitchell Sharp. In addition to these regular Cabinet committees, there were a number of ad hoc committees. I was involved in one on GATT, one on employment in eastern Canada, and another on shipbuilding subsidies.

Our responsibility in the Privy Council Office was to serve Cabinet. We drew up Cabinet agenda and steered documents through departments. At the meetings we prepared minutes and decisions. Normally at committee meetings when eight or ten ministers interested in an issue came to a decision, it was automatically approved by Cabinet.

On a number of occasions when Gordon Robertson and Gerry Stoner were away, I found myself required to fill in at meetings of the full Cabinet when discussions were on trade and economic issues. These meetings took place in the historic and impressive East Block Cabinet room with its great oval table dominated by the high velvet-covered prime minister's chair on which prime ministers had since 1867 sat with their Cabinets.

My office overlooked the lawns in front of the Centre Block of Parliament with its majestic Peace Tower and flag towering over downtown Ottawa. In my first few days, I doubted if I would be able to put in a good day's work, because every morning in the summer months, there was the changing of the guard, with all the band music, pomp, and ceremony that went with it. There was also the onslaught of tourists an hour or so before the ceremony started. All of this soon became humdrum, and it wasn't long before I no longer knew that the soldiers and the crowd were there.

I was impressed by the ease with which a junior officer in the PCO could have access to the prime minister. I believe that in my case this was due largely to the very long leash Gerry Stoner gave me. I recall that during my early days in the PCO, the Ottawa media was preoccupied with the public's concern about bilingual road signs. There was great controversy regarding, for example, whether parking signs with such cumbersome language as, "No Parking Between This and the Next Sign," should also have the equally cumbersome French wording. I clipped from an old Swiss road map a copy of the international road signs, which used symbols instead of wording. This I attached to a short memo to Gerry, suggesting that all the bitterness surrounding the question of bilingual signs could be overcome if we were simply to adopt the internationally approved signs. Gerry gave the memo to Prime Minister Pearson, who next day sent it back to me, having scrawled in the column, "Great idea, push it!" We did, and within a few months, with absolutely no fanfare, the international signs started to appear on federal roads in national parks and around airports. Before long the provinces also adopted them.

I got to know many of the Cabinet ministers. Sitting next to them several days a week for a few years, you could not help observing their strengths and weaknesses in dealing with their colleagues and with issues. I was very impressed with the friendship that existed between many of them. Perhaps it was that they faced and dealt with immense problems together and were individually and collectively subjected to constant media and public scrutiny and criticism, that tight bonds were formed. The friendship between Judy LaMarsh, Guy Favreau, and Jack Pickersgill (Newfoundland's minister in the Pearson Cabinet) appeared particularly close. They would wait for one another after Cabinet meetings, much as kids would wait for their best friends after school. I saw a lot of Jack Pickersgill at meetings, but we never developed a close relationship. On one occasion when we were alone (in the washroom), he asked me whether I ever considered returning to Newfoundland to enter politics. I told him that I was happy with what I was doing.

Paul Hellyer, the minister of defence, served on few of the committees I worked on, but I did see him in a number of full Cabinet meetings and was always impressed with his ability if not always with the policies he championed. Particularly controversial was his policy on the unification of the armed forces and the common uniform for the army, navy, and air force. Walter Gordon was close to the prime minister and, while finance minister, chaired our Finance and Economic Policy Committee. He tended to use the committee to encourage support for his many unorthodox policies, which I silently considered dangerous. He was preoccupied with what he saw as the financial and economic takeover of Canada by the United States and was bent on having the government take counteracting measures. I feared that if he got his way, it would damage Canada's international relationships, particularly those with our major trading partner, the United States. He soon ran into serious opposition, not only from the conservatives in Parliament and from the financial and business community, but from members of his own party.

Mitchell Sharp, the Cabinet minister, was like Mitchell Sharp, the senior civil servant. As a former deputy minister of Trade and Commerce he knew the trade and economic issues as well as or better than the civil servants who were advising him. I looked at Mitchell Sharp as one of the few who had the power and the knowledge to serve as a moderating influence on Walter Gordon.

Edgar Benson was for a time finance minister. I liked him, but we had a run-in a few days after I arrived at PCO. When we were introduced, he noted that I was from Newfoundland and made some flip remark about another Newfie coming to Ontario for employment. I flared, saying I would have hoped that the minister would have been pleased to see the federal service represented by people from across the country and not only from Ontario and Quebec. He was a bit taken aback by my reaction.

Future Prime Minister Jean Chretien joined the Cabinet in 1967 and sat in on our Cabinet committee meetings as minister of state attached to Finance. Although struggling with English and the ways of government, he fitted in well. The prime minister and Mitchell Sharp made every effort to help him. Future Prime Ministers Pierre Trudeau and John Turner were appointed at the same time but were in portfolios unrelated to my area of work. I met Trudeau when he was parliamentary assistant to the prime minister.

One of my favourite ministers was Jean Luc Pepin. I got to know him well in later years when he was minister of Trade. Our first contact was at a Cabinet committee when the discussion was on the Baie d'Espoire power development on Newfoundland's south coast. When he referred to the name, he understandably used the proper French pronunciation. I lightheartedly corrected him, saying that in Newfoundland we pronounced it "Bay Despair."

He said, "That is incorrect."

I said, "It might well be, sir, but three hundred years of common usage makes it correct."

He said with his usual disarming smile, "If you called it 'Bay Despair' for three hundred years, it would be only fair for us to call it 'Baie d'Espoire' for the next three hundred."

These were the years when federal overspending really got underway. One got praise for concocting new spending programs, whereas nowadays, the applause goes to those who cut them back. Some ministers were better than others in picking up program money for their ridings and provinces. At my time, the champions were Jack Pickersgill for Newfoundland and Arthur Laing for British Columbia. I'm sure that Pickersgill had a federal wharf built in every Newfoundland outport. The story goes that he was ready to build one in Buchans until he learnt it was fifty miles from the sea!

George McIlraith I liked very much. He had time for small talk and took an interest in people. Little wonder the Liberal party relied on him for so many political chores. He was moved from Transport to the Privy Council in 1964. Maurice Sauve moved into Forestry at the same time, and I saw a lot of him in the Trade and Resources committee. He later served as the "spouse" of Madame Sauve when she became governor general.

The 1965 election resulted in another minority government for Prime Minister Pearson. The Liberals, I felt, had made the terrible mistake of campaigning on the need for a majority government. This was an appeal that excited nobody. The solid measures on the government's agenda, such as the proposed new flag and Medicare, became subsidiary to the appeal for a majority. The election did bring in some badly needed new blood. Pierre Trudeau was elected that year and joined the PMO as parliamentary secretary to the prime minister. About the same time, Marc LaLonde and Michael Pitfield joined the office, and the three of them were thereafter very close. I'm sure that Marc LaLonde and Michael Pitfield had far greater insights about Pierre Trudeau's future than the rest of us.

Just before the 1965 election, the prime minister was invited to Newfoundland by Premier Joey Smallwood to open the newly completed portion of the TransCanada Highway. The ribbon-cutting ceremony was to take place at a spot about eight miles west of my hometown of Grand Falls. The prime minister invited me to accompany his group. Also included were Ministers McIlraith and Winters. Joey had named the spot, "Pearson's Peak," and had a monument erected on the site. We flew to Gander on a government plane. I had alerted my parents and was pleased to see them on the runway when we arrived. I had very little time with them, for cars were awaiting to take us to Gander Lake, where there were float planes to take us to Rushy Pond, a few miles west of Grand Falls. The Mounties drove us from Rushy Pond to the site.

Joey was there to greet us with a crowd of several hundred. There were the usual speeches expressing optimism about the good things the new highway would bring to Newfoundland, and the cutting of the ribbon. We then boarded cars for the drive back to Gander. We took a rest stop at a service station at the edge of Grand Falls. I asked Minister Winters whether I might be dropped off at the home of my sister Janet, where I would meet my parents who would drive me back to Gander. The minister turned to an accompanying Mountie and asked him to take me to my family.

My mother and father were delighted that I had returned to Newfoundland in the company of the prime minister, although some of my relatives and friends took this as an indication that I was now a committed Liberal and a friend of Joey's. They couldn't accept that a federal civil servant could serve without being dedicated to the party in power.

My father insisted that we drop into Lewisporte on our way to Gander, to pick up four fresh salmon, two for the prime minister and two for me. On the aircraft, I had the steward put the salmon in the refrigerator, and next morning in Ottawa, I drove to the prime minister's residence at 24 Sussex Drive. A Mountie at the gate escorted me to the kitchen, where I presented them to the cook, explaining that they were a gift from my father. Several days later, I received a very nice note from the prime minister, saying how much he had enjoyed them and asking me to thank my father. I sent the note to Dad, who, I am sure, showed it to everybody in Lewisporte and Grand Falls.

The new Canadian maple leaf flag had been raised at Pearson's Peak and, indeed, was flown across Canada since February 1965 with ever-increasing acceptance. The big flag debate that raged across the country ended almost as quickly as it began. When Prime Minister Pearson established a Cabinet committee to choose a new flag in September 1964, neither he nor anybody on the committee had any clear idea of the flag they wanted. The only points of agreement among ministers (strongly opposed by the conservatives) was that it had to carry no links with Britain or France, and it must be clearly Canadian.

A colleague in the Privy Council Office, Alan Winship, whose office was next to mine, did much of the secretariat work for the Flag committee. It sounded straightforward enough, but the opposition to the new flag was strong and vocal. Those opposing could rally around the existing red ensign with the Canadian coat of arms and the Union Jack under which Canadians "fought and died." Those favouring a new flag had nothing to point to except their own favourite design; there was nothing uniting them except that they wanted something new. The leader of the Opposition, former Prime Minister Diefenbaker, had great support in his emotional appeals for the retention of "the old flag." Canadian veterans were on his side.

Newfoundland went the other way and adopted as their provincial flag the straight Union Jack. I remember that Alan had a multitude of designs that the Cabinet committee whittled down to just a few. A postage stamp was actually issued with one of the designs, depicting three maple leaves; it was immediately labelled "Pearson's pennant." The prime minister, while ready to accept anything that was simple and readily recognisable as Canadian, did eventually lean to a design that was very close to the one eventually adopted. The difference was in the number of points on the red maple leaf and the shade of red. He had this flag raised for a weekend at the prime minister's country residence at nearby Harrington Lake in Quebec's Gatineau Hills. Here, against the blue winter sky and a typical Canadian snow-covered landscape, he became convinced that this flag should be the basis for the new Canadian emblem.

After tinkering with the number of points on the maple leaf and tone of red, the design was adopted by the Cabinet committee. The decision was then taken that all of the competing and often controversial designs should be destroyed. This was a very sensible and politically wise decision.

I was in Alan's office when the various designs and flags, including, to my horror, the flag flown at Harrington Lake, were being discarded. Unknown to Alan, I grabbed from the disposal bin the flag that had been flown by the prime minister. I took it to my office and locked it in my bar-lock cabinet. I felt strongly that this flag had to be preserved. I struggled for years about what to do with it. It ended up, a decade later, in the archives of Queen's University in Kingston but that is a story to be related later.

Like all enjoyable working periods of my career, my time at the Privy Council too quickly came to an end. On the day before I was to return to Trade and Commerce, the prime minister's executive assistant, Mary Mac-Donald, threw a farewell party for me. Virtually everybody in the PCO and PMO was there except the prime minister. He was preoccupied in Cabinet with a national railway strike that had just been called. Mary went into the Cabinet chamber and suggested he might want to come out for a few minutes to say good-bye to me. He did. With a glass of sherry, he toasted me and expressed the hope that I would "get back to Geneva, which for somebody from the Trade Department had to be the centre of the world." He told me about his time in Geneva; the highlight being when he played for one of the Geneva hockey teams; hockey for him was second only to baseball. I was overwhelmed that the prime minister, burdened as he was with a national railway strike, should bother to take time to attend my farewell party.

Chapter Seventeen
Heart of the Trading World

On my return to Trade and Commerce, I joined the United States division as assistant director. The job was short-lived, for within months, I received a call again from the deputy minister's office. I was told that the assistant deputy ministers responsible for Trade Policy in Trade and Commerce (Maurice Schwarzmann), the Department of Finance (Rodney Grey), and External Affairs (Jim Langley) had selected me for the number-two position at the Canadian Permanent Mission to the United Nations in Geneva. I was pleased yet a little stunned. I was pleased because the work was interesting and familiar, and I knew that my family would easily make the transition back to life in Switzerland. I was stunned a little because I would be the officer at the Mission responsible for Canada's involvement in the international economic organisations in Geneva. The most important of these was GATT, but they also included the United Nations Conference on Trade and Development (UNCTAD) and the Economic Commission for Europe.

It was the summer of Canada's one hundredth birthday, and Montreal was entertaining the world at Expo '67. We sailed from Montreal on the *Carmania* and, fortunately, were able to spend the night on the ship before sailing, and thus take in Expo.

We bought a car for export and it accompanied us to Le Havre. From there we drove to Geneva. I arrived relaxed and rested. This was just as well, for I was immediately thrown into what proved to be the craziest international meeting I was ever to attend.

There was a cabled instruction sitting on the desk of my new office in Geneva. I was to attend that afternoon, as the Canadian representative, the recently formed UNCTAD committee on synthetics. I was instructed to do what I could to kill the committee. I hardly had a chance to meet my new colleagues and staff at the Permanent Mission before I had to rush off to the UN's Palais des Nations, where the meeting was already underway.

They were in the process of electing a chairman. I had hardly found my seat when the British representative, seeing a new, green committee member and rightly sensing that I was unaware of the internal politics of the committee, proposed me as chairman. I felt it would be rather difficult for me, given my instructions to end the life of the committee, to take the chair. I declined. Pressure nevertheless built up for me to take the position, because they wanted a Western representative. All the other representatives of Western industrialised countries had the good sense to decline. In the end, I compromised and accepted the position of vice-chairman. I might have saved myself the squirming that I went through to avoid the chair, because a few days later the new chairman (from Sri Lanka) was posted back home, and I automatically assumed the position.

I was horrified when the first proposal from the floor, following my installation as chairman, was a most ludicrous and unattainable recommendation from the representative of Chad (who was a French professional troublemaker in the employ of Chad) that all synthetic production throughout the world be banned. This would mean, if passed, that the United Nations would go on record in favour of a phase-out of, for example, Canadian synthetic rubber production. I was about to point out that such a ridiculous proposal could only waste the time of the delegates and bring the UNCTAD into disrepute, when several representatives from developing countries asked for the floor to support Chad's proposal. I could now understand why Ottawa was intent on the destruction of the committee. Clearly the solidarity of the developing countries would result in this crazy recommendation going onto the books of the United Nations as an UNCTAD-approved position supported by a great majority. I immediately called for an adjournment. As was the practice in UNCTAD, all delegations separated into groups. There was a Western industrial countries' group, one for the Communist countries and, largest of all, a group for the developing countries. This was all so foreign to me, for in GATT, friends and foes changed every few hours, depending on the issue. The UNCTAD groups were rigid and generally voted as a bloc.

Our Western group agreed categorically to vote against the resolution and go on record condemning it. This was in the full knowledge that we would be overwhelmed by the developing country majority. I was asked by the chairman of the Western group to approach some of the more sensible developing country representatives to try to have them vote sensibly or abstain. The "sensible" developing countries agreed with me individually that for a United Nations organisation to go on record prohibiting synthetic production was farcical. Nevertheless, they felt compelled, in the interest of developing country solidarity, to support the proposal. Similarly the Eastern European representatives I spoke to agreed privately that the proposal was senseless, but they were under a general instruction not to oppose the developing countries, so they would either back the proposal or, at best, abstain. I reported this to the Western group. Putting the best gloss on it, they agreed that a positive vote would only serve to bring the committee on synthetics into disrepute. I was sure that Ottawa would be happy to have the committee held in low esteem.

As soon as the committee reassembled, I called for the vote. After the predictable result was announced, I expressed my disappointment that the committee could not have addressed the problems confronting synthetic and natural products in a serious way. The sort of resolution just adopted would never bring about a solution but would place doubt on the ability of UNCTAD to undertake serious work. In good conscience, I could not waste more of my time considering such meaningless proposals that were unhelpful in arriving at mutually acceptable solutions. I resigned as chairman. I did thus conclude my short career as an elected officer of UNCTAD. Thereafter, I tried to leave it to others at the Permanent Mission to handle UNCTAD. I was determined to devote my time to the more serious work on trade problems in GATT.

It was not difficult for me to carry through with my decision to concentrate on GATT, since the ambassador, who would normally be expected to do much of the GATT work, looked to me to take full responsibility for GATT. It suited me to have a free hand, and it quickly became known in the GATT Secretariat and in other Permanent Missions that I was the Canadian officer to deal with on GATT issues. Within weeks, I was elected chairman of the Balance of Payments Committee, a position I held for the duration of my posting. I also chaired a number of Working Parties, such as those on the accession of countries to GATT; I felt honoured when both Israel and the Arab countries asked me to chair working parties dealing with the accession of countries in the Middle East.

We lived in the village of Vesenaz, directly across the lake from the UN's Palais des Nations. Our house was in a lovely rural area. Within minutes on bicycle or on foot we could be in the Swiss countryside or in France, for the French border to the east or south was but a kilometre or two away. I used to wonder about life, so full of contrasts; wonderful carefree hours bicycling or walking with the family along Swiss and French country lanes, and involvement in international negotiations at the Palais des Nations late into the night.

We registered the three older children (Janine 14, Chris 12, and Julie 11) in the English stream of the International School. Jennifer 7, we placed in the Geneva English School that we had helped found seven years earlier. This school was now located in our village and had grown from the original several students to several hundred.

Knowing Geneva and the GATT environment, Peggy and I set out to become the most effective Canadian representatives possible. I drew up a list of all the foreign representatives and Secretariat people we should get to know well. We listed twenty-five countries that really mattered on trade issues to Canada and picked the representatives from these countries who made an impact at GATT. Some of these were ambassadors and some third secretaries. We didn't differentiate. We set up a schedule of dinner parties and, every week, would entertain four couples from our list. We intermingled foreign representatives with influential members of the Secretariat. Within two months, we were on close friendly terms with every country representative and Secretariat member who was in any way important to Canada. For the other seventy or so country representatives and lesser influential people in the Secretariat, we held receptions every few months. The result of our effort was that I could call on anyone in the GATT circle and be on close personal terms with them, within a few months of our arrival. This was to be particularly important when delegations from Ottawa descended upon us and wanted to meet the individuals involved in this or that international trade issue.

I arrived in Geneva immediately after the GATT Kennedy round had ended in 1967. Indeed, the last of the Canadian delegation made such a rapid departure that they left a few loose ends that hit me during my first few weeks. The European Community delegation, for one, descended on me. They claimed that some of the concessions that Canada had given them (in the form of reductions in the Canadian customs tariff) had been given to them before. These were in payment for concessions that Canada had received from the Community in the form of reductions in the Common External Tariff of the EEC.

It was not surprising that this sort of thing happened, when our negotiators were dealing with thousands of items with dozens of countries. However, I had no sympathy for the Community when their representatives came close to accusing the original Canadian negotiators of dishonesty.

117

Ottawa confirmed to me that we were in the wrong and asked me to renegotiate a number of items. I enjoyed this very much, for I found that when you were negotiating with the Community, you had a tremendous advantage. You had to satisfy only one country, whereas the Community representatives had to satisfy many. With a little homework and help from my friend Joe Loomer, who headed the Tariff Division of our Department of Finance in Ottawa, I found it easy to conclude a deal favourable to Canada. The Community would tend to turn down a good offer simply because it would satisfy only a few member states; a less meaningful offer that gave a little to all members of the EEC would often be most acceptable.

Interlaced with the normal GATT work were a number of attempts to tackle major problems facing international trade. One area in which I was involved was an attempt by the major dairy-producing countries to overcome the depressed market prices for skimmed milk powder. While this was but a small part of the terrible problems facing trade in the dairy industry, I was pleased to see the beginnings of international consideration of dairy products. Most dairy-producing countries were subsidising their production and exports with the obvious result of depressed prices and drains on their treasuries.

Canada was requested to chair a committee of producers. I was titular head of the delegation but in reality, Cliff Barry from Canada's Department of Agriculture was the chairman, since he was the well-informed individual who sat with me and guided me in everything I did or said. He was a delight to work with, as were the other Canadian agricultural trade experts, Earl Stewart, Gordon Dobson, and Mike Gifford. We had some success in setting minimum prices and designating areas where each country might sell its product. I could never understand why there was no great outcry from the consuming countries, particularly in the developing world, for the deal struck was designed to stiffen their prices and, in a sense, manage the market. Perhaps the developing countries were busy trying to score political points in UNCTAD rather than following developments on the real trade stage. The agreement was short-lived, not because of the opposition of consuming countries, but because of a general upswing in prices of dairy products.

We were in Geneva for about a year when our ambassador had a serious illness. He returned to Ottawa, and I was named chargé d'affaires of the Permanent Mission. I was to serve as chargé until I returned to Ottawa some two years later. Now my responsibilities were broadened to cover all aspects

118

of our relationship with the United Nations and other international organisations in Geneva. On the evening the ambassador became ill, he and his wife were to host a reception at Montana-Crans in the Swiss Alps. There was a world hockey meeting and all the notables of world hockey were to be there. The meeting was to decide whether or not professional players should be permitted to play on national teams in world championships. Our position was that since the national teams of the Soviets, Czechoslovaks, and some of the Scandinavians already included professional players, for Canada to use National Hockey League players would simply put things on an even footing.

Peggy and I set off in the ambassador's car, which was already loaded with supplies for the reception. I don't recall many of the hockey personalities. The members of Hockey Canada were there with their opposites from the other countries. Many of the Canadians were jockeying for position in our Canadian receiving line. They were all intent on making an impression on the Soviets and others who would pronounce on the issue. This was fine, but I was determined that Peggy and I would not surrender our places as hosts. If the Canadian government was paying, then we would fulfil our duty as hosts. With a lot of undiplomatic pushing and shoving, we kept our positions at the head of the Canadian receiving line. The best that can be said for the evening was that it was a solid but bumpy start to a change of attitudes towards professionals in world hockey.

In the early hours of one morning when the Nigeria-Biafra war was at its height, I was summonsed to the office of the head of the Red Cross. He was most concerned about a threat from the Nigerian government to shoot down a relief plane that was on a mercy mission to Biafra. The reason for his call was that the plane was Canadian. I had Len Houzer from our mission with me, and although he knew as little as I did about the issue, we were at least two to lean on the Nigerian ambassador, who was most reluctant to intervene with his government. We pressed him throughout the remainder of the night, during which time we were in constant touch with Ottawa. We finally succeeded in having the ambassador contact Lagos. In the end, good sense prevailed, and the plane was given safe passage. I would be glad to get back to GATT work.

Two individuals from Ottawa whom I saw regularly and got to respect very much for their knowledge and work in the trade policy field were Maurice Schwarzmann and Rodney de C. Grey. Maurice was assistant deputy minister in the Trade Department, and Rodney held much the same position in the Department of Finance. I believe the reason I saw so much of them (generally together) was that while they certainly liked and respected one another, they didn't really fully trust each other professionally. (Trade and Finance often held opposing views on certain trade issues.) Maurice had a highly successful way of winning his way over friend and foe by heaping confusion on an issue. Rodney tried to accomplish the same through brilliance, logic, and what many people saw as unnecessary toughness. I was never the recipient of any unfair toughness from Rodney; I was, however, often battling Maurice's efforts to confuse, divide, and conquer. I liked working with both of them, but work with Maurice could be exasperating, particularly if you were required to work with him in the early morning, for Maurice was a "night" person.

On one occasion Maurice came to Geneva to act as the Canadian representative for a major meeting with Germany. Germany had long been free from balance of payments' difficulties, yet continued to retain measures against imports more akin to those imposed by developing countries rather than by a country on a swift climb to being one of the foremost economic powers. I picked up Maurice at his hotel and briefed him in the car on the way to the Palais des Nations on my discussions with delegates the evening before. He made notes on the back of a pack of cigarettes.

As we entered the conference room (a few minutes late) and walked to our seats, the chairman requested that the Canadian representative lead off, since Canada was one of the countries that had requested the session. As we were shuffling our papers, Maurice asked me to do the speaking. I quietly reminded him that it would look bad in Ottawa when it became known that he had flown all the way to Geneva to take on the Germans and then had passed the responsibility over to me. He quickly rallied and delivered a magnificent, strong, balanced attack on German trade policies. He ended with an appeal that the Germans take their rightful place in the international trading community and live up to the great expectations we all had for this growing economic power. Maurice emerged as the catalyst and leader of the committee members in their efforts to move Germany towards a more liberal trade policy. I was very proud of him and as usual any annoyances quickly evaporated.

Among the enjoyable holidays we had during our years in Switzerland were the exchange arrangements we had with the Latimer family. Bob had been my director in Ottawa and had been posted to London as minister-economic at the Canadian High Commission. We used to exchange homes. Living in London, Bob and Eleanor liked to get away to the more countrylike atmosphere of Geneva, and we looked forward to a few days in London.

In addition, for several Christmas holidays, the Petrie and Latimer families took accommodation together in the Alps. The six Petries and the four Latimers would fill the entire floor of a pension. In Lenk we certainly did. We had the top floor of a beautiful pension at the bottom of a chairlift. During the day the restaurant below was a beehive of activity, but as soon as the chairlift shut down for the day, you could hear a pin drop. We ate our evening meal together in the restaurant below, which was most memorable, not because of the food, but because there was a jukebox with only two records that the children played over and over. I shall never forget "Little Arrows" and "Those Were the Days My Friends." Bob, at the time, smoked a pipe and was subjected to much abuse from some of us, but Eleanor made the best of it, even claiming that it made him look distinguished. I heard Jennifer, who was about five, asking Shelly Latimer, who was about the same age, "What is 'distinguished'?" Shelly responded that she thought it meant, "old and smelly."

We prepared to leave Geneva in the summer of 1970. Our new ambassador was to be George Ignatieff, who had distinguished himself as our ambassador to the United Nations in New York and ambassador on disarmament. Now he would take on additional responsibilities for GATT and other international organisations. He would be ably assisted by my good friend and veteran of many GATT meetings, Percy Eastham, who was an officer with a thorough knowledge of GATT. I spent my last month in Geneva bringing George Ignatieff into the GATT picture, for he had worked little in the trade field and did not know the personalities in the GATT circle. He was a very quick learner.

After two postings and six years in Geneva, we regretted leaving. Maurice Schwarzmann, my senior in Ottawa, encouraged me to stay, indicating that if I did, he would pursue proposals that were being launched at senior levels in the GATT Secretariat, supported by the Americans and others, that I should take the chairmanship of the GATT council. I felt honoured, to be sure, but after serious family discussions, decided to return to Ottawa and move the children back into a national environment.

I left Geneva feeling that I had spent six good years working in an area that had been not only personally enjoyable, but was making a definite and positive contribution to the growth of world trade and consequently to increased global prosperity.

Chapter Eighteen
Into South Africa

In Ottawa I was assigned as director of the Pacific, Asia, and Africa Branch of the Trade Department. This gave me responsibility for our trade relations with much of the developing world other than Latin American and the Caribbean. I also was responsible for Australia, New Zealand, and South Africa. I felt that in this position I would have little to do with GATT. Yet, on my first few days in the office, I was told by my assistant deputy minister, Maurice Schwarzmann, that I was to head a team to renegotiate our trade agreement with South Africa.

Among the duties I had enjoyed most in Geneva were the renegotiations required when Canada or one of its trading partners introduced measures that changed or eliminated commitments to maintain tariffs at negotiated levels. These were known as Article XXVIII negotiations, and their aim was to restore the balance that had been violated by the newly introduced measures. Every few months in Geneva, I had been required to enter into such negotiations with numerous countries. Now I was faced with a similar but major renegotiation with South Africa.

The South Africans were in the process of abandoning their elaborate protective system of import controls that they had applied for balance of payments' reasons. They stated that it was their intention to rely solely on the tariff for the protection of their domestic industry. They believed it necessary to increase certain tariffs; in doing so, they violated agreements previously struck with a number of countries, including Canada. Canada's access to the South African market would be adversely affected for exports of lumber, newsprint, salmon, sulphur, and a range of manufactured goods. Our responsibility was to negotiate an acceptable rebalancing of trade concessions.

I was fortunate to have as my right-hand man on the South African negotiations, David Knowles, who had a great interest in, and a detailed knowledge of, Canada's industrial capabilities. What he didn't know, he knew where to go to source the information. When we left for Capetown in September 1970, we had briefing material sufficient to enable us to pronounce on the spot on South African offers.

South Africa at the time was being shunned by the international community because of its apartheid policies. Canada was in the forefront, since Prime Minister Diefenbaker had taken the lead in forcing South Africa from the Commonwealth. We pressed the politicians to separate trade from the political relationship with South Africa. As our minister of trade, Jean Luc Pepin, put it when he was asked why we continued to trade with South Africa, "If we only traded with those we loved, we wouldn't even trade interprovincially." We were continually under pressure from academic, church, and labour leaders to cut off trade with many countries. We argued that with one-third of Canada's income coming from exports, we couldn't afford to lose any customer.

We knew full well on our departure for South Africa that any agreement we negotiated would have to run the gauntlet of extreme opposition in Canada. This opposition across the country was much greater than that against any other country, whether Communist or right wing. The opposition in Ottawa came, not from ministers, but from Prime Minister Trudeau's advisors, who seemed to be less concerned about loss of exports and employment than were our elected representatives.

En route to South Africa, I dropped into Geneva, where my colleague, Percy Eastham, arranged meetings for me with the Americans, British, and others who were also negotiating with South Africa. I wanted to ensure that we were not alone in our planned tough demands. They were all under instructions to take a tough stand. I flew to Zurich for the flight to Capetown. Zurich airport was an armed camp. The Palestine Liberation Organisation had just blown up hijacked planes in the North African desert. The security checks were most thorough. Everybody had to identify their luggage personally on the runway and have it searched before it was loaded with them onto the aircraft.

A most beautiful sight was spread before us on both sides of the runway as we landed in Capetown. The ground was a carpet of colour with brilliant wild Livingstone daisies. It was springtime, and the flowers were at their best. I was met by the South African authorities and our embassy people and driven to the beautiful Mount Nelson Hotel. There, David Knowles, and Jean Marc Dery, the department of finance man on our delegation, awaited me. We closeted ourselves for several hours of final preparation before heading for the residence of our Ambassador Harry Carter for dinner and an embassy briefing.

The next day we opened our meetings with the South Africans. We found our hosts and opponents congenial but tough. Their leader, Mr. Stein, was an acquaintance from Geneva. He was a senior official at the deputy minister level, a man who was very highly respected in GATT circles. His wife was a Canadian, and while he was tough in his official dealings with us, he and his wife were most kind socially after-hours.

We spent a week or so in negotiations. Clearly the South Africans wanted a settlement. Our instructions were to "hang tough" in our demands, so we had many hours for sightseeing while the South African negotiators brought our demands to their ministers for consideration. On one of these occasions, they provided transportation to the Cape of Good Hope. It was always a dream of mine to visit this southernmost point of Africa. The moment that sticks in my memory was not when I saw the magnificent view from the cape, but when we had to barricade ourselves in our cars in fear of the apes that crawled all over the vehicles, trying to get at the snacks we had inside. Cape Province was very beautiful and reminded me of Australia with its lovely beaches, wonderful climate, and very different fauna and flora.

We recessed the negotiations to give both sides time to study proposals and to consider alternative offers. The South Africans were to meet us in Ottawa in a month in an attempt to finalise an agreement to be put to ministers.

Jean Marc and I flew home via Angola and Lisbon. We stopped in Lisbon overnight after a twelve-hour flight. Arriving in Lisbon in the early morning, we checked into a very reasonable hotel near the railway station. Although exhausted from the flight, we took a train to one of the beaches at Estorel. We stretched out fully clothed on the sand. We were very tired and fell into a deep sleep. We were awakened with a start when a huge wave crashed over us. We jumped up all too late to avoid a soaking, and much to our embarrassment, everybody on the beach was roaring with laughter. They had obviously been watching the incoming tide creeping in on us as we slept, in the certain knowledge that we would get a soaking.

I had many matters awaiting me in Ottawa. There was no question that when you were on a mission, you were excused from other duties. I had to start the preparation of a ministerial mission to China, for we were on the verge of diplomatic recognition of the People's Republic. I did, however, want to see a successful conclusion to the South African negotiations, for it seemed a deal was well within reach.

The South Africans joined us in Ottawa in the late fall, and we were able to achieve an agreement that we could put to ministers. We had an embarrassing moment during our last meeting when we were finalising the text. A temporary secretary rushed into our meeting room and told me in a very loud voice, "External Affairs wants to talk with you urgently about trade sanctions against South Africa." The South Africans looked nonchalantly out the window as if they had not heard. I excused myself for a few moments to take the call and get rid of the temporary secretary.

We took a half-day to show the South Africans around Ottawa. They were most impressed with Prime Minister King's estate in the nearby Gatineau Hills, where one of them pronounced, "Now, there was a good prime minister." He was implying that the recent lot of prime ministers, who were anything but friendly to South Africa, could never measure up to Prime Minister King.

Officials were convinced that the agreement with South Africa offered many benefits and opportunities for Canadian exporters. We had obtained duty-free entry into South Africa for our traditional ocean and forest products. We had won free entry or low duty rates for a number of our manufactured exports. South Africa, like Australia and New Zealand, was an important outlet for Canadian manufactured goods. The agreement was never to be ratified. It was shelved for political reasons, not by ministers, but by the prime minister's office. I had great respect for Ivan Head, Prime Minster Trudeau's special assistant, but obviously we were never to see eye-to-eye on the subject of trade with South Africa. I was then and remain strongly of the view that if there were United Nations or other multilaterally imposed sanctions against South Africa, we should support such measures. Unilaterally to deny our exporters the right to export under the best possible conditions such as we had negotiated, was merely to pass the business to the French or other nations that were not as intent on boycotting South Africa as were many Canadians.

The attitude of the export community and trade officials was probably best illustrated by Bob Latimer, our future assistant deputy minister, Trade Policy. Bob was invited by the World Council of Churches to attend one of their conferences. He was to explain why Canada traded with South Africa. Bob explained that Canada was like the general store in his hometown of Seeley's Bay, Ontario. In order to stay in business, the owner had to sell to everybody. He couldn't refuse to sell to customers because they beat their wives or otherwise behaved badly. Bob, aware that it was one of the first times a senior Roman Catholic observer was in attendance, said that the only reason the Seeley's Bay general store owner might refuse to sell to a customer was if the customer was a Catholic. The clergy and others attending broke into laughter, and the Catholic representative was said to have laughed the loudest. I doubt, however, whether he or any other of the church representatives was persuaded to agree with us, that there were no grounds to refuse to sell legal and peaceful goods without multilaterally imposed sanctions. This issue was to plague me all through my career in the field of international trade.

Trade with South Africa continued but on a greatly reduced basis. Numerous actions were taken by Canada to frustrate it and to win political kudos at home and internationally. Trade promotion activities in South Africa were no longer permitted. The Export Development Corporation was shackled in its attempts to assist Canadian exporters. On the Canadian import side, South African products, particularly wines, were shut out of the Canadian market. When a new Democratic Party government was elected in British Columbia, they ordered liquor stores to take South African wine off their shelves. Next morning, the South African ambassador called on me and advised that if the wine trade was shut down, they would have to retaliate against Canadian products. They picked lumber, newsprint, salmon, and other products of major interest to British Columbia. Nobody wins a trade war.

Chapter Nineteen
The Chinese Puzzle

Most children during my youth were informed at home, at school, and, certainly in my case, at Sunday school, about the misery of the teeming masses in China, where millions died each year of disease, civil war, flood, and famine. We were also made aware of the Sino-Japanese war, which seemed to be heaping additional misery on the already suffering Chinese people. My earliest recollections of things international (that is, outside the island of Newfoundland) were my grandfather Petrie's stories about that terrible war. I remember walking to the post office with my grandfather in the early 1930s when I was only four or five years old and asking him who were the "good" fellows and who were the "bads"? Without hesitation, he told me that the Chinese were the "goods" and the Japanese were, in every sense of the word, the "bads." These views or prejudices, strengthened by the shocking Japanese behaviour during the Second World War, have been with me ever since. However, my favourable view of the Chinese never did stir within me a wish to visit their country. Yet, visit it I would on many occasions.

In 1950, Canada decided to proceed with negotiations to recognise the People's Republic of China. The decision was shelved because of the Korean War. The mood in the aftermath of the war, particularly on the part of the Americans, was that China should be isolated and kept out of the United Nations. Future Prime Minister Pearson, then secretary of state for External Affairs, held that nonmembership of China in the United Nations was doing nothing to lessen world tension. Canada's inclination in 1956 was to recognise China, but the decision was again put off when United States President Eisenhower threatened to withdraw the United States from the world body if China entered. Prime Minister Diefenbaker was confronted with a similar American intransigence when he raised the issue with President Eisenhower. No further attempts were made by Canada until

1970, when Prime Minister Trudeau indicated his intention to establish diplomatic relations.

A number of Western countries in Europe already had diplomatic relations with China. Like the United States, most of our friends around the Pacific had not. We were to be the first of the second wave of countries to normalise relations.

Wheat had for years dominated the Canada-China relationship. China was a huge and valued market for Canadian grains. We had great hopes and rather unrealistic expectations that Canadian recognition would result not only in greater Canadian grain sales but also in large sales of Canadian manufactured goods. We felt that the Chinese were hungry for North American technology. Our thinking was that we would get established in the market before the United States got around to dismantling all of its restrictions against doing business with this giant of a country with one quarter of the world's population. (The United States was so restrictive on trade with the People's Republic that Canadian wig makers, who favoured Chinese hair, had to keep mainland hair in different warehouses and well away from the indistinguishable Taiwanese hair if they wanted to ship their wigs to the United States; they had to certify that there was no mainland hair in the wigs.)

Recognition of the People's Republic meant that we had to abandon our diplomatic relationship with Taiwan (the Republic of China). One of the very few things that the People's Republic and Taiwan agreed upon was that there was only "one" China. The problem was that both claimed to be the "one." The choice for us was whether to recognise that the one China was governed from Beijing or Taipei. We chose Beijing.

Our recognition came in October 1970. We immediately began to lay the groundwork for a major trade and economic mission. As director of the Pacific, Asia, and Africa Affairs Branch of the Trade and Industry Department, I was given responsibility for organising the mission. It was to be led by our minister, the Honourable Jean Luc Pepin. Our work was continuously hampered by sometimes overt, and often ingeniously obscure, actions by the Taiwan-Chinese and their Canadian supporters. Many of these Canadian supporters were not easy to deal with, in that they often included, or were supported by, provincial governments.

A number of the provinces were not very sympathetic to the federal government's decision to recognise Red China. They would sometimes act to cause us embarrassment. A provincial trade show or cultural event would feature the Taiwanese flag, or a provincial government would threaten to set up a trade office or send a ministerial mission to Taipei. Officials of the new embassy of the People's Republic would call on us almost daily to complain, always suggesting that the incident would not bode well for Canada–China friendly relations. I worked closely with Arthur Andrew in External Affairs, who had been involved in the negotiations for recognition and was now responsible for the political relationship. We talked every morning about Chinese or Taiwanese activities that were likely to give us cause for concern during the day.

In addition to the minister, our mission included representatives of the House of Commons (Ray Perrault); the Senate (Bill McNamara); the deputy ministers of Industry, Trade and Commerce (Jake Warren); Agriculture (Sid Williams); National Revenue (Ray Labarge); and Energy, Mines and Resources (Jack Austin); and business leaders of national trade and industry associations such as the Canadian Exporters, the manufacturers, and the chamber of commerce; and from the forestry, mining, chemical, engineering, and banking sectors. As secretary of the mission, I feared that I would be heading into an unfamiliar area with a lot of prima donnas. This certainly was not the case. I learned then what has been confirmed for me many times, that the more senior the people, the easier is the task for a junior officer.

I was ably assisted in organising and running the mission by Bob Burchill, the regional coordinator of the area for our Trade Commissioner Service, and Bob Kelly, the minister's executive assistant. We set out for Hong Kong in late June 1971. I made the mistake of seating myself immediately in front of Minister Pepin on the flight across the Pacific. I had given him briefing galore, prepared in Ottawa and by our embassy in Beijing. He devoured every word of it and continuously pressed me for more. He kept me awake during the entire flight, quizzing me on every conceivable subject that might be raised. I spent the night running about the plane, waking up the deputy ministers for answers or elaboration. I had the greatest admiration for Minister Pepin's appetite for facts and the ease with which he devoured them both night and day.

When we boarded the train in Hong Kong for Kuang-chou (Canton), our Hong Kong-based trade commissioner presented us with a huge metre-long box of sandwiches to take with us into China. It was explained that ours was the first major Western government mission to enter China since the Cultural Revolution had reached its extremes. Consequently nobody was sure where we might get our next "bite to eat." We were also given a large thirty-pound, scarlet, sealed, diplomatic bag containing secret and confidential material for our embassy in Beijing. All the way from Hong Kong to Kuang-chou, Bob Burchill and I clutched the bag, particularly when going through the formalities of the border crossing. The Chinese knew what we were carrying and made no attempt to inspect it, but we kept flashing our diplomatic passports at them just in case.

We certainly didn't need our sandwiches on the train, where there were trays of delicious fresh litchis; these were as different from the canned product as chalk was from cheese. At the border crossing, the Chinese had food for us, and at Kuang-chou, we were royally entertained at an official banquet. With full stomachs and with our diplomatic bag and the sandwiches, we boarded the Chinese flight to Beijing. We didn't make Beijing that day. We had an unscheduled stop and overnight stay near the birthplace of Chairman Mao Tse-tung in Hunan province. Mao was born in Shaoshan; we stayed in nearby Changsha.

While the stop was not on our program, as guests of the Chinese, we had no alternative but to relax and enjoy it. To my questions about why we had not flown directly to Beijing, the Chinese responded that we were prevented from doing so by the terrible weather in Beijing. (Our embassy people later told us that the weather in Beijing had been wonderful during the days before our arrival as it was when we arrived.)

By the time we reached Changsha, our sandwiches were getting a little "high." Bob had placed them in the overhead rack. On departing the plane, we decided to cover them with pillows and a blanket and make our escape without them. When we reached the hotel, we were of course "delighted" to see the sandwiches in my room. We agreed that we would leave them on the wastepaper basket when we left for Beijing in the morning.

That evening the entire mission of twenty-three gathered in my room. The Chinese had provided us with cold beer to help us cope with the hot weather and the lack of air-conditioning. When people started drifting back to their rooms, Deputy Minister Jake Warren asked how Bob and I were going to secure the diplomatic bag during the night. It was agreed that I would take responsibility for the bag, and my security would take the form of the bag being tied to my wrist and the empty beer bottles being piled against the locked door so that any would-be intruder was bound to awaken me if he entered the room. So I passed my first night in China in a fitful sleep but secure in the knowledge that my country's secrets were safe in my hands.

131

Next morning in Changsha, we were treated to a Western breakfast. I'm sure it was the first one they ever served. Among the best meals I have ever had were those served in China. This breakfast had to be the worst. Our "bacon and eggs" consisted of pigeon's eggs and strips of pork fat deep fried in more pork fat. The pièce de résistance was hot buffalo milk served as a substitute for hot coffee. Thereafter I always demanded Chinese breakfast.

My most vivid memories of that first breakfast in China were not of the food but of the staff who descended on those of us with "hairy" arms. They even came out of the kitchen to see the hair on the arms of these foreigners, undoubtedly confirming their belief that foreigners were indeed "barbarians." Some of the staff, like children, touched our arms. This, combined with their poor attempt at a Western breakfast, suggested that we were probably the first Western guests in Changsha.

Bob and I sat together with our diplomatic bag as the plane revved up for departure. They closed the door and we were congratulating ourselves on having gotten rid of the sandwiches, when the door reopened and a man from the hotel jumped in and handed the box (by now putrid and smelling rotten twenty feet away) to the flight attendant. The Chinese on board cheered at the great efficiency of the state hotel and state airline for ensuring that no foreign property was lost. Most of our delegation joined in the cheering. Bob and I almost wept. When we arrived in Beijing, we unloaded the smelly box onto the first junior embassy officer we saw. The story goes that the only way he could get rid of them was to put them through the shredder for classified material at the embassy.

We worked hard in Beijing (which we then called Peking). Our Ambassador Ralph Collins and our trade people in Beijing and Hong Kong had prepared a schedule that kept us going ten hours a day. This was always followed by official dinners. On arrival we were met by Chinese Trade Minister Pai Hsiang-kuo, who was a general in the Red Army and always wore the uniform. We got to know each other fairly well over the next few years; I was to accompany him on his official visit to Canada a year or so later, when he was to have the honour of being the first Communist Chinese minister to visit North America.

Beijing had been a town for some three thousand years and a capital for seven centuries. It was China's second largest city and was extraordinarily rich in legacies from its past. Beijing's Tiananmen Square was the largest plaza in the world, site of the Great Hall of the People, and the

Forbidden City that housed the opulent walled palaces of the emperors of China, with acres of massive halls and gaily painted pavilions.

We stayed at the old Peking Hotel just off the square. From there we were within short drives from most ministries and trading organisations that were the sites for most of our meetings. Our four days were filled with meetings, and only at one that I attended was there a negative aspect. The incident, which involved a reference to Taipei, was very minor and would not have been seen as an incident by most. However, I was very sensitive to the relationship between Beijing and Taipei, and became concerned when the word was mentioned by one of our businessmen. He happened to be an American citizen, resident in Canada. When going through our usual ritual about, "How nice it is to be here in Peking," he said "Taipei" instead of "Peking." The interpreter mentioned "Taipei" and went on to say something unintelligible to me, probably that the Canadian didn't know where he was. The Chinese seemed to pass it off as a slip of the tongue, which it was.

Of our numerous meetings, two will always stand out in my memory. One in particular, a three-hour meeting between Minster Pepin and Premier Chou En-lai, I will always remember because of the opportunity it gave us to meet and listen to one of the great leaders of the twentieth century. The other, that I shall refer to first, impressed me, not for its substance, but for the sheer horror of seeing the Red Guards in real life and witnessing the terror they spread throughout academic life. This was a meeting with Red Guards and university professors at the Peking University of Chiang Hua.

Minister Pepin, a former university professor and always the academic, requested a visit to Chiang Hua University, and the Chinese concurred. While, as usual, the Chinese tried to show everything in the best possible light, they couldn't hide the fact that the Chinese academics were petrified of the Red Guards, who were present at all times.

The ten years from the mid-1960s to the mid-1970s, during which time the Red Guards held sway in China, must be recorded as one of the worst regressive and destructive periods of recent Chinese history. As a result, Mao Tse-tung, who launched the Great Proletarian Cultural Revolution, lost the support and respect of virtually all of the intellectuals and old-time revolutionaries. He lost all those who wanted to build on what had been accomplished by the Communist revolution and at the same time wanted to move closer economically to the outside world.

Mao's purpose in unleashing the Cultural Revolution was to renew the spirit of the Communist revolution. He doubted the revolutionary commitment of his colleagues, who were bent on bringing China out of the economic depression caused by such destructive Maoist policies as the Great Leap Forward. He sought to replace the current leaders with leaders more faithful to his own thinking. He also wanted to provide China's youth with a revolutionary experience and wished to make education, health, and cultural systems less elitist. He pursued these goals through a massive mobilisation of China's urban youth. The result was the Red Guards.

At a rally in 1966 in Tiananmen Square, one-half million youths assembled, and Mao accepted from them a "red" band. He encouraged them to carry out the objectives of the Cultural Revolution. Mao ordered the party and army not to suppress the movement. The result was to throw China's cities into turmoil. His action shut down the schools and encouraged the Red Guards to attack traditional values. The Chinese refer to this as the attack on the four O's, old customs, old ideas, old culture, and old habits.

The Red Guards were also to test party officials by criticising them publicly. Deng Xiaoping, whom Chou was later to bring back for the leadership, had survived several attacks. At a Lushan meeting when the minister of defence and vice premier, General Peng Dehuai (former Chinese commander in Korea) was ousted, Deng was saved because he had been unable to attend because of a leg injury he received while playing Ping-Pong. Deng was, however, criticised by Mao for trying to keep him in the background on economic matters, and he was dismissed in March 1967.

The Red Guard movement quickly escalated, and many intellectuals and elderly people were not only verbally attacked but physically abused. Many died, and many more were banished to the countryside to do hard labour on the communes. In later years I was to talk personally with distinguished academics who had spent up to a decade doing the most menial work and forbidden to do anything of an intellectual nature. One told me of a friend, a teacher, who was instructed to deliver to the Red Guards the most reactionary person in the class. Unwilling to select any of his students, he named himself. He was tried and banished for twenty years. The waste of such life was incalculable.

The Red Guards eventually splintered into rival factions, each purporting to be the true representative of Maoist thought. Mao's own personality cult assumed religious proportions, and again it was explained to me in later years, by academics and intellectuals, the nonsensical actions they had to undertake and the meaningless words they had to utter to "prove" their unquestionable support for Mao. The resulting anarchy completely disrupted urban life with a shocking impact on the entire Chinese economy.

Deng Xiaoping and other leaders, old revolutionaries, and teachers were humbled, as planned by Mao, aided and abetted by his wife, Jiang Qing, and the defence minister, Lin Biao, and others who emerged later as leaders of the infamous Gang of Four. Chou En-lai survived, perhaps as much because of his essential role in keeping the country running as for his immense popularity with the masses. He ran the country as well as could be expected during years of extraordinary chaos. Our mission arrived in China just as Chou was nudging China back towards stability. He encouraged a revival of the educational system and an increase in trade and other links with the outside world. In a sense, Canada, being the first country in years to normalise relations, was among the first to be caught up in Chou En-lai's process.

Uppermost in our minds as we met at Peking University with the Red Guards and their cowed professors was, as Minister Pepin put it, "Why, given the desperate need for all types of education in China, should the existing teaching resource be wasted by relegating it to menial tasks in the countryside that could be better done by the farmers themselves?" The Chinese answer to our question was always the same, whether given by the Red Guards or the frightened professors. They simply mouthed Chairman Mao's thoughts on the matter, "It was time to rekindle the revolution, and to do so meant ridding the revolution of the elements that undermine it, namely, the old ways." They continuously stressed that all comrades without exception should spend time learning the ways of the common peasant.

We agreed that this in itself was not entirely a bad thing if it meant working alongside the man in the field for a few days or weeks, but to do so for years didn't make sense to us. They had no satisfactory answers to the waste of talents and skills, the disruption of personal, family, and public life, the loss of educational opportunities for countless students, and the chaos in factories and government offices. Our unspoken conclusion after talking to and observing the Red Guards was that the presence of the numerous, belligerent, bullying, interfering, unqualified state-backed youths in the few institutions that still remained open, was all that was needed to bring any positive activity to a halt.

Chapter Twenty
Premier Chou En-lai, the Great Administrator

By the time we met Premier Chou En-lai, we were all convinced that dealing with the Chinese was straightforward enough as long as you did not confuse the ritual with the real. With Chou En-lai there was no confusion; he was real. He was a giant of a man in every sense of the word. During my five or six visits to China, I had never heard a word of criticism of him, as one does of all other leaders past and present. His features, bushy eyebrows, and wavy hair were unusual for a Chinese. He was affable and had a great sense of humour (which I was particularly to witness during a later visit).

He was the great administrator, having been premier of that vast country since 1949 (retaining the position until he died in 1976). He was also foreign minister from 1949 to 1958 and has been generally acknowledged as one of the great negotiators of the twentieth century. He was a leader in the Long March that ended in 1935. In 1936, when Chiang Kai-shek was arrested in Shensha by his generals who wanted to stop the civil war, Chou flew to that city and persuaded the dissident generals to release Chiang on condition that he cease military attacks against the Communists and cooperate with them in a united front against the Japanese. Chou was the Communists' chief representative to the national government after Japan surrendered in 1945 and was a leading participant in the unsuccessful peace negotiations.

Our meeting with Chou En-lai was to last almost three hours, which proved to be a bit of a record. China watchers timed such meetings to get an indication of the seriousness with which the Chinese took their newly established relationships. Minister Pepin beat some of China's new European friends by an hour or so. Chou spoke only in Chinese through excellent interpreters, whom he kept correcting, thus revealing that he still maintained a good understanding of both English and French. He said that he now spoke only a few words of English that he learned first as a foreign language. He claimed he had forgotten the French he had learned while a student in France. (On one of my later visits to China, he did say a few words to me in English.)

Chou had a surprising knowledge of Canada. He was either well briefed or well informed; probably a bit of both. On several occasions, he mentioned that he had learned his facts on Canada from Chester Ronning, who was born in China, the son of Canadian missionaries and, prior to the revolution, head of the Canadian Diplomatic Mission. Chou was obviously very fond of Ronning and spoke very warmly of him and his family.

He went through the list of persons in the Canadian delegation and said, "I see from your names that some of you are of French origin, British origin, and maybe some of German or Dutch origin." He showed a detailed knowledge of the Canadian political scene when he was introduced to Senator McNamara, who had been chief commissioner of the Canadian Wheat Board. Chou said he understood that "McNamara was a senator for life," which was a fact about which few foreigners were aware. The senator told him of the recently introduced requirement that he had to retire at the age of seventy-five. Chou mentioned that he knew of another McNamara, the American defence secretary, but he "preferred the Canadian one."

Premier Chou spoke about what he felt must be a difficult matter for Canada, a country of twenty million, maintaining sovereignty when living alongside a giant of two hundred million. It was natural for such a vast underpopulated country, with a big powerful neighbour, to want to develop closer relations with other countries. He referred to a speech that Prime Minister Trudeau made in Moscow about the need for Canada to diversify its interests.

Chou En-lai interrupted his conversation with Minister Pepin to request permission to smoke. He ignored the fact that most of his colleagues and some of the Canadians were already filling the room with clouds of smoke. He said the ladies present should feel free to smoke if they wished, recalling that "Chester Ronning allowed his daughters to smoke in public." Few of us in those days objected to people smoking at meetings, but a practice that all the Canadians found disgusting was the continuous hacking, very loud throat-clearing and spitting, particularly by the older Chinese. About the only exception was the premier, who seemed to be oblivious to the terrible noises and spittle coming from many of his compatriots. The numerous spittoons were objects of great focus and constant use.

Chou recalled that one of the Ronning daughters had married a

137

foreigner, and understood that Canadians had fewer inhibitions in this regard than Chinese. He apologised for the fact that "Chinese were rather conservative on this point; Chinese who lived abroad not only rarely intermarried or learnt the local language, but they had their bodies sent back to China when they died; hopefully this thinking was changing."

Minister Pepin made several valiant attempts to nudge the premier away from discussions on Canada and things Canadian. He succeeded when he jumped in, stating, "When I have the pleasure of meeting a prime minister, I like to ask him, what are his dreams for his country?" Chou reminded the minister that China was a Socialist state. He said, "The economy is rather weak, and our important agriculture is backward, depending almost entirely on man and animal power." He warned us that the model communes we would be shown in the coming days were not representative of the state of agriculture. While China's output of food grains was the highest in the world, it was low, given China's huge population. China had serious storage problems; grain in storage at the moment seemed adequate, "but the composition of China's food grains was inferior to Canada's." Sweet potatoes were regarded in China as food grain, being a staple in some areas. "China must advance towards mechanisation but not too quickly; every year more and more peasants were leaving the land for industry, but it can't be too fast."

Minister Pepin raised the possibility of using the service sector to increase employment for country people. Chou explained that the service sector in China was very small. He said, "In estimating the gross national product, we don't even include services; I mentioned this to Edgar Snow" (author of the controversial book, *Red Star over China*). Chou explained that China's Gross National Product was "just a little bit more than Canada's, which includes services; the GNP to population was very high in Canada but extremely low in China." Chou stressed, "Our development must be based first on our natural resources and national market; we may in this way bring about rapid development and perhaps achieve something in twenty years." He jokingly said he wouldn't be around at that time. A year later he learned that he had a fatal malignancy.

Chou went to great pains to convince the Canadians that the philosophy of "relying on your own resources," didn't mean that China would close its doors to the world. This seemed to us to be a bit of a contradiction; if they relied solely on their own resources, they wouldn't need a trade relationship with Canada or any other country! Chou argued that his Canadian guests had to realise that there still remained an international embargo and block-ade against China, "But I don't want to go into that!" He went on to say, "The Soviets tore up all agreements with us in 1959, but we don't complain." He added, "We thank Khrushchev for compelling us to rely on our own efforts."

Chou turned to the subject of trade. He looked towards his officials and half-jokingly criticised his minister and Ministry of Foreign Trade. He said, "My trade people don't do their job well." He expressed interest in seeing "a Chinese trade delegation go to Canada to see what your country needs; we can't depend only on the contacts made at the (annual) Canton Trade Fair; we need to improve packaging, quality, et cetera." It was interesting that Chou thought of foreign trade only as exports from China and not imports. As if anticipating this thought of ours, he went on to explain that foreign goods accounted for only five percent of China's total consumption, whereas in Canada, "the proportion was much higher; Canada was the fifth largest world trader." Chou was to turn to the inadequacies of his trade department when we again met with him during Prime Minister Trudeau's visit in 1973.

The premier got sidetracked into a discussion of the comparative sizes of countries. He mentioned that only Canada and the Soviet Union were bigger than China, but China was first in population. He then categorically stated that China, despite her size and population, "will absolutely never be a superpower; if coming Chinese generations want China to become a superpower, the Canadian press can say they (the Chinese) are violating Mao's undertaking that China will not become a superpower!"

Minister Pepin turned the discussion to Chinese domestic politics and focused on the current chaotic situation for education in China. He recalled his meeting the previous day at Peking University, where "young people who are involved in the Cultural Revolution were expressing how they felt about education." As a former university professor he said he had tried to balance in his mind the benefits and drawbacks of the actions of these students. They had said that professors must show great humility and join the students in being close to the masses. He said, "I am not totally at ease about this position," and he wondered how a great specialist, a scientist, could keep up in his speciality and, at the same time, do all demanded of him by the Cultural Revolution.

For the first time I really wondered whether Chou was convinced about the arguments he was putting forward. They certainly paralleled the "Party line." Chou said, "The Cultural Revolution does not completely negate the achievements of the last twenty years." (I wondered whether the word "completely" was the premier's or the interpreter's.) He said, "Because the educational system is an old system and the methods old methods, education was divorced from socialism and was not serving the proletariat." He added, "The professors, by going to the factories and the farms, learn anew their speciality, because until now their knowledge has been confined to (what is available in) books." He said, "There is a great gap in their outlook and the demands of the people." In the past, "the great inventors and scholars did not gain their knowledge in university, but through their own hard toil."

Minister Pepin, like all of us, questioned how a highly skilled surgeon, scientist, or artist could improve his ability to serve the people by doing hard manual labour in the countryside, not for weeks but often for years. The premier never did answer the question but said, "Through the new methods of education, they will be able to gain new knowledge and experience and thereby be able to make new contributions." He said he realised what Minister Pepin was asking. "How is it possible for teachers, professors, or students to engage in so much physical labour, to engage in so many prescribed activities while engaging in study; and how is it possible at the same time to have so much energy to do that?" He continued, "It's a question of allocating time; for me, and this is very subjective, I've had a tight schedule for fifty years; work is tempering."

The minister asked, "To what extent was the Cultural Revolution planned?" Premier Chou replied. "Chairman Mao made the decision, and 'we' made a lot of preparatory work for it." He went on to say, "It was after we had carried out transformations in the three main fields, of the collectivisation of agriculture, cooperatives for handicraft industries, and the joint ownership of private enterprise, that we saw that the general orientation, trend, and desire of the masses was for socialism." He added, "We also noted that quite a few persons wanted to take the capitalist road; at that time the Soviets withdrew all their experts and relations deteriorated in 1961–1963." He explained, "This brought on difficulties in industry and agriculture. At that time we needed imports of food grains." At this point Premier Chou thanked Canada, not only for the delivery of grain, but for the credit terms that Canada had provided. He said, "We have repaid all our debts to Canada and to the Soviet Union: China now has no debts, internal or external."

Chou was so caught up in the dialogue that he waved aside translation from English to Chinese. Whenever Minister Pepin spoke in English, Chou answered in Chinese. When the premier did speak, there was always much noisy throat-clearing and use of spittoons that might have led one to speculate that the premier's officials disagreed with his comments or his support for Chairman Mao's policies. There was no doubt that the need to expectorate superseded respect for Western manners or respect for the premier, his foreign guests, or Chairman Mao's policies.

Minister Pepin observed that everything the premier said would indicate that he was continuously exploring how to do his job better. Chou said he was simply following the leadership of Chairman Mao. "Such a leader did not fall from the sky!" He explained that as prime minister he used to have ninety separate central agencies reporting to him. To assist, he had ten vice premiers. With such a bureaucracy, "the party's policies cannot truly be carried out." The central agencies had 100,000 personnel and "we were too busy looking after these people and not serving the people of the country; so there (had to) be a 'revolution.' " He explained that he had "a small office of twenty," and Mao advised him not to have so many or he would be "busy serving them and not the Chinese people." Now he had only two. He turned around and said, "One of my secretaries is sitting behind me; he knows English, so he asked to come and listen." He said that with such little staff, "I can have more direct contact with ministers." He explained that the ninety central agencies had now been reduced to twenty-six, and the number of vice premiers had been reduced significantly.

The discussion between Minister Pepin and Chou En-lai drifted into ancient history. The minister had made a reference to the Chinese possibly first populating the Americas by crossing the Bering Straits. Chou jumped in with the slightly annoyed comment, "For the Chinese to claim that they first settled the Americas would be as arrogant as saying that Columbus 'discovered' the new world." He said that while "China had a long history, if we look at it from the point of view of what has been unearthed, Mexico has five-thousand-year-old relics and the Incas go back seven thousand years; no nationality should have the arrogance of thinking they were first." He went on, "It would be easy for us to commit the mistake of 'big nation' chauvinism."

Chou was obviously launched on a subject he enjoyed. He said, "Although China's written history cannot be compared to Egypt, Babylon, the Greeks, Aztecs, or Incas, China's written language has remained for over four thousand years; and because it is a symbol language, China's

141

recorded history has been continuous." While China "had been ruled by nationalities other than the Han, they were all assimilated." He said that having a common and continuous written language for so long throughout the country has "made us conservative." The result was that "the bureaucracy has become a serious problem; it is highly stratified from the central government down, making it a difficult country to govern." As a consequence he championed the division of authority.

Minister Pepin asked Chou how he would describe a Maoist. Chou rambled a little, replying, "Sometimes when I carry out Chairman Mao's policies, I make mistakes. When I come to realise these mistakes, I correct them, because Chairman Mao has repeatedly said a person must be able to criticise himself before criticising others." I'm not sure whether Chou was addressing Minister Pepin's question on Maoists, but he went on to say, "If in our country an elderly person was to retire, that is not strange; if in China an elderly person disappeared, there could be a lot of gossip at home as well as abroad!" He went on, "Our foreign minister (who had retired) reappeared on May Day" after many rumours about his "disappearance," and now that he is again off the scene, they say that he is ill. Because of such difficulties in retiring, "in China the old generation of revolutionaries remain at top levels." The premier ended the meeting, suggesting that our journalists check any of his comments with the interpreters. He invited all present to a Peking duck dinner.

During our remaining days in Beijing, we were able to see most of the sights around that historic city. Probably best known throughout the world is the Great Wall, which snakes for several thousand miles in various states of disrepair across the mountains of northern China. A repaired and most impressive portion can be reached by a short drive from the city. I've visited this imposing structure on at least four occasions, but this first visit was the most impressive, in that we were virtually the only foreigners there. One could visualise the wall as it was when the Chinese relied on it as their line of defence against the foreign hordes from the north. On my most recent visit, while the wall remained as ever, it was swarming with tourists, and there was very much the appearance of Disney World, with colourful banners, soldiers dressed in period costume, dancers, and jugglers.

The roads to the wall from Beijing have been improved, but on this first visit, one side of the simple provincial highway was covered with drying grain for much of the way; agriculture obviously took precedence over transportation or tourism. For some considerable distance before you reached the wall on the old road, you could see it meandering across the mountaintops from east to west. With all its branches it runs for about 6,400 kilometres or 4,000 miles from the northwestern arm of the Yellow Sea to a point deep in central Asia. It is one of the largest construction projects ever carried out. Parts of it date from the fourth century B.C. In 214 B.C., the first emperor, Shih Huang-ti, connected a number of existing defensive walls into a single system fortified by watchtowers, which served both to guard the rampart and to communicate with the capital, then near Sian, by smoke signal by day and fire by night. It was originally built of masonry and earth and was faced with brick in its eastern portion. It was substantially rebuilt in later times, especially in the fifteenth and sixteenth centuries. The basic wall is about nine metres high and five to twelve metres wide.

On the outskirts of Beijing is the Summer Palace in an eight-hundred-acre park popular with the people of Beijing. Its artificial landscaping provides an inimitable blend of woods, water, hills, and architecture. Most impressive are the richly painted promenades that parallel a picturesque lake generally covered with rented boats.

Beijing consists of two old walled cities, the inner Tatar city and the outer Chinese city. Within the inner city is the "Forbidden City," surrounded by a wall four kilometres or two and one-half miles on each side. The Forbidden City was so called because no commoner was permitted to enter without special permission. It contains hundreds of buildings, the main ones of which served as the imperial palaces of China from 1421 to 1911. The nine thousand rooms in the Forbidden City housed the entire imperial court. When we made our visit, we were the only group present. Our embassy staff told us we were the first foreigners to tour the City since the start of the Cultural Revolution.

I found the Temple of Heaven impressive. This structure is unique, both for its unusual geometric layout, which embodies the age-old belief that heaven is round and the earth square, and because it represents the supreme level of Chinese architectural enterprise. This was another one of the sites that was better on my first visit than in more recent years, for without the crowds of tourists, it was then possible to experience the genius behind the construction. This lovely temple is surrounded by a courtyard and circular wall. Both of these were constructed with such mathematical precision that it is possible to stand on a stone in the courtyard in front of the temple and clap your hands once and get one echo; on the next stone one clap returns two echoes; and on the next three. One can whisper against the wall and someone standing several hundred feet away opposite you near the circular wall can hear you distinctly. I tried this again during a visit with Peggy in 1992, but the noise of the tourist crowd was such that we could hear little.

Premier Chou En-lai hosted us for an official dinner in the Great Hall of the People, a two-block-long building whose grand auditorium seats the National People's Congress (the supreme organ of state power). Its banquet hall, where we dined, seats five thousand people. We had the traditional Peking duck dinner, one of the most celebrated dishes of Pekinese cuisine. In its classic form, the dish calls for a special breed of duck, the Imperial Peking, that is force-fed and confined to a small cage so that inactivity will ensure tender meat. Chou En-lai was in great form and moved from table to table, touching glasses with every Canadian and wishing each good health.

Minister Pepin hosted the Chinese officials at the Summer Palace. It took place on Canada Day in most beautiful surroundings, marred only by the ever-present gaudy Communist propaganda banners and posters which adorned the walls.

On our final evening in Beijing, when we were all in our rooms at the Peking Hotel writing our reports, our deputy minister, Jake Warren, invited us all to his room for a "presentation." I was very surprised, and my colleagues amused, when he presented me with a beautifully wrapped gift in appreciation of the work I had done in organising the mission. Jake, however, was a man who never allowed anyone to have more than a few moments of glory; when I opened the gift before my smiling colleagues, I couldn't believe my eyes when I saw a Newfoundland-packed can of seal flippers. Where Jake got this great Newfoundland delicacy I never learned.

We were all impressed with the feeling of personal safety and security for our possessions during these early days in the new China. Unfortunately the same cannot be said for the situation now. Our rooms were left open when we were out and we had many stories of mission members throwing away old holed socks or underwear only to find them retrieved, washed, darned or mended, ironed, and placed neatly in their dresser drawers. One of our members was actually presented with discarded personal belongings as we crossed the border going back to Hong Kong.

When our four busy but interesting days in Beijing ended, we flew to Canton. There we toured a commune devoted mainly to the growing of rice and other grains. It had a population of over sixty thousand. The commune was virtually self-sufficient, having its own small hydroelectric plant with small lakes and a stream supplying the water. The waters were thick with grain-fed carp and covered with ducks. That evening the Revolutionary Committee of Canton entertained us at another of those magnificent Chinese banquets, in what was said to be one of the largest open-air restaurants in the world!

The next day we left by train for the border with Hong Kong. When we walked across and boarded the Hong Kong train, the train staff circulated amongst us with appetising ice-laden British gin and tonic. In spite of having had the best of hospitality the Chinese could bestow upon us, as we settled down with our gin and tonic, we were all pretty pleased to be again in the "free world."

Chapter Twenty-one
Commuting to China

Carl Ruffelds was a big man, in terms of both his capabilities and his sheer size. It is the latter I think about when I recall the challenge that faced the Chinese when they promised to outfit him in winter garb for a cold, windy December day visit to the Great Wall. Carl was a former football player and would have been difficult to outfit in a few hours even in North America, the land of football players. We chuckled when we thought about the trouble Chinese officialdom would have in dressing Carl for the Wall. Yet, dress him they did, and the big fur coat and hat they delivered to Carl fitted him as if made just for him. Maybe it was.

I was back in China, following up on the beginnings of the trade relationship launched by the Pepin mission. There were two agreements we had reached with the Chinese that we were eager to pursue. One was that we should have periodic (annual) trade and economic consultations, and the second was that Canada should hold a "solo" trade fair in Beijing as soon as possible.

We saw the annual consultations as a way of familiarising the Chinese with Canada's industrial and export capabilities. I led a small group into Beijing in December 1971, just a few months after the Pepin mission, to lay the groundwork for what we hoped would be regular meaningful meetings. With me were Lindsay MacNeil, a colleague in the Trade department who had worked with me for years and was a close personal friend; Carl Ruffelds, one of our outstanding Trade commissioners; and David Lee, a very competent officer from our External Affairs department. We attempted to establish a mechanism with the Chinese, whereby they would inform us of the potential trade areas in their overall economic development plan where they could look to Canada for product. It was a most frustrating exercise. The Chinese always reverted to the position that China purchased huge quantities of Canadian grain and the bilateral trade between the two countries was consequently heavily in Canada's favour. It would simply worsen the situation if they were to buy locomotives, road graders, or other major items from Canada instead of from their friends in Western Europe.

The other major task was to make arrangements for a Beijing Solo Canadian Fair. The Chinese had agreed during the Pepin mission that Canada could mount a fair, showing Canadian machinery and equipment, and well over one hundred Canadian companies were anxious to participate. The major problem was that the Chinese had said that there were to be no American or American related companies participating.

We went to great lengths to explain to the Chinese, who were very anti-American, that only Canadian "corporate" citizens would be involved. We tried to get them to appreciate that Canada not only had a free flow of goods across its borders but also a free flow of investment. We explained that it was not unusual for Canadian industry to be foreign owned or to have some degree of foreign ownership. Indeed, the daily changes in the stock market caused changes in company ownership, since shares were generally traded internationally. Despite all of our explanations, the Chinese held to their very rigid position that there must be no American companies participating.

We were getting nowhere with the Chinese until a reception at our Ambassador Ralph Collins' residence. There, I was called aside for an informal discussion with the Chinese delegation. I told the leader in front of the others that if they were to insist that certain Canadian "corporate" citizens could not participate in the Canada–China relationship because of ownership, then much of the Canadian labour force was going to be excluded from any relationship with China. They had to accept that under our different economic system we couldn't discriminate on grounds of ownership. If they didn't, we would have to abandon any plans for a fair in Beijing.

Before the reception was over, members of the Chinese delegation came to me, saying that Mr. MacNeil, Mr. Ruffelds, and Mr. Lee would be going to the Great Wall next morning and I was to remain in Beijing for further negotiations. I agreed and half-jokingly noted that it was very cold, and I wasn't sure that my friends had warm enough clothes to venture around the Great Wall. My concerns were for naught because not only did they find clothing for Lindsay and David, but as I mentioned before, they had no problem dressing Carl. Next day, in an environment where the leader of the Chinese delegation was not overshadowed by his colleagues, he soon agreed to our demands regarding "corporate" citizens and gave us the exclusive right to select or reject companies that might participate in the Solo Fair.

When the Solo Fair took place a year or so later, we had over two hundred firms exhibit. While I would like to say that it was a great success, it was not. Some companies certainly laid the groundwork for future sales, but the Chinese purchased very little. It was almost impossible to get to the end-users, since all dealings had to be with the state trading corporations that had monopolies over imports. It was a sad epilogue that during the fair, the two hundred Canadian firms did more business with each other than with the Chinese.

There was one incident during this visit to Beijing that might shed some light on Chinese thinking during the early 1970s. It was the practice for delegations to host dinners in each other's honour. It was suggested by our colleagues in the embassy that the famous Peking Duck Restaurant would be a most acceptable site for our entertainment. On the appointed evening, we were joined by the Chinese delegation at our hotel and driven to the restaurant. I would not be exaggerating if I said there were ten thousand people assembled outside the restaurants, cheering us as we made our way towards the entrance.

When we waded through the crowd and got inside, I said to the Chinese leader, "Please explain why such a huge crowd was there to greet such a relatively unimportant group from Canada." I added, "Surely you must have encouraged them to assemble, because otherwise how would they have ever known of our presence in China?"

He made the ridiculous response, "If these people came on their own, it's because the Chinese people think highly of you; if we encouraged them, it's because the Chinese government thinks highly of you."

After much prodding, he admitted that all the authorities had to do to bring out the crowd was to inform the local communist network that Chinese officials were being entertained that evening by friends "from the land of Norman Bethune." He explained that the Canadian doctor's status was such that people would come from all over the neighbourhood to see someone from his country of origin. Bethune was idolised by the Chinese for his great work with the revolutionary forces during the war against Japan.

The following year, we held a full-blown Economic and Trade consultation in Beijing. Claude Charland, our assistant deputy minister, Trade Development, headed our delegation. I was with him. This also was a rather frustrating exercise and led to no great breakthrough in expanded trade.

Thereafter, although we continued to attend annual consultations with the Chinese in Ottawa and Beijing, we became rather cynical regarding the possibility of meaningful results.

Minister Pepin followed through with his invitation to the Chinese trade minister, Pai Hsiang-kuo, to visit Canada. Minister Pepin really had absolutely nothing in common with the Chinese minister, an army general, who had little knowledge of trade and absolutely no interest in political or economic relationships. He was the first Chinese Communist minister to visit North America, so we had to ensure that all went well.

Minister Pepin spent a good deal of time shepherding his Chinese guest around the factories and farms of central Canada; I took Minister Pai to similar establishments in western Canada. Minster Pai's visit ran like clockwork, but I always wondered whether Pai was sufficiently influential in Beijing to make all of our efforts worthwhile.

On top of our uncertainties about Minister Pai were our very real concerns about security for the Chinese minister; there were a number of serious threats against him. Our Royal Canadian Mounted Police Security Service had already suffered the embarrassment of seeing Soviet President Kosygin grabbed from behind on Parliament Hill in Ottawa by a deranged man, and despite fast action by the Mounties that prevented any serious harm, the president, the government, and the Mounties were shaken. The incident, which was recorded on film, provided the security force with material to feed recruits about the seriousness of personal security for years.

One of the threatening groups was an extreme right paramilitary one that, thankfully, the Mounties had infiltrated. This gang was determined to do harm to our guest when, like all official Chinese visitors, he would be visiting Gravenhurst, Ontario, the birthplace of Dr. Norman Bethune. My confidence in the Royal Canadian Mounted Police security people skyrocketed when I learned how they peacefully diverted the troublemakers away from Gravenhurst and the visiting Chinese minister. As the senior official responsible for the visit, I was briefed daily by security. Inspector Barry Moss was detailed as the senior Mountie for our group, and I got to know him well and grew to respect him and his colleagues more and more every time we met.

Few people appreciate the work and responsibility these officers had in ensuring the personal security of visiting dignitaries and our own leaders. Years have now passed, so I might mention that the Mounties, while concerned first and foremost with the well-being of the visitors, were also eager to learn who amongst the Chinese embassy staff were security officers themselves. I remember an incident at the Chinese pavilion at the Canadian National Exhibition in Toronto that was being officially opened by Minister Pai. Some of the Canadian security got close enough to "bump" the Chinese surrounding Minister Pai and were able to determine that some of them were armed. For a foreign security man to be armed was contrary to law and international practice. There was an understanding that the security people in the host country did the protecting. There was no incident, but the Mounties took careful note of the embassy individuals involved.

Another occurrence that demonstrated the thoroughness of the security screen took place at a reception at one of the main hotels in Ottawa. My wife Peggy, while talking to Ministers Pepin and Pai, glanced towards the ceiling only to see a face peering down at her and the ministers. She quickly reported this to me, and I in turn went to Inspector Moss. It was one of our security officers.

Our next major move towards China was to be a visit by Prime Minister Pierre Trudeau in 1973. As a forerunner to this visit, it was agreed that since China was not a member of GATT and could not legally claim Most Favoured Nation (MFN) tariff treatment for its exports to Canada, we would negotiate an MFN trade agreement with China. Bob Joyce, assistant deputy minister of Finance, Roger Bull, head of the Economic Division in External Affairs, and I were to negotiate the agreement in Beijing just before our prime minister arrived. We were to have it ready for signing by the prime minister and Premier Chou En-lai. We would then join the prime minister's group.

Bob, Roger, and I had what must have been one of the most frustrating commercial flights ever taken in an effort to reach Beijing. In order to avoid the well-known slower route by train from Hong Kong to Canton and then by air to Beijing, we were routed from Montreal to Paris and then by Pakistan Airlines through Karachi to Beijing. It certainly didn't work out to be as straightforward as the schedule suggested. A fog patch settled on the runway in Ottawa for just long enough for us to miss the last flights out of Montreal overseas. We took the first available plane to New York in the morning to pick up a day flight to Paris. All went well until over Saint Anthony, Newfoundland, we lost an engine and had to return to New York. By the time we finally approached Paris's Orly Airport, it was closed for the night, so we were diverted to Charles de Gaulle. After a bus ride to Orly, having missed our plane to Pakistan, we booked ourselves on an early morning flight.

To go from bad to worse, the boarding cards we were provided for our Pakistan International Airlines flight proved to be for a flight that had ceased to exist several weeks previously. We kicked up such a fuss that the airline personnel scrambled to get us on another flight to Islamabad, Pakistan, via Istanbul, Turkey. They hoped in this way we might, just might, pick up the Beijing plane that they would try to persuade to touch down in Islamabad. We carried all of our bags aboard, and when we landed at Islamabad, we were very pleased to see the Beijing-bound plane sitting far out on the runway. Against all regulations in the Western world, we descended from our plane with our bags and climbed aboard the plane for Beijing.

From there on, all went well. Indeed it was a most spectacular flight over the Himalayas, up the far western borders of China, and over the Gobi Desert to Beijing. The only negative thing about the flight was that the washrooms were full of cockroaches! I marvelled that these creatures could live, even in a pressurized cabin, at such altitudes.

On arrival in Beijing, we were taken to our hotel to freshen up and then whisked off to dinner by our Chinese hosts. I'm sure that our hosts had no idea of the time-changes between Canada and China for they entertained us as if we were residents of Beijing. Next day we were deep in negotiations on the text of the agreement. Things were complicated by the fact that while the Chinese gave some indications that they had an import tariff and promised to get us a copy, they never did table it, if indeed it existed. I believe they were talking of a tariff that existed in pre-Revolutionary days that had absolutely no meaning at present. It would have, in any case, been meaningless, since all imports were decided upon and made by state trading companies under the overall "plan," so a tariff could not play the role it played in a Western country.

We sat in a smoke-filled conference room for much of a week, drinking endless cups of Chinese tea. Hour after hour, attentive staff poured boiling water over a pinch of tea leaves at the bottom of our covered cups until all taste of the tea was steeped from them. Only then would the staff set before us new cups with new leaves.

The Chinese were as keen as we were to have an agreed text, since our leaders intended to sign a trade treaty within days. Our Canadian objective was to get agreement on a text that reflected GATT in substance and deviated as little as possible from GATT in text. This was difficult, since

China was still in the throes of the Cultural Revolution and fond of revolutionary language that was, of course, completely unacceptable to us. Also they did not see eye-to-eye with the Western world on international institutions. GATT, if nothing else, was a Western institution, drawn up to deal with trade relationships between market-oriented countries. Despite many attempts, it has always proved difficult to accommodate state trading countries, like China, in GATT in a meaningful way. In the end, after the proposal and rejection of numerous "final" texts, we were able to reach agreement. This agreed text, we felt, provided China with MFN treatment in the Canadian market; gave Canada similar (if less meaningful) rights in the Chinese market; and (important to us) could be accepted by our Western trading partners and GATT as conforming with our international obligations. We put it to Ottawa for approval.

Agreement came through in a day, and we were able to initial an agreed text with the Chinese on the very afternoon that the prime minster and his entourage arrived. Indeed, as we completed our final meeting, we could hear the sound of the prime minister's procession approaching Tiananmen Square. After initialing each and every page of the agreed text, we raced to our cars (provided with chauffeurs by the Chinese) and slid into the traffic-free stream behind Prime Minister Trudeau's official fleet of vehicles and waved, as he did, to the cheering crowds.

We were housed with the others of the delegation in individual suites in the several buildings that made up the government guest complex. We didn't see our newly arrived colleagues for several hours, for they were all exhausted after the long flight from Vancouver. Next day when we fully integrated ourselves into the delegation, I was pleased to see my good friend Tom Burns, the associate deputy minister of Industry, Trade and Commerce; Ivan Head, the prime minister's special assistant; Michel Dupuy; and a number of other colleagues from Ottawa. The prime minister was accompanied by his wife, Margaret, and a Royal Canadian Mounted Police security detachment headed by my acquaintance from other Chinese missions, Inspector Barry Moss.

Our first major order of business was a meeting between Prime Minister Trudeau and Premier Chou En-lai. Deng Xiaoping, China's future leader, was also present. Bob Joyce, Roger Bull, and I were included. The discussion was wide-ranging, covering all aspects of international affairs. My interest was particularly aroused when Premier Chou started to chaff his trade minister and trade officials for not doing a good job in exporting

Chinese goods. The premier drove home the point by contrasting their efforts with the great job that "our cousins in Taiwan were doing in producing and promoting products that met the needs of overseas customers, such as the Canadians."

To demonstrate his point, he reached up the arm of his Mao jacket and pulled down the sleeve of his long underwear; at the same time, he reached down and produced from the bottom of the leg of his trousers, the leg of his long underwear bottoms. Amidst the roaring laughter of all the Canadians (but not the Chinese), he said that while their Taiwanese cousins seemed to be able to produce such items as underwear to meet Canadian standards, Chinese producers had difficulty producing them to the satisfaction of less-demanding Chinese customers like himself. He said that insofar as his underwear was concerned, it should have been sold with a pair of scissors, for rather than shrinking when he washed it, it stretched with each wash. He had continually to keep cutting off the cuffs and the bottom of the legs to avoid embarrassment when he met with foreign guests.

Premier Chou presided over a dinner for Prime Minister Trudeau and the delegation in the Great Hall of the People. As he did during the dinner for Minister Pepin, he circulated and toasted each Canadian. Later after he and the prime minister signed the new trade treaty, he broke ranks and came to Bob, Roger, and me and thanked us individually for the work we had done in so short a time to make the agreement possible.

The best way to travel anywhere is with your prime minister. The Chinese at the direction of Premier Chou En-lai had "laid it on," as the Chinese certainly can do. After the meetings in Beijing, the Chinese were eager to show the prime minister a little of their country. We had the usual tours of the Great Wall, the Ming tombs, and the Forbidden City, but in addition, the Chinese had asked the prime minister what he particularly wished to see. He wisely chose the Luoyang Caves, Kweilin (Guilin), and the Kuei River.

Premier Chou En-lai accompanied us on the first part of the journey from Beijing to Luoyang. This was by private train. The delegation and our hosts gathered on a private platform at Beijing Station where Chou En-lai spotted his old Canadian friend Chester Ronning. The two of them embraced on the platform as only old sincere friends can. We were all introduced to this well-known and respected Canadian diplomat who worked in China during the years of transition from the Nationalists to the Communists.

We boarded the train, whose several carriages were sleeping cars and a diner for the overnight trip to Luoyang. These were the most beautiful and best-maintained railway carriages I have ever seen; they would have been a railway buff's delight. We didn't see any more that night of the two prime ministers, who were quartered in Chou En-lai's own carriage. We took advantage of the great food and service and had a most enjoyable exit from Beijing. (It was certainly better than a trip Peggy and I did by train from Beijing many years later, although we travelled "soft class.")

Next morning when I lifted the window blind, I was pleased to see a beautiful day, but as I glanced at the countryside, I noticed that every several hundred metres along the embankment, there were sentries stationed with their backs to the train. The Chinese left nothing to chance when their premier and his guests were concerned. Later, at breakfast in the dining car, I was able to confirm that the sentries were stationed along both sides of the track. My first thoughts were that Premier Chou En-lai and Prime Minister Trudeau deserved such protection, but then I wondered why, in a country where the Party had such strict control, such extreme action in the country-side should be considered necessary. It was an indication that all was not perfect in the new China. Anyway, there we were, fully armed soldiers lining the tracks for hundreds of kilometres. I argued that they used the same few hundred soldiers, moving them when the train passed, several kilome-tres down the track, but as some of my colleagues mentioned, the Chinese had terrible transportation problems and would have trouble moving any-thing anywhere.

Almost all of our time in Luoyang was spent at the Long Men Caves on the Yi River at a spot where high cliffs on either side form a pass. Work began on the caves in 494 A.D. There were now more than thirteen hundred and almost one hundred thousand statues of Buddha ranging in size from one inch to fifty-seven feet. These caves and the stone sculptures ranked as one of the few great remaining masterpieces of Buddhist culture in China. The caves, entirely hollowed out by man, had suffered a great deal of deterioration from natural causes and vandalism. Many precious pieces were removed and could now be seen in most of the great museums around the world.

Chou En-lai gave us a personally conducted tour of the caves. Two instances stand out in my mind during the tour. One involved Margaret Trudeau, who was in the middle of a pregnancy and constantly under the protective care of Inspector Barry Moss. As she walked along the river, viewing the sites, a friendly Chinese official walked over to her and was about to touch her on the arm and explain the surroundings. Inspector Moss and his assistant grabbed the poor fellow and whipped him away. Barry later explained to me that he had to be most strict in the matter of protecting the prime minister's wife during her pregnancy, for it would cause a terrible situation between Canada and China if anybody, even inadvertently, was to harm her.

The second strong memory I have of the tour of the caves was a brief chat I had with Premier Chou En-lai as we were ascending steps at a cave site. There was nothing of substance in our few words, but what impressed me was that it was the first and only time I heard him speak in English.

Chou En-lai left us in Luoyang and returned by plane to Beijing. It was the last time we were ever to see him. He died three years later. He did, however, leave us in the care of the future Chinese leader, Deng Xiaoping. During the waning years of the Cultural Revolution, Chou had sought to restore Deng Xiaoping and other former moderate leaders to positions of power. We did not then appreciate that he was Chou En-lai's choice for future leader. Deng accompanied us to Kweilin and down the Kuei River and stayed with us until our return to Canada.

The Kweilin area was without question one of the most impressive places I have ever visited. The city itself was nothing out of the ordinary, but the surrounding countryside and the Kuei River were most spectacular; the scenery was unique. The river flows through an agriculturally rich valley set in a landscape that nobody would believe if it was presented to them in a picture. Deep erosion and the limestone plateau had left a multitude of tall, needle-shaped pinnacles, out of whose steep sides trees improbably sprouted. These mountains have long been memorialised in Chinese paint- ing and poetry. There are also many caves; we visited the largest, Lu Ti Yen, or Reed Flute Cave.

Our trip down the river took the entire day. It has to be one of the most beautiful river trips in the world. We were on two comfortably furnished barges. I was most impressed with the navigation of the barges; they were kept in often fast-flowing channels by strategically located streams of water flowing between piled stones. These streams entered the channel at the very moment the barges were about to go off course. They would keep the cumbersome craft in midchannel. I was told that these channels and the supporting streams had been in use since time immemorial, as the river provided the best route south from Hunan. All along the river were the most picturesque scenes imaginable, with small villages and fishermen offshore in their boats fishing with cormorants. These birds fascinated me. They would dive for fish, but because of rings around their necks, the fishermen were sure of retrieving the catch. The rings prevented the birds from swallowing the fish. Birds and fish were reeled in, and the fish confiscated. After a good catch, the rings were removed and the cormorants were allowed to fish for their own dinners.

When we were traveling in and out of the cities of China in the prime minister's procession, Bob Joyce and I shared a car. Each car in the cavalcade was numbered, with the prime minister and his wife in car one. Car five or six was always allocated to us. The streets of Kweilin, like the other places we visited, were lined five or six deep with cheering onlookers, mostly school children, let out of school for the occasion, or factory workers, let off to welcome a "friend" of China's.

In the fifth or sixth car in the procession, Bob and I found that by the time we rolled past the crowds, the clapping and waving was always waning. We found that whenever we stuck our arms out of the car window, the level of clapping and general noise would increase. After hours of driving through cheering crowds, we amused ourselves by sticking our arms in and out so as to get almost a "tune" from the increasing and decreasing noise. We never did quite achieve an "Oh Canada," but we did find that our slightly cynical, if harmless, pastime was interpreted by the Chinese lining the route as indications of great friendship.

This was my last visit to China for many years. When I was to return some twenty years later, China would no longer be one of the most isolated countries on earth. Mao's reign would be well over, and the "Little Red Book," which had been the Chinese "Bible," would no longer be waved by chanting crowds; it would be only one of the many souvenirs of revolutionary days sold by free-market entrepreneurs on the street corners of Beijing to the countless tourists who invaded China.

Chapter Twenty-two
All Around the Rim

It must appear that my days were devoted entirely to China. My wife certainly thought so, for even when I was in Ottawa, we seemed to be spending much of our social life at the Chinese Embassy. I had to focus also on our trade relations with other countries of Asia and the Pacific, as well as Africa and the Middle East. I had been placed in a position that required me to follow Canadian trade interests in this vast area.

The next several years I spent on missions across and around the Pacific. I made several visits to Manila in order to negotiate a Most Favoured Nations (MFN) agreement. Like China, the Philippines was not a member of GATT, and we had no MFN relationship. The Philippines was very much within the American sphere of influence, so we felt we should do all we could to have them look to Canada as a possible alternative to the United States when meeting their import needs. Lindsay MacNeil was with me on several of these missions. We usually flew from Ottawa to Hawaii, where we broke our trip overnight before taking the long flight via Wake Island to Manila. Whenever we could, we stayed in the old wing of the Royal Hawaiian Hotel. With the discounts that our department travel man, Charlie McCullagh, was able to negotiate, the rate was reasonable. It was one of the great hotels of the world, in a most beautiful tropical setting. This at least was the case until Hawaii became the Mecca for Japanese and American tourists, bringing the high-rise hotels that now overshadow the Royal.

I recall one interesting flight from Honolulu to Manila, with a refuelling stop at Wake Island. Lindsay, who was keen on military history, wanted to see Wake Island, which featured so prominently in the early years of the Japanese sweep around the Pacific. When we landed, we were surprised to see such a small and narrow piece of land all alone out there in so much ocean. As the plane touched down, we felt that the wings overshadowed the beaches on both sides of the island. One couldn't help wonder how the American defenders could have held onto this speck of land for as long as they did; it looked indefensible. We spent the refuelling hour wandering about both sides of the island, finding it impossible to visualise the slaughter that took place in this beautiful tropical setting.

Wake Island aside, what made the flight so memorable was the company we ran into on the plane. We left Honolulu at 11:59 P.M. so after a nightcap, we decided to stretch ourselves out on the many empty seats in the back of the nearly empty aircraft. While we were waiting for the washrooms at the rear of the aircraft, a man standing nearby said, "You fellows sound like Canadians; I'm from Canada myself!" He introduced himself as Donald Sutherland, the actor, and asked what we were doing in this part of the world? When we explained that we had business in Manila and Beijing, he waved to a hippie crowd at the front of the aircraft and yelled, "Jane, come here and meet some of my fellow Canadians." Jane Fonda, the actress, came back to join us.

Jane Fonda walked up the aisle, accompanied by about a score of hippie-looking black and white friends. There were very friendly introductions all around. They explained that they were holding anti–Vietnam War demonstrations at American bases around the Pacific. Their first stops were to be at bases in the Philippines. We tried to look as if we got mixed up in this sort of thing every day. It was immediately obvious that they were all very left-wing. Any mention on our part of our trips to China was received with great interest and enthusiasm.

Lindsay and I spent the remainder of the night in our seats with Sutherland and Fonda (in army fatigues) kneeling on the seats in front of us, surrounded by their weird-looking colleagues. We discussed the affairs of the world with particular emphasis on China and the Vietnam War. They must have thought our views quaint. We found the whole thing entertaining until we arrived in Manila, where the crowds meeting the group at the airport delayed our entry.

Manila was and still is a city of stark contradictions. Makati, the city's financial centre, has its wide, well-kept boulevards, high-rise apartments and office buildings, and ultramodern shopping centres. It also has a well-guarded, walled enclave of the extremely rich. Many of the diplomatic residences, including our own, were inside the walls. To enter and exit was reminiscent of crossing a border between unfriendly independent states. In contrast to the Makati area was the large slum of Tondo, dominated by a huge pile of garbage known as Smoky Mountain because of the endless burning of garbage fires. The poor lived here in cardboard shanties and scavenged for a living.

Despite the good and the bad, Manila had a joie de vivre that transcended the day-to-day battle for survival. The blend of Latin and Asian temperaments make for an easygoing atmosphere. Indeed, as far as the political situation was concerned, we felt life was too easygoing. For example, interspersed amongst the luxury hotels along Roxas Boulevard were numerous casinos, all illegal, yet tolerated because they were owned or controlled by senators and members of the government.

It was really most difficult to get the Philippines to place real importance on a formal trade link with Canada. They felt, with some justification, that their special trade relationship with the United States was all they needed. We knew that we would never be able to negotiate the type of agreement we wanted until we were able to demonstrate that Most Favoured Nation (MFN) access to Canada would give them very real benefits. We attempted to draw a parallel for them with our own situation, where the bulk of our exports went to the United States and where we felt it was in our interests to diversify our markets without in any way turning our backs on the American market.

To demonstrate the potential market for the Philippines in Canada, Lindsay and I did a statistical review of Philippine exports to the United States showing that many hundreds of millions of dollars' worth of the same items were imported by Canada from sources other than the Philippines. We impressed upon them that they could compete with other developing countries for this large market. The message was received, for interest in an agreement with us picked up, and we were able to conclude one that we felt was in line with our Cabinet instructions.

I returned to Manila several months later with a member of Parliament, Mr. Howard, who was the parliamentary assistant to the minister of Industry, Trade and Commerce. Mr. Howard was designated to sign our new agreement. I remember on that occasion having meetings with Foreign Minister Carlos Romulo, the Philippines' great statesman-author-educator. He told me that in his youth he had crossed Canada by the Canadian Pacific Railway and was intrigued that all of the silverware and china were marked with his initials, "C.P.R."

For several years I was involved deeply in our relations with Australia and New Zealand. Both countries, as members of the "old" Commonwealth, granted Canada "preferential" tariff treatment; that is, our goods generally

159

faced much lower customs tariffs than the exports of our non-Commonwealth competitors in Western Europe, the United States, or Japan. We in turn granted Australia and New Zealand preferential treatment in our own market. Because of the advantage that preferred treatment gave us, the two markets were amongst the most important for our manufactured exports. A large number of branch plants had been established in Canada, not only to supply the Canadian market, but to enjoy the preferential treatment granted to Canada in the markets of Australia, New Zealand, Britain, and certain other countries of the Commonwealth.

We seemed to be forever tending these preferential relationships and were virtually in constant negotiations with Australia and New Zealand in attempts to stem or slow the unravelling of the preferences. Both these countries and Canada in the 1970s maintained very high tariffs, and Australia and New Zealand seemed to be forever attempting to increase protection for their already overprotected industry. At the same time, we were tending to lower our tariffs, either because of negotiations in GATT or in an effort to lower costs to our industry or to reduce inflation.

The real crunch for the Commonwealth preference system came when Britain entered the European Community in 1973. Britain made it clear that they would be abrogating the preferential trade relationships. While certain of the preferences we had in Australia and New Zealand were contractual between Canada and these countries and would be unaffected by Britain's entry into the Community, many other preferential rates had been extended to Canada after these countries signed separate agreements with Britain. These derived preferences would have no legal basis when Britain abolished its preferential regime. We sought and received Cabinet authority to bring these derived preferences into our formal agreements with Australia and New Zealand.

I was on the delegation selected to negotiate these "derived" preferences. I was designated to lead the delegations to New Zealand and to Fiji. While we had no formal agreement with Fiji, we did enjoy preferential treatment as a result of preferences the Fijians had given to the British and extended to us. Our first meetings were with the Australians, and our Assistant Deputy Minister Bob Latimer led the delegation. Also involved, in addition to myself, were Joe Loomer and Craig Oliver from the Department of Finance; Roger Bull from External Affairs; Fred Light from Customs; and David Knowles from the Trade Department. Harry Horne, our man in Sydney, joined us in Canberra.

We spent several days in Canberra on the floor of Bob Latimer's hotel room, tediously fingering through the Canadian and Australian tariffs. We were trying to assess the changed positions the Australians presented to us without warning on the first day of our meetings. Australia was concerned that commitments on preferential tariffs not stand in the way of negotiations they might enter into with their major non-Commonwealth trading partners. On the other hand, they hoped to have non-Commonwealth countries pay for the removal of their preferential system. This was a rather naive position, given that Britain's entry into the Community signalled to the world that the preferential system was finished.

The Australians agreed to maintain the existing system for us but without any legal commitments. This satisfied our finance people who wanted the flexibility to eliminate or reduce Canadian tariffs in the attack on inflation. As a trade officer, I was unhappy that our exporters would have no assurances that their preferred access to the Australian market would continue for any prescribed time.

In New Zealand, the situation was no easier. New Zealand was facing the loss of its huge market in Britain for dairy products and lamb. It couldn't count on Canada to fill the gap. Indeed Canada imposed severe restrictions on many of New Zealand's exports, particularly on dairy products. New Zealand was beginning to think about cutting its tariffs and exposing its overprotected industrial sector to the fresh air of international competition. If it were to move in that direction, it wouldn't want to be encumbered with new commitments on tariff preferences. We did strike an agreement, but it was clear to all that we were witnessing the beginning of the end of the Commonwealth trade relationship.

Fiji was an interesting case. We had no contractual preferences with Fiji, but we did exchange preferential tariff rates. On our way to New Zealand, I took a small delegation to Suva to get the Fijians to agree that we should not allow the British act of joining the European Community to dictate the treatment of trade between Fiji and Canada. They were particularly interested in the preference we gave them on sugar. We were interested in the lower tariffs they applied against a range of Canadian processed and manufactured goods. They agreed to strike an agreement to preserve the preferences until such time as they might associate themselves with the European Community as a former British dependent territory, as did former French and Belgian territories; this would give them preferred access to the entire Community. At least for a short time, we were able to continue to enter the Fijian market under conditions more favourable than those faced by our competitors.

Our deal with Fiji paid off for us the day after we reached it. At breakfast I met an American businessman who was building a resort in Fiji. I asked him where he was buying the equipment and furnishings, and he said, "In the States, naturally."

As diplomatically as I could, I told him that he might be making a wrong decision, since his imported goods would face twenty or thirty percent duties if imported from the United States and only ten percent if imported from Canada. I learnt some weeks later that my new-found friend imported several hundred thousand dollars' worth of equipment and furnishings from Canada.

Fiji was one of my favourite spots in the South Pacific. I got to know well a number of ministers and senior officials. On my many trips to Australia and New Zealand, I switched my overnight rest spot from Honolulu to Nadi. Honolulu airport was becoming difficult with long lineups when the early morning flights arrived from the Far East. Nadi airport was small and friendly by comparison.

At Nadi Airport, I had a very amusing moment on one occasion when I was checking in for the small South Pacific Airlines flight to the capital, Suva. I wasn't amused at the time, but later, as is often the case, I had a good laugh about the incident.

The man behind the counter said to me, "Sir, if you don't mind, would you please hang on to your bag for ten minutes or so, because there is a plane about to depart for New Zealand, and if I send your bag out there now, it will most probably end up in New Zealand."

I guarded my luggage and asked the man to let me know when it would be safe to check it. A few minutes later, he called me over and said, "It should be safe now." I could hear the New Zealand-bound plane warming up for takeoff. The thoughtful man placed my bag near the small baggage exit behind him.

As soon as it touched the floor, a dark hand reached in and grabbed it and, with great efficiency, threw it aboard the New Zealand-bound aircraft. The poor man behind the counter yelled through the small baggage exit, but the noise of the departing plane drowned out his appeals. He raced out the door of the departure lounge and ran towards the departing aircraft, but he was too late! My bag went to New Zealand and back; it was delivered to me as I was about to depart Suva on the way back home.

When flying to Australia or New Zealand, I would generally arrive at Nadi at six in the morning after about fifteen hours of flying from Ottawa. I would take a day room at the Regent Hotel. A kilometre or so down the beach from the hotel, a schooner in full sail would leave about nine in the morning for a several-hour voyage to Castaway Island, where the day is spent in swimming, snorkelling, or just lounging about in a most beautiful South Sea setting.

Towards sunset, the schooner set sail for Nadi. The Fijian crew would get out their guitars and drag a fishing line, and everybody would be most relaxed. The Fijians were all six-foot plus and wonderful specimens of men. They sang like the true Methodists that most of them were, having been converted to Christianity by the London Missionary Society. (My wife Peggy and I once attended a Fijian church service where we were treated to some of the most harmonious singing I've ever heard. Incidentally, we were the only ones in the church wearing shoes.)

Like most "paradises" in this world, Fiji was not without its problems. The native Fijians found themselves to be without a majority in their own country. The history was that when Fiji was taken into the British fold, it was found to be an ideal place for growing sugar cane. The Fijians, however, did not take easily to such large scale agricultural production, so the British imported indentured labour from India. The result is that, now, over half of the population is East Indian. While on many visits to Fiji, it appeared, at least on the surface, that the two racial groups got on well enough; there was, politically, a great divide between them. In the minds of the native Fijians, the only true Fijians were themselves. Yet for the majority East Indians, Fiji was the only home they knew, for they were by now many generations in the country.

Many Indians, particularly the richer, maintained contacts with India and understandably kept the customs and beliefs that their forefathers brought from the old country. This, coupled with the fact that the Indians tended to be more entrepreneurial and richer, added fuel to the political fires. When the government, which was always controlled by the native Fijians, fell under the control of the Indians, the military, controlled by the Fijians, took over. The situation now dictates that minority Fijians will always have political control. Thus Fiji has moved from being one of the few truly democratic countries in the developing world to join the host of others where a large part of the population is virtually disenfranchised.

Chapter Twenty-three
Sheikh and Shah

One autumn day, when the entire world was in the grip of the oil crisis, Tom Burns, our senior assistant deputy minister and a close friend, forced me to change my focus from the Pacific to the Middle East. He called and told me that the minister of energy, the Honourable Donald Macdonald, was to visit the oil-rich countries of the Middle East. Tom wanted me to join the minister as the representative of the Trade Department.

We were to visit Saudi Arabia and Iran and en route drop into Cyprus and Lebanon. Minister Macdonald had been defence minister and wanted to take the opportunity while in the eastern Mediterranean region to visit the Canadian United Nations Forces that had been for years positioned between the Greeks and Turks on Cyprus. Our visit to Lebanon was scheduled because it was not politic to fly from Saudi Arabia to Iran over Iraq, even in a Canadian government plane; indeed it would have been foolhardy to attempt to do so. Beirut was to be our staging point between Saudi Arabia and Iran.

We flew from London to Cyprus, where in addition to our visit with the Canadian troops, we were to pick up a Canadian military propeller-driven aircraft for our trip through the Middle East. For the few days in Cyprus, we were in the hands of the Canadian military. There was no trade component to the visit to Cyprus, so I tagged along with the minister and his charming wife, Ruth, in a day-long inspection of the "Green Line," which separated the Greek and Turkish Cypriots. Canadian and other UN troops were stationed along this line; a very thin line between the two opposing forces. I was impressed with these eighteen- and twenty-year-old men, particularly when they stood on lonely sentry duty outside the populated areas, separated from their closest colleagues by hundreds of yards. Along one lonely stretch, I met and chatted with a company of Newfoundlanders.

Cyprus was one of the most frustrating United Nations peace-keeping missions. This was unfortunate, for it was one of the first areas where the UN was to set up a multinational force. This force, which was given a mandate in 1964, had to have it extended for three decades because of the continuing conflict between the Greek and Turkish Cypriots and the external interventions by Turkey. Certainly without the UN, the area would have been a continuous bloodbath. However, without parallel and forceful international attempts to bring about a political settlement, much of the UN effort must be viewed as having been largely in vain. Canadians were for the entire period among those manning the Green Line.

From Cyprus, we flew in our small Canadian forces plane to Riyadh, the capital of the kingdom of Saudi Arabia. We were to be the guests of the oil minister, Sheikh Yamani, who had been at Harvard Law School with Minister Macdonald. Sheikh Yamani had shaken the world with his pronouncement on oil production and prices. He was the leader of the newly established cartel of oil producers, OPEC. The next few days were to prove that the two ministers were not only college acquaintances but close friends.

This was my first of several visits to Saudi Arabia, and every day I spent in the country, I was both impressed and annoyed. One had to be impressed with the good use to which much of the new-found oil wealth was being channelled in those days. Emphasis was placed on education and the living standards and quality of life of the people. On the other hand, there was a complete intolerance of non-Muslim religions. Religion permeated all aspects of daily life, but public worship and display of non-Muslim faiths was prohibited. The population was almost entirely Sunnite Muslim; that is, orthodox, and the only Christians were amongst the foreign industrial employees, diplomats, and businessmen. These people had absolutely no freedom of religion. If Americans and Canadians truly believed that their principles were as important as their political objectives, then Saudi Arabia would have long ago been stamped as one of the most intolerant of nations.

Amnesty International, as recently as 1993, noted that "Religious intolerance is deep rooted in Saudi Arabia, and the government must take a strong stand to show that the pattern of arbitrary arrest, detention, and torture must stop." Amnesty was commenting on the fact that Christians (workers from the Philippines and Sri Lanka) were victims of persecution and torture by the state-sanctioned Saudi religious police.

Another area that impacted on a Westerner was the Saudi attitude towards women. Women were said to play a dominant role inside the home, but outside, they were to be unseen and unheard. They were covered from

165

head to toe, veiled and dressed in black caftanlike garments. To show a few inches of flesh at the ankle would invite a swish of green paint by the religious police, who were ever on the lookout for such indecency. I heard of two German ladies, dressed most conservatively, who were so abused by these officious thugs. Women were chattels and not permitted to do such common things as drive a car or buy an airline ticket without an authorising note from their husbands.

Saudi Arabia was swarming with foreign workers, mainly from overseas countries with Muslim populations, such as Pakistan and the countries of Southeast Asia. They came on temporary visas and did all of the physical labour. There was a story circulating amongst the foreign community about a Saudi being asked whether sex was work or pleasure. His fast response was that it must be pleasure, because if it was work, the Saudis would have somebody else do it.

The government was based on the law of Islam, the Shariah, derived from Mohammed's pronouncements and practices and from the traditions of Islam's first adherents. Muslim law prescribed civil as well as religious rights, duties, obligations, and responsibilities for the ruler and ruled. To preserve the country's purist religious position, many prescriptions of behaviour and dress were enforced. Alcoholic beverages were prohibited, and the theatre and public cinema did not exist. Educated Saudis were well informed on issues at home and abroad, but public expression of opinion about domestic matters was "not encouraged."

The kingdom exhibited a certain aloofness to outsiders; a foreigner could only secure a visa to enter the country if invited to visit for an official or officially approved reason. The king was all powerful. He combined legislative, executive, and judicial functions. As prime minister, he presided over the council of ministers, whose appointment or dismissal were decisions only for the king.

Modern Saudi history dates only from 1932 with the creation of the kingdom from two lesser kingdoms and their dependencies. Ibn Saud was king until his death in 1953. He was succeeded by his eldest son, Saud, with his second son, Faisal, being declared heir apparent. In 1964, King Saud was deposed and Faisal was proclaimed king. He was considered to be more competent than his predecessors perhaps because of his great exposure to the outside world during the time he served as foreign minister, and his support for modernisation. He developed the ministries for government and established for the first time an efficient bureaucracy. These were positive changes, but as was the case during the rule of Faisal's father and brother, there was no move whatsoever towards the introduction of democratic institutions.

Oil Minister Ahmed Zaki Al-Yamani, or Sheikh Yamani, as he was known to the world, was an expert on international law. He was a soft-spoken, handsome man with very piercing eyes, dressed in Saudi robes and was forever playing with his "worry beads." He spoke perfect English. He was a powerful man domestically and internationally. This was not only because of his considerable intellect but because of Saudi Arabia's place in the world of oil; Saudi ranked first with twenty-five percent of the world's known reserves. He was a moderate, certainly when compared to his opposites in Libya and Iraq.

At the time, we had only one ambassador in the area, accredited to Lebanon, Syria, Jordan, Iraq, and Saudi Arabia. He was Jacques Gignac, resident in Beirut.

Marshall Crowe, the chairman of the National Energy Board and the senior official accompanying Minister Macdonald, was informed by Gignac on arrival in Riyadh, that he (Gignac) would be the only person joining the minister for the meetings with Sheikh Yamani. Marshall exploded and, not in his usual diplomatic language, said that he and Petrie were to attend.

We had an all-morning meeting in Riyadh with Sheikh Yamani. Minister Macdonald, while primarily interested in the world oil situation, lost no opportunity to stress our interests in expanding our overall trade with Saudi Arabia. Saudi Arabia at this time was not only flush with money, but was swarming with American advisors telling them how and where in the United States they should spend their wealth. Our message was that they should ensure that their sources for both technology and equipment were diversified, and if it was North American they wanted, Canada was the only alternative to the United States. We started then to set the stage for a concerted trade effort in Saudi Arabia.

Sheikh Yamani invited us to a magnificent luncheon. His wife and the wives of the other Saudi Arabian officials were present, as was the minister's wife, Ruth. My recollections of this luncheon are limited to the nervousness of the Canadians, who were concerned that one of them might be called upon to eat the "bite-of-honour," the sheep's eye. Everybody got along so well that, at the conclusion of the luncheon, Sheikh Yamani announced that we were all invited to dinner at his home in Jeddah, where we would meet all the men who ran the country. It didn't seem to concern him that Jeddah was about eight hundred kilometres away. Minister Mac-donald accepted the invitation and invited Sheikh Yamani to join us on our Canadian forces plane. He accepted, but when he got to the airport and saw our old and slow propeller-driven aircraft, he said that he had better take his own jet in order to get there first and prepare for our arrival.

Sheikh Yamani's dinner and party were amongst the most interesting social events one could attend. By the time our slow aircraft arrived in Jeddah and we were driven to the Sheikh's home, he was awaiting us with his wife and young daughter. His wife, a middle-aged Arab woman, left no lasting impression on me, but I shall never forget his relationship with his daughter. She was around ten years of age and was by his side all evening. She was an adopted child from Indonesia. Apparently her parents died while on a pilgrimage to Mecca, and one of the greatest things a good Saudi can do is to adopt a child so orphaned. The little girl sat clinging to her father; there was obviously great love and affection between them.

Everybody who had an important role in managing the Saudi Arabian economy was at the dinner. I chatted with the head of Saudi Airlines, the governor of the central bank, and ministers and senior officials of various economic ministries. It was a very informal affair, and everyone was seated Eastern-style on cushions on the floor. Chivas Regal whisky was served, but I noted that no Saudis accepted a drink. (It was illegal even to have alcohol in the home, let alone to serve it.)

I was seated near the front entrance so was able to observe closely the arriving guests. Each of the Saudi men was followed by a wife. It was interesting to see the men enter the living area and be introduced while their veiled and black-shrouded wives disappeared into a room behind closed doors. Minutes later, the women reappeared, transformed as the most beautiful spring day is from the gloomiest winter night. They were dressed in the finest French and Swiss creations and carried themselves like models. I was told that almost all of the wives were Arab, mostly from Lebanon or elsewhere in the Middle East outside Saudi Arabia. They all spoke excellent English or French or both and had been educated mostly in Switzerland. To talk with them was like talking with the most sophisticated ladies at diplomatic receptions in London, Paris, or Geneva. It was difficult to think of them as the same women who disappeared into the cloak room in their black caftanlike garments with only their eyes showing.

Music has always been a part of Saudi life, and a small group of musicians enthusiastically played traditional numbers. Sheikh Yamani and

168

his daughter led in a Saudi dance, joined by many of the guests, including Minister Macdonald and his wife. It was strange to see these generally very serious Saudi leaders dancing and enjoying themselves.

Next day we departed for Beirut, Lebanon. Sheikh Yamani was at the airport to bid farewell, and one couldn't but be impressed by his open friendliness towards Minister Macdonald and his wife. The few days of meetings together and the party the night before certainly had brought to life the old college friendship the two had known at Harvard. The visit gave me an opportunity to meet most of the movers and shakers in the economic life of Saudi Arabia and would help later when we were to establish a task force to focus on trade with the Middle East.

In Beirut we stayed downtown at the Hotel St. George, a Swiss-style hotel equal to the best in that country. The sad thing was that when I visited Beirut a few years later, the beautiful hotel had disappeared. It had been totally destroyed in the senseless civil war. The city was divided between the Christians (Maronites and Greek Orthodox) and Muslims (Sunnis). The overwhelming majority of both religious groups was Arab, and at that time they lived in relative peace. We spent a day calling on Lebanon's leaders, who were most friendly towards Canada, many having relatives or friends living there and some having aspirations someday to live there themselves.

Over the next several years, I was to visit Iran several times. This first visit left few memories other than days of continuous meetings with ministers associated with the oil industry and the economy. I was, however, most impressed by Prime Minister Hoveda (who was to be executed by a revolutionary mob). He was a very well educated and cultured man, not only in his native Pharsee, but in French and English. While he was most proficient in French, he conducted the meetings with us in English. I shall always remember his comment when we were discussing the political situation in the neighbouring Arab states. He said the Arabs were fine people except that they had trouble coordinating the mind (and he touched his head), the mouth (and he touched his lips), and the heart (and he touched his breast). As we left he presented me with a paperweight on which were the raised images of the Shah and his queen. Prime Minster Hoveda's life and fate were bound to the fate of his Shah.

My next visit to the Middle East was several months later with the Honourable Allister Gillespie, minister of Industry, Trade and Commerce. As director general of the Pacific, Asia, Africa, and Middle East Bureau, I had to organise a mission with accompanying businessmen and journalists.

As an indication of the need to get involved with every detail of a mission I might relate the saga of the Hudson Bay blankets!

It was customary for a minister on an official visit to take with him gifts for his opposites in the host countries. The department had, or had access to, an array of Canadian-made artefacts, the most popular of which were soapstone carvings produced by the Innu people. Mrs. Gillespie, who generally accompanied her husband, was unhappy with what was being offered and prevailed upon her husband to get something different, mentioning specifically Hudson Bay blankets. What could be more Canadian than a Hudson Bay blanket? Where had I found it colder in bed than in overly air-conditioned Saudi Arabia, where I had to wear my raincoat over my pyjamas to keep warm in bed? So we took along a few blankets, and Mrs. Gillespie was happy.

Luckily we also took along other possible gifts.

Once en route, the officer who had purchased the blankets asked to speak with me. He said, without any fanfare, "The blankets were made in England." As I was catching my breath, he quickly added, "You are not to worry, Mr. Petrie, because I have cut the 'made in England' labels off and nobody would ever know the difference." I went into slight shock. I would have to inform the minister and, despite his wife's love for the blankets, I would have to advise him not to offer the blankets as gifts from Canada.

I had a strong feeling that the journalists with us knew that we had blankets and that they were not made in Canada. My feelings were strengthened when we stayed overnight in London and I joined some of the press fellows for a beer. They continuously pestered me (with smiles) to let them know when we planned to give out the blankets. I spoke to the minister and made the recommendation that we leave the blankets with the staff who were setting up our new embassy and trade office in Saudi Arabia. He was "not amused" but quickly saw that he had no option but to stick with my story that the blankets were for our new embassy and that we would be giving soap carvings and other Canadian artefacts to our hosts in the Middle East. Mrs. Gillespie never again mentioned blankets.

Our first stop was in Beirut, and we stayed at the beautiful Phoenicia Hotel. This wonderful hotel boasted, with justification, one of the best restaurants in the world. It was ironic that we had our press conference and reception for our Canadian exporters and their Lebanese contacts in the restaurant's Age d'Or, or "Golden Age," room. The Golden Age of this famous hotel and its competitor, the St. George, and indeed of Beirut itself, was quickly coming to a close. When I was next to visit Beirut, the Phoenicia, as the St. George and much of Beirut, would lie in ruins.

At its peak, Beirut had been an important trade and financial centre, and most of the major Canadian banks still maintained offices there. A short time before our visit, a left-wing mob had attacked and stoned most of the Western banks. The representative of the Bank of Nova Scotia had proudly told me that the only bank bypassed by the mob had been the Bank of Nova Scotia. The mob assumed that the word "Nova" was Russian, and being a Russian bank, it was to be spared.

It was Good Friday evening when our delegation of about thirty-five arrived in Beirut. We had some twenty-five businessmen, five journalists, and five officials. Next morning after briefings by our embassy staff and Canadian bankers resident in Beirut, our businessmen headed out for calls on the local business community. I accompanied the minister and the ambassador to meetings with economic and trade ministers. As we did our rounds, it was clear that the political situation was quickly deteriorating. The government buildings were armed camps, with soldiers everywhere. The airport had the appearance of a fortress prepared for the worst. We were relieved when we were on our way to Saudi Arabia.

We arrived in Jeddah, on the Red Sea. It was the Saturday afternoon before Easter. We stayed overnight, spending the evening with Jean-Pierre Lefebvre, our chargé d'affaires, who gave us a briefing on Saudi Arabia, including the do's and don'ts. One of the "don'ts" was not to work on Easter Sunday. While it was an ordinary working day in the kingdom and the Saudis had no tolerance for non-Muslim religions, they would have thought badly of us had we worked on this most important of Christian holidays.

So on Easter Sunday, we flew to Riyadh, the capital, and spent the day sightseeing and preparing ourselves for the next day's work. I was friendly with a lot of the businessmen, including Ray Frigon, Ian Ross, Bob Stedman, and Jean Paul Gordeau, and with Alan Lutfy on the minister's staff, and our departmental officers, Alan Lever (who was later to be our ambassador in Saudi Arabia), Dan Janigan, Phil Ghatas, and Keith Gardener. Many of us spent part of Easter Sunday at the souk, or bazaar. The shopkeepers, their wares, the crowds, and the sounds and smells of the souk always fascinated me.

Minister Gillespie impressed me with his often successful attempts to get our exporters (and journalists) into his meetings with ministers and heads of state in the countries we visited. I recalled the success his predecessor, Minister Jean Luc Pepin, had in China of including exporters and journalists in his meeting with Premier Chou En-lai. The greatest opponents of this practice were some of our External Affairs people, who generally felt that only officials (senior) should be present during ministerial discussions. It was felt that ministers would not speak as openly in the presence of nonofficials. I found the opposite to be true, and, obviously, so did Minister Gillespie. Business people were often able to bring to bear knowledge and points of view not directly available to politicians and officials. When Minister Gillespie would ask the Saudi minister of finance or of trade whether he could be accompanied by several of his key delegation members from the private sector, the response was generally most positive. This practice was followed by all of Minister Gillespie's successors, and I never had any indication that discussions were any less substantive because of the presence of exporters; the contrary was the case.

As experienced during my first visit to Riyadh, I was never so cold in winter when camping in Newfoundland as I was in the Riyadh hotel. I was wishing I had several of those Hudson Bay blankets we had left with our people in Jeddah. The temperature hovered around forty degrees Celsius, or one hundred degrees Fahrenheit, outside, but all public buildings, including the hotels, were excessively air-conditioned. When I went to bed, I ended up wearing all of my clothes again including my raincoat. Oh, for the good old days when you could open a window.

One group of Canadian engineers had a small reception for us in one of their homes, and I was a little surprised when we were offered alcoholic beverages. I'm not sure how these drinks entered the country, although diplomats did bring alcohol in with their diplomatic supplies. The story was that the Saudis in charge of the docks, being devout Muslims and against alcohol, would "accidentally" have the crates dropped when they suspected they contained alcohol. I was told that one ingenious British diplomat imported his supply in a lead-lined case. If the workers on the docks dropped the case and smashed the bottles, he would strain the contents and serve the terrible mixture of several different beverages as his "special."

Without much warning, we were advised that eighteen of us would be received by King Faisal Ibn Abdul-Aziz. We were driven to the palace and ushered straight into the receiving room. The king was there in Bedouin dress, standing on the edge of a raised platform, so that when you approached him he towered over you. He was surrounded by a retinue of Bedouin guards, and the entire scene was rather theatrical with subdued bluish lighting and facial makeup liberally applied, as if it were amateur theatre. I was reminded of an illuminated Christmas manger scene; as I approached the king to shake his hand, the vision of my childhood flashed through my mind of the three kings of the Orient. He was standing perfectly still, bathed in that bluish light. He was unsmiling, and his face under the makeup was gaunt and wrinkled; his eyes were tired-looking and his eyelids heavy. He didn't say a word. He shook our hands, and as quickly as we had entered, we were ushered out to an adjoining room where Crown Prince Khalid awaited us. Little did we know that on March 25, 1975, King Faisal would be assassinated by a nephew and Prince Khalid would become king.

Prince Khalid sat on a thronelike chair that was the only indication of his royalty. He chatted with us without an air of superiority. He was well informed or well briefed on Canada and reviewed very professionally the Saudi-Canadian relationship. He gave us a very thorough rundown of his expectations for Saudi Arabia. He didn't visualise that in a few short years Saudi's seemingly inexhaustible oil revenues would diminish to the point where the kingdom would carefully have to husband resources. King Khalid was to die in 1982, and Crown Prince Fahd would succeed him.

We flew from Riyadh straight to Baghdad, which was not really a well-travelled route because of the hostility between the two Arab states; we had to follow a very circuitous course. Our Canadian forces plane enabled the minister's entourage of exporters, journalists, and officials to travel together. During these flights, I scheduled fifteen-minute meetings between individual exporters and the minister. This gave the minister a better understanding of the export capabilities of each exporter and helped to ensure that we all "sang from the same songbook" when we met with officials and private sector representatives in the countries we visited.

Baghdad was the setting for many of the stories of *The One Thousand and One Nights,* when during the eighth and ninth centuries it reached the zenith of its economic prosperity and intellectual life. It was then the richest city in the world. Shortly thereafter, it was captured by the Turks and experienced a long, slow decline from which Baghdad did not recover until the oil boom in the 1970s. Even the great expansion and economic development of the 1970s was to be curtailed by the bitter war with neighbouring Iran and its confrontation with the West.

Baghdad was a city of marked contrasts in architecture and lifestyles, combining bazaars, shrines, and mosques, riverside cafés, Western-style hotels, and modern high-rise apartments. At the time of our visit in April

1974, Baghdad had all of the trappings of a third-world or Communist dictatorship. It was easy to imagine being behind the iron curtain. There was a well-treed avenue leading from the airport to the city, lined with arches, statues, and flags such as were seen in newly independent countries striving for identity, or in Eastern Europe.

Most of our delegates stayed at the Hotel Baghdad, and you could tell it was run by the state as soon as you stepped inside. The staff had none of the hustle or determination to please which is so evident in private establishments. I didn't stay at the Baghdad but accompanied the minister to a palace that had been converted to a government guest house, on the River Tigris. This was a beautiful residence with lovely gardens and a magnificent view of the river. Our splendid accommodation was not however paralleled by a friendly reception such as one might normally expect to receive as a visitor from abroad.

On our two days of calls on ministers and senior government officials, the reception was anything but friendly. I have, during my career, made visits, albeit often very short ones, to some eighty countries, but I look back on our official reception in Iraq as being undoubtedly the coldest. The ministers with whom we met had to be either cowered or just plain unfriendly. It wasn't that they were belligerent or sharp with us, but they were passive to the point of rudeness. They left the impression that, despite the very good interpreters, they were not listening and could not bother to join us in a discussion. There were often long, embarrassing periods of silence while we waited for their responses, during which times they would just sit there staring at us. I mark it down to an official position of general hostility towards Western countries, for it is hardly in the nature of Arabs to be unfriendly to guests. We tried to ignore the attitude, for we had our eyes focused on the vast sums commanded by Iraq as a result of the quadrupling of oil prices in 1973. These funds were being spent liberally on a wide variety of projects; we had a lot to offer and were determined that, despite the unfriendliness, we would get "a piece of the action."

On April 18 we flew to Isfahan in Iran. Among Middle Eastern countries, Iran is unique in many ways. Its official language, Farsi, is Indo-European, and while Iran adopted a modified version of the Arabic alphabet, it refused to lose its identity after the establishment of the Arab empire in the seventh century. When conversion to Islam began, Shi-ism was adopted, even although it was considered heresy at the time to be supporting the house of Ali, Mohammed's son-in-law, whose claim of

174

succession to the Prophet was disputed by the Sunnite majority. The Shiite branch became the official religion.

Isfahan has to be one of the most interesting cities in Iran. It was the capital of Persia at the time of Shah Abbas I (1587–1629), and we stayed at the very beautiful hotel that bears his name. The Shah Abbas was decorated by Iran's most distinguished artists and was virtually a museum of national treasure. The gardens of the hotel were superb. The entire setting was in the shadow of one of the most beautiful mosques in Iran.

Our stay in Tehran was as usual taken up with meetings with ministers and business representatives, all of whom spoke perfect English or French. They gave the immediate impression of being well motivated and well disposed towards Canada. I was able to meet once again Prime Minister Hoveda who spoke in most positive terms about the economic development of his country and the opportunities for Canadian involvement. Despite the prime minister's optimism, there was, even then, a sense of trouble brewing. You could not escape the feeling that although the Shah's regime appeared to be well entrenched with one of the largest and best equipped armies in the world, all was on shaky ground.

We tended to push such negative thoughts aside, since there appeared to be such great opportunities for Canadian exports, ranging from agricultural products and equipment, pulp, and paper mills, chemical plants and flight simulators. A number of our companies were able to discuss real possibilities for economic cooperation through joint ventures. We had positive responses from the Iranians on the setting up of a joint economic commission and an agreement on export credits as vehicles to put us on a par with our competitors in Western Europe. Indeed the stage was set for the development of a considerable amount of business, and we had some real success over the following few years, until the glowing coals of discontent that we sensed then, burst into all-consuming flame, engulfing the Shah's regime. He left Iran on January 16, 1979. Khomeini arrived on February 16, 1979, bringing to an end our promising economic relationship.

I have visited Iran on four or five occasions, and each time I was taken to the Central Bank of Iran (Bank Markazi Iran) for a viewing of the Crown Jewels. The jewels were said by their protectors in the bank to be the richest collection in the world. I certainly would not dispute this claim; it was a most dazzling collection. The invaluable treasure had a fascinating history. When, in the middle of the seventh century the Arabs conquered Iran, they found wealth as had rarely been seen by a conquering army. There is one account of an immense one-hundred-and-eighty-foot-long carpet covering the main hall of one of the palaces. The carpet was jewel-encrusted. The invaders cut it into pieces and distributed them amongst the soldiers after a major portion had been reserved for the leaders. In the Safavid period (1501–1736), Iran was once again united into a coherent, mighty force and embarked on a series of conquests. The most important figure of this period was Shah Abbas. He was a lover of jewels, and he built his collection to unprecedented dimensions. Foreign envoys, travellers, and gem dealers have left glowing accounts of bejewelled thrones, crowns, harnesses, and utensils. In our own time, a team of scientists from the Royal Ontario Museum made a study of the Crown Jewels and joined the long list of those who marvelled at this great collection.

It is not surprising that much of the original treasure disappeared into the hands of invaders who overran Iran on several occasions. Some of these jewels found their way to the courts of Mongol kings in India, to be later recovered by Nadir Shah. He sent a number of these jewels to reigning monarchs. The famous diamond, Kooh-i-Noor, or "Mountain of Light," found its way into the British Crown Jewels.

On my last visit to Iran in late 1978, I could hear the sound of gunfire at night. It was just a few months before the flight of the Shah, and yet there was still little acceptance amongst the international community that the physically mighty regime of the Shah would come to a speedy and inglorious end.

One of our well-known Canadian engineering firms, Statler Hurter, had built a pulp and paper mill complex in northern Iran on the Caspian Sea. They had won this contract through international competition; there were tens of millions of dollars worth of Canadian engineering services and equipment sold to Iran because the project came to Canada. The time had come for it to be commissioned, and the Shah had agreed to open the mill. The Honourable Tony Abbott, minister of Small Business, was delegated to represent the Canadian government at the opening, and I was to accompany him. Tony was a close enough friend that I could half-jokingly tell him that I would be pleased to join him if we could introduce him in Iran as the Canadian Minister of Business and not "Small Business." The term "Small Business" was, I insisted, popular at home, but overseas it would do nothing for Tony's image or for Canada's efforts to sell abroad.

There was a very disturbing side to our "mission" to Iran. The Canadian engineering firm Statler Hurter had been taken over by an American financial group. This normally would not have been a cause for concern. However, the American company seemed to have little interest in Statler Hurter as a forestry-based engineering firm. Fred Hurter, the company's founder and previous owner, and the man who won the Iranian project, was an acquaintance of mine and was to join Minister Abbott in Iran.

When Tony and I arrived in Tehran, we were shocked to learn that the new American owners of the company had "sent" Fred Hurter back to Canada, not permitting him to participate in the opening of the mill that he engineered, designed, and had built. We had a hurried meeting with our Ambassador Ken Taylor (who in a few months was to be propelled into the world's headlines for harbouring some of the escaped American hostages from the seized American Embassy). We agreed that time would not permit any action on our part before the opening ceremony, which was to take place next day. We were determined that even without Fred Hurter, we would keep the Canadian image up front, and after the event, we would have a very serious meeting with the American owners.

The new prime minister of Iran, Shalpur Bakhitar, provided us with his personal plane to take the Canadian (and American) party to the mill site. The American owners were represented by a very well known Washington lawyer, David Morris. Morris had been secretary of labour in President Truman's Cabinet. He was a most congenial man and a difficult man to dislike, although all of us at the time were determined not to befriend him when we first met him as we boarded the plane. He readily agreed to join us at Ken Taylor's residence as soon as we returned to Tehran following the opening of the mill and the planned audience with the Shah.

The prime minister's plane was a relatively small executive jet, so it was possible to get a good view of the airport and runway as we landed. It was a fairly large airport on the shores of the Caspian Sea, several miles from the mill site. We had a textbook landing, and yet it was the most eerie landing I've ever had; there was an absence of any activity whatsoever near the runway. A quick glance told us that this was probably one of the most securely protected runways anywhere. Every ten or twenty metres along both sides of the runway were members of the Shah's "crack" personal guard, all with their backs to our landing aircraft. When we entered the terminal, it was like a mausoleum, with soldiers stationed here and there, but absolutely no civilians or airport staff anywhere.

The Shah's political situation was not as secure as we all thought, or he was getting paranoid concerning his well-being. Why in the world would such extraordinary security be necessary unless one were expecting the worst? We were whisked from the empty air terminal by jeeps to the mill site at Gilan, on the Caspian Sea. Next to the entrance of the mill, they had erected platforms for the planned ceremonies. The Shah was being shown around the town that was being created because of the employment generated by the mill. We followed him, looking at kindergartens, day-care centres, and staff housing.

We then all went into the mill, where we joined the Shah on a tour. We were introduced to him as the Canadian group involved in the "construction" of the mill (without Fred Hurter). After admiring the Canadian equipment and the work of our engineers, the Shah and his followers travelled in their jeeps to the newly constructed stands, where there were several thousand workers assembled. The Shah was on a platform about five metres above the ground. I noticed that about thirty metres in front of the stand and between the Shah and the assembled multitudes there was a deep newly-dug ditch. The reason for the ditch didn't register on me at the time. Tony, Ken Taylor and I were to the left of the Shah on the Shah's side of the ditch, which, as it turned out, was the right place to be.

The Shah addressed the crowd, and their reaction seemed to me to be that of great enthusiasm. There was loud cheering (or in retrospect perhaps it was jeering) and waving of hands. I felt that the Shah must be the most popular man in Iran. Suddenly the crowd started to rush forward towards the Shah's raised platform. Just as suddenly, our side of the ditch was lined with soldiers, and even more quickly, the Shah disappeared off the platform into a waiting jeep and was hurried away. The few thousand workers were now no longer a crowd, but a mob. The poor fellows in the front rows had no choice but to move forward into the ditch or be trampled on by those behind. You could see the fear on their faces as they were propelled towards the soldiers in front of them by the trampling feet of their fellow workers behind. We didn't wait to see the outcome but jumped into the nearest jeep and raced away after the Shah and his entourage.

I couldn't believe that the program would continue after the Shah's experience with the workers. We were all assembled in a hall, where the Shah was briefed on the economic impact of the mill on the region. He sat a few feet in front of me, and I was impressed that he showed no sign of distress or of being upset by his experience a short time before. It was as if he had that sort of thing happen to him regularly. Perhaps it did!

Back in Tehran, we were driven to Ambassador Ken Taylor's residence. Our American friend, David Morris (who claimed to have met me in Geneva), came with us. Ken and I had been close colleagues for many years, and we had in common the fact that we both had Australian wives. Ken's wife, Pat, was there and had a Persian meal laid on for us in their Persian-style dining room. The room was covered with cushions and beautiful Persian carpets that Ken had purchased from his favourite rug merchants, two Jewish brothers. (He actually later introduced me to them and had them show me their stock, which was impressive; I often wondered whether they survived the extreme revolutionary period.)

Before, during, and after dinner, we tackled poor old David Morris. We stressed to David that we had been embarrassed by the actions of the new owners of Statler Hurter. They had diminished the image of Canada in the forestry sector in Iran. We impressed upon him that the Canadian private and public sectors had spent a good deal of money, time, and effort building a relationship. Clearly the new owners had no interest in using the good name of Statler Hurter to pursue further business in Iran or anywhere else, building on Fred Hurter's great success in winning the project we saw today in Gilan province.

We discussed this all evening, and by the early hours of the morning, David agreed to press his principals to sell what remained of Statler Hurter to an engineering company in the forestry sector that would have the capability and the willingness to pursue projects of interest to Canada. I undertook to explore with Canadian engineering firms whether they might be interested in acquiring the company. Tony undertook to set up a meeting for David and his principals in Ottawa with the Honourable Donald Macdonald, who was familiar with Canada's interests in Iran and certainly had the political clout to bring together the various elements required for a resolution of the problem.

We had our meetings in Ottawa with Donald Macdonald, and the American company agreed to cooperate. I didn't have much success in getting a Canadian group to take over what remained of Statler Hurter but was successful in working out an arrangement with the giant German firm Klockner to have them absorb the Canadian group and, through them, do much of their forestry projects out of Canada. Klockner-Statler Hurter Limited was the outcome and with such competent Canadian staff as Al Curleigh in charge of their project financing, and Bill Barton, our former ambassador to the United Nations on the board of directors, they were soon able to win a several-hundred-million-dollar forestry project in Sabah, Malaysia.

Before "leaving" Iran, I might comment on the traffic. It was terrible in Tehran, but I was told that one of the most dangerous drives in the world was through the long, dark, single-lane tunnels that connect Tehran through the mountains to the north with the Caspian Sea. There was a lot of heavy truck traffic, and these vehicles were driven by macho types who would never allow mere automobiles to pass them. The tunnels were not only dark, but full of exhaust fumes, so it was essential to use one's lights. The only way one could pass the trucks was to turn off the lights so that the truck driver in front was unaware that you were behind him. It was thus the practice of many cars to extinguish their lights and speed past the unsuspecting trucks. The problem was that trucks and cars coming the other way played the same game. The result was numerous head-on crashes and the "temporary" closure of the tunnels much of the time.

Tiananmen Square before China was opened to tourists.

The honourable Jean Luc Pepin and Chou En-lai

On the Great Wall before the crowds.

On a commune.

Philippine Foreign Minister C. P. Romulo and Howard M.P. signing Canada-Philippine Trade Agreement.

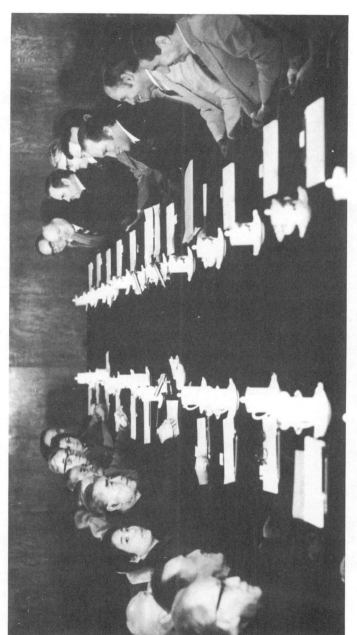

Formal meeting between Prime Ministers Trudeau and Chou En-lai.

Prime Minister Trudeau and Premier Chou En-lai after signing Canada-China Trade Agreement (from L to R in background: Ambassador John Small, Petrie, Michel DuPuy, Ivan Head, and Mrs. Trudeau).

Prime Minister Trudeau and Premier Chou En-lai at Luoyang (1973).

Prime Minister Trudeau in Trinidad.

Meeting President Suharto of Indonesia.

The honourable Donald C. Jamieson's visit to Indonesia (February 29–March 3, 1976).

The honourable Don Jamieson meeting with President Marcos, Philippines

Discussions with Datuk Hussein Onn, Malaysian prime minister

Don Jamieson in Singapore. Seated L to R: Dick Thompson (president Toronto Dominion), Derek Burney (future Canadian ambassador to U.S.A.), Bob Thompson (Canadian high commissioner), Jamieson, myself, David Macnaughton, and Rodger Hatch (CEA chairman).

Malaysia. Signing of Double Taxation Treaty with Su Sen, minister of finance.

In the permafrost of Northern Siberia.

Chapter Twenty-four
The New World South

Rio de Janeiro is one of the most beautiful of the world's larger cities and the least safe. Rio has a magnificent harbour, with the conical Sugar Loaf Mountain standing at its entrance. The city's setting between mountains and sea forms an extremely attractive sight. A beautiful promenade of marble, eight kilometres long, lines the waterfront. Equally impressive is Copacabana Beach that forms a concave half moon for many kilometres, lined with beautiful hotels and restaurants.

John Raynor of our Department of Finance and I arrived in Rio after an overnight flight from New York. We took rooms at a small hotel on Copacabana Beach for a break before continuing on to a GATT meeting at Puenta del Este, Uruguay. In Rio, the advice was not to wander from the beachfront promenade. We did take a tour of the city and felt secure as part of the tour group. However, we left the tour at the far end of Copacabana Beach several kilometres from our hotel. My Newfoundland taste for salt cod led us to a restaurant whose speciality was "bacalao." This is dried cod soaked overnight, cut into pieces and cooked with garlic, chopped tomatoes, peppers, and onions. It was delicious for me and, I hoped, for John.

After our bacalao dinner, we had to make our way several kilometres back to our hotel. It was already dark but a beautiful night, and the promenade paralleling the sea was well lit and crowded. We felt that if we followed the advice not to wander off the promenade, we would be safe from the infamous street criminals of Rio. We were fine for the first half-mile or so, and then we were confronted every few yards by "ladies of the night." We counted one hundred such confrontations before we gave up counting. They generally took no for an answer and seemed to be in no way threatening. Indeed, the walk would have been good for the male ego if we forgot for a moment that it was not us they were after but our money. We were more than a little careless to have taken that walk at night. Contrary to the advice we were given, one could get into trouble even on the beachfront.

Some Canadian engineering friends, who were attending an international conference at one of the grand hotels on the beachfront, told me about an experience they had while lined up with their wives to board their buses when going out to dinner. Two "beautiful" and very well-dressed transvestites walked down the line of couples right in front of the hotel. One of the transvestites would grab the man between the legs, and as he bent over, the other would relieve him of his wallet. By the time the offended and robbed couple recovered, the transvestites were several couples down the line, similarly relieving others of their cash. Some thirty couples were robbed in a matter of a few minutes.

Latin Americans are generally subjected abroad to many misconceptions. They are thought of as more-or-less Spaniards or Portuguese or as descended from Spain or Portugal with Indian blood. There is some truth in the latter; the great mixed race of Europeans and Indians forms the bulk of Latin American nations. They are too far removed from the original stock to be identified with either. There are, however, large important exceptions to the European and Indian blood mix. Latin America is one of the great immigrant recipient areas of the world. Italians, for example, have greatly changed the composition of the people of Argentina. Founded by the Spaniards, Argentina has always been overwhelmingly European. British, Germans, French, Austrians, and Slavs have all played their roles, as have the Spanish, but today there are more people of Italian background than any other. Uruguayans also are predominately of European descent.

It was almost impossible to fly to Uruguay from anywhere except Buenos Aires. It was, at the time of our visit, impossible to fly commercially, even from Buenos Aires, because the militant labour unions had picked the time of our international conference to close the airports. Not to be outdone, the Uruguayan government had organised flights for the delegates from the international airport at Buenos Aires. It was by the Uruguayan Air Force. I never dreamed that I would one day be flying with the Uruguayan Air Force.

John and I flew from Rio to Buenos Aires, where we stayed overnight, with arrangements to take the Uruguayan flight next day. I was to visit Buenos Aires several times later, but this first stop was a short one. Situated on the Rio de la Plata, or River Plate, about one hundred and fifty miles from the Atlantic, Buenos Aires has grown into one of the world's largest cities. It was a handsome city, more northern European than Latin, with many well-designed open spaces and parks, boulevards and squares.

Uruguay is just across the River Plate from Buenos Aires, and we were shuffled aboard Uruguayan Air Force troop carriers for the flight across. It was amusing to see delegates from seventy or eighty countries, many of whom were well known to me, strapped into bucket seats along the sides of the aircraft. These didn't look like the ambassadors and other senior officials I knew from the Palais des Nations in Geneva. We were packed into three of these planes, which took off together and flew in formation across the wide expanse of the River Plate to Uruguay.

Uruguay reminded me very much of Australia. There were the sheep and cattle ranches and the beautiful rugged coast, where the broad ocean pounded the sandy shore. It was only when one listened to the background of the Spanish language and saw the very different habitation that you knew you were in South America. The surrounding ocean abounded with seals and whales, and between the rugged headlands were some of the finest beaches in the world. Puenta del Este, where all of this came together, was a holiday-maker's paradise, and the Argentines certainly had discovered it!

Puenta del Este was in reality a resort for Buenos Aires. The wealthy of Buenos Aires had beautiful summer homes nestled among the gigantic pines that were all around Puenta del Este. They supported the fine hotels, restaurants, and the casino. Without the Argentines, Puenta del Este would be just another fishing village. The international community had also discovered the area. I give Uruguayan Ambassador LeCarte credit for its popularity as an international conference centre. LeCarte was the ambassador to the United Nations and GATT during my years in Geneva, and I knew him well. He was always pressing for international conferences to take place in the developing world (specifically Uruguay), and he was successful in attracting the current one. He was now a minister in the government of Uruguay. He was on the runway to greet us when we descended from the transport planes.

Uruguay used to be called the Switzerland of Latin America. Its three million people had a standard of living before the Second World War comparable to Switzerland's or Canada's. Like the Swiss, they had adopted a national council of nine ministers instead of a president. Six of the nine were from the majority party and three from the leading minority party, all with equal powers. The majority members took turns annually presiding over the council. Unlike the Swiss, the presiding council member tended to leave difficult and unpopular decisions for the next chairman, who in turn left them for his successor. The result was that little was done to correct the many problems facing the nation, mainly as result of an overambitious welfare program.

Before other countries in the Western Hemisphere even considered such welfare measures, Uruguay had introduced a comprehensive welfare system that the country could ill afford. They maintained such measures as old age pensions at sixty, family allowances, and financial compensation for dismissal. I was told by our trade commissioner, Ben Shapiro, in Montevideo, that because of nondismissal, the bureaucracy was larger than Canada's, even though the population was only one-fifth of Canada's. The fishing industry had been nationalised, and even its members were considered government servants.

The difficulty to dismiss workers meant that there were always more civil servants than offices or desks. Those who got to work early got the desks, and the rest went home on full pay. The result was superinflation. Before the Second World War, the Uruguayan peso was worth a United States dollar. At the time of this visit, it was equal to about one United States cent, and the downward plunge was only beginning. Most businesses demanded payment in United States dollars that never entered the coffers of the country but ended up in foreign bank accounts as a hedge against the local inflationary situation.

The GATT meetings in Puenta del Este were devoted entirely to finding solutions to the trade problems of the developing countries, covering barriers to trade in tropical products and such products as wool and beef that were important to Argentina and Uruguay. The Uruguayans were certainly successful in demonstrating the high quality of their beef. They entertained us at a "gaucho barbecue." It differed from other barbecues in that the beef was cooked with the skin (fur) left on the side away from the fire. It was said that in this way the juices were trapped as the flames cooked the meat on the other side. It was certainly delicious but a little disconcerting to have animal fur on your dinner plate.

Chapter Twenty-five
Cuba

In the mid-1970s, I was assigned as director general of the Western Hemisphere Bureau of Industry, Trade and Commerce. One small market in that area that was attracting a lot of attention from our exporters was Cuba. Cuba was off-cover for American exporters and seemed to offer a unique opportunity for a range of Canadian products and services.

In March 1975, Trade Minister Gillespie asked Claude Charland, our assistant deputy minister (Trade Development), and me to organise a mission of some thirty businessmen and journalists that he would lead to Cuba. We assembled a strong departmental supporting team. We had George Blackstock, Dick Porter, Max Smith, Allan Lever, as well as Charlie McCullagh and Doris Ladouceur, who were the best arrangers of travel and accommodation in the business. Bob Shaw was in charge of the media.

The minister agreed that following the mission, I could take a previously arranged vacation in Cuba with my wife and two of my daughters. The timing fitted since the mission would end four days before our family's scheduled "week in the sun." I was booked on a charter flight to Havana with Peggy, Janine, and Jennifer. I arranged to go ahead with the minister's mission and then join my family for a stay at Varadero Beach. This sort of arrangement would have been easy in any Western country. In Cuba, all visitors were in organised groups; to remain alone for several days after the departure of our mission would cause great confusion amongst Cuban officialdom and bring me into combat with them.

Our ministerial mission went off better than planned. We were very well received by nine cabinet ministers and the president of the Republic. A real surprise was a meeting with Fidel Castro. Clearly, the Cubans were intent on normalising trade relations with Canada, seeing us as a source for North American technology and equipment that was now unavailable from the United States. We felt that their needs and our capability to supply "peaceful" goods and services could be meshed very well as long as the

Soviet Union continued to pump money into Cuba that the Cubans could use for the payment of purchases from Canada.

Cuba was being bankrolled by the Soviet Union and continued to be so until the Soviet Union's breakup. Consequently, Canadian exporters were able to develop business with some certainty of being paid. The Soviet Union, Cuba's *tio rico,* or "rich uncle," was to provide eighty billion dollars during the 1970s and 1980s. During this period, Cuba pursued its Socialist experiment with little concern for cost or efficiency, and it was only with the collapse of the Soviet Union that their illusionary world was shattered. In the meantime, we were able to develop business in such fields as cattle, swine, and poultry breeding stock, seed potatoes, auto parts, and hotel and airport equipment.

One of our mission members, Billy Rix, from Charlottetown, Prince Edward Island, succeeded in winning a large contract to build a fish-processing plant for Cuba. The difficulty he ran into, not only with the Cubans, but with his own authorities, is indicative of the problems encountered when developing a business relationship with a country like Cuba. Billy visited Cuba many times before a deal was struck. He manufactured all of the parts for the plant at his facility in Charlottetown. Finally it was time for a Cuban ship (the Cubans insisted on using Cuban ships) to take on board what was to be the largest export of manufactured goods from Prince Edward Island. However, on its way up from Cuba, the ship visited the Cuban fishing fleet on the Grand Banks.

For some inexplicable reason, it took on a huge quantity of fish from the fleet, and it was found when the ship arrived in Charlottetown that there was insufficient room for all of Billy's equipment. Billy was confronted with possible penalties for not delivering on time. He was understandably adamant that all the equipment be loaded. The only way this could be done was to off-load the fish for pick-up by another Cuba vessel. The problem was that to off-load the fish would constitute an importation into Canada, and the Cubans or Billy would be liable for Canadian customs duties. Billy, in a flap, telephoned me in Ottawa. I called a senior friend in Customs. Within a few hours, he had the wharf and storage facilities in Charlottetown declared a temporary bonded area for customs purposes. Billy was delighted. The fish were off-loaded and Billy's equipment went off on time to Cuba.

The highlight of our visit to Cuba was a meeting with Fidel Castro. We were told several hours beforehand that a meeting might be arranged, but we were not told when or where. It happened when we were having a snack and drinks in the garden of our Ambassador Malcolm Bow's residence with Chris Spencer, Sam Pattee, and others from the embassy. Suddenly we realised that the property was surrounded by armed men who had permeated the garden and house. As this was happening, we suddenly found Fidel Castro, in his battle fatigues, in our midst. He settled in the dining room at one end of the dining table. Minister Gillespie sat at the other end. Interpreters were stationed between them, and the rest of us stood around the table.

The minister and Castro covered virtually every issue. The only downside was that one of our bankers asked Castro for an autograph for his granddaughter. This is never done at an official meeting, but Castro complied. What impressed me about the event was, not so much the substance of the discussion, but that Castro would take several hours to meet with a delegation that had already been well received by nine of his ministers. He clearly wanted to show the world that his regime could have a normal relationship with a country closely allied with the United States.

The Cuban regime showed its extreme bureaucratic nature as soon as I said good-bye to the minister and our delegation, who were on their way without me to Venezuela. I had four days to wait before Peggy, Janine, and Jennifer would arrive on the charter from Canada to join me for our short vacation. Although my few days alone had been agreed to at senior diplomatic levels, and I was provided with a room at the Havana Libre (the old Hilton), lower ranking Cuban officials resisted accepting me. I had to show my diplomatic passport a dozen times. I stuck out as a sore thumb, for every visitor in Cuba was with a group, and here I was all alone. My "group" wasn't to arrive for several days, so I was required to explain over and over again what I was doing in Cuba before my charter's arrival. Fortunately, I had some knowledge of Spanish and had local currency and knew my way around to some extent.

I took advantage of my few days alone to walk around Havana to see first hand as much as I could of the "new Cuba." The people on the street were friendly enough, although I felt they were a little distant, possibly because they knew that I was likely being watched by their security people. This didn't stop someone every few minutes from offering to buy various articles of my clothing, offers which I refused. I have never thought of myself as a very snappy dresser, and I placed little importance on having the latest styles. But this didn't seem to deter the Cubans, who offered large amounts of local currency for everything I wore. The Cubans, like citizens of Communist countries generally, seemed to have lots of local currency but little on which to spend it.

The Havana Libre (Hilton), like the city itself, had seen better days and was badly in need of refurbishing. It was comfortable enough until you needed to go to the bathroom. All of the toilet seats were missing. I took it as an indication of the plight of the people in the countryside that they took with them, when they checked out, the toilet seat from their rooms. I reported my missing seat on arrival, but it was still missing on my departure.

The Havana Libre was filled with honeymooners. It was explained to me that the state provided "qualifying" newly married couples from the countryside with a few days' honeymoon in Havana. In addition to the toilet seats that they obviously considered theirs, each couple was given a brand new radio. I believe I heard every one of them playing at the same time while we all sat around the Havana Libre swimming pool. Fortunately they were tuned in to the same station, Radio Miami, which boomed out Cuban music and anti-Castro propaganda.

Cuba then had many advantages as a holiday destination. There were wonderful open air concerts and stage shows in Havana and a good floor show in the main hotel at Varadero Beach. Varadero had to have one of the finest and, certainly at the time, cleanest beaches anywhere. Accommodation varied from the hotel to small beach apartments to the state-owned villas of the once rich and famous. These villas could be rented with full meal service and housekeeping for a reasonable amount. Close by and open to the public was the once luxurious Dupont estate with its beautiful parklike gardens. Virtually all of our fellow guests were Canadians, since Cuba was not a destination open to Americans. There were many Russians and Eastern Europeans, but we were segregated from them; they lived and played at a very separate area of the beach. This alone said very much for the state of things in Cuba.

Chapter Twenty-six
Of Queen and Commonwealth

Press reports had Margaret Trudeau on the prime minister's plane to Guyana. I knew she wasn't, because I was with the prime minister's party. Many articles written about her on this trip were obviously written before the journalists left Canada for the 1975 Commonwealth Conference in Kingston, Jamaica. Mrs. Trudeau was indeed to join her husband in Kingston, but prior to this, he was to pay official visits without her to three other Commonwealth countries (Guyana, Barbados, and Trinidad and Tobago), which, with Jamaica, were jointly hosting the Commonwealth conference. A number of the media people accompanying the prime mister to Kingston seemed more interested in filing material on Margaret Trudeau than reporting on the prime minister's substantive itinerary.

We landed in Georgetown, in the former British Guiana. When I was at school, it used to be the only bit of South America in the atlas painted "British Empire red." We arrived amidst fanfare and music from a wonderful steel band. Guyana's Prime Minister Forbes Burnham and most of his Cabinet were at the airport, all calling each other and each of us "comrade."

Burnham had taken the colony of British Guiana into independence as Guyana in 1966. He declared his government to be Socialist. Given relations with the Communist world that had from the start of British Guiana's move towards independence been close, the exchange of the "comrade" greeting was just a part of Guyana's problem.

We moved from the airport to Prime Minister Burnham's residence, where a first-class garden party was underway. Any true socialist would have had serious concerns for the ninety-nine percent of Guyanans who were not there. There was much food and rum passed around all in Prime Minister Trudeau's honour. He was not a "drinker." (On occasions over the next few days when refreshments were served, I would ask if I could get him anything, and he would only sometimes take a beer.) Our High

Commissioner Ormond Dier and his wife Jean returned the Guyanan hospitality the next evening.

The newly independent country of Guyana was caught in its colonial past. Its economy was dominated by sugar. The growing bauxite industry, like most other commercial activity, was being stifled by government controls. As for the people, the indigenous population was small and not integrated, and the people on the coast, where ninety percent lived, were mostly descendants of African slaves or indentured East Indian labourers who had been imported to work the sugar plantations. Guyana's major external problem, other than its flirtations with Communist nations, was with Venezuela. That country periodically claimed large tracts of Guyana's territory.

There wasn't much to discuss with Guyana other than the forthcoming conference. The economy was in bad shape; so much depended on the international sugar market. The climate for investment wasn't good, given the government's tight control of the economy and its negative attitude towards the free market. About the only positive element was that Guyana was supplying the new secretary general of the Commonwealth. He was Sonny Ramphael, the foreign minister.

Prime Minister Trudeau wanted to see something of the sparsely inhabited interior, so two Canadian-built DeHaviland short takeoff and landing (STOL) aircraft were made available to take him and his group south. Sonny Ramphael was with us. Our first stop was at a small airport on the Rotaro River, a tributary of the Essequibo, where we saw the famous Kaieteur Falls. These are most spectacular, having a total fall of eight hundred and twenty-two feet, nearly five times as high as Niagara Falls. Bob Joyce, from our finance department, and I walked over to the top of the falls and lay on our stomachs, peering at the falling water as it made its impressive drop. For hundreds of feet around the falls, there was a miniclimate created by the eternal spray that grew vivid green moss and plants in a small world of their own. We were offered a bird's-eye view when we took off and our pilots made several passes over the falls and the winding course of the river below.

We flew further south to savannah country that was inhabited by the Amerindians. Landing close to a village, we had an opportunity to see the way they lived in this remote area. It was interesting to see black Guyanan patrol officers and administrators rather than the Europeans you find in similar situations in much of Africa or northern Australia. Not far from this site, we went swimming in a fast-flowing river below a beautiful wide waterfall right on the border with Brazil. Prime Minister Trudeau was the first to jump in.

While in Georgetown, I contacted an old university roommate, Rama Maraj, who ran his family sugar estate near Georgetown. I hadn't seen him since university days, at Mount Allison, in New Brunswick. Rama could not expect visits from many of his old colleagues; Guyana was not a favourite tourist destination. It had a long way to go to provide the infra-structure that was so well established in areas of the nearby Caribbean. There have, however, been a number of international conferences held there, and one that had an amusing incident associated with it was a Commonwealth finance minister's meeting.

The story goes that at the end of the meetings, the Guyana government treated all the delegates to a moonlight river cruise with a steel band playing and the rum punch flowing. At the end of the cruise, as the ship was moving towards the dock, one of the Canadians (who shall remain nameless) fell overboard. The ship stopped and suddenly went silent as the crowd peered over the side to see the Canadian swim towards the dock and be pulled from the water by two burly policemen. There wasn't a sound when one of the policemen asked, "And which delegation would you be from, sir?" Without any hesitation, and to the great delight of his Canadian colleagues, the soaking wet Canadian said, "Australian!"

Prime Minister Trudeau was able to do some electioneering in Bar-bados. We had luncheon with Barbados Prime Minister Barrow and some of his ministers at a hotel in Bridgetown. When Prime Minister Trudeau emerged from the luncheon room, there were some fifty or sixty Canadians in the lobby to greet him. He spent ten minutes chatting with them and, in this environment, was a different person than he was when you spoke with him one-on-one. He was normally a very shy and private person, but encircled by a group of ordinary Canadians, he opened up and could give and take with the best of them.

We stayed some distance from Bridgetown, although everything is close in Barbados, an island only twenty miles long and fifteen miles wide. We were at Sam Lord's Castle, which was one of the finest mansions in the Caribbean. Built in 1820 for Samuel Hall Lord, it was now a hotel.

The prime minister had been quite taken with the "Jack shirts," which were worn throughout the Caribbean and Guyana and generally acceptable as daytime business wear. He had a dozen shirts sent to the hotel, from which he picked several. Bob Joyce and I were more or less his size, so we bought some of his rejects. We wore these for much of the remainder of the visit.

We really got into substance on trade in our meetings with Prime Minister Barrow. We reviewed the multilateral, regional, and bilateral relationships. On the latter, Prime Mister Barrow had some tough questions about Canada's failure to comply with international efforts to help developing countries upgrade their exports. They wanted to have the value added by upgrading or finishing their products before export where this made economic sense. Prime Minister Barrow stressed that it did make economic sense for Barbados to be able to sell its finished bottled rum to Canada rather than be required to ship rum in bulk for mixing, as Canadian regulations often required, with "inferior" Canadian rum, and bottled in Canada.

This had been an issue that had concerned me for years. My concerns were not only about Canadian imports, but about the treatment imposed upon Canada's sizeable whisky exports to the United States. American border practices favoured bulk shipments for bottling in the United States rather than the finished Canadian bottled product. Prime Minister Trudeau turned to me and asked what could be done. I explained that this was primarily an area of provincial jurisdiction. The provinces looked upon their liquor boards as a major source of revenue. They controlled the listings, pricing, and markups on domestic and imported products. The best we would promise was to use our best endeavours with the provinces. (I mentioned privately to the prime minister that we had done this many times to no avail.)

On our return to Canada, we wrote to each of the provincial ministers responsible for the liquor boards, mentioning that we were doing so at the request of the prime minister; it accomplished little. Indeed, it took years and a number of dispute panels brought to GATT by our trading partners before there was any movement. Even today, foreign suppliers claim that Ontario, for example, places discriminatory restrictions on the sale of non-Ontario wines. While Ontario wines might be sold in private wine stores, imported wines do not have the same right. Similarly, only Ontario wines were allowed to be sold in the four-litre containers with the built-in tap.

Our last stop before the opening of the Commonwealth conference in Jamaica was in Port of Spain, Trinidad. Trinidad's economy at the time was much more diversified than that of Guyana or Barbados. Sugar was no longer "king." Oil and asphalt deposits had greatly increased Trinidad's earnings. There had also been considerable growth in manufacturing, which employed over ten percent of the active labour force. The population, which numbered about a million, had a similar makeup as the other countries in the area of blacks and East Indians, with smaller numbers of whites and Chinese. It was noteworthy that while English was spoken throughout the country, there were a few areas where a French patois and Spanish were still heard. Whereas the Spanish speakers were there because Trinidad was a Spanish possession until 1802, the few French speakers were there in spite of the fact that the island was never French. They originated when French families were driven from Haiti and elsewhere as a result of the French Revolution.

In Port of Spain, I took time to meet with my university friend Dan Ramesar, who was now practising dentistry in Trinidad. He assembled friends from university days, and we all had a beer together. Just before our departure, Dan arrived at the hotel with his wife Margaret to say farewell, and I was able to introduce them to Prime Minister Trudeau.

In Kingston, Jamaica, the Canadian delegation was accommodated in a hotel next to the conference centre with several other Commonwealth groups. The hotel was to be turned into government offices immediately after our departure. This was still in the period when governments were ever expanding; privatisation, particularly in the developing countries, was not yet even a dream. The prime minster and Mrs. Trudeau had a suite on the top floor. I only saw Mrs. Trudeau on a couple of occasions in the elevator and when I attended meetings in their suite. One of the Mounties charged with her security told me one evening when the Trudeaus were secure for the night that he was having a lot of trouble with the prime minister's wife, who was forever trying to give him the "slip."

Much of the trade discussion at Kingston was on the problems of the less developed countries. This was not surprising, since the vast majority of Commonwealth countries were countries in that category. We spent time preparing briefing and speaking notes and accompanying the prime minister to the meetings when items in our field were under discussion. Only one or two officials from each country were allowed in the conference room at any one time, and for certain items, officials were excluded. The absence of officials gave prime ministers a better chance to get to know each other. There was also the longing amongst many of them to return to the informalities of the days when the Commonwealth was a smaller, more intimate "club." Thirty or more presidents and prime ministers with their officials didn't permit the old "fireside chat" approach of the first Commonwealth conferences. I was impressed during the meetings with Ivan Head, the special advisor to the prime minister on foreign affairs. He orchestrated the attendance of officials at the meetings and was absolutely fair, ensuring that everybody was given the chance to play their role.

When we returned to Ottawa, I received from the prime minister a "Dear Frank" letter, which I am sure was written by Ivan and probably was similar to letters received by other members of the delegation involved in economic affairs. It encouraged me "to continue to do whatever possible to ensure that Canadian economic policies toward less developed countries are wise, effective and compassionate." I really feel that, unlike his somewhat lesser interest in the subject of trade, the prime minister had his heart set on Canada doing something meaningful to help the developing world.

The queen, as head of the Commonwealth, and Prince Philip flew into Kingston and stayed aboard the Royal Yacht *Britannia*. We had an evening reception aboard the ship to meet the royal couple. We went out to the ship on one of *Britannia*'s launches with fellow delegates from all over the Commonwealth. Once aboard the royal yacht, Bob Joyce and I joined the reception line. Immediately in front of us was the Fijian delegation. When they were announced for the queen, instead of shaking hands, they did what we would describe in Newfoundland as a "jig." It was some form of Fijian greeting and demonstration of loyalty. It made our shaking of the queen's hand seem a little inadequate.

After the introductions, we were offered a drink and taken on a quick inspection of the royal yacht. It had to be the best cared-for ship afloat. Everything was polished and spotless. When the queen and Prince Philip had greeted the last of their arriving guests, they wandered separately amongst them. Suddenly the queen walked over to Bob Joyce and me. She remembered that we were Canadians and made us feel completely at ease with her comments and questions. Obviously she had perfected the art of small talk. I asked her lightheartedly about the little "jig" that the Fijians had performed when introduced to her. She told us it was a greeting and went on to say that the various members of the Commonwealth had customs that, to the uninitiated, must appear to be strange indeed.

She said that she had received the prime ministers of all the Commonwealth countries individually that day and was particularly impressed with the dress and customs of the man from Swaziland. I said, "Oh, is that the man with the feather sticking up on the back of his head?"

The queen said, "Oh, no, your man must be a lowly official, because my man had two feathers!"

She seemed to be in no hurry to move along, so I said, "I understand that you are going from Jamaica to Japan via Hawaii."

She said she was a bit concerned about the visit to Japan, because she would be required to ride on one of those very fast trains, and that worried her. I mentioned that in Hawaii, she would be staying in the Royal Hawaiian Hotel. Her comment was "A 'royal' hotel in the United States? Now that's a misnomer!" I didn't have the presence of mind then to remind her that Hawaii had a royal family before the arrival and takeover of their islands by the British and Americans.

At that point, she glanced towards the wharf, where we had boarded the launch for the *Britannia,* and asked whether we could see the building near the dock with the scaffolding. She said, "When I came aboard, there was a man hanging off the scaffolding, waving a huge Union Jack and yelling at me; I was afraid to wave at him in fear that he would wave back with his other hand and lose his grip. Obviously British!"

I couldn't help noting that all the time the queen spoke to us, although she appeared most relaxed, she held her glass with one hand and continually tapped it with three fingers of the other. I was impressed with the attention she gave one even during small talk. So many people spend such moments looking over your shoulder for somebody more important. You had the feeling that you had her complete attention. I had always been an admirer but had thought of the queen as very serious, very remote, and, as required by her position, a somewhat pompous person. I found her to be just the opposite. I was most impressed!

Chapter Twenty-seven
A Newfoundlander at the Helm

There were eight different ministers in the position responsible for Canada's international trade during the 1970s and early 1980s. This caused me to look back longingly at the days a decade or so before, when a minister was in the job for many years and built up a great degree of expertise for trade policy issues and for trade development and got to know well the Canadian export community. During the 1970s, we felt we had a revolving door for trade ministers and a situation that was almost as bad for deputy ministers.

I got to know all the trade ministers, travelling overseas with most of them. Contrary to some views amongst the electorate, they were hard-working individuals who were dedicated to expanding Canada's exports and who looked upon trade as a most sensible way of maintaining and increasing employment and general economic well-being. Understandably, they differed very much in knowledge and ability.

Nobody doubted that Jean Luc Pepin would be assigned a senior portfolio in the Trudeau government, but few would have picked this academic and intellectual for Industry, Trade and Commerce. Yet, he made a fine minister in that portfolio. I really enjoyed working with him. No task was beneath him. On one occasion I recommended strongly that he not take, as he planned, a Chinese minister and his officials to *Jesus Christ, Superstar* at the National Art Centre. He reluctantly agreed and took all the tickets that had been purchased by the department and went up and down the lineup at the Arts Centre, selling them. He delivered the money to the department next morning.

Allister Gillespie, I have already mentioned as being popular with exporters, since he was one of the first ministers to insist on including them in virtually all his meetings when abroad.

Don Jamieson, who had little formal education, more than made up for it with good common sense and his "golden tongue!" He was an outstanding speaker, able to bring an audience at home or abroad to tears or laughter at will.

Jack Horner had different strengths. He was very friendly and could be one of the boys with exporters, officials, and foreigners alike.

Jean Chretien was very good at generating positive publicity for the trade effort; he had good news to offer to the media almost daily. He was not, however, with us long enough to make a real impact and was very busy with the industry portfolio.

Herb Gray was solid and a pleasure to brief but was also preoccupied with the industry side of the Department of Industry, Trade and Commerce.

Ed Lumley was one of my favourites, perhaps because he at first held only the trade portfolio and was able to give trade his undivided attention. Some of my colleagues considered him to be unfairly tough with officials. He never was in his dealings with me, but I must admit he was a little rough with the language at times, although never in the presence of foreigners. Nobody could criticise his performance when abroad; he was an excellent Canadian representative. He had his heart in his work and was one of the first ministers to give trade development rather than trade policy priority emphasis.

Mike Wilson was only with us for the nine months of Prime Minister Joe Clark's government, but I got to know him very well and liked him. He would tend to bug us to come up with ways to measure the efficiency of trade officers, but, that aside, I believe he would have been an excellent trade minister if his government had not been so quickly thrown out of office.

Gerry Regan I knew from university days when we were both at Dalhousie, in Halifax, Nova Scotia. We knew him then as "Gabby" Regan for he had a gift for the gab. I thought highly of him. He was not only a minister with both feet on the ground, he had the strength of his convictions. He demonstrated this when he took the very opposite position of his leader, John Turner, and the Liberal party, and supported the Conservative proposals for a free trade agreement with the United States. He was later elected chairman of the Canadian Exporters Association.

Almost all of these ministers developed a love affair with the Asia Pacific region. This was understandable, given that the trade and output of our traditional partners slowed in the 1970s, and all the world was predicting an upsurge of economic activity around the Pacific, particularly in Southeast

Asia. I was to accompany almost all of them (and the prime minister) on missions to practically all the countries in the region.

The most memorable trip was one to Southeast Asia, led by fellow Newfoundlander, Minister Don Jamieson. It was a large group of twenty-four exporters, six representatives of national business associations, five journalists, and ten officials. As one of the journalists, William Heine, headlined in an article in the *London Free Press,* "Trade Trip to Far East Not Just Another Junket." He wrote that the trip cost the government and business about a quarter of a million dollars but generated sales of about ten million. He said that many other contracts already under negotiation were concluded during the minister's visit, mentioning a gas-collecting, storage, and distribution system that was signed for $34.6 million. Bill wrote that "Jamieson had the capacity to get to the heart of matters (he saw 27 ministers and all five heads of state in less than two weeks)." He continued, "The staff had arranged hundreds of interviews during the two weeks, with individuals matched to cars and to government and office buildings and to senior officials in the host nations, and not once during the trip was there a failure." This was good stuff for our eyes and ears, given that journalists were not always kind when writing about government and bureaucrats. It showed appreciation for the professionalism of our team, particularly of our trade commissioners at the posts who had to arrange many meetings daily for each of our twenty-four businessmen and five journalists in five countries.

We used a Canadian forces aircraft, which surprisingly was under the command of an American air force pilot, who was with us through an exchange program between the Canadian and United States forces. The minister was accompanied by Mrs. Jamieson, who was a delight to travel with.

Also with us was David MacNaughton, the minister's executive assistant, who became a close colleague while he and the minister remained in Trade. David was more than an executive assistant; he was really the minister's alter ego. David's support on an issue meant that the minister would support you.

Among the officials on the mission were several whom I considered to be among the most competent in the trade and economic field in Ottawa. Our External Affairs office was Derek Burney, whom I had known for some time as a likeable, capable, solid, and down-to-earth officer who was destined to hit the top. Derek's capabilities were immediately recognised by Minister Jamieson, who would later take him into his office as press secretary when the minister became secretary of state for External Affairs. Derek would eventually spearhead Prime Minister Mulroney's drive for free trade with the United States and be a major contributor to that successful effort.

I often wondered whether Derek's meeting with Don Jamieson on our Southeast Asia mission had been the beginning of Derek's long journey towards free trade with the United States. Minister Jamieson certainly had no hang-ups about the United States, having in the late 1940s campaigned for economic union of Newfoundland with the United States. He was definitely the most pro-American minister in the Cabinet. Anyway, Don Jamieson and Burney became very close, and after the change of government, Derek would become Prime Minister Mulroney's chief of staff and ambassador to the United States and, in these capacities, be a driving force for free trade with the Americans.

Lindsay MacNeil, my friend and veteran of many flights around the Pacific, was with us. The minister liked him and would ensure that Lindsay and I joined him every evening for a nightcap in his suite. We would discuss the content for the next day's speech, and Lindsay and I would labour half the night writing the text, only to have the minister good-naturedly wave it at his audience next day, thank us profusely for our good work, and then throw it aside! He did extract facts and figures from our night's work, which we felt was largely a labour for naught. The next evening we would go through the same ritual with the minister. I hoped he would relieve us of the nightly chore, but he never did.

Gordon Keyes, who was shortly to join me in the office of overseas projects, was also along. Gordon, an engineer, had an encyclopaedic knowledge of Canadian industrial capabilities, and if anyone could put together a group of Canadian companies to pursue successfully an overseas project, it was Gordon.

Allen Lever was our mission coordinator and was the best in the business. Like Burney, he so impressed Jamieson with his organisational and administrative abilities that when later Jamieson was assigned to External Affairs, he would take Lever to run his office. Allen's ability in the policy and international relations field, which was never tested in the Department of Industry, Trade and Commerce, would later be recognised when he was named ambassador to Saudi Arabia.

Some of the countries we were visiting were recipients of Canadian aid, and we were to spend some time with the Asia Development Bank, so we had an "aid" officer with us. It was Vic Lotto, an old friend and colleague, who had been seconded to the Canadian International Development Agency by the Trade Commissioner Service. The service often seconded officers between postings to such positions, which gave us a good point of contact when dealing with such nontrade-oriented institutions.

Among the businessmen were many career-long friends and associates. There were proven exporters, such as Roger Hatch, who represented the Canadian Exporters Association; Roy Phillips was there for the Canadian Manufacturers Association; Dick Thompson, president of the Toronto Dominion Bank, who represented the bankers association. We had, to mention a few, Rom Vuia of Combustion Engineering; Hal Godwin of Consortex; Ed Bennett of Delcanda; Ben Ball of Federal Pioneer; Jack Nodwell of Foremost; Bob Kelly of Interimco; and Henry Valle of Montreal Locomotive.

We flew to Hong Kong, with a refuelling stop at Nagoya, Japan. It was the last day of February 1976, and the sun had already set when we approached Hong Kong. The tricky approach, over the mountains that surrounded the harbour and the descent down between towering buildings on the runway, was both frightening and very beautiful. In the distance around the harbour were a million lights, and just beyond the wingtips you could see into apartments where people were preparing their evening meal oblivious to our encroachment on their privacy.

I had been there many times and never ceased to marvel at this jewel of the Orient. It's a city of contrast, with glamorous shopping arcades, and shops and clubs along hundreds of narrow, winding streets. A tram took you to the top of Victoria Peak, where before you was a magnificent panorama of Hong Kong. The Star ferry to Kowloon, across the harbour, brought you amongst junks in full sail, naval vessels, freighters, and cruise ships. Then there was Aberdeen with its floating restaurants and the fishing vessels of the boat people.

We were received by our trade commissioners, Mike Spencer and Colin Russell, who I am sure didn't relax a moment until they packed us aboard the aircraft next day for the flight to Indonesia. We left midafternoon, and at the time, I don't believe that any of us other than the cockpit crew were aware how very close we came to not making it! Our plane was on the end of the runway, waiting for the incoming traffic to ease sufficiently to allow us to take off. After takeoff, I was with the minister when the pilot came in and told him that while we were on the runway, an incoming

Lufthansa flight, on touching down, bounced violently towards us, coming within a hair's-width of hitting us. He said that had the German plane touched us with our full load of fuel, we would not have known a thing. After that piece of news, I joined the minister in a very early predinner cocktail.

Jakarta had changed radically in the twenty years since Peggy and I had stepped ashore off the Italian ship en route to Europe from Australia. The reminders of the old Dutch city of Batavia were all but smothered by the development that had taken place. The city at the time was around five million in population and going through growing pains, with much disruption to communications and transportation. We got first-hand knowledge of this from our car windows, for we seemed to spend much of our time in cars going to and from offices of Indonesian ministers. We called on several, including the minister of finance, with whom we signed a Double Taxation Agreement. We extended to Indonesia a two-hundred-million-dollar line of commercial credit from our Export Development Corporation (EDC) to be used for the purchase of Canadian goods and services.

On the mission was Don Keill from EDC. Don was a very nice man, and I felt a little sorry for him, for he was under very strict instructions from his president, John MacDonald, and his vice president, Ron Sumner, not to discuss the line of credit with the government members on the mission nor with the officers at the post. This was considered most peculiar by all of us, not least the officers at the post, and in particular, Reg Dorrett, our senior trade commissioner. EDC was, after all, a government agency. This was one of the biggest developments in the trade relationship with Indonesia. Reg and his officers would be working hard to ensure that the line of credit was drawn down as quickly as possible. Under John MacDonald, EDC was playing its cards very close to its chest. John favoured a greater separation of EDC from the government, whereas the trade people simply looked upon EDC as one of the tools for exporters, albeit a very important one.

I was caught in the middle of all of this. I was first and foremost a trade officer, but I was also an alternate director on the board of EDC, designated by Order In Council to represent Industry, Trade and Commerce when the deputy minister could not attend. In fact, I attended all the board meetings, even those the deputy minister attended. I had been bombarded by Mac-Donald and Sumner with the view that trade commissioners couldn't be trusted with financing information because they were so intent on seeing the deal concluded, they were not above leaking to the host country the fact that EDC often had room to reduce its rates or extend its terms, rather than see the negotiations collapse. If this did happen, it could result in considerable losses of funds for Canada.

I believe that this position of EDC was based on one isolated incident when something of the nature described did happen. Rather than having it out with the trade officer at fault, EDC chose to adopt a general policy of excluding our trade commissioners from any discussions not only of the rates and terms, but about how the credits might best be used in the interests of Canada and the host country. Indeed, in some instances, EDC went so far as to attempt to hide from the post that they were in the country meeting with officials about financing. This happened when I was head of post in Australia, and I reacted appropriately. This EDC activity really undermined the post in the eyes of local businessmen, bankers, and officials.

In Jakarta, EDC performed the inexcusable act of ordering Commercial Counsellor Reg Dorrett from the room in front of the Indonesian delegation before they got down to substantive negotiations. If EDC really felt it necessary that Reg not be present, there were ways of having him withdraw without causing embarrassment for Reg and for the Indonesians, who looked upon Reg as a very senior and influential officer at the embassy, which he certainly was. I am happy to say that under later presidents, Syl Cloutier and Bob Richardson, things were handled differently and certainly more cooperatively and diplomatically by the Export Development Corporation.

On our last day in Jakarta, the minister called on President Suharto at the Cendona Presidential Residence. The Indonesians restricted our number to three; the minister asked me to accompany him with Ambassador Peter Johnston. I felt a little badly about being there instead of Derek Burney, who I thought would benefit more and be able to make a better contribution to any political discussions. There was, however, little discussion of any substantive nature. (I reported this to Derek, jokingly suggesting that with no substance to the meeting, an External Affairs officer like himself would have been more at home there.) My only involvement was to be the bearer of a letter from Prime Minister Trudeau, which Minister Jamieson presented to the president.

I shall always remember the devilish look on Don Jamieson's face when Derek, Lindsay, and I were briefing him about Malaysia, just a few minutes before we landed at its capital, Kuala Lumpur. He looked my way

216

and said, "Enough of all the facts and figures; tell me, Frank, is this the old Malaya we used to read about in our Newfoundland geography books?"

I didn't know how to respond, because I couldn't recall what our Newfoundland geography books said about Malaya. I replied that geographically, Malaysia was indeed the old Malaya except for some additions on the island of Borneo and the loss of the island of Singapore. It was still part of the Commonwealth. The minister seemed to grab onto the Commonwealth bit and, indeed, next evening had his Malaysian and Canadian audience giving him standing ovations for his Churchill-like references to the Malaysian-Canadian relationship within the Commonwealth.

As usual, Lindsay MacNeil and I, with contributions from Derek Burney, drafted the minister's speech. He summoned Lindsay and me to his suite an hour or so before it was to be delivered. He was only half-dressed and in his undershorts when he opened the door. This didn't bother him, but poor Mrs. Jamieson was in her slip and in the midst of getting dressed for dinner. He poured drinks. We sat down. He started to read the draft. He didn't say a word. After reading the text he closed his eyes and sat back in his chair. We knew from experience that he was now drafting in his mind the speech he would deliver. After twenty minutes of silence, he politely dismissed us, thanking us for all our work, and retained our text.

At the dinner we saw the same routine; the waving of the text at the audience, a grateful nod to Lindsay and me for all the work we did in preparing it, and then the gentle tossing of the text in our direction. The audience loved it, especially our fellow bureaucrats. The stage was now set for the best possible reception for what we knew would be a wonderful speech. Wonderful it always was! It obviously included bits and pieces of what he had picked up from our draft. It reflected his conversations with us, with Derek, with the businessmen, with our chargé d'affaires, Ian Robertson, and with our trade commissioner, Mike Vujnovich. It undoubtedly also included contributions from the chambermaid and bellhop in the hotel (he used to be a bellhop in his youth in the Newfoundland Hotel).

At the end of his speech, amidst the standing ovation and cheering, he leaned over to me and, in a truly hyperactive state into which he had worked himself while speaking, said, "Frank, I want you to join me in my suite in fifteen minutes, and bring MacNeil." I knew that the next day was about to begin.

That evening in Malaysia, I arrived at the minister's suite ten minutes or so before Lindsay. Minister Jamieson poured us drinks and said to me in a relaxed but very serious way, "Frank, you and I have come a long way; I'm talking geographically." He went on, "If we were any further from Newfoundland, we would be on our way home again." He said something then that I had not heard since I was a child in Newfoundland. He said, "Frank, we have gone as far as ever the puffin flew!"

I told him that I had heard the expression before but was really unclear about what it meant. He explained that in the old days, around the Newfoundland coast, if someone was to journey to a distant bay, they would say that he had gone as far as ever the puffin flew, which in Newfoundland was, "the end of the world." He said, "Frank, we have gone to the end of the world."

Any meeting with Minister Jamieson was interrupted frequently by his stories. He could tell a story like he could make a speech. Many of them were laughs on himself that were particularly enjoyed in his native Newfoundland. He told about the time he sang at the old Nickel Theatre in St. John's. The Nickel was Newfoundland's first silent movie theatre, where the films were accompanied by live piano music. Before the program started, the management would invite well-known local singers to entertain the audience. Don Jamieson had a good voice and was always in great demand, singing songs called for from the floor. After the "Old Gray Mare" and "You Are My Sunshine," someone yelled, "Hey, Don, do you know your fly's open?" Don replied, "No, but if you hum it, I'll sing it!"

Friendship and good relations within the Commonwealth all aside, we got into some pretty tough discussions with the Malaysians. The talks were a microcosm of negotiations being held in Geneva, London, and elsewhere on all the major problems facing international trade. Since both countries had resource-based economies, we shared an interest in upgrading, and we attempted to get the Malaysians to view the current GATT Tokyo round of multilateral trade negotiations as the vehicle to achieve this objective. Malaysia, like most developing countries, was looking at GATT with diminished interest since the advent of the United Nations Conference on Trade and Development (UNCTAD), the forum where the developed, developing, and Communist countries faced one another in endless sessions, where in my biased view, everybody spoke but nobody listened.

The Malaysians raised a subject that they placed on every international agenda, that is, the treatment by developed countries of tropical products imported for the developing world. Malaysia had submitted a list of twenty products to the world community appealing for better import treatment. We had responded on only four. All we could give them at the time were the well-worn words, "The matter is still under review."

As partners in the Commonwealth, we had more positive things to say about tariff preferences. We made the point that although the United Kingdom had abrogated the trade agreements under which the Malaysians and others qualified for preferential tariff treatment in Canada, Canada continued to grant Commonwealth preferences to Malaysia. These preferences, we stressed, were better than the internationally accepted General Preference Scheme that had been extended to all developing countries. It was better, because items under restraint in Canada (textiles and footwear) still qualified for Commonwealth Preferences whereas they didn't qualify for the General Preference. (We didn't dwell on this point, since the "restraints" against textiles and footwear were imposed because the values were so low that tariffs had little impact on trade.)

Malaysia's major area of interest was international price stabilization for commodities. They relied very heavily on exports of rubber, tin, palm oil, and timber. We were involved with them in the international rubber and tin agreements, and we were able to inform them that as a consuming country we were considering a voluntary contribution to the tin agreement buffer stock. We hoped to encourage others to do the same and to push for greater international participation in buffer stock financing through the World Bank.

I cite these details of our discussions with the Malaysians not because they were of great importance, but as an indication of the range of issues a delegation had to deal with when undertaking an official visit to a foreign country. This was particularly so when you were with a senior minister, and Don Jamieson certainly was a senior minister.

The area around Kuala Lumpur was luxuriously tropical. You could expect to see Somerset Maugham or his characters behind every tree. Somerset Maugham might well have been out there for all we saw of the area outside Kuala Lumpur. The city itself, originally a small, tin-mining town, had grown into a cosmopolitan city of quiet charm. One had the pick of the food of the East, the best of Malaysian, Chinese, and Indian!

We did visit, while in Kuala Lumpur, a most impressive factory complex that I felt indicated the way of the future. There were a number of several-story buildings. Each floor was split into different "apartments" to accommodate, condominium style, small industry in individual production areas. The cost of infrastructure and common services was shared, in some

219

way proportional to the space occupied. I couldn't help compare this site to the often empty industrial parks that can be found on the outskirts of virtually every Canadian town or city. What we were shown may have been a model, which I doubt, but the cleanliness, efficiency and overall attractiveness of the complex impressed me. I believe that the proof of the worth of such centres has been demonstrated by the quality Malaysian high-technology products now on the shelves of the shops of the Western world.

In Singapore, we were told that a Canadian diplomat went to meet his son at the airport to find the youth without his passport. The Singapore immigration people had taken it, telling him he could have it back next day when he reported to a police station with his long hair cut to Singapore standards. In the city-state, men's hair was considered too long if it touched the eyebrows, the shirt collar, or if the ears were covered. Posters told you this as you went through immigration. The boy had no recourse but to visit the barber.

Our reporter for the *London Free Press,* Bill Heine, wrote, that the hair-cutting regulation was a reflection of Singapore's "almost paranoid preoccupation with the discipline of its young people." Bill wrote, "The state is determined not to let its young people degenerate to what Singapore's leaders consider to be decadent Western standards." They believe that "long hair leads to sloppy hair, to smoking, promiscuous sex, drugs . . . you name it." Singapore wants "no hippies on the island's 226 square miles at high tide, 229 at low tide."

In Singapore, we stayed at the magnificent Shangri La Hotel. It was my first visit to Singapore since Peggy and I, with our four children, came ashore five years previously en route from Europe to Australia. Then, Singapore still had many of the vestiges of the old colonial era. These now were largely gone. Before this visit my strongest impressions of Singapore were those imprinted on my mind by my readings of Somerset Maugham or from what I heard during my time in Australia from former prisoners of war who had suffered the Japanese atrocities in Singapore's infamous Changi Prison. Now I had to switch my mind from this very real, but fading, world of twenty years ago to the one outlined in the notes and facts prepared for us by our people in Ottawa and Singapore. I was sure that Don Jamieson's images of Singapore were as dated as my own. By the time we drove from the airport to the city centre and witnessed the great changes of recent years, old memories and impressions gave way to the new.

Singapore became a state of the Federation of Malaysia in 1963 but seceded in 1965. It was run by Prime Minister Le Kuan Yew. He had a lot in common with Malawi President Banda, with signs at customs and immigration such as "Males with Long Hair Will Be Attended To Last." Our High Commissioner Bob Thompson laid on a meeting for Minister Jamieson with Prime Minister Le Kuan Yew, the author and enforcer of all that went on in Singapore. This time Derek Burney accompanied the minister.

Before we left Singapore, we met with our Canadian bankers who were resident there. I joined them in trying to convince the minister that we should be doing something about trade representation in Taiwan. Other countries were getting around the Chinese insistence that there be no official contact with the Taiwan regime, but we avoided any confrontation with the Chinese. We did, of course, have a very big stake in the China grain market, which we wanted to safeguard, but we were losing out on opportunities in the growing Taiwanese market. The bankers actually offered to serve as the unofficial Canadian trade office in Taipei, but the minister wouldn't hear of it. I guess it was an idea ahead of its time.

We had only one full day in Bangkok, and we seemed to have spent most of it in traffic. Our Ambassador Bill Baur and our First Secretary Commercial John Hill, kept us on the move. We stayed at the Siam Intercontinental, and Lindsay MacNeil and I spent much of our stay in Bangkok in the hotel. The minister again was guest speaker at a government of Thailand luncheon, so we laboured through the night preparing the speech that we knew the minister wouldn't deliver. As usual he took parts of it and stuck these together with things he picked up from all and sundry and came up with a terrific speech that won him a long standing ovation.

Manila was for me more interesting. The Philippines was really familiar ground for Lindsay and me, but we were not prepared for the welcome mat that our embassy laid out for us. They even had a small band playing as we walked down the steps of the aircraft. Our Ambassador Irwin was always most supportive of everything we did, but I knew him well enough to realise that he hadn't arranged for the Philippine band. It had to be our Trade Commissioner Art Perron and his Assistant Commercial Secretary Margaret Huber.

Lindsay and I had met most of the ministers and senior officials who were to be involved in meetings with Minister Jamieson. We noted a little surprise on Minister Jamieson's face when the newly introduced Philippine ministers rushed from him to greet us like long lost friends. One who had always impressed me and whom I held in the highest regard was Cesar Virata, who was at the time minister (secretary) of Finance. Minister Jamieson signed a Convention for the Avoidance of Double Taxation with Minister Virata, whom I had met years before, when Frank Clark, a former trade commissioner, was ambassador in Manila.

On one of my visits, Frank had a dinner party with the technocrats who had recently been appointed to the Philippine Cabinet. President Marcos had seen the wisdom of these appointments, after suggestions by the United States, the World Bank, the International Monetary Fund, and others that it would be a good idea. Cesar's curriculum vitae was very modest, and he listed his hobby as "Golf, but no time to play."

We had several evenings together, and when, later, he visited Ottawa I showed him around. Cesar Virata was later to become prime minister; I was not surprised to see a report at the end of the tumultuous Marcos era that said simply that unlike the president, he "lived modestly and blamelessly and now is a trusted advisor in private practice."

The Manila Hotel, where we stayed, was haunted by the ghost of General Douglas MacArthur. It was famous because he had made his headquarters there, but I would rate it one of the best hotels in the world with or without General MacArthur's ghost. It had to have one of the best locations in Manila. By the time of our visit, the authorities had cleaned out most of the illegal casinos and had placed an official casino on a ship moored off the Manila Hotel's front entrance.

Lindsay and I talked Minister Jamieson into a few hours on the ship before official evening engagements. We took a launch to the ship, and while it was certainly not up to the standards of some of the illegal casinos that had been closed, it served us well for an hour or two. Indeed it was all our colleague Claudio Valle needed. He put the equivalent of ten cents into a slot machine, and it jammed, giving a two-to-one payoff each time he played. It would have taken him a few days to become a rich man, but he stuck to the machine for the time we were on the ship. There was a lineup of a dozen people behind him, waiting for him to abandon it. Later he did when the minister signaled that we had to go. Apparently, the casino authorities could not close down a machine, even if it was malfunctioning, until it ran out of money. We never did learn when it ran out. Duty had called us away from a sure winner.

A highlight of the visit was a call on President Ferdinand Marcos at the Presidential Palace. Unlike Cesar Virata's curriculum vitae, the Presi-

222

dent's filled three pages. He had been president since 1965. In 1954 he was chairman of the Philippine delegation to the Colombo Plan Conference in Ottawa. He had an active war record, having fought in Bataan and having been taken prisoner by the Japanese in 1942. He escaped to work with the guerrillas until the end of the war. He was in good form on the day we met with him. He and Minister Jamieson seemed to hit it off.

Suddenly, in the midst of our discussions, his wife Imelda rushed excitedly into the room with the news that oil had just been struck in Philippine waters. The president and his wife (who at the time was mayor of Manila) could hardly contain their enthusiasm. They were particularly struck with the coincidence that at the exact hour of our visit with the president, it was announced that Canadian oil exploration companies had played a role in the discovery.

Chapter Twenty-eight
Code Named OOPS

We had two important family happenings in the summer of 1976. One was a very happy one and the other our greatest family tragedy. In July of that year, our eldest daughter, Janine, was married to Peter Churchill-Smith. Janine and Peter went off to Britain and Europe on their honeymoon. In Britain they went to Oxford to see our son Chris, who was at the university for the summer. Janine and Peter were the last of the family to see Chris alive. He was a student at Queens in Kingston and was due to return from Oxford in early September. Being a keen bicyclist, he decided to take a bicycle tour of Holland before his return to Canada. On his second day in Holland (about which he wrote fondly), while crossing from one bicycle route to another through a village, he was hit by a car and killed.

Amongst Chris' cherished possessions was the actual maple leaf flag that Prime Minister Pearson had flown at his country residence at Harrington Lake when he decided that the new Canadian flag should be based on that design. The adopted flag underwent a few changes in the number of points on the leaves and the tone of red, but basically, the one Prime Minister Pearson flew was our first national flag. It was to have been destroyed together with the other competing designs, but I had retrieved it from the disposal bins of the Privy Council Office. Chris had "borrowed" it and placed it on his wall at Queens. I felt it would be fitting to have the flag placed in the archives of Queens. The university readily received it, and with a brief note I wrote on its history it now complements documentation on the new flag, including the J. R. Matheson papers. Mr. Matheson was parliamentary secretary to Prime Minister Pearson and took great interest in the choice of the maple leaf flag. Indeed he wrote a master's thesis on the subject.

I was at the time director general of the International Financing Branch of the Department of Industry, Trade and Commerce, working on financing for Canadian exporters. This brought me into working relationships with domestic financing entities, such as the Canadian banks, the Export Development Corporation (EDC), and the Canadian International Development Agency (CIDA). I was on the board of EDC as an alternate director over the years to Deputy Ministers Gerry Stoner, Mickey Cohen, and Gordon Osbaldstein.

My work also brought me into regular contact with the international financial institutions, such as the World Bank and the regional development banks. Our purpose was to ensure that the policies of institutions, domestic and foreign, were not contrary to Canada's export interests. We wanted to be sure that opportunities were open for Canadian exporters to use financing from all of these sources. We worked closely with our exporters as well as the institutions. We helped exporters obtain, not only export financing, but the political and diplomatic support needed to win contracts against international competitors.

I was very pleased to see the International Financing Branch, whose mandate was almost entirely financial policy, evolve into a trade development unit. Barry Steers, who was our assistant deputy minister at the time, played a major role in this evolution. We very quickly became, to the amusement of everyone in the trade field in Ottawa and in our posts abroad, OOPS (Office of Overseas Projects). The heading-up of this group was certainly one of the most satisfying periods of my years in government. The proof of its need was that our offices were flooded daily with visiting exporters, while in some of the other parts of the department, the cry was, "Where have all the exporters gone?"

The change was fully supported by the senior management of the department, including the Deputy Minister Mickey Cohen and the Associate Deputy Minister Bill Teschke. It went without saying that the assistant deputy ministers of Trade, Barry Steers and Claude Charland, supported what we were doing because they, and Barry in particular, were the instigators.

I had the task of melding several overlapping branches into one group. I was shocked by the inflexibility of the system. I found that it was virtually impossible to introduce cost savings and efficiencies into a government department without destroying your own position. I had at the outset over one hundred officers and a support staff to fit into my new organisation. With the assistance of our senior staff, Gordon Keyes, George Eeles, Mike MacDonald, and Ed Gorn, were able to work out an organisation plan and

225

advise the deputy minister within a few days that we were able to do without some forty people.

The bureaucracy couldn't handle this. The only way we could reduce our number was through attrition or postings or by giving bodies and positions to other parts of the department. When, after three years, we had reduced our number by forty, I was informed by the civil service commission that my own position commanded less pay because I was responsible for fewer people and consequently a smaller budget. I went screaming to the deputy minister, telling him what he already knew. A civil servant was rewarded for empire building and not for reducing costs and introducing efficiencies. Mickey Cohen saw to it that I didn't suffer for doing what he agreed was the right thing!

The Office of Overseas Projects, or OOPS, was in my judgement, one of the more successful units in the trade field in Ottawa. Without diminishing in any way the role played by the private sector, the Office was sometimes able to bring to bear for the exporter, all of the political, diplomatic, and financial elements necessary to win projects overseas. There were a number of government programs, such as the Program for Export Market Development (PEMD), which were very helpful for exporters. I chaired the PEMD committee dealing with support for bidding overseas. When a company or group was accorded PEMD support of an overseas project, the entire government apparatus swung behind them in Ottawa and in our posts abroad.

We were thus sometimes able to beat the Japanese in their "high-low" game, in which they would often have two groups bid, one priced high and the other priced low. If there was no competition below the Japanese higher bid, the Japanese lower bidder would withdraw. If there was non-Japanese competition between the two Japanese bids, the lower Japanese bidder would be awarded the contract and would then work on negotiating higher prices. If this failed, they would have the Japanese group with the higher losing bid "subsidise" the lower bidding group. There were all types of games being played, not only by the Japanese, but by countries, like France, that were expert at mixing commercial and aid financing to achieve the lowest possible bid. We had to be similarly organised to compete.

I found most helpful the information gathered by our intelligence people. This at times enabled us to obtain details on the competitive positions of a number of overseas competitors. A man with a locked suitcase would drop into my office and behind closed doors would present to me material gathered by "unorthodox" means. On one occasion, I had the text of a telephone conversation between a Latin American head of state and his girlfriend that was most interesting but of little commercial use. On another occasion, I read a report that a foreign diplomat had written about an interview he had with me a few days earlier. He had it terribly mixed up, and I was able to call him in again, and without divulging to him that he had misunderstood me, set him straight. Perhaps the most dramatic example of the intelligence that came our way was when our Export Development Corporation was so protective of the details of their loans to Indonesia that they kept the information from all but their own inner circle. I was able to place on the deputy minister's desk the details of the EDC financing agreements that had been purchased on the streets of Jakarta for ten dollars!

Through such a concentrated and coordinated approach, we were able to claim success on many overseas projects amounting to many hundreds of millions of dollars, which I am convinced would not otherwise have come to Canada. Our overseas competitors were always the Japanese and the French, and often the Germans and the British. They were rarely the Americans, whom our exporters generally considered noncompetitive for a number of reasons. Their export financing was often good, although unlike our EDC their Eximbank had many political constraints imposed on them. Eximbank could not finance exports to the Soviet Union. Consequently much of the business for North American type mining equipment and the like for that market came to Canada.

I have been told by many American businessmen that they did not receive the political and diplomatic support that our exporters took for granted. Indeed, I have heard of cases where American exporters had approached our Trade commissioners abroad, saying that they were representing the Canadian branches of their companies to get assistance that was not forthcoming from their own embassies or trade representatives. Another major problem facing American competitiveness was the need for exporters to add to their prices high contingencies to cover the eventuality of being sued. They were preoccupied with catastrophic loss brought on by the failure of their own or a partner's equipment. Companies joining to pursue overseas project work had to carry heavy, expensive insurance coverage that often put them out of the running on foreign projects.

We were in daily contact by cable with most of our posts abroad, and while both sides talked the same language, I do remember an exception, when we had an amusing exchange with our post in Saudi Arabia. David

McCracken, our senior trade man in Saudi, sent us a cable asking for details on a "turkey" project one of our exporters was pursuing in his area. We signalled back, asking whether he meant "turnkey" project. He responded, "No, I mean turkey/gobble-gobble/turkey project." There was no further reason for confusion.

The officers of OOPS had a close and, I believe, mutually beneficial relationship with Canada's international aid agency, CIDA. Through participation in commercially viable activities in the developing world that were being pursued by experienced Canadian exporters, CIDA was able to assist developing countries with infrastructure, the purchase of competitive equipment, and the construction of export oriented plants. By using even a small amount of concessional financing, we were often able to establish an overall competitive rate of interest for Canadian financing that was essential when competing with the Japanese and French.

I continually impressed upon our officers and exporters that we must not look upon CIDA as a crutch for noncompetitive exports. Certainly there were Canadian exporters who could not sell abroad without CIDA, and these were generally well known to us. Maggie Catley-Carlson, then president of CIDA (and in my view the best of their presidents) and her very able deputy, Geoff Bruce, discussed with me regularly the need to exclude from aid financing, companies that were not competitive.

We worked with companies that were internationally competitive; they were already competing in overseas markets. We would go to CIDA with them to ensure that Canadian aid funds, when available, would be used to help finance competitive Canadian goods and services. Again we would only do this if economic development plans in the developing country called for such equipment or services and if foreign exchange funding was required for such purchases. There was unbelievable competition amongst aid donors for good projects, so we sought to work with CIDA in a constructive way to help ensure that Canadian aid was best used.

Chapter Twenty-nine
The Land of the Lake

In November 1976, CIDA's West Africa office asked me to accompany them on a small mission to Malawi and Zambia. The mission was led by Nick Hare, the director. The purpose of the visit was to inspect a railway construction project that CIDA was financing in Malawi, complete with locomotives and rolling stock. We were also to examine the possibility of a very large order for road graders and mining equipment in Zambia. In the company of CIDA officials, because they held the "aid bag," I knew that I could have access to the very top political levels in these countries, so I gladly went along.

An overnight flight across the Atlantic is not my idea of enjoyable travel. I did, however, enjoy the trip because my seat companion was a long-time friend and colleague, Ken Taylor, who was on his way to London. Ken was later to make headlines and many American friends for Canada. While he was Canadian ambassador to Iran, he sheltered at great risk, American embassy personnel who had eluded the Iranian mobs who had stormed and ransacked the American embassy in Tehran. Most of the staff was taken hostage. I was to visit Ken in Tehran just months before the fall of the shah and the slide of Iran into chaos.

Malawi was, by African standards, a small country but one of Africa's most beautiful. Contributing greatly to this beauty was Lake Malawi, which stretched some three hundred and sixty miles, almost the full length of the country. It was nestled amongst the majestic mountains and rolling hills of the Great Rift Valley. The fifty-mile-wide lake was the heart of Malawi. Around the end of the eighteenth century, Arabs came to Malawi from the coast to establish depots for the slave trade that was eventually to devastate large tracts of East Africa. Later, in 1859, the famous missionary-explorer David Livingstone arrived, spearheading British influence that was to leave its mark religiously, administratively, and linguistically on much of south-east Africa. Livingstone called the country Nyasaland ("land of the lake").

He named the capital Blantyre, after his birthplace in Scotland. After independence in 1964, the country's name was changed to Malawi, meaning, "reflected light of blue haze," an apt description for a country the size of Newfoundland, of which a quarter is covered by the magnificent Lake Malawi.

We arrived in Blantyre, which impressed me as the cleanest city I had seen in Africa. The country's Life President, Dr. Banda, might justly be criticised for running the country as would a schoolmaster and for his authoritarian ways, but one had to respect him for the importance he placed on such tried and true values as cleanliness and law and order. This may seem a minor positive compared with the many negatives levelled against him locally and internationally. He has been accused of complete intolerance of any opposition to his policies, and stories abounded about human rights abuses.

Malawi was the only country in Africa where someone tried the "Singapore approach" of ensuring that people behaved publicly in a well-defined way. Critics would point to the often-ridiculed notices in public places and in hotel rooms regarding strictly enforced regulations applying to residents and visitors alike. Dr. Banda insisted that ladies not wear slacks except at game parks and at beach resorts. They were required to wear dresses or skirts that completely covered the knee. Dr. Banda was no easier on the men. "Gentlemen" were not to wear trousers of the bell-bottom variety; nor were they to have long hair (defined as hair in bulk falling to the collar).

The life president was generally viewed as a homburg-hatted disciplinarian who was an African Victorian. His government actually barred the Simon and Garfunkel song "Cecilia" as offensive to Cecilia Tamanda Kadzamira, who was the "official hostess" of the bachelor life president. Besides being head of state, he was minister of almost everything. He was also the rector of the national university, and his face stared from coins and banknotes, from office walls and from the backs and fronts of the dresses on many ladies. However, most of his critics would concede that in spite of all the criticisms towards Dr. Banda, Malawi, as a country, compared well with some of her postcolonial African contemporaries. Malawi was peaceful, tidy, hard-working, with little crime or tribal warfare.

Our host in Malawi, John Tembo, was at the time governor of the Central Bank. He was the alter ego of Dr. Banda and second only to the president in authority. I got to know him quite well on this visit and during the next few years during his visits to Ottawa. He impressed me as a very well informed, hardworking man who had the best interests of his country at heart. Tembo was so closely allied to Dr. Banda that the life president's critics included him in their condemnations.

Tembo took several days from his busy schedule to conduct us on a tour of the railway that was being constructed with the help of Canadian aid funds. On the completed portions we travelled by a train made up of one engine and a lone railway car. Where the track hadn't been laid, we made our way by jeeps. I very much enjoyed this trip that took us far into the countryside, allowing us to see it before it was opened up by the railway. We were able to see villages and speak to villagers far off the beaten track. I was not only impressed with the trip but with the overall Canadian project and the positive impact it was having on the country.

This was in direct contrast with the railway project that the Chinese had undertaken in neighbouring Tanzania. The Chinese had moved in by the thousands to build the Tanzanians a railway. (It was said that the Chinese workers had set up house in the containers in which they had shipped the equipment and railway rolling stock.) There was little in the Tanzanian project for the locals other than to have a new railway; there was a minimum of contact between the giver and receiver. In Malawi, the Canadians built the first bridge with the Malawians looking on; the second bridge was built by Malawian engineers with the Canadians assisting; and the third and subsequent bridges were built by the Malawians alone, with a few Canadian advisers standing by if needed. When we arrived, you could count the Canadian personnel on your fingers. It was basically a Malawi project.

One French Canadian working on the railway project, who was older than the rest, ran the equipment repair and maintenance depot. He told me that all the work at the depot was done by Malawians whom he personally had trained on the job. The people who had left his service had returned to their villages and set up garages or small motor repair shops, thus ensuring that the Canadian aid would have a lasting impact on the Malawi economy.

At the end of the railway line, at Salima, one of Malawi's lake holiday centres, we stopped for a night. I was fascinated with the beauty of the lake. The weather was very hot, and the waters were inviting. It was claimed by all that this lake was completely free from bilharzia, which is a disease transmitted by a worm from water to the blood and bladder. It is common in a number of African countries. It finds its way into lakes and rivers and can be picked up from these waters by swimmers. This dreaded scourge kept me out of all African waters, so I was not tempted into the clear inviting lake.

Here, however, my mind was fixed, not so much on bilharzia, but on the hippopotamuses, which seemed to be all too common. A few days before our arrival, a swimmer had met his death when attacked by a hippopotamus. It was true that the careless swimmer had entered the water that was the animal's place of refuge. However, when walking along the beach, I saw several hippos going through their rituals in the water. Just to see the size of them was enough to confirm me in my decision not to enter "their" lake.

All along the railway construction site, I made it my business to crawl through the spare-parts sheds. I mean "crawl," because to see all, you had to make your way along the shelves with a flashlight. I was troubled to learn that although the locomotives, tracks, road graders, and earth moving equipment originated in Canada, most of the spare parts were not Canadian. Manufacturers often find the after-market as important as the sale of the initial equipment, so I was disappointed to learn that the spares and parts were often from Britain, France, or the United States. In the developing world, the difficulty for Canadian exporters to maintain depots for spares favoured the well-established former colonial powers, such as the British and the French, who had long-standing commercial relationships and followed up initial sales with spares and fast service.

At the end of our visit to Malawi, Governor John Tembo had us to luncheon at his home in Blantyre. I discussed with him the range of aid issues and found his views refreshing after years of listening to the official lines of the developing countries at international meetings in Geneva, New York, and Paris.

On the very touchy question of the untying of bilateral aid, that is, allowing other developed countries, such as Japan and France, to compete with Canadian suppliers for Canadian aid funds, he felt that this was unreasonable to request. He held that if Canada was giving aid to purchase Canadian equipment and services in areas where Canada was internationally competitive, then it was reasonable that Canadian taxpayers should see the bulk of their funds spent at home. If Canadian funds could be used to purchase products produced locally, then they should be so used. However, many "local" products were often foreign goods warehoused locally with little or no developing country content. Perhaps he knew he was talking with someone who was of this belief, but I found his views realistic and "music to my ears."

After five days in Malawi, we spent two in Zambia. My interests were focused on road-building equipment and machinery for the mining sector. We knew that the Zambians needed about one hundred road graders and were being offered them under aid financing by several countries. The wealthy mining sector, which was for the most part in private hands and outside the Zambian economy, also needed machinery and equipment, but the depressed nature of the world market for copper meant cash sales to these people were unlikely. All we could hope for was to position ourselves for sales later; Canada was not among the countries they would normally look to, so I made calls on several companies to make them aware of Canada as an eventual source for a lot of their equipment needs when world market conditions changed.

As for road graders, the Zambians were playing several would-be donors off one against the other. CIDA had the funding, and I felt if the Zambians were to have road graders, they should be Canadian. The CIDA funding would not only benefit Zambia but would make a major impact on Goderich, Ontario, where they were produced and sold to over sixty countries around the world. I felt that such an internationally competitive company would be a good candidate for the CIDA funds. Through the good offices of my CIDA colleagues, we were able to meet with Zambia's prime minister and persuade him to have his people buy Canadian.

Chapter Thirty
Troubleshooting

Our work in the Office of Overseas Projects (OOPS) put us at the beck and call of Canadian exporters doing project work abroad. We were required to make frequent visits with companies to project sites and to country capitals in all corners of the world. We would meet with senior officials of the countries for whom the work was being done and with the institutions that were financing the work, such as the World Bank, the regional development banks, and the Arab Funds that were available to countries with Muslim populations. We also called on the engineering firms and contractors on the job. Many of the projects were in the hundreds of millions of dollars and could involve goods and services from many Canadian subsuppliers. A serious request to accompany exporters demanded a serious response. Consequently we had officers continually in the air. In 1977, for example, I was required to join firms in Islamabad, Pakistan; Bandoung, Indonesia; Damascus, Syria; Bangkok, Thailand; and Manila, Philippines.

In August of that year, one of my colleagues, Mike MacDonald, and I were asked to fly to Islamabad. One of our large companies had bid on some tens of millions of dollars' worth of equipment for a major power development. Mike was a most valuable officer on such a trip, for he had a deep knowledge of international financing and we would be meeting with the World Bank and the Asia Development Bank.

Inexplicably, when the company had put together its bid, the freight costs from Canada to Pakistan were quoted at the high level that a freight forwarder would ask of someone seeking freight costs for a small shipment. The huge quantities that our company was to ship would have demanded considerable discounts. The Canadian bid was higher than a Japanese bid by roughly the amount of the error made on the freight estimates.

Mike and I had a tight schedule, for we had to meet the responsible Pakistani deputy minster who was leaving Pakistan for an extended trip abroad the day after our scheduled arrival in Islamabad. We flew to Paris and connected within the hour with a flight to Karachi. I had never seen such bedlam as greeted us at Karachi airport, with the result that we missed our connecting flight to Islamabad. When we arrived in Islamabad, we were exhausted, having travelled for more than twenty hours. It was early morning, and our appointment with the deputy minister was in a few hours. In the meantime we had to meet with our embassy staff.

At the appointment, we could hardly keep our eyes open. I apologised to the deputy minister for our exhausted state, and he completely understood, since he was himself leaving next day for Europe. He was also very sympathetic to our problem regarding the incorrect freight rates in the Canadian bid and arranged for us to meet with local World Bank officials and the responsible Pakistani authorities. Then it happened. In the middle of our conversation I nodded off. It must have only been for a few seconds, but when I opened my eyes, the deputy minister and Mike were smiling at me. I had no idea whether I had been asleep for a second, a minute, or an hour. I was very embarrassed, but the deputy minister just made a joke of it. It had only been a few seconds.

Pakistan's capital was really two cities. There was the new emerging city of Islamabad that stood on the Potwar plateau between Rawalpindi and the foothills that stretch northward towards the Hindu Kush. Here were the brand new embassies, diplomatic residences, and government buildings. A little to the south was the city of Rawalpindi, which was, in contrast with the unfinished new capital, an old city full of life and interest. We stayed in Rawalpindi and commuted to Islamabad. Our embassy and the ambassador's residence were in the new city.

Our ambassador was absent, so the staff arranged for me to use the residence to host a small dinner for the Pakistani ministers and senior officials who were involved in the power project. Clearly the Pakistanis were all on our side, mainly because earlier phases of the power project had been done by Canada with Canadian equipment under our aid program. They generally felt that the next phase that had a lot of international financing should also go to Canada, so that the equipment for the entire project would be from a single source. After our visit to the World Bank office, it seemed that almost everybody was ready to do everything necessary to see that the project went to Canada. I say "almost" everybody, because the only group that wouldn't cooperate with us was the project engineering firm that had drawn up the call for tender. What hurt us was that the engineering group was Canadian.

The Canadian engineers first refused to see us. Only after persistent pressure would they allow us inside their doors and grant us a hearing. It was a one-way conversation. They didn't say a word until I said in exasperation that it was the most unfriendly meeting I had ever had with a group of fellow Canadians. Their response was that they hadn't asked for the meeting and that they would treat us no differently than they would treat the Japanese. I was shocked. I can understand the need for project engineers to be absolutely fair-handed and neutral, but I couldn't believe that we were being treated no different than if we were Japanese. I have worked closely with dozens of engineering firms (and on retirement, served on the board of directors of one) and have always considered them the best in the world, but I felt that the unfriendly attitude of this group was abnormal. I reported on the incident to the Canadian head office of the group that we worked with around the world. They couldn't believe the extreme unfriendly behaviour of their staff in the field.

From Pakistan, Mike and I flew to Manila, where we had meetings with the Asia Development Bank, which had money in the Pakistan power project. We were well received and, after a one-night stay, flew to Hawaii, where we collapsed for a night before continuing on to Ottawa. From Ottawa to Ottawa, with only three stops where we stayed overnight, the round-the-world trip had taken us eight days. I guess it was worth it, because Canada got at least a portion of the project.

That October we were asked by a western Canadian group to help them in their efforts to win a pipeline contract in Syria. Syria was not on the friendliest terms with Canada or any other Western nation. However, despite the unfriendly relationships, some of our Western friends had very lucrative trade relationships with the Syrians.

We had no embassy in Syria. Our ambassador responsible for that country normally resided in Beirut, Lebanon, but because of the civil war, he was no longer in residence. Our trade commissioner responsible for Syria and Lebanon resided in Cairo. I was beginning to wonder, when I arrived in Beirut, which was the jumping-off point for Syria, what I was doing there, given the withdrawal of all our Canadian embassy personnel. Our Trade man from Cairo, Dean Browne, whom I had known for many years as a good, competent trade officer, joined me as did another trade commissioner, Marc Pelletier. One of my officers, Jack Mcleod, who was an expert on oil and gas projects, accompanied me from Ottawa.

None of the beautiful hotels that had welcomed me when I had last been in Beirut was standing. The destructive civil war had destroyed all. The hotel we stayed in was certainly not one to be recommended. It was a temporary building swarming with journalists and United Nations personnel monitoring the civil war. We made the mistake of following some of the English-speaking journalists we had been chatting with into the hotel bar. It was a long room in which the bar itself ran the full length and took up about a third of the place. The journalists deserted us to join some of their colleagues at tables.

There were no tables available for us, so Dean, Jack, Marc, and I strung ourselves out on seats along the bar and ordered a beer. On either side of us, several young Arabs settled. They had come in off the street. One of them asked whether we were Canadians. This was not surprising, since we were all wearing Maple Leaf pins or other ensignia that identified us as Canadians, for we worried about being mistaken for Americans, who were most unpopular at the time. We proudly acknowledged that we were Canadians, and one of the Arabs shouted, "We detest Canadians!"

With great indignation, I asked, "Why?" The Arab began to quote word for word a speech that he claimed Prime Minister Trudeau had made. He said it was anti-Palestinian and pro-Israeli.

One of our number started to argue with him. The bartender, who was British, leaned over to me and whispered, "Get your boys out of here, mate; these guys are really looking for trouble, and they are armed!"

I gulped my beer and grabbed my colleagues and pushed them out into the street. Our not-too-friendly neighbours on the bar stools were close behind us. I explained the situation to my friends, and we quickly retreated to the front entrance of the hotel.

I couldn't get out of Beirut fast enough, but next day we had to visit the Canadian business group involved in Syria and get a briefing about the latest developments for their project in Syria. I found it a little peculiar that senior representatives of the Canadian company did not wish to accompany us to Syria. They felt that we would make more of an impression on the Syrian authorities if they were not present. It wasn't money that prevented them from accompanying us, because they were quite willing to cover our expenses.

In order to visit with the Canadian company representatives, we were required to travel by taxi from the eastern area of Beirut across the line that separated the Muslim and Christian areas of the city. I felt safe enough on our way from the hotel, because we travelled during daylight hours. Even then I was a little unsettled when the taxi ground to a halt at the "line" and the driver announced that this was as far as he would go. We had to walk across the street that marked the boundary between the two warring factions and pick up another taxi on the other side. I must say that I felt, in spite of the lull in the fighting, that every gun-sight in Beirut was focused on us as we crossed that street.

Returning after our meetings was even more disconcerting, because we had to cross the line after dark. Again we had to pay off the taxi before we crossed. As we entered a taxi on the Muslim side, soldiers surrounded the car, and with guns in the windows demanded identification. It was, to say the least, disconcerting to see a seventeen-year-old pointing a gun at you and realising that he probably had insufficient education or experience to tell if you were friend or foe, or worse, that he probably didn't care. On the way back to the hotel, the taxi driver insisted that the inside lights of the car be left on and that our windows remain open. We were stopped at several check points, usually manned by Syrian soldiers, who looked just as young and unconcerned for our welfare as were the local militias.

Dean Browne had been our trade commissioner, resident in Beirut sometime before, and had been taken from his car by militiamen. He was driven to a sandpit, where he was certain he was to be executed. He had some knowledge of Arabic and recognised, by their dialect, that the thugs who had kidnapped him were from his area of Beirut. He was able to convince them that they were supposed to be protecting people like himself who were from their area of the city. They let him go.

The ambassador's chauffeur arrived at the hotel with the car to drive us to Damascus. I found it a little disconcerting when I saw him put a revolver in the glove compartment as we stored our luggage for the trip. I couldn't help compare the revolver to the automatic weapons that every thug in Beirut seemed to flash around.

We called at the Canadian embassy on our way out of the city. It was deserted except for a guard. The parking garage below the building said it all. Canadian-owned cars and those of other tenants were shells, having been stripped of their wheels, motors, and any other movable part. Dean showed us around the Chancery, pointing out where he and others had been held at gunpoint, with their hands against the wall for many hours, by a disgruntled Lebanese immigrant who was having difficulty returning to Canada. I'm not clear about the case, but Dean was still furious at the thought that the individual concerned was now a landed immigrant in Montreal. Dean felt that if the villain was in Canada, he should be in a top security prison, in view of the misery he had caused in the embassy.

The drive to the Syrian border was uneventful. We didn't stop until we were well out of Beirut and up the Lebanon mountain range that ran along the Mediterranean Sea. We had coffee in a terrace garden with a magnificent view of the coastal area that looked to be perfectly peaceful. Over the mountains to the east was the Bekaa Valley, a very fertile ten-mile-wide valley across which was the Anti-Lebanon mountain range that formed the boundary between Lebanon and Syria. We had a bit of a wait at the border, where the crossing traffic seemed to be predominately large transport trucks, each as bad as the next at filling the air with black poisonous diesel fumes.

Damascus was on a terrace seven hundred metres above sea level. Its position on the edge of the desert and on the only easy route through the Anti-Lebanon mountains down to the Mediterranean Sea made it a trade centre for many centuries. It had been conquered by the Babylonians, Persians, Greeks, and Romans. Roman temples, Byzantine churches, and Muslim mosques were built one on the other. Still preserved was the chapel commemorating the conversion of Paul of Tarsus (Saint Paul). It stood near the east entrance of the street called "Straight," mentioned in the Bible.

We stayed at the very French Meridian Hotel. Much to the surprise of everyone in the hotel, we were associated with a hijacking. A plane had been hijacked over India, and the poor souls aboard had been jockeyed throughout the Far and Near East for several days. Eventually, in a desperate attempt to refuel, they approached Damascus. It happened on the night of our arrival, and it was in our hotel that the passengers were being received. The authorities had surrounded the plane and categorically stated that the plane would never take off, so they had best surrender. The hijackers agreed. When the released passengers arrived, the hotel was an armed camp, in case some of the hijackers were passing themselves off as passengers. I have never seen such a sorry group of individuals as those that came off that plane. They were relieved, yet it was obvious they had gone through a terrifying experience. Within an hour, they were interviewed and sent to bed.

Our days in Damascus were involved in eternal meetings with Syrian minsters and officials. We certainly were given access to everybody in a position to make a decision. We met senior people in the ministries of Foreign Affairs, Finance, and Planning. We also met with representatives

239

of the United Nations. Our final appointment, which was one we hadn't counted on, was with the deputy prime minister for foreign affairs, Jamil Shaya.

Given that the political relationship between Canada and Syria was not good, the reception we received was better than we could have expected. We felt that because of our efforts and our presence in Damascus, there would be no automatic exclusion of Canada as a contender for the project. The Canadian group were successful in winning contracts in Syria, but I shall always remain of the view that the company should have been with us on all of our calls. I was determined never again to call on a foreign government on a specific project without the presence of senior officers of the Canadian company concerned.

My most memorable hour in Damascus was my visit to the souk (bazaar). The Damascus souk is one of the best in the world. It stretched for what seemed to be miles. I was not ready for the riot that suddenly stormed through the souk. While trying to match wits with the best of traders in this wide, indoor, crowded street, it was disconcerting, to say the least, suddenly to hear a noise as that of an oncoming express train. It was a political mob rushing down the souk, carrying or trampling everything in its path.

As the noise got close, the shoppers got more and more worried, realising that the mob was going to steamroller through. The shopkeepers quickly secured their shutters and doors. I jumped through a doorway just before it was bolted as the mob raced past. It didn't appear to be an unfriendly crowd, but the sheer weight of numbers was enough to put the greatest fear into anyone. Reports in the papers next day were that several people were trampled and killed.

On our way back to Beirut, we stopped on the Lebanese side of the border, at the small town of Baalbek. The town had been inhabited since the Stone Age. It was the location of the Roman Temple of Jupiter that was said in Baalbek to be the largest Roman temple in the world. The Phoenicians occupied the area about 3000 B.C. They built a temple dedicated to Baal Bucas, their sun god, and thus the name of the town, Baalbek. Traces of one of their temples could be seen in the centre of the Temple of Jupiter. The Greeks built a temple on top of the Phoenician temple, dedicated to Zeus, their greatest god; the walls of this temple could also be seen. All the temples on this location were virtually destroyed by an earthquake in 552 A.D.

During 1978 and 1979, I visited, in the company of exporters, such diverse markets as Trinidad and Tobago, Brazil, Iran, Hong Kong, the Philippines, New Zealand, Australia, Argentina, and the Soviet Union. We pursued an airport project on the very beautiful island of Tobago. Tobago was reputed to be the site of Daniel Defoe's Robinson Crusoe's shipwreck and life on the tropical island that captured the imagination of every schoolboy in the English-speaking world, at least in my generation.

George Eeles and Mike MacDonald pursued this project, although they did involve me in a visit to the Trinidad and Tobago government people in Port of Spain and with the airport authorities in Tobago.

The Hong Kong project, a vessel traffic management system, eluded us for several years.

We eventually got the Canadian Commercial Corporation involved as the Canadian contractor, and they won the contract for Canada. The Canadian Commercial Corporation was a Crown corporation established by the government of Canada to serve as an international trade facilitator and prime contractor for the sale of Canadian goods and services to foreign governments and international agencies. (I was to be a member of the corporation's board of directors for many years after my retirement from government.)

Chapter Thirty-one
The Ebb and Flow of Governments

Jack Horner was a very controversial figure. He used to laugh at a report that said he was so narrow-minded that he could look down a whisky bottle with both eyes at the same time. What really made him a national figure was his switch from the Conservative party to the Liberals who were for much of his career the butt of his fire and fume. Few people love a deserter, although in politics it is not unknown, and often a few years can erase the public's memory of the defection. Not so for Jack Horner; his western constituency pronounced on him twice after he defected from the Tories and ended his political career.

Many in the government shared the public's criticisms about Jack Horner. Former Prime Minister Diefenbaker said it best, "The sheriff has joined the rustlers." However, it was not for us as public servants to question such a move; we were to give full support to all members of the government in power, including now Jack Horner. He was appointed minister without portfolio, responsible for Alberta, where the Liberals had been desperate for representation. Months later in a Cabinet shuffle caused by Donald Macdonald's departure, Jack Horner was appointed minister of Industry, Trade and Commerce.

I enjoyed working with Minister Horner. He was friendly, down to earth, and put on no airs. He was aware of his lack of background and expertise on many international issues and was always receptive to a briefing. I went with him on a mission to Southeast Asia as I had done several times before with other ministers. He performed well, but he did have trouble with names. I advised him to call ministers with unpronounce-able names, "Excellency," which they all liked. He was at home in the Philippines, where fellow ministers often responded positively when he invited them to call him "Jack." The Philippine trade minister was known to him as "Teddy." It wasn't only the Asian names he had trouble with. One of our officers on the mission was Bill Laskaras; Minister Horner could never get his tongue around his name, so he always called him "Mr. Bill."

My best memory of Jack Horner was when in 1983, he was out of government and chairman of the Canadian National Railways, which was a political plum given to him by a grateful Liberal government for his defection from the Tories. I was at the time Canadian consul general in Sydney, Australia. Out of the blue, I received a call in my office, and a voice said, "Frank, this is Jack Horner." I asked, "Canada's Jack Horner?" He laughed and acknowledged that it was indeed.

He said he was in Australia looking at the railway system and that his wife was looking up a few old "pen pals." It was just before lunchtime, so I asked whether he and his wife could join Peggy and me for lunch. I phoned Peggy, and realising that it was too late to put on a luncheon at the residence, I asked her to make a reservation at the Royal Sydney Golf Club, where we had an honorary membership. When my driver pulled up in front of the Sydney Hilton, where the Horners were staying, he said to me, "Mr. Petrie, I don't think, sir, that you will be going to the Royal Sydney." I glanced towards the hotel, and there was this tall, former Canadian minister in white shorts with black ankle socks. Clearly we would not be admitted to the Royal Sydney, whose dress code would not even allow Jack Horner on the grounds, let alone into the dining room.

We drove to the residence, and while Peggy showed the Horners around the garden, I phoned and cancelled the Royal Sydney and made reservations at Doyle's, which was the largest fish restaurant in Sydney. The owner, Peter Doyle, was a friend of ours, so I asked him to "lay it on." He did, and we had one of the best luncheons we had while in Sydney. The Horners were great company and we talked for hours about every issue and personality in Canadian political life. I was glad that Jack Horner had worn his black ankle socks.

I have two recollections of the trip around the Pacific with Minister Horner, and neither involved the minister. Both recollections concerned events in Hong Kong at the end of the Southeast Asian mission. The minister was going into China, but I wasn't going with him. I was to head for Australia and New Zealand. On our last night, we had a dinner at our Canadian commissioner's residence. He was a colleague, Bill Warden. Bill's teenaged son and my daughter Jennifer had been counsellors at a church summer camp at Gracefield, Quebec. Jennifer had a "pet" stuffed snake she called Snaky.

Unknown to Jennifer, Bill's son "borrowed" Snaky and took him on their posting to Hong Kong. Shortly after their arrival in Hong Kong, Bill's son had taken a picture of Snaky curled up on the stern of the Star Ferry, with a magnificent view of Hong Kong harbour in the background. There could be no doubt that Snaky was in Hong Kong. The boy sent the picture to Jennifer with a note made up of print from newspapers saying something about her never seeing Snaky again.

While I was at the dinner party at Bill's, his son gave me the stuffed snake and suggested I take it to Australia with me and send a similar note to Jennifer. I did. In Sydney, I had some of her cousins dress in sinister-looking coats and hats and had their picture taken holding Snaky and a copy of the newspaper, *The Australian.* They sent it to Jennifer. Snaky sure got around. I took it back to Jennifer on my return to Canada.

The other incident happened when I left Bill Warden's residence and returned to the hotel. At the desk I asked the clerk for my key, giving him my name and room number. I ascended the twenty floors or so to "my" room. When I unlocked the door and entered, I was shocked to see a man in "my" bed. When he gathered his senses he was doubly shocked to see a stranger in "his" room. He was a Frenchman and addressed me in French, asking what I was doing bursting into his room. I answered in belligerent French, saying that the room was mine, and to prove it, I held up the key.

He gathered enough of his senses to say, "Look at the clothes in the closet to your left." I opened the door and saw immediately that the clothes were not mine. I suddenly realised that I was in the wrong room and none too graciously retreated to the hallway and the elevator. I had asked for and received the key for the number of the room I had stayed in the night before in another country. As they say, "If it's Tuesday, we must be in Hong Kong."

Prime Minister Joe Clark and his Conservatives were elected as a minority government on May 22, 1979. His government was to survive only nine months, when it was defeated on a vote in the House of Commons. Mike Wilson was named minister of International Trade in the Clark government. We got along very well. I accompanied him on his first trip abroad as a minister when we flew to Washington on a government aircraft for a day of meetings with the embassy, the World Bank and the Interamerican Development Bank. I was organising a trade mission for him to Australia, New Zealand, and Southeast Asia when the government was defeated. (His successor, Ed Lumley, led the mission and, on my recommendation, took Mike Wilson along.)

The minister of finance in the Clark government was John Crosbie from Newfoundland. The International Monetary Fund and World Bank meetings in the summer of 1979, during the short life of the Conservative government, took place in Belgrade, Yugoslavia. John Crosbie, as finance minister led the Canadian delegation, and I was named a member. These annual meetings were command performances for every finance minister and Central Bank governor. They and their retinues of officials mingled for a week with each other and with thousands of international bankers.

I persuaded Peggy to accompany me to Belgrade, with the plan that we take a week of vacation in Portugal on the way home. We arrived in Belgrade a day or two before the meetings were to begin. It was Peggy's first visit in the Communist world, although Yugoslavia was hardly representative of countries behind the Iron Curtain. President Tito (who was to open our meetings) had stood up to Stalin and broken with Moscow and drawn his country more closely to the West. He had also made Yugoslavia one of the leaders of the nonaligned developing countries that played an influential role in such institutions as the United Nations Conference on Trade and Development (UNCTAD). Tito was certainly a dictator and a committed Communist (albeit with his own peculiar brand), but he did bring some four decades of peace to the Balkans, knitting together a territory that proved before and after Tito to be almost ungovernable.

During the Middle Ages, Belgrade was to be conquered by virtually all of its neighbours and, from the 1500s to 1867, was occupied much of the time by the Turks. Belgrade is, in general, a modern city, having been rebuilt since the severe German air bombardments during the Second World War.

The weather was perfect, although the early August air was heavy with pollution from the brown coal widely used by industry throughout the region. We stayed in a typical, massive Communist-style hotel that stretched along the Danube. It was comfortable, and from its public rooms, you had a magnificent view of the river. We did a little sightseeing, walking the kilometre to the centre of the city. On our way back to the hotel from this first outing, Peggy stepped into a hole in a park and hurt her ankle; it was broken. Peggy emerged from the local hospital with a cast from knee to toe. Our well-laid plans for sightseeing in Yugoslavia and Portugal "went out the window."

Peggy did mange to hobble down to a reception in our hotel to meet Mister Crosbie and the others in the Canadian delegation. However, on most of the evenings after my business meetings, we installed ourselves in a hotel restaurant and listened to Gypsy violins and gazed at the Danube flowing past our window. We did stop at Lisbon, but after a day's attempt at sightseeing, we realised that, given Peggy's cast, we would be better off at home. We cut short our visit to Portugal and headed back to Ottawa.

The minority Conservative government was defeated in the House of Commons on December 13, and the resulting election at the beginning of 1980 brought back Prime Minister Trudeau and his Liberals, giving us a new minister of international trade, Ed Lumley. Some referred to Ed Lumley as "an unguided missile," probably because he was so full of energy and new ideas. I considered him to be one of the most effective trade development ministers we ever had. In the next few years he would insist that I accompany him in his efforts to increase exports to all corners of the earth. We got along very well even though he always called me "a closeted Tory."

Chapter Thirty-two
Siberia—Land of Permafrost

When I checked into my hotel room in Moscow, the atmosphere in the room was like that of a steamy, tropical rain forest rather than the cool May afternoon it was outside. As I entered, I could hear the noise of fast-running water coming from the bathroom. I raced to turn off the tap. I saw a stream of scalding water flowing into the tub, filling the air with steam. Try as I did, I couldn't turn the tap. When I left Moscow three days later, the water was still pouring out of the faucet, in spite of my appeals for help to virtually every member of the hotel staff. It was a good demonstration of the wastefulness and lack of responsibility bred by the Communist system. There was no concern whatsoever amongst the hotel staff and management for the comfort of the guest or the cost of such waste. There was no bottom line. The hotel was, in effect, just another branch of government with all staff in government employ, but certainly not as servants of the public.

My Moscow hotel experience was not unique. I was told by a colleague that he had stayed in what had been a beautiful hotel built by the Finns. The Finns had lined the lobby with attractive wood panelling, only to have it destroyed in a few months. The cleaners who mopped the floor had sloshed around the dirt every morning with filthy mops transferring most of the dirt onto the first few feet of the panelled walls. The wood just rotted.

It was May 1979, a few days before Prime Minister Joe Clark's Conservatives formed their short-lived government. I was in the Soviet Union with a small delegation of Canadian businessmen involved in the hydroelectric field. Our purpose was to have a look at what the Soviets had done in the construction of hydroelectric dams in the permafrost. This was to take us to northern Siberia.

Minister Don Jamieson, after discussions with the Soviets, had set up with them several joint commissions to look at ways in which the two countries might cooperate in fields where we had a common interest. One such field was hydroelectric power. Our people had shown the Soviet members of the Joint Commission on Hydro-Electric Power virtually everything they wished to see, but there had been no quid pro quo. The Canadian members had visited the Soviet Union but had seen little and learnt less.

Much to my surprise, I was asked to take over the Canadian chairmanship of the group. I was surprised because I had no real knowledge of the hydroelectric power field. I was told that this shouldn't concern me, because the Canadian commission members would together have all the knowledge and expertise needed. I was required just to play a leadership role. I had negative reports about the commission. I agreed to take on the task (on a part-time basis) if I could have a free hand to try to make the commission work meaningfully, and be equally free to end its work if in the view of the Canadian members its continued existence served no positive purpose. This was agreed to by my superiors. My first act was to consult the Canadian commission members who included representatives of northern Canadian hydroelectric authorities, power equipment manufacturers, and consulting engineering firms. All agreed that unless we could get the Soviets to address our demands meaningfully, we should walk away from the joint commission.

My next act was to call in the Soviet ambassador, who was very senior in the Soviet hierarchy; he would later play a leading role in the transitional period following the break-up of the Soviet Union. He congratulated me on my appointment as cochairman of the commission. I thanked him and said that regrettably my first act as cochairman would have to be to propose that the work of this particular commission be ended. I explained that I couldn't chair a group whose Canadian members saw no useful purpose in its work. I said that, for a year or so, our people had attempted to show the Soviet members everything they were interested in, yet our people couldn't even get their Soviet counterparts to show them Soviet work on hydroelectric dams in the permafrost. It would be my proposal that the work of the joint commission be ended.

The ambassador expressed great surprise and disappointment and left me with an appeal that we put off any decision for at least a few weeks. I agreed and reported on my meeting to our embassy in Moscow, asking them to reiterate my views and intentions to the Soviet deputy minister of power who was my cochairman. Within a week or so, the Soviet ambassador handed me an invitation to visit Moscow for talks with relevant ministries and for a visit to northern Siberia to view first hand, dams in the permafrost

248

near the Lena River. I accepted, and on the eve of our departure, the ambassador had our small delegation of six to the embassy for dinner and a briefing.

In Moscow it was interesting to view first hand the "classless" society. We were, of course, staying in a hotel designated for foreigners. There was a restaurant and bar area near the street entrance, and every time local citizens even glanced towards it, they were very impolitely driven away. What shopping we did was at shops reserved for foreigners. When driven to and from meetings, it was in those large black Russian Zhiguli, or "seagull," automobiles, which had rights to a lane on the main Moscow streets reserved for senior party officials and official visitors.

In the evening, many of the bars of the hotels that housed the foreigners and that were out of bounds for locals were swarming with Russian prostitutes looking for foreign currency. It was clear that while the ordinary citizen was excluded, the prostitutes carried out their age-old business with the blessing of the state. We were told by the hotel staff that they were permitted in the bars because they possessed foreign currency. We could see that they earned it here, but they certainly didn't spend it.

On our first evening in Moscow, the Soviet deputy minister and cochairman of the joint commission took us to the Bolshoi Theatre of Opera and Ballet (founded in 1780). You had to be impressed when you considered that the performance before you was just one in the theatre's two hundred years of fame and that top performances had been staged in good times and bad. I was struck not only with the excellence on stage and in the orchestra pit, but with the enthusiastic audience that seemed so appreciative. During intermission there was an exodus to a large open area downstairs, where they liberally poured and sold glasses of vodka. It was the most efficient retailing operation I was to see in the Soviet Union. Everybody seemed to be in good spirits and very much enjoying themselves even before they downed their vodka. The only negative thing about the whole evening was that in such a magnificent old building, with beauty and excellence in music and dance, that the foyer and bar areas should reek with the smell of urine, which gave one the impression that the nearby lavatories had never been properly cleaned.

Besides the engineers and equipment manufacturers, our group included a colleague from the Department of Industry, Trade and Commerce, who was an expert on power production, "Chip" Chiperzak. He had all the technical knowledge that I lacked and consequently was a tremendous right-hand man. He was also fairly familiar with the Soviet Union, having travelled there on business several times. Also with us was Joe Wong, a Chinese Canadian, who headed one of our most northerly hydroelectric corporations. Joe was a third-generation Canadian, but because he was of Chinese origin, he was to experience the all-too-common Russian prejudice against the Chinese.

Our flight from Moscow to Siberia was to say the least, different. Like all internal flights in the Soviet Union, ours was with Aeroflot. The cabin crew, men and women alike, looked and performed as if they were sergeant majors just transferred to the airline from the army. They were very officious and behaved as if the last thing on their minds was the comfort and well-being of their passengers. Aeroflot has been compared to a dilapidated bus service with wings. Passengers are said to sometimes outnumber the seats, but unlike buses, there are no straps to hang onto if you are standing in the aisle. You can feel the knees of the person behind you if you recline your seat. One-seater toilets in the country are preferable to some of the toilets on the domestic flights.

The joie de vivre of our fellow passengers made up for the conditions on the plane. The passengers were either Russians or nationals of other Soviet Republics heading home or going to Siberia to make their fortune. There were many incentives that enticed workers from the European parts of the Soviet Union to Siberia, and although most tended to stay once they reached the wide open eastern lands, they had left western Russia "temporarily" looking for a nest egg, which was almost impossible to obtain back home.

As soon as we were airborne, the passengers passed around food and vodka bottles to everybody within range including us. The airline staff just stood around and watched. An hour or so into our flight, all the passengers were happy and already enjoying the "good life" they were heading for in Siberia. I felt a little guilty that these people, whose incomes were but a fraction of ours, should so generously share their few luxuries with us.

We had several stops en route, including, for some inexplicable reason, an overnight stay in Omsk in western Siberia. We were driven to one of "the" hotels in town, which in Western Europe or elsewhere certainly wouldn't have made the *Michelin* guide. The view of the town on the drive from the airport was, however, enough to make you appreciate the hotel. I was not too impressed with what I saw of Omsk, Siberia's biggest city of three-quarters of a million on the Trans-Siberian Railway.

Before leaving Omsk, we had the opportunity to stand in a departure lounge above the arrival gate and were given a perfect view of the rigours that arriving local passengers were subjected to when disembarking at Omsk. They may as well have been arriving in an unfriendly foreign country when they went though passport control.

The end of our commercial flight across the Soviet Union was at Bratsk, where we were to visit a huge power site. Bratsk was described to us as a new city of a quarter million, roughly the size of Ottawa, but that was where any comparison ended. It had nothing in common with any Canadian city, not even the winter climate. Bratsk was much colder. It was in Irkutsk province, almost directly north of Lake Baykal and Beijing. It was on the Angara River, which flowed through Lake Baykal. Settlement remained unimportant until 1954, when the Tayshet-Lena railway was built through Bratsk and work started on the Bratsk hydroelectric station, which was completed in 1964, one of the world's largest. An aluminum works and a timber-processing plant was built to utilise the power.

We were housed in a very fine guest house. I say "very fine," but this was by Russian standards. It was comfortable and the food was good, but there were a number of things that were only surface-perfect. When we went to our assigned rooms, it was obvious that all was not socialist in the socialist world. I shared the biggest and best room with Chip. Our poor Canadian interpreter was at the bottom of our diplomatic list and was given the least desirable room. I accompanied him to his room, and it looked fine enough, but when he turned on the tap over his basin, he soaked his feet. There was no pipe under the sink! Water went straight to the floor or to the feet if they were in the way.

We spent the weekend in Bratsk. Throughout the town, there were rows and rows of desolate-looking apartment buildings, each an exact copy of the one next to it. There was no landscaping around the apartments or along the streets. From the front of the very austere buildings to those across the street it would have been several hundred feet, as if they were expecting someday to have a superhighway run between the buildings. From the buildings to the street was a sea of mud. The street itself was very narrow, which mattered little, since there were few cars. Indeed there was little sign of life on the streets except for a few women in shawls on their way somewhere. There was no evidence of a "downtown," as we would know it. There was a huge cenotaph with thousands of names on it, commemorating those who had lost their lives during the Second World War. Uniformed guards marched to and fro before the great monument.

Accompanying us from Moscow was a Russian interpreter and a young man we identified as the security officer assigned to "cover" us; we called him the "spook." The interpreter was not in the same league as ours from Ottawa. He told me that he was a Communist party member, so maybe that made up for his imperfections as an interpreter. He was a very serious young man but grew friendlier with the passage of time and distance from Moscow. Towards the end of our visit, we had him almost fully integrated.

Sunday morning at breakfast in Bratsk, we decided to cause our hosts a little embarrassment. This sounds awful, but both sides constantly played games to keep the other side off balance. It was as if we had a duty to keep our overseers uneasy by continually challenging them. In the full knowledge that there would be no churches in the new city of Bratsk, we told the spook that we all wanted to go to church. Chip was an elder in a church in Ottawa, and one of our engineers was a strict Methodist, but most of the others probably hadn't darkened the door of a church in years. We could see that the spook was concerned that our request couldn't be accommodated. After much nervous discussion amongst the spook, the interpreter, and the officials who ran the guest house and the hydroelectric plant, they politely informed us that since Bratsk was a new town, there were no churches, as there were in the older cities of western Russia. We expressed great disappointment but indicated that we accepted the sorry situation. Our Methodist engineer, much to the surprise of the rest of us, noting that there was a piano in the guest house, asked whether our hosts would mind if we sang a few hymns. They gladly agreed, so I made my way to the piano and played hymns while the others, with varying degrees of enthusiasm and capability, sang. I believe that the Russians enjoyed the hymn-sing as much as we did. Our request to attend church made a great impression, for on our return to Moscow after our Siberian tour, the deputy minister of Power was to apologise for the fact that we were not able to attend church on our Sunday in Bratsk.

The gloominess was behind us when we drove out from Bratsk into the countryside along the beautiful and still partly frozen river to see the workers' private weekend cabins. It was a perfect spring day in mid-May. In that remote northern region, the air was pure and still. You could hear the sounds of hammers and saws miles away. It seemed that every worker in Bratsk had a small piece of land and was either building or repairing a small cabin. These cabins were all privately owned and showed it. The enthusiasm and pride of workmanship going into them was in direct contrast to that which went into the government-owned apartments they left behind in the town. In the conifer bush along the lake, the worker was for a few hours master of his own castle.

We visited the Bratsk hydroelectric station on the Angara River just below its confluence with the Oka. The dam was four hundred feet, or one hundred twenty-five metres, high and over two and half miles, or five and a half kilometres, wide. It was built under very difficult circumstances. Winter temperatures fall as low as -72° F., or -58°C., and there was frost on average over 280 days a year. The consensus of our engineers and equipment manufacturers was that the station was well-built and well-equipped. Although it was recently constructed, it was a copy of a Western power station of the 1920s. There were none of the technological improvements introduced over the past fifty years that were in comparable Western stations. The Russians were proud of this site, but it held little interest for our people; in spite of the 280 days of frost, it was still well below the latitudes of permafrost.

That evening we were warmly entertained by the local Communist party officials and officials from the power station. I'm sure they were glad to see us, for it gave them the perfect excuse to throw a big dinner party and to break out the best vodka. We were told that the vodka glasses got larger the further north you went. They were large enough in Bratsk, and I wondered what was in store for us when we got up near the Lena River.

There was much toasting of Canada and the Soviet Union, and Canadian-Soviet relations. After the formal speeches and toasts, the Russians got into story-telling, which really tested our interpreters. Our man really performed well. The stories that poked fun at various people of the Soviet Union were almost identical to the Newfie stories that I was regularly subjected to by my colleagues. We matched them with tales of our own for every one of theirs. We must have told some good ones, or the Russians were affected by the vodka, for they roared with laughter. When back in Ottawa, I was told by a close business friend, Colin Smallridge, that when he was at an energy conference in East Berlin, he was approached by a Russian and asked whether he knew any Newfie jokes. The Russian was our friend, the spook. When Colin asked him where he had heard about Newfie jokes, the spook said, "In Siberia, from Frank Petrie."

We flew north towards the Lena River to the Soviet Union's diamond-producing area that extends from Mirny to the Vilyui and Markha Rivers. These rivers flow into the Lena that in turn flows north into the Arctic Ocean. Someone mentioned that the terrain and rock formations there were identical to the diamond-bearing areas of South Africa.

We landed in a town, of about thirty thousand people, that was in the permafrost. I was surprised to see the countryside covered with small Christmas-tree-size conifers. These grew in the several feet of soil that thawed during the brief summer, but below that depth was permafrost. There were buildings of several floors, throughout the town, built on stilts. To build them on the ground would disturb the permafrost and cause melting and collapsing of the structures. We stayed long enough in the town for me to spot and inspect several giant off-highway trucks. I was pleased to see that they were made in Canada, although they were described to me as being American. They were trucks that our Export Development Corporation had financed, causing the American-owned company concerned to set up production facilities in Canada. It was not possible to build and export the trucks from the United States, because the American official export financing agency, Eximbank, was not permitted to finance exports to the Soviet Union.

The site of the dam in the permafrost was much further north, west of the Lena River. We reached there by a smaller plane that gave one a very good view of the Siberian countryside, which was truly the "land of the little sticks," for as far as the eye could see, there were short straight conifers. In the permafrost, these were only eight or ten feet high. The name of the town built around the dam and power station escapes me, some unpronounceable name, but it had a population of about six or eight thousand. The town seemed to be filled with children. They were all smiling and well dressed for the still-cold weather of May. It certainly appeared that they had been well provided for, because, besides their schools, there was a large sports complex with an indoor swimming pool and a gymnasium. The townsfolk were very proud of this complex, and it was first on our list when we did a tour of the town.

If Bratsk had 280 days of frost a year, this small town, situated as it was in the permafrost, had to have a very short summer indeed. It was said that in these parts of northern Siberia, where snow cover was often thin or absent, permafrost sometimes extended to depths of one thousand feet. Yet, the short summers could be warm, and the stunted Christmas trees that peppered the countryside obviously thrived in the brief, warm season and in the shallow, thawed ground.

The prairielike countryside covered with conifers stretched in every direction as far as the eye could see; this was known as the "taiga." You heard the word in every conversation, in Russian or in translation. It was as if western Canadians were talking about the "prairies" or Newfoundlanders were referring to the "sea." For the people of this vast northern region of the world, the endless taiga stretched from their back doors.

We spent most of a day touring the hydroelectric station and the dam site. The members of our mission were upset that our hosts wanted to restrict us to one shore of the dam site and seemed intent on keeping us away from the other. When the Soviets finally gave in to our demands, we saw why they were reluctant to show us all. The other side was a mess (for which they apologised). There were pieces of lumber and machinery strewn around the site. They obviously had intended, but failed, to clean it up before our arrival. Our people told me that any site in Canada left in such a mess would have required the firing of all concerned. Our engineers and experts gave the Russians full marks for the dam in the permafrost, but they made it clear to me that they were not overly impressed. There was little technology in Siberia that Canada did not already possess.

After our tour of the site, the Soviets took us up in a helicopter over the dam site. They even allowed us to take pictures. It was impressive, and I said so to the Russians. (The result was that they later presented me with a piece of metal on which was worked the picture I had admired from the helicopter.) They then flew us north for many miles towards what they said was to be the site for a bigger dam. During the flight, the chairman of the local Communist committee invited me to join the pilot in the cockpit to take in the sight of the endless taiga. I gladly accepted. While chatting through our interpreter to the pilot, who was a Soviet military officer, I viewed the surrounding country.

What struck me was that in this virtual wasteland, every ten kilometres or so there would be straight cuts across the taiga where trees had been felled, making lines like grids on a map. These cuttings went off in perfectly straight lines into the horizon. After ten minutes of chatting with the pilot, I decided that Joe, our northern Canadian resident, would probably get more out of this flight across northern Siberia than I would.

I vacated my cockpit seat and told Joe to take my place. Before he could make a move towards the cockpit, the local Communist party chairman intercepted Joe and refused him entry into the cockpit. There was no question that it was because Joe was "Chinese." That he was third generation Canadian didn't matter. He was singled out for closer observance than the rest of our delegation. Joe took it well. Obviously he was used to, or expected, such treatment, so he let it pass. I was fuming with anger and disgust at the Soviet major domo. Joe had to calm me down.

We landed on a shelf of snow on an island in a frozen river. There was no sign of habitation or of construction activity. It was left to the imagination to determine where the dam would go. The Russians brought out a folding table from the helicopter and several bottles of vodka. These they threw into the snow. After showing us the site, they retrieved the vodka bottles, opened them, and poured generous portions for everyone (including the pilot). They toasted everything Canadian and Soviet until the bottles were empties.

On the morning of our departure from the guest house in the town, the Russians served us a huge breakfast. All the civil and Communist officials and the people who operated the hydroelectric station were there. The food was good, and we were enjoying it until, again, they produced the vodka bottles and large glasses and started on the speeches and toasts. As leader of the Canadian delegation, I was expected to respond to all of this. I did, but I couldn't help concluding that these lonely people, in this far northern land, were using us to exact as much vodka and good food from the system as the level of our delegation would allow.

I was pleased that I had the opportunity to travel across the Soviet Union and to get a glimpse of the vast territory before it came apart, as I was sure it would. The mammoth union of such diverse republics and states bound together only with communist glue couldn't work. The Soviet Union was like the church bell and the cannon shown to visitors to the Kremlin. They are both proudly described as the world's biggest. This may indeed be true, but both the bell and cannon were too big ever to work.

Chapter Thirty-three
Flying with Minister Ed

Ed Lumley was a minister "to keep up with." As minister of international trade, like Mike Wilson before him, he could concentrate on foreign trade and leave the industry side of the department to another minister. Herb Gray was that "other" minister, having been named Minister of Industry, Trade and Commerce. Those of us on the trade side were delighted to have a minister who could devote himself entirely to pushing Canada's exports and not be diverted from the job by industrial development concerns and the huge regional and industry programs the minister responsible for industrial development had to administer. Ed Lumley would eventually take over the industry, as well as the trade responsibilities.

Ministers Lumley and Gray were both from Windsor, Ontario, although Lumley represented the Cornwall area in the House of Commons. He had been mayor of that city on the Saint Lawrence. I learnt quickly that there was little love lost between the two ministers. Possibly it was Minister Lumley's perception that Minister Gray considered himself the senior minister, although the position of minister of International Trade as created by former Prime Minister Joe Clark was, in effect, a ministry in its own right. Minister Gray did get involved occasionally in trade matters, and I did travel with him to Israel on one occasion, but for the most part he didn't interfere with Ed Lumley.

The trade mission of businessmen that we had set up for Wilson to Australia and New Zealand, just before the defeat of the Conservative minority government, was taken over by Lumley. He was impressed that Canadian exporters still counted these countries among their most important markets for manufactured goods. At the time, these two Commonwealth countries ranked next to the United States and the European Community as markets for our finished products. They were certainly much more important for exporters of manufactured goods than was Japan.

I very much enjoyed working with Ed Lumley. We generally got along well. One difficulty I had in dealing with him when organising missions abroad was when selecting mission members. In my office we would assemble a list of Canadian companies interested in the market. This list would be based on recommendations from our posts in the area and from our industry experts as well as from our own knowledge of the markets. The minister, rightly, would vet these lists thoroughly. He would send the names of the companies to other ministers and members of Parliament who represented the areas where the companies were located. He would invite the parliamentarians to submit other recommendations. While we generally ended up with a good list of mission members, I dreaded that some firm that could really profit from a mission would be pushed aside to make space for a political favourite. In retrospect, I'm sure many of my concerns stemmed from the arrogance of the bureaucracy, that it felt it was better placed than our political masters to make such selections.

I suggested to Minister Lumley that he take his predecessor, Michael Wilson, with him on the Australia and New Zealand mission. He readily agreed because he liked Wilson and because he thought that Wilson's presence would silence opposition criticism in the House of Commons that Lumley was taking a mission to South Pacific in the dead of the Canadian winter. It always disturbed me that ministers should be so sensitive about being abroad, seeking export business, because missions led by ministers often resulted in contracts for Canadian exporters that would not have been obtained otherwise. The result was generally increased production and employment in Canada, with all the positive economic fallout generated by sales overseas.

The mission to Australia and New Zealand was most productive. I spent my evenings writing the minister's dinner speeches for all the major cities we visited in both countries. He used to get rather annoyed at me for giving him the same material for most of the cities. My response was that if you got a standing ovation for what you said in Sydney, why not try the same lines in Melbourne? This never satisfied him, and he got me out of bed on one occasion in the middle of the night to rewrite his speech. He was concerned about the Canadian press members who were hearing the same old line every night. I couldn't have cared less about the press; my concern was to impress upon the local business community the wisdom of doing business with Canada; but he was the boss. The businessmen on our mission were certainly pleased with the doors that the minister opened for them. I

258

was more than pleased with Lumley's performance with the Australian and New Zealand political and commercial movers and shakers.

Former Minister Mike Wilson's presence certainly was positive. Minister Lumley used him on a number of occasions to sub for him and there was no political nonsense between the two of them for the duration of the mission. Lumley used to get a little annoyed with me when he would be confined to the hotel with his charming wife while the rest of us would go on the town with Mike Wilson. The next morning I would, while briefing the minister, say what a fine fellow Mike Wilson was and would delight in seeing him fume. He would have loved to have been with us "on the town" in Sydney or wherever. He might have known that we were generally all too tired to do much more than have a few beers, a good meal, and a good laugh when we thought how the minister was restricted to his quarters. All the laughs certainly were not on Ed Lumley. In New Zealand, he almost collapsed in laugher when he pointed out to me a bumper sticker on a car that read, "Help fight inflation, drive over a civil servant today!"

Most people if asked where, this side of heaven, was the harp played as a national instrument, would, I'm sure, have trouble responding. Some of British extraction would perhaps mention Wales, but I am sure that very few would point to Paraguay. Yet, in Paraguay, I have never heard music played so beautifully as they play it on the harp. The harp there was as common as was the guitar in other countries of Latin America.

Minister Lumley had with him a small group of six or eight businessmen in the power sector pursuing one project. It was a giant hydroelectric development on the border of Paraguay and Argentina. This project, known to us as Yacyreta, held the promise of hundreds of millions of dollars worth of Canadian exports. The minister, of course, aimed to get it all. Gerry Rowe of GE (General Electric) Canada, who was one of my favourites in the private sector, told me many years later that the initial orders for his firm had been about eighty million dollars and that, thereafter, since they were already on the ground, new orders kept coming. Necessary for the Canadian sales was Export Development Corporation (commercial) financing, so we had with us a veteran of EDC, Roger Paquette. I was also pleased to have with us a friend and long-time trade commissioner very familiar with the area, John Treleaven.

We flew from Ottawa via Miami. We had the best part of the afternoon and evening to wait in Miami for our flight to Asuncíon, Paraguay; via Lima, Peru; and Buenos Aires, Argentina. In Miami, we took a day room in a hotel directly above the airport terminal. The entire delegation jammed into the room to await our flight. An hour or two before our departure, there was an almighty racket in the hallway outside our door. I wanted to peep out to see the source of the noise, but the minister, who obviously was more streetwise than I was, barred my way. It was just as well, because two Cubans had been in a fight over a woman, and one had been pushed through a plate glass window. The police arrived, signalling that the nightlife of Miami had begun.

We stopped in Lima, Peru, just long enough to meet at the airport with our Trade Commissioner Tom Parrot. I arranged an overnight stop and visit to the post on my return. It was almost impossible to fly to Asunción, Paraguay, from anywhere other than Buenos Aires, Argentina, so we had to go all the way down to Buenos Aires and retrace our steps north to Asunción. When we arrived at Asunción, we were all very tired. Our Ambassador Dwight Fulford, who was responsible for Paraguay, as well as Argentina, boarded the aircraft immediately upon its arrival and told the minister that he had to inspect a Paraguayan guard of honour. Nothing could have been further down on the minister's wish list. He did the rounds of the gathered troops, mumbling all the way, words that thankfully only an English-speaking person could comprehend.

The Paraguayans rolled out the welcome mat, which augured well for our involvement in the power project, for we had to win the favour of Paraguay as well as Argentina if we were to be involved. Besides the guard of honour, it was arranged that we would meet with the president, General Stroessner, who ran the country as his private domain.

Paraguay must be one of the least known countries of South America. It lies in the centre of the continent, bordered by Bolivia, Brazil, and Argentina. It shares with Bolivia the peculiarity of being landlocked. The smallness of the population, which was between two and three million, was said to be the result of the devastating war of 1865–70 against Brazil, Argentina, and Uruguay, when the population of over one and a half million was reduced to two hundred thousand. As Canadians, we were interested to learn that in this remote country, there were thousands of Canadians or people of Canadian descent. These were members of Mennonite farming communities. I met some of them and was told that while many of the present generation had been born in Paraguay, most maintained their Canadian passports. There was amongst the Mennonite community, as there was elsewhere, great uncertainty about the future of the country under

General Stroessner. The Mennonites were among the most prosperous farmers in Paraguay, having, through hard work, turned often inhospitable land into model farms.

We spent the best part of a morning with President Stroessner and the economic members of his cabinet. He seemed to be very much impressed that a country like Canada should pursue such a huge project as the Yacyreta. My major concern was that our Department of External Affairs wanted us to raise with General Stroessner the concerns that we (and the rest of the world) had about human rights abuses by Stroessner's government.

There was no doubt that there were abuses galore. I feared that to antagonise Stroessner would do little to reduce the abuses and would most surely mean the end of our chance to have the Paraguayans turn to Canada for the Yacyreta project. Minister Lumley did and said all the right things. He said what he had to say but certainly didn't antagonise General Stroessner. He satisfied our ambassador (who naturally wanted to be able to advise External Affairs that we had raised human rights). Lumley also was able to calm our businessmen who, like me, were concerned that we must not "put a foot in the wrong direction." The minister never did.

For the hydroelectric power project, it was equally important for us to persuade the Argentines, as well as the Paraguayans, that we could deliver what they wanted in equipment and services. It was my second visit to Argentina, and I was so impressed with Buenos Aires that I was determined one day to have a holiday there with Peggy. (We made the trip together shortly after my retirement.) Buenos Aires struck me as a Germanic, rather than Latin, city. If you could ignore the Spanish language, you could imagine yourself being in north central Europe.

At the time of this official visit, we were unable to enjoy the city because everything was so terribly expensive, due to a ridiculous rate of exchange. The Argentine currency was pegged at such a high rate against the dollar that it actually paid people to buy an air ticket to New York for shopping. The air tickets plus the New York prices were less than the prices to be paid for the same goods in Buenos Aires. I remember that the minister had some shirts laundered, and he was charged twenty-five dollars for each shirt. A beautiful "coffee table" book on Argentina caught my eye. Its price was equivalent to eight hundred and fifty dollars.

When Peggy and I visited about ten years later, all this had changed, and prices were most reasonable in dollar terms. Indeed you could have a great steak dinner for two and a bottle of excellent wine for about ten dollars.

We left Argentina well satisfied that our chances of winning at least some of the huge project were excellent. The business members of our mission all stressed to me that their efforts were greatly enhanced by having a minister open doors and stress to senior ministers and officials details of Canada's industrial and export capabilities. The exporters themselves would have had difficulty delivering such a message at such levels.

On my way home, after an overnight stop in Lima, Peru, I stayed in Bogotá, Colombia, as a guest of our Ambassador Doug Valentine and his wife Beverly. I found Bogotá a frightening place from the security point of view, but Doug and Beverly seemed to enjoy living there. My concerns were not solely grounded on the terrible reputation that Bogotá had for the drug trade; I was more impressed (in a most negative way) by the stories of children being trained to pick pockets and steal and that there had been "schools" established for the purpose. These stories, while probably a little exaggerated, were made more believable when Doug told me about the problems that car drivers had with children stealing their watches off their arms when stopped at traffic lights. There was little air-conditioning in cars in those days in Bogotá, so drivers had their windows open. Kids would pick a watch off an arm in a flash. To avoid this, some drivers would wear their watches on their right wrists away from the window. This did not deter the kids, who would press a lighted cigarette on the left hand, and when the driver reacted by grabbing the burnt hand with the right one, the kid would relieve the victim of the watch.

The following month I was on the road again with Minister Lumley. We went to Egypt, where he brought his many talents to bear on a range of opportunities for Canadian exporters, including such important items as passenger aircraft and diesel locomotives.

The Egyptians like to advertise their country as the "outdoor museum," and the title is more than justified. No other nation can boast monuments spanning a period of six thousand years from the dawn of first civilisations. Cairo was said to offer a Westernised facade, but was not a Western city. It was unruly, vibrant, dirty, exotic, alive with the teeming poverty of the millions who had migrated from the countryside. The villagers who swarmed the streets, still liked "to keep their foot in the countryside" by often raising their farm animals and storing their grain on their urban rooftops. At the same time, Cairo was a city of striking beauty and serenity,

262

with handsome buildings and broad, leafy Nile-side boulevards. Perhaps no city of comparable size offered such startling contrasts.

The pyramids of Giza and the Sphinx are undoubtedly on the top of every visitor's list. A rather shocking site closer to the city is the City of the Dead. Here among the tombs and burial sites of the recent dead, live thousands of people. They have taken from the dead their final resting places and turned them into living quarters. In great contrast to the living conditions of many of the residents of Cairo, we were housed in the Meridien Hotel, on the banks of the Nile, with a magnificent view of that great river that has been the lifeline of so much of early civilisation.

Not far from the Meridien Hotel, situated on a houseboat on the Nile, was the Papyrus Institute. Here you could see a fascinating demonstration of the making of paper from papyrus, which means, "the growth of the river (Nile)." It is a reedlike plant, which in ancient times grew profusely near the Nile. The earliest books known were written on rolls of papyrus back in the first half of the third millennium B.C.

We seemed to spend our time, when not tied up in traffic, in government offices, for government departments and agencies held the key to market access. Our Export Development Corporation was crucial in all of our meetings, since sales of heavy equipment such as we were offering required export financing.

On our last evening in Cairo, the delegation had dinner at the residence of Larry Dickenson, our trade commissioner. After dinner, the minister's departmental assistant, Bob Fournier, who was a career trade officer "on loan" to the minister's office, strolled over to the piano and started playing beautiful nightclub music. Bob was known to all of us as "Stretch" because of his six-feet-plus height. He was a bit of a character and took an awful lot of "soft abuse" from the minister. I felt they liked working together, but Bob was always searching for little ways to "bug" the minister. When Bob started to play, Lumley said, "Bob, I didn't know you played the piano; you are a man of many talents and full of surprises." Bob continued playing but quietly responded, "Yes, minister, and it may also come as a surprise to you to learn that I am a closeted Tory." The minister laughed and said, "Well, that makes two of you; don't fall over Petrie because he's in the same closet!"

Bob and I had a lot of laughs over the gifts the minister carried with him for his opposite numbers when travelling abroad. He objected to the usual gifts of soap stone carvings and, instead, opted for coloured glass-blown figures, usually of animals, that were produced by someone in his riding around Cornwall. There was one the minister really liked to give to his hosts. It was a horse. Bob and I would ask him every time we saw it if it was a "donkey." He was not amused. We always were.

From the point of view of exports or, at least, opening up opportunities for exports, Minister Lumley's mission to Egypt was a success. I was to visit Cairo several times, following up on the many opportunities opened by the minister's mission generally in company with Export Development Corporation officers.

Chapter Thirty-four
Zimbabwe

In March 1981, I started what was to be a long association with southern Africa. Years later, when I was appointed president of the Canadian Exporters Association, I would put great effort into Canada's relations with that part of the world, mainly to stave off trade sanctions that various Canadian governments threatened to impose against Canadian exports to South Africa. I had already worked on South Africa, Malawi, and Zambia, but my first introduction to Zimbabwe was when I was appointed a member of a Canadian delegation led by one of our senators. We had been invited by newly independent Zimbabwe (Rhodesia) to their capital, Salisbury (about to be renamed Harare). All the Western industrialised countries had been summoned to discuss how they proposed to support the new Zimbabwe. The Western world had given strong verbal support for the black disenfranchised majority before and during the bitter civil war. Now they were being asked to back up their rhetoric with aid funds and investment.

The man behind the "Zimcord" Conference was the new minister of finance, Bernard Chidzero. He was a colleague of mine from our Geneva years. He had been one of the bright lights in the Secretariat of the United Nations Conference on Trade and Development (UNCTAD) when I was at the Canadian Permanent Mission to the United Nations. Bernie, as he was known to his friends, was a brilliant and likeable man. He was a graduate of McGill University in Montreal and had a French Canadian wife.

Zimcord was masterfully planned and executed. Bernie Chidzero must have achieved all he set out to do, for many millions of dollars were pledged to launch the newly independent country economically.

We were pleased that many of the whites who had just fought in the terrible civil war were prepared to stay and live under a predominately black government. I met and had many discussions with the white Cabinet Minister Norman, who for some years held the agriculture portfolio before being moved to the senate. I also met with a number of white Zimbabwean farmers and found them positive and determined to help make the new country work. This was not surprising, given that many of them could claim to be from families that had been in the country or in southern Africa for many generations. They had nowhere else to go! England or Europe was as foreign to them as it was to most third or fourth generation Canadians. I was also impressed with a number of cabinet ministers I met. They were brand new in the job but were well educated and well motivated.

The great downside for me was the attitude of the new head of state, President Robert Mugabe. He had been educated in a Roman Catholic mission school, but somewhere he had picked up Marxism. He had many good administrative qualities but could not put aside his Marxist ideals. I know that Bernie Chidzero as finance minster was particularly restricted in what he could do in opening up the economy because of Mugabe's views. I used to press Chidzero for specific written guidelines and undertakings by his government regarding foreign investment. He understood perfectly the need for would-be investors to have some assurance on repatriation of profits and capital. Chidzero could give us oral assurance but no more. Mugabe refused to allow such written guarantees. Consequently foreign investors held back and many local investors pulled out.

The day after Zimcord ended, I received a telephone call in the early morning from Chidzero. It was Sunday, and he asked me to assemble what remained of the Canadian delegation and to bring them over to his home for brunch. There, for several hours, he opened up as among friends on the problems and hopes he had for his new country. Of all the black African countries, Zimbabwe probably held greatest promise. It had the industrial infrastructure. It was virtually self-sufficient in many products, after being boycotted by the international community for years, although much of this industry was outdated and needed huge investment if it was to become competitive.

Zimbabwe had a tremendous degree of good will in the international community. There were well-educated people, black and white, capable of getting the country up and running. The country needed the quarter of a million whites, who had the required technological expertise, and they seemed prepared to stay. The country was fairly well-endowed with natural resources, particularly with good agricultural land. Zimbabwe was the only African country that was self-sufficient in agriculture. Indeed, a large part of its foreign exchange earnings came from the export of corn. This was not without its problems, since agricultural production was largely in the hands of efficient white farmers who owned and operated some of the most efficient operations in the world. To break up these farms for distribution to the poor blacks would cost the country dearly. Yet not to do so was bound to lead to growing frustration and disappointment amongst the blacks.

One evening during a reception in Harare, I was approached by several white farmers who asked whether I would like next morning to have a quick air tour of the Zimbabwe corn belt. I accepted and early next day met them at the airport, where they flew me by a small aircraft over magnificent farming country. They showed me the opening in the back of the aircraft, where a short time before, they had mounted guns when the plane was part of the Rhodesian air force. We landed at one of their farms, where a Mercedes met and drove us around the farm. The setup was most impressive. Indeed, the corn yield in this area was greater than in the highly considered corn belt of the United States.

The white Zimbabweans took me to the homestead for tea and scones. Afterwards, they drove me to show me the accommodations of the farm labourers that, they proudly stressed, were much better than that lived in by farm workers anywhere else in Africa. They explained how they provided land and opportunity for some of their more promising staff. They were determined to show me what they, as successful farmers, could contribute to Zimbabwe's future. The only thing they asked of me was whether they could expect any help from Canada for the education and training of their workers and their families. I didn't give them any encouragement in this, pointing out that their sector of activity was undoubtedly the best off in the country, and I couldn't see either the Canadian or Zimbabwean governments putting money into it.

What they were really seeking, I knew, was the widest possible support internationally against the expropriation of their efficient farms for distribution to the landless blacks. The conventional wisdom was that such action would not only be unfair to the white farmers who had given their all to the land, but it would "kill the goose that laid the golden egg" as far as Zimbabwe's production and foreign earnings were concerned. Deep down, I felt that the terrible gap between the standard of living of these people and the miserable conditions of the landless blacks meant that the days of the whites were numbered. I felt that there would be at best a gradual easing of the white farmers off their land. I only hoped that the result would not be a levelling of living standards down to the lowest.

Chapter Thirty-five
Trudeau the Trader

Prime Minister Trudeau was in his Japanese dressing gown when I joined him for breakfast in his private cabin on the Canadian forces flight from Alaska to Korea. The prime minister's quarters were in the forward section of the aircraft, where the bulkheads had been rearranged to give him privacy including a bed and sitting-eating area. I was glad to see the prime minister so treated, because I had heard of Prime Minister Pearson and his wife travelling overseas on normal commercial flights and trying to work and catnap with absolutely no privacy from the media or officials. These most senior representatives of the country were, of course, expected to be "on deck" immediately on arrival, behaving as if they had just stepped out of a comfortable bed after a great night's sleep.

I already had my first meal of the day aft. When word came back that I had been asked by the prime minister to join him for breakfast and to brief him on our trade with Korea, I felt it was a "command performance" to have a second breakfast. I felt it would be impolite just to sit there and watch him eat while I told him all I knew on the subject of trade with Korea.

We had spent the night in Anchorage and were due to land in Seoul within a few hours. Having spent twelve hours in a comfortable hotel, we were all relatively fresh. The prime minister seemed fresher than the rest of us. He told me when I joined him in his quarters that his first meeting in Korea within an hour or so of our arrival would be with the Korean prime minister. He anticipated that much of the discussion would be on trade, and he would like to have my views on which subjects the Koreans were likely to raise. I had come armed with briefing galore. I juggled my books as I attempted to respond to the prime minister's questions while buttering my toast and eating my second meal of scrambled eggs.

I told him that the Korean prime minister was bound to raise the issue of restraints that Canada imposed against Korean textiles. He asked penetrating questions on the restraints and on trade in textiles. I explained that since the Americans and Europeans imposed restraints on producers in the developing world, there would be a great diversion of products from the United States and Europe to Canada, unless we took similar action. I mentioned that per capita imports of textiles into Canada from the developing world were much higher than per capita imports into the United States or Europe, except for Sweden. Indeed, except for Sweden and Australia, we took in more textiles per capita than any other country. He asked why Sweden was such a large importer? I explained that Sweden served as a pass-through to the Communist East.

He glanced at the statistics and quizzed me on them for about a half-hour or so (during which time we were joined by my colleague from External Affairs, Tom Delworth). The prime minister thanked me, and I packed up my papers. I then made the terrible mistake of saying to the prime minister, "Sir, would it help if I prepared for you a card with a few notes and figures?"

In slightly annoyed tones, he said, "Frank, don't you feel I have all the information I need?" Indeed he had!

A few hours later, after we had landed in Seoul and were received by the Korean prime minister, events unfolded along the lines I had predicted. Our host spent most of the time with Prime Minister Trudeau, discussing trade matters. He expressed the hope that Canada would liberalise our imports of textiles from his country. Prime Minister Trudeau, like a computer, explained in great detail the textile trade, gushing out all the per capita import figures and all the statistics I had mentioned to him. He was terrific! When he finished and the Korean prime minister had no alternative but to accept his very detailed explanation, he turned to me and said in a slightly challenging manner, "Mr. Petrie, do you have anything to add to what I have said?" I certainly didn't, and even if I had, I would have limited myself to the response that I gave, which was a simple, "No, sir!"

About twenty Canadian exporters turned up in Seoul at their own expense following a general invitation from our office to join the prime minister if they felt his presence could help their export efforts. We had persuaded the prime minister's office and the Privy Council office to press the prime minister to hold an hour-long meeting in Seoul with the Canadian businessmen, so that he could be briefed by them personally on the problems they faced on penetrating the very restrictive but lucrative Korean market. The hope was that the prime minister would raise their concerns with the Korean ministers he met. I was convinced that the exporters would be responsible to the point where they would only raise with the prime minister general issues of trade policy and demonstrate these by their own particular problems.

It came as a great surprise to me that the prime minister's immediate handlers had readily agreed that he should meet with the businessmen. I tend to give some of the credit for this to Michael Pittfield, the prime minister's close friend and future clerk of the Privy Council (head of the Civil Service) and Liberal senator, although I had little evidence to support my assumption. Michael did call me into his room while in Seoul to thank me for my participation and to say that it was his view that it was "valuable to have a trade man" on the prime minister's visits aborad. I said how pleased I was to see the prime minister so heavily involved in trade questions.

Given the very special relationship between Korea and the United States, it took a prime minister to pressure the Koreans not to continually discriminate in favour of the United States and, consequently, against Canada. I had known for some years that although the prime minister had taken economics as well as law at university, economic and trade matters were not at the top of his list of interests. I had pressed his office previously to have him intervene when we felt that only intervention at the highest level would make a difference on a major trade question. He or his immediate advisors always responded that he had a trade minister to do what I was requesting. He was now really breaking new ground by involving himself personally in international trade questions, and I was very pleased about it.

At the meeting in Korea with the Canadian exporters, the prime minister was first class. Deep down I had the feeling that his heart wasn't in it and that he would have preferred to be dealing with broader international political issues, but he did rise to the occasion. I arrived at the meeting about a half-hour before the prime minister and attempted to orchestrate the twenty or so exporters. I pointed out that if each took more than three minutes to explain their presence in Korea to the prime minster, we would be hours getting through our agenda and lose his interest. Everyone was asked to be brief and to the point. They were. When the prime minister arrived, he invited each person around the table to tell him about the problems they faced and the opportunities they saw in the Korean market. He handled it all beautifully. He had a way of ferreting out the real issues. I came away most impressed, and I am sure the businessmen appreciated his direct involvement. My only regret was that Prime Minister Trudeau left it until almost the end of his mandate as prime minister to get directly involved with exports, an area of activity that brings to Canada about one third of its wealth and employment.

Of great interest for me was a day-long visit to the South Korean border with North Korea at Panmunjom. This was one of the great trouble spots of the world. My only experience with North Koreans had been while sitting amongst their soldiers at a Chinese opera in Beijing when it had been the practice to seat foreign "friends" together. The North Korean soldiers had numbered several hundred; we Canadians had numbered four.

At Panmunjom, straddling the border, was the conference room where meetings were held between the South Koreans and their American and other Western allies, and the North Koreans and their Chinese backers. The border between North and South Korea ran straight through the conference table, so that the south end of the conference table was in South Korea, and the north end in North Korea. Each side could enter by separate doors and avoid venturing into the other country. My diplomatic passport specifically excluded me from visiting North Korea, but I couldn't resist the temptation to walk into North Korea by walking around the conference table. I glanced out the windows of the conference room and could see peace-keeping foreign soldiers patrolling the border area around the building. The soldiers were divided between those from countries friendly with the North (Czecho-slovakia) and the south (Scandinavia).

We strolled along the heavily defended border for several hundred metres. I was intrigued with the propaganda directed at us from across the border. The North had a "model" village that we could see. Everybody was well dressed and lived in beautiful houses, and you could almost see their smiles from where we stood. The Communists claimed that the village simply demonstrated the good life enjoyed by the people in the North. Loudspeakers in the village continually blared out loud annoying music and speeches aimed to convert the South from their decadent ways to those of the brave new world. How the Communists could pretend that people actually lived and slept in this noisy model village made the propaganda ludicrous. Our American military guides told us that the entire village population was loaded onto trucks each evening and driven away. They returned at daybreak. Only the loud music and recorded speeches remained overnight.

Of more interest to me were the crowds of tourists on the other side waving at us. They were East Germans, who for the North Koreans had the deep pockets and free spending habits that in the West we tended to associate with the Americans and more recently the Japanese.

En route to Australia, we landed for refuelling at Guam, where the American military took us in hand. They brought us to a beautiful club, where we were able to relax for an hour's break from the long flight to Melbourne, where the prime minister was to attend the Commonwealth heads of government meetings.

The meetings in Melbourne involved most of the players and much the same agenda that we had at the Commonwealth meetings in Jamaica a few years before. The focus was, for the most part, on the plight of the developing countries in the world economic community. We were in Melbourne only for several days before heading north back across the Pacific. On our way back to Canada, we made an official stop in Fiji. I recall that Prime Minister Trudeau obliged the Fijians by drinking with them their traditional drink of *kava,* a diuretic beverage from the roots of a Polynesian shrub. I had tried it on an earlier visit and found its muddy appearance tended to put me off. When you did swallow it, you were left with a slight numbness of the mouth. This could be devastating for a politician who was expected to be ready to say a few words at a moment's notice.

At Honolulu, the prime minister was driven to the Royal Hawaiian Hotel in the security car that had been sent there for the use of Queen Elizabeth as she passed through on her way to and from Melbourne. United States security was tight when we arrived at the hotel, but it didn't stop the prime minister several hours later from appearing on the beach in front of the Royal Hawaiian, where we were all stretched out on the sand, trying to recover from the flight from Melbourne. He asked whether any of us wanted to go surfing. Bob Joyce, my colleague from the Department of Finance, jumped up, and the two of them, followed by several secret service officers, jumped into the sea and swam several hundred yards offshore, where the prime minister and Bob rode the waves. It was interesting to watch the security detail covering both the beach and the area of ocean around the prime minister. I sat with my acquaintance, Inspector Barry Moss of the Royal Canadian Mounted Police, who had no alternative but to relax and leave the security worries to the Americans. He had obviously warned them that the prime minister was likely to bound into the surf like a twenty-year-old.

Immediately on our return from Australia and Korea, the Korean ambassador to Canada held a dinner in honour of the prime minister's visit to his country. Peggy and I were invited. On arrival at the ambassador's residence and after shaking his hand, I was greeted by a loud voice from across the room, "Frank. I got you!" It was Michael Pittfield.

I really didn't understand his greeting. I asked him quite innocently, how he "got" me. He told me that the prime minister had just approved the moving of the trade elements of the Department of Industry, Trade and Commerce into the Department of External Affairs.

Like many of my colleagues in Trade and in External Affairs, I had concerns about the integration. My main concern was that we must not diminish the very close relationship that we had with the export community. I was also concerned that emphasis on security in External Affairs might interfere with our ability to maintain close contact with exporters. I was to spend the next six months along with many of my senior colleagues in both departments, trying to fit the trade function into the overall thrust of External Affairs. While it was rather unrealistically hoped in many quarters that the trade mentality might permeate overall foreign relations I feared, as did many of my colleagues in Trade, that while trade policy might fare well in the expanded department, trade development would be swallowed up by External Affairs.

During the Korean ambassador's dinner, at which time I was seated well away from Michael Pittfield, I thankfully got into discussions of other subjects. It was a very informal evening, despite the prime minister's attendance. We were at small tables seating four or six. Peggy and I were seated with the prime minister and his "date."

To get the conversation well away from Korea, I asked the prime minister whether he had ever taken his sons trout fishing in the ponds around Harrington Lake, where the prime ministerial country residence was located. His response was that he had no interest in fishing. I suggested that probably his sons did. I told him that when Mr. Diefenbacker was prime minister, he had a pond near the residence stocked with trout. I had been assigned to the Privy Council Office shortly afterwards and had heard that he had the pond "foamed" with some chemical to clean out the coarse fish and make room for the trout. Prime Minister Trudeau suddenly became interested in the subject and told me that while cross-country skiing with his boys he had come across some pipes leading into a pond that possibly had to do with the trout-stocking to which I referred. I hoped that what I told him would nudge him to take his boys fishing in that lake, but given his complete lack of interest in fishing, I doubt if his boys ever did go after those trout.

Chapter Thirty-six
The Holy Land

I had a few breaks from my travels with Minister Lumley in the early 1980s, but not from travel with other ministers. In January 1981, I went to Jamaica with the secretary of state (minister) for External Affairs, Mark MacGuigan, and in early 1982, I accompanied Industry Minister Herb Gray to Israel. The Jamaican trip had minimum interest from the trade point of view because of Jamaica's terrible foreign exchange situation and its under-standable tendency to dwell on aid rather than trade. Israel was another matter, holding potential for the development of two-way commerce.

The Honourable Herb Gray had been a powerhouse in the Liberal government for many years and was to be influential in government into the Chretien years. Back in early 1982, when he was minister of Industry, Trade and Commerce, he made a visit to Israel to follow up on the Joint Economic Commission that had been set up between that country and Canada. He invited me to join him. Israel was at that time Canada's third most important market in the Middle East. During Minister Gray's meetings with the Israelis, he undertook to send a Canadian government-sponsored trade mission of exporters and importers to Israel. Within three months of Minister Gray's visit, I was asked to lead a mission of about a dozen Canadian businessmen.

Israel was one of the most interesting countries I was to visit, and I was to return several times. Peggy and I made a private visit there on my retirement. Of greatest interest for me was the area around Jerusalem, the Sea of Galilee, the Jordan River, and the Dead Sea. No city has been coveted and fought over as often as has Jerusalem, the "City of Peace." Babylonians, Macedonians, Romans, Byzantines, Persians, Arabs, Crusaders, Mongols, Turks, British, and Jordanians were only some of the conquerors whose flags have fluttered across the pages of Jerusalem's bloodied and anguished past. Jerusalem has played a role in history out of all proportion to its economic importance and size.

Jerusalem remains the centre for three of the world's great religions, Jewish, Christian, and Islam. The magnet for all three faiths is the Old City and its close surroundings. On my first visit to Jerusalem, I had but one quick glance within the walls of the Old City. This was no fault of Minister Gray, but rather of the tight, ridiculous schedule that we had set for ourselves, which gave us no time to visit the places where our Western way of life got its start.

It was almost as bad when I returned three months later, leading a delegation of businessmen. We visited factories galore, particularly arms plants, for the Israelis were trying to sell us arms. We also visited numerous high technology plants that were both hungry for North American technology and able to offer impressive products, particularly in hospital equipment. But I only got a glimpse of the Old City of Jerusalem, on a Sunday afternoon when I slipped away from the delegation. The short visits were enough to make me determined to come back with Peggy and to spend a week or so combing through everything between those city walls.

Peggy and I did return in 1987, just before I was to retire. We made all the arrangements ourselves. On arrival in Tel Aviv, we ran immediately into the religious disputes of that ancient land. A shared taxi was to take us from Tel Aviv airport to Jerusalem. There were five of us with the driver. Peggy and I sat in the back with a young Israeli man. A young Israeli woman sat in the front. Our fifth passenger was a very strict Jew, who refused to sit in the front with the woman or in the back with Peggy. The driver had to shuffle her to the back seat and move the man to the front before the strict Jew would get into the car and allow us to get underway. It was not a very congenial group that set out for Jerusalem.

We had booked a small hotel about half a kilometre from the Damascus Gate of the Old City. It was an Arab hotel in a generally Arab area. It surprises many visitors to Jerusalem to learn that most of the Christians in Jerusalem are Arabs. In the early mornings, I was just a little disappointed that all the Arabs around us were not Christians, because we were awakened very early by the *muezzin,* the cryer calling to the faithful of Islam from the top of his slender minaret, proclaiming the hour of prayer.

We spent three or four days in and around the Old City. We walked along the four kilometres of the city walls wherever they were accessible, descending into the various quarters and exploring the seven open city gates. We entered the city each day through the Damascus Gate, on the top of which were always stationed a couple of armed Israeli soldiers. You were

276

reminded of the Six-Day War, when the Israelis took over the entire Old City by the presence of young armed soldiers on the walls and in the streets.

After combing through the Old City, Peggy and I set out to explore the surrounding countryside. We took a local bus to Bethlehem. Like the Church of the Holy Sepulchre in Jerusalem, I found the Church of the Nativity and the Grotto marking the place where Christ was born to be spoiled by the gifts and decorations of centuries. It is difficult to associate the scene in the Grotto with the simple descriptions of cave or stable and manger in the Bible. I was more impressed with the Garden of Gethsemane, which had not changed significantly from the days when Jesus would gather there with his followers. Similarly the site of the Last Supper on Mount Zion greatly impressed me, probably again because of the simple and unadorned nature of the room. The Upper Room is in a medieval structure marking the site. In the fifth century, the site was linked to the Pentecost and the Last Supper. It is said that the earliest Christians had their headquarters on Mount Zion.

Peggy and I had booked several days at a kibbutz near the Dead Sea. The day we were to leave Jerusalem was the Jewish Sabbath, so we had problems with public transport. In the end, we negotiated a reasonable fare with an Arab Christian driver. He spoke English and, as it turned out, was able to show us, on our way to the Dead Sea, a lot of the sites recorded in the Bible that we surely would have missed had we taken a bus. We stopped at the supposed site of the hotel used by the Good Samaritan. Next to it was a Bedouin camp, into which our driver invited us to join him for a traditional coffee with the Bedouin.

We also visited Qumran, where there was great excavation activity following the discovery of the Dead Sea Scrolls in caves above the site of Qumran. In 1947, an Arab shepherd stumbled on a cave and brought to light seven ancient scrolls. Many others were found later in other caves in the area. They proved to be part of the library of a fundamentalist Jewish religious sect (Essenes) that was in existence in Qumran from the second century before and during the time of Christ. These scrolls indicate that many of the characteristic Judaeo-Christian ideas were cradled in just such a religious environment.

Our kibbutz was Ein Gedi, situated on the side of the hills of Judea overlooking the Dead Sea. Ein Gedi is mentioned in the Old Testament. It is an oasis in an otherwise barren land. The area around was known as the Wilderness of Judea. I had grown up hearing about the Wilderness of Judea but could never visualise a wilderness such as the sight before us. For me, a wilderness couldn't be anything but thick woods. Here, outside the fences of Ein Gedi, there wasn't a blade of grass. Below us, we had the most magnificent view of the Dead Sea. This is the lowest body of water on earth, about four hundred metres (thirteen hundred feet) below sea level. It was eighty kilometres (fifty miles) long and attained a width of eighteen kilometres (eleven miles). The fresh waters of the River Jordan flowed into the Dead Sea.

There were many sulphur springs, and the waters were extremely saline. This salinity excluded any animal or vegetable life. Fish that were carried in by the Jordan died instantly. It was not possible to swim as one would in another sea or ocean. You were able to sit in the water and read a newspaper, for there was no fear of sinking. We would go down by a kibbutz bus to the Dead Sea daily. I would plaster myself with sulphuric black mud, which was said to be good for the skin, and soak in the sea.

Life at the kibbutz was simple. We had a self-contained unit but took our meals in a common dining room. After dark, we enjoyed sitting outside looking across the Dead Sea. You could see the twinkling lights of Jordan that was forbidden territory for anybody in Israel. The beautiful view was only occasionally interrupted by loud Israeli fighter jets zooming up and down the Israeli side of the Dead Sea.

We took a day-long trip south along the Dead Sea to Masada. Because of movies and television, Masada is probably well known to people the world over. However, it has to be seen to be truly appreciated. In a nutshell, Masada is a plateau on the top of a mountain with almost perpendicular sides. During the Roman persecutions at the time of the destruction of Jerusalem, a number of Jews took refuge at Masada, and it took the complete might of Rome for three years to dislodge them. In the end, the only way the Romans could get to the top of the mountain was to build a ramp, using Jewish prisoners as shields against bombardment from the top. When it was certain that the end of their brave defence was imminent, the Jewish defenders came to an agreement to commit mass suicide rather than be taken prisoners by the Romans. They drew lots for who should do the killing of their fellows and their families and to be the last to commit suicide. They had all died by the time the Roman ramp reached them. Peggy and I went to the top and spent several hours exploring the plateau.

Among the most impressive views from Masada were not only the Dead Sea and the hills of Jordan across the sea, but the sites of the Roman encampment that can be easily identified from above. The passage of time has not obliterated the markers that encircled the Roman camps. We could look down on a site that, except for the camp itself, had not changed in two thousand years. Peggy and I also were most impressed with the underground reservoir where the defenders stored their water supply. You descended hewn steps into a huge underground cavern, where enough water was stored to maintain the defenders for years. It certainly wasn't water, or food, or determination that spelled doom for the defenders. It was the ramp.

From Masada, we travelled by public bus north along the Jordan River. Peggy immediately got a seat. I was left standing with a dozen or so passengers, including a young soldier. He carried his rifle that was mandatory in this war-torn area. The young soldier was so careless with the way the rifle was slung over his shoulder that it was virtually sticking in Peggy's ear. She was startled but said nothing, simply moving away from the gun. Several of the soldier's fellow countrymen noticed her discomfort and gave the young man a tongue-lashing, demanding that he be more careful with his weapon. They all apologised for the boy's carelessness. We could see the need for armed soldiers on the bus (although the soldier concerned was only going on leave).

When we stopped at Jericho, a girl got off the bus, leaving a small bag. This was forbidden for obvious security reasons, so the driver went into a bit of a panic when the bag was pointed out to him. He yelled to the girl who had not gone far and instructed her to return to the bus and collect her bag. It obviously was just carelessness on her part, but her fellow passengers were not amused.

We got off the bus at Tiberias, on the western shore of the Sea of Galilee. The Sea of Galilee was everything that the Dead Sea was not. It was fed by mountain streams, and the River Jordan flowed from it to the Dead Sea. The Jordan (a "stream" by Canadian standards) gave life to the Jordan Valley before ending its own life when it flowed into the Dead Sea.

Our interest was not so much in Tiberias, but in getting across the Sea of Galilee to Capernaum. We sought the instructions of our hotel keeper about how best to cross Galilee. He was very vague, so we decided to look for ourselves. We were glad for his vagueness, because in our ignorance, we stumbled upon a most pleasing experience. We walked down to the dock area and saw three busloads of English-speaking people boarding a boat. We went up to some people who appeared to be in charge, and before we could ask whether we could join the group, we were told that it was getting late so we must hurry and board the boat, for they wanted to push off immediately. They obviously thought we were of their number. We did as we were told.

Once in the boat, a gentleman opposite me leaned over and asked, "Which group are you people with?" He was an American.

I said, "We are not with any group, so we must be on the wrong boat!" The friendly American explained that he was a Baptist minister from Colorado, and he and another minister were conducting a group of fellow Baptists on a tour of the Holy Land. He explained that the other two groups were from England. One was Anglican and the other Roman Catholic. He asked what denomination I was. I told him Presbyterian. He smiled and said that Presbyterians were close to Baptists, so we might wish to consider ourselves a part of their group for the day. We thanked him and had one of the most enjoyable days we had ever had.

We were introduced and shook hands with the thirty or so Americans and were most touched by their friendliness. We no sooner met them all, when the boat stopped. The captain emerged from the wheelhouse and said that since we were in the middle of the Sea of Galilee, it might be appropriate if one of the clergy amongst us would come forward and offer a few words of prayer. I have never seen men move so fast as did the two Baptist ministers, the Anglican, and the Catholic priest. The Anglican minister got there first, so the other three good-naturedly retreated. He gave a very simple and moving prayer, and I do believe that everybody on that boat would have thought it perfect, given our location and the interdenominational nature of the people on the boat. While he prayed, I glanced around me at the calm and quiet sea and the beautiful shoreline and mountains beyond.

We landed at Capernaum, and Peggy and I joined the Americans for a tour of the ruins of the temple and what was thought to be site of Peter's house. The two Baptist ministers quoted the biblical accounts of Jesus' presence in the area as no ordinary tour guide could. We joined the Baptist group on their bus. At first, their driver was a little nervous about this, being under instructions for security reasons not to allow people who were not part of the group onto the bus. Practically all the Americans came to our rescue and explained to the driver that we were indeed now with them.

All the way on the bus, the two ministers explained the countryside and its connections with the Gospels. We stopped on the side of the mountain on the Sea of Galilee where Jesus had preached the Sermon on the Mount. The younger of the two ministers read from the gospels and gave a touching sermon, sitting on a rock under the trees, with the Sea of Galilee below forming the perfect backdrop. The bus tour took us all around the Golan Heights to a point where we could actually see Canadian Peace-Keepers with the United Nations on the border between the Israelis and the Syrians.

We travelled along the eastern side of the Sea of Galilee to the point where the Jordan started its flow from Galilee. Here, many of the Baptists intended to have their second baptism, this time in the River Jordan. Amongst the most determined was a very elderly lady everyone affectionately called Granny. The ministers changed into ministerial garb and waded into the Jordan at a spot obviously reserved for such purposes. One by one, men and women, young and old, including Granny, having changed from their normal clothes, waded in for the baptism. It was touching.

Chapter Thirty-seven
Sydneytown

Peggy and I arrived in Sydney, where I was to serve as Canadian Consul General, in the Canadian summer and Australian winter of 1982. I had visited the house that was to be our home many times before and rated it one of the best of Canadian diplomatic residences abroad. This was not only because of the house itself but because of its location. The view from the residence was of the full sweep of Sydney's harbour, from the heads that stood like sentinels at its entrance, all the way for the five or so miles to the Sydney Harbour Bridge and the other internationally known landmark of Sydney, the beautiful Opera House.

Also appealing was that on the front lawn was a one hundred-year-old operating lighthouse. Peggy's sea-faring grandfather had used the light of "our" lighthouse to line up his approach when he entered through the heads into Sydney Harbour nearly a half-century before we claimed it as "ours." One of my early Canadian predecessors had struck a deal with the Maritime Services Board that allowed us to incorporate the lighthouse and its surrounding property into that of the residence, on condition that we always recognise it as New South Wales government property and maintain it as we would our own. Peggy and I, who were both keen gardeners, spent much of our spare time caring for the property and, while doing so, waving to the busloads of tourists who stopped to admire the old lighthouse and watch what they thought were the consul general's gardeners hard at work.

Peggy's paternal grandfather Roberts had been a sea captain. As a young boy, he had sailed from England to make his home in Australia. After a sea-going career that took him over the Far East, he came ashore in Sydney, where he served as a harbour pilot. He ended his career as harbour master of the port of Newcastle, which was New South Wales' second city. The sea must have run in the veins of the Roberts family. One of Peggy's uncles, Ted Roberts, also was a captain. When I knew him, he was commander of the largest ore carrier on the Australian coast. His son Cecil followed in his father's steps. Peggy's father also had a close connection with the sea. He was an economist with the Maritime Services Board. He had many interests, not all related to the sea; he wrote several books on the Australian stock market.

I had decided to take an overseas posting. I felt that I had done many of the tasks in the trade policy and trade development fields and perhaps the time had come for me to move. Bob Johnson, who was Deputy Minister of International Trade, was most cooperative and suggested a number of positions as head of post that I might consider. Barry Steers, the assistant deputy minister, was more focused and made a pitch for me to go to Sydney, Australia. Sydney was a large post, concentrating mainly on trade in the South Pacific, but with an element of all of the activities found at a large post, such as consular and immigration work. Indeed, on immigration, the post was responsible for Australia, New Zealand, and all the islands of the South Pacific. It had a staff of some thirty people, including Canadians and locally engaged Australians. I couldn't think of anywhere else I would have preferred to go.

I left my position in Ottawa in early summer, and since we had several weeks to wait for my predecessor in Sydney to vacate the post, we decided to take a vacation on two of the islands of the South Pacific that we had not visited before. We flew to Tahiti, where we had booked a Tahitian-owned hotel on the outskirts of the capital, Papeete. We arrived after midnight, only to find that our hotel reservation was recorded for the next day. We had no alternative but to bed ourselves down on a couple of lounges in the open-air reception area. This would have been fine, for the temperature was perfect and we were so tired from the long flight that we could have slept standing, but the lounge was crowded with hotel guests, staff, and locals. They were all glued to the television, watching the world soccer finals. It wasn't until this ended, as dawn approached, that we could stretch out and sleep.

Tahiti was as French as France itself. In Papeete on a Sunday morning, it was interesting to witness the work of the London Missionary Society over a century ago, for the entire local population seemed to appear on the streets, decked out in their Sunday best for church. The ladies wore beautiful, pure white dresses and huge hats, and the men, dark suits, more suitable for the far north than this very tropical isle. They sang the same Methodist hymns that their neighbours sang far away on the English-speaking islands; the only difference was that they sang them in French.

We flew from Tahiti to Nouméa, New Caledonia. This island, east of

283

Queensland, Australia, was France's largest possession in the South Pacific. At the time, about a third of the population was European and you had the feeling of being in southern France on the Mediterranean. We were there for the French National Day, July 14. The military parade and activities of naval ships and helicopters clearly underlined the French position that, despite a separatist threat, the island was very much part of France. After exploring the town, we took long walks in the countryside surrounding Nouméa. One day we were surprised to see a most unusual soccer match. It was unusual in that all the players were ladies, they were native islanders playing in bare feet, and all of them wore "mission" dresses. These were ankle-length colourful dresses that had been introduced by the missionaries, none other than the London Missionary Society. It was surprising that this custom should survive for a hundred years on an island steeped in the culture of France. They were beautiful dresses, with the loveliest floral designs of the South Seas, but they certainly were not the latest Paris fashions. I was glad that they weren't.

Life in Sydney was not at the hectic pace it had been for me during the past decade or so in Ottawa. I found it easy to find my way through the political system that was almost identical to Canada's. I had no problem getting access to most ministers and the governor.

I used to call regularly on the governor. My chauffeur, John, enjoyed these calls very much. He would say, "Then this is a flag-job, sir?" It was about the only occasion when I would allow him to fly the Canadian flag on the official car. Peggy and I were always amused with the "instruction" on the governor's invitations, "Carriages at Eight." I used to tell John that he had to have our "carriage" in front of the Governor's Residence exactly at eight o'clock. I wasn't aware of the hierarchy amongst chauffeurs until these calls on the governor. They sorted themselves out to ensure that the most senior heads of post were picked up first. Seniority depended on the length of time a head of post had been at the post. The chauffeurs did this on their own. We all waited for our "carriages" in the knowledge that the drivers knew more about precedence than we did. John took his position very seriously, which I appreciated. He used to tell me that he was friendly with the driver of the American consul general who had taken "a shine to him" and that whenever we had to go to the American consulate general, he was given priority parking.

I had good reason not to fly the flag more than absolutely necessary. While Australians generally couldn't have been friendlier, I did have threats from some of the Australian animal protection and environmental groups. I also had very serious threats from an Armenian terrorist group.

I realised that opposition to Canada's annual seal hunt was very widespread. I felt that most of those opposed were sincere in the views they held, but they could get dangerously emotional when seeing television or magazine articles of seals being killed. There seemed to be a deluge of such material in Australia. The people who got overly upset over the seals had no problem eating the products of their own slaughterhouses and wearing the leather from the hides. They certainly didn't seem to get as worked up over the "culling" of the kangaroos as they did about the "killing" of the seals. The kangaroo cull could be justified because these animals played havoc with pastures and competed with cattle and sheep for grassland, whereas seals were only cute little animals that ate codfish.

There had been a commercial seal fishery for pelts, meat, and oil since the fist settlers landed on the island of Newfoundland. It came as a great surprise and shock to us that people like Brigitte Bardot, who had no concern about the French customs of eating horse meat or of force-feeding geese to obtain the most appetising livers, were almost paranoid in their opposition to the hunting of seals.

The hatred and violence stirred up by people against the "seal hunt," even in Australia, led to serious threats against me as the representative of the Canadian government. It was worst when it was learned that I was from Newfoundland. Some of this group published papers calling for violence. One Australian radio station even suggested that listeners, "Club a Canadian to death today!" We threatened this station with legal action and they quickly retracted, but it serves to demonstrate how a group can work up a population to contemplate violence.

Across the street from the consulate general, scrawled and painted on the walls, were a number of nasty messages for Canadians about the seal hunt. When we reported these to the authorities, their advice was that under no circumstances should we ever admit representatives of any of these groups into the consulate general for discussion. They told me that one group with a television crew was going to request an interview in my office. The police said that the routine would be for someone to throw red ink over me and for the cameras to roll, recording the Canadian consul general covered in the "blood" of the seals.

More serious were the threats of Armenian terrorists. These thugs had recently killed the Turkish consul general and his driver in Sydney and were now threatening to "get" a Western diplomat. The new Turkish consul general was a friend, but it was always disconcerting to have him to dinner, for he had a standing threat against his life for the atrocities committed by the Turks against the Armenians some hundred years ago. He had to travel everywhere with several Australian security people. When he came to my place, our garden was like an armed camp. His plight really struck home when he told me that on his visits in the countryside, where he liked to paint, behind him while he painted were always three armed security men.

My Turkish friend's concerns suddenly became mine. I was advised confidentially by Ottawa that following the murder in Ottawa of a Turkish military attaché, I would have to take particular precautions. The poor Turk was driving to work and stopped for a traffic light at the corner of Island Park Drive and the Ottawa River Parkway when he was gunned down. The Canadian government had offered a reward for information leading to the arrest of the persons concerned.

The reaction of the Armenian terrorists was that Canada would "pay" for their "unfriendly" action. Information obtained by the Canadian authorities suggested that the terrorists were threatening to hit Canadian targets in California or Sydney. In Sydney, the likely targets were the consulate general or Canadian Pacific Airlines. There was a large Armenian population in Sydney, although I'm sure that all, except a crazy few, were as law-abiding as their fellow citizens of other ethnic backgrounds. These terrorists could hide and hit anywhere, for well over half of the world's nine million Armenians lived outside today's Armenia.

For several months Australian security people followed me around. John, my driver, became expert at spotting them. I only wished he had the same expertise spotting those who were out to get us. He was under instructions to take me by a different route to and from the office each day, and often he would mention that one of "their" (Australian security) cars was behind us. I must say that I got to know Sydney's King's Cross, or "King's Bloody Cross," area very well because we meandered through the Cross on our way home every night. This was the nightclub and "good time" area of Sydney. It was made famous or infamous by American soldiers, who favoured it as one of their main recreational areas when on leave. In several months, the whole issue of Armenians and their threat seemed to quiet down, and we became more relaxed. I was, however, left with the conviction that if armed terrorists were determined to do you harm, there wasn't really much you could do about it, unless you wanted to live in an armed camp.

I was always struck by the similarities between Canada and Australia, in spite of the great differences between the two in climate. Australia was one of the driest of continents, with thousands of square miles of hot desert country, and Canada one of the coldest, with great tracks of white frozen wasteland. Yet the two countries had much in common. They were the only two countries with parliamentary systems of government superimposed on a federal system. Both had relatively small populations. The Australian population stretched along the southeastern and eastern coast and the far southeastern corner of the country. Canada's population was largely strung along its southern border with the United States. In neither country did you have to venture far to be in the wilds. Both countries shared the problem of a relatively small population supporting a great infrastructure of rail and road trying to knit together its disparate parts.

In the lead up to Canada's participation in Australia's Bicentennial celebrations in 1988, we asked Peggy to do a little research (gratis). She dug through material on Canada's relations with Australia in Sydney's libraries. She found that there had been little contact in the early days owing to the "tyranny of distance." A voyage from the settlements of eastern Canada to Australia involved five to seven months on a sailing ship around Cape Horn, the southernmost tip of South America. The Panama Canal was not yet open, and Vancouver did not become the Canadian outlet to the Pacific until the late 1800s, when the Canadian Pacific Railway brought contact with eastern Canada.

The events that really developed contacts, albeit deplorable contacts, were the War of 1812 against the Americans and the 1838 rebellion in Upper Canada. There was a recruiting of convicts in New South Wales in 1812 to bring the 103rd British Regiment (the notorious Rum Regiment) up to strength. This regiment that now included the New South Wales Fencibles was sent to fight in the War of 1812 at Niagara. They had the reputation of being the worst regiment ever sent to Canada, particularly because of drunkenness and desertions. That convicts would desert the Americans or seek a new life in Canada should have surprised nobody.

After the rebellion of 1838 in Canada, fifty-eight French Canadians and ninety-two English-speaking Canadians and Americans were sent to Australia. The French Canadians went to Sydney, and the English-speaking deportees, to Hobart, Tasmania (then called Van Diemen's Land). Nine of these prisoners wrote detailed accounts of their experiences in Australia as political prisoners. Sir George Arthur, who had served as governor in

Tasmania, was instrumental in helping to repress the 1838 rebellion in Upper Canada, where he was lieutenant governor. He may have had some part in the decision to send the political prisoners to Sydney and Hobart.

Sydney, at the time, had a population of under two hundred thousand. According to one of the prisoners, some one-third were the vilest criminals from Britain. The surrounding woods were "infested with the scourge of bushrangers." Robbery was "common and very often accompanied by bloodshed," according to the convict writer who had suffered such an experience with "his mates." Eventually all except one returned to Canada on French and American whaling ships. Joseph Marceau stayed in Australia and married. Some of his descendants attended the unveiling of a memorial plaque by Prime Minister Trudeau at Concord in 1970.

In Tasmania, or Van Diemen's Land, the treatment of the English-speaking Canadian and American political prisoners was much harsher. One of the convicts stated that almost all the prisoners were Americans who had been attempting to free Canada from "British bondage and misrule." One of the convicts describes seeing scaffolds on the main street on his arrival in Hobart, and another describes the terrible situation which existed after eleven years of Sir George Arthur's term as governor. Prisoners were fed like dogs, lodged in the meanest huts, worked almost to death, and lashed to posts for flogging, with brine poured into the lash wounds. Some suffered complete physical collapse and death through overwork. Three men escaped and were picked up by an American ship and arrived in the United States seven months later. In 1843 two pardons were granted to members of the group for helping to capture bushrangers. In that year, twelve of the Canadians died, some of ill-treatment. One of the convicts describes in his journal that Van Diemen's Land society was "loathsome," with "drunkenness, debauchery and vice of all kinds run riot." These political prisoners, not being criminals, were often used to uphold the law in the Hobart streets and were recommended early for pardon. Again, only one, a Moses Ducher, married and remained in Van Diemen's Land.

It can be said that the granting of responsible government to the Australian colonies in the 1850s was a direct result of the Canadian Rebellion of 1838. The British Commissioner to Canada in 1839, Lord Durham, recommended that responsible government should be granted to a Union of Upper and Lower Canada. He said that the same principle must be applied in Australia, New Zealand, and South Africa. This was the first move in changing the British Empire into a Commonwealth of independent nations.

Canada decided to exhibit at a trade fair in Sydney in April 1877, the forerunner to the Royal Easter Show, which is today one of the world's great agricultural shows. A government minister, the Honourable J. Young, went with the trade mission. He publicly urged the Australian colonies to federate as the Canadian colonies had done in 1867 to eliminate tariffs and other barriers to trade. (He seemed to ignore the fact that confederation in Canada did not rid the new country of interprovincial trade barriers.) The minister returned to Canada feeling that the absence of a federal system in Australia hindered him from achieving what he had hoped for in expanding trade between the two countries. Nevertheless, a Canadian government trade office was opened in Sydney in 1895, making Australia the first Canadian trade post abroad.

The name "Chaffey" wasn't restricted to eastern Ontario, where in the beautiful Rideau Lakes area on the Rideau Canal, we have Chaffey's Locks. The Chaffey brothers made an important contribution to Australia. They irrigated the Murray Valley in Victoria, and they irrigated land in South Australia. George Chaffey, born in Brockville, Ontario, in 1848, was an irrigation pioneer, being an engineer, inventor, and entrepreneur. His brother William was an agriculturist and irrigation planner.

The brothers travelled to California, where they were partners in developing model irrigation projects. The state of Victoria, in Australia, suffered severe droughts in 1877–85. Alfred Deakin, a Victorian government minister, visited California, where he met the Chaffeys. He persuaded them to move to Mildura, in Australia.

In 1887, Sir John Downer, the premier of South Australia, offered them a block of land at Renmark, South Australia. With great energy, the Chaffey brothers developed the desert at Mildura over the next four years. Eventually, the settlements of Mildura and Renmark became very prosperous. There are monuments to the Chaffeys in Mildura and in Brockville, Ontario.

Another Canadian who made an extraordinary contribution to Australia was Simon Fraser. He was born in Pictou, Nova Scotia, in 1832. He went to the Australian gold fields in Bendigo in 1853 when only twenty-one years of age. After two years, he had sufficient capital to move into business in Melbourne. In 1865 he went to Queensland, where he brought property. The western parts of Queensland were badly stricken by drought in 1882 and for a number of years thereafter. The government had dams built to keep stock routes open and attempted well-boring without many positive results. In Sydney, in 1886, Simon Fraser met J. S. Loughead, a Canadian well-borer who had come to New South Wales with Canadian well-digging equipment, hoping to find petroleum. Fraser contracted with Loughead to sink five bores to a depth of five thousand feet on some mount formations on his Queensland property that he suspected had subterranean water. The drilling was a great success; at a depth of just over one thousand feet was found huge supplies of excellent fresh water that flowed two feet deep over the surface of the ground.

At the age of 82, in 1914, Sir Simon Fraser wrote that the discovery of artesian water in Australia was due to private enterprise, and the Canadian system of using a "pole tool, maintained its supremacy to the present day." In 1909, there were five million gallons of fresh water made available daily because of the system. The changes to beef and sheep farming and exports were astonishing. Simon's grandson, Malcolm Fraser, was to keep the family name in the headlines. He became prime minister of Australia.

There is nothing Canadian that has more impact abroad than a red-coated Mountie. We had four of them join us in Sydney on their way to take part in the Commonwealth Games in 1983 in Brisbane, Queensland. They were members of the famous Royal Canadian Mounted Police Musical Ride and were to lead the Commonwealth parade at the opening of the games. Due to Australia's very tough and rigid quarantine regulations, the Mounties couldn't bring their horses from Canada. The New South Wales Police offered theirs. We were very friendly, through Peggy's parents, with Cec Abbott, who was Commissioner of the New South Wales Police. They had a mounted detachment, and Cec offered the Mounties superb horses and invited them, while in Sydney, to accompany the New South Wales Police when on mounted patrol duty in "the Rocks" area of Sydney. The Mounties made the front page of every paper in Australia. Cec told me that the Mounties, as ordinary policemen, helped raise the prestige of his force in the eyes of the public. The Mounties were superb ambassadors for Canada.

Peggy and I had the Mounties and their hosts from the New South Wales Police to luncheon at the residence. After lunch, they emerged from the kitchen, where they had gone to thank the staff. The youngest said to Peggy, "If one more lady asks me whether I know how to sing 'Rose Marie, I Love You,' I'll scream!" That question, and whether they personally knew Jeanette MacDonald and Nelson Eddy, the stars in that popular movie where

Nelson Eddy starred as a Mountie in the Canadian Rockies, seemed to haunt them.

I asked the young Mountie where he was from. He said Ottawa because, as he explained, nobody would know the small close-by village where his family lived. I said, "Try me." He said, "Ramsayville."

I said, "Where in Ramsayville?" I was able to single out the very house where he had been raised.

We had a visit at the same time from the Canadian navy. Four destroyers docked in Sydney for several days, on their way to the Commonwealth Games in Brisbane. Protocol required that the officer in command should call on the senior Canadian representative in the port. He and his senior officers visited us at the Consulate General. In return, I had to join them with my senior staff for luncheon aboard ship. The four destroyers were tied together, so it was possible to visit all four using the one gangway.

After a good luncheon, we got down to serious business. I mentioned that the ships would provide an excellent site for us to entertain Sydney's top business and government people. The commander said they would be pleased to make the ships available for such a reception for some one hundred and fifty and to provide the stewards and drink on one condition! He would expect the Canadian Consulate General to provide some one hundred SYTs. I asked what were "SYTs"? He said they had some one hundred young officer cadets on the four ships and would like, besides the businessmen and government people, to entertain some "sweet young things."

We agreed and next morning stationed our consular staff at points where the ferries docked during morning rush hour in downtown Sydney. Any young lady who resembled a "sweet young thing" was handed an invitation to the reception aboard the ships. About one hundred turned up, along with virtually all the business and government invitees. Peggy and I were "piped aboard" and joined the commander and his senior officers welcoming the guests. It was a unique setting for a reception and the weather cooperated beautifully. I'm sure that all the other consuls general in Sydney were most envious of the wonderful facility we had to host the important and the beautiful in Sydney. We did a repeat performance in Brisbane.

We faced what could have been a major consular problem when some one thousand Canadian sailors came ashore in Sydney and in Brisbane each night the Canadian ships were in port. In Sydney we worked out with Commissioner Abbott's officers and the Canadian commander's officers an arrangement whereby any Canadian sailor picked up by the local police for anything but a major chargeable offence would be escorted back to the ships, where he would be dealt with by the navy. We made similar arrangements with the police in Brisbane. When the four destroyers sailed for home, I was proud to be told that not one Canadian sailor ended up in an Australian jail. Many were escorted back to their ships, where, I was told, they faced disciplinary treatment much more severe than they would have received from the Australians.

One sailor came close to spending the night in jail in Brisbane when he and an Australian sailor he met in a pub decided, for either patriotic reasons or mere curiosity, to sneak aboard the royal yacht *Britannia*. Both had consumed a little too much of the strong Aussie beer and were swimming out to the *Britannia* when they were apprehended. The Australian was taken to jail, and the Canadian escorted back to his ship where he was "dealt with."

The only thing that went wrong for the navy while in Australia was the outcome of an ice hockey game in Queensland. The Canadian sailors offered to put on an exhibition game on the Gold Coast. The Queenslanders said they could organise a team to play the navy. Peggy and I were there and were horrified by what we saw. The Queensland team was made up of every Canadian beach bum that could be found on the beaches of southern Queensland who could play hockey. From the moment the puck was dropped, the referees, who were not very effective, let the beach bums off with everything but murder. The Queensland team committed every illegal offence known to hockey. They were obviously intent, not on playing hockey, but on harming as many navy players as possible. The navy stopped the game after five minutes and announced that their team was made up of men who had to work next day running four ships, and they were not going to subject them to injury by people who seemed to have injury as their sole objective. They would agree to return to the ice if the referees would strictly enforce the rules and if the players would attempt to abide by them. The game continued and was completed without too much more violence. The Queensland team won by an embarrassingly large margin.

During the Commonwealth Games, Peggy and I were required to be in Brisbane for several days. We shared a small efficiency with our good friends Ray and Joyce Anderson. Ray was our high commissioner in Canberra. One event that both Ray and I involved ourselves in was boxing. Ray was from Saskatchewan and noted that Canada's great hope in boxing was a Saskatchewan boy, Sean O'Sullivan. We were having dinner with our wives in a restaurant across the street from the stadium where the boxing event was to take place. The Canadian boxer was to compete within the hour. We started our dinner, leaving word with the staff, who were watching the Games on television, to let us know when the O'Sullivan match was about to start.

As we finished our soup course, we received word that O'Sullivan was entering the ring with an African opponent. Ray and I excused ourselves from Peggy and Joyce and raced across the street to the stadium. We hadn't tickets but talked our way in, and we were just seating ourselves when the bell sounded to start the first round. Our Canadian hero rose and walked towards his opponent, delivered one punch and the poor opponent went down for the full count. Ray and I followed the Canadian to his dressing room and warmly shook his hand in congratulations. We then raced back to the restaurant and our wives. The waiters were just serving the main course as we sat down. It was difficult to believe that we had had our soup, seen an entire bout and congratulated the winner, between courses. We had been away less than ten minutes.

In Australia, I spent a lot of time with fellow officers Michael Fine and Art Perron, chasing various export opportunities. We seemed to have a steady stream of federal and provincial trade missions. We also had to make frequent political representations on behalf of Canadian companies and consortia. These were often successful, but there was one project in particular that we found most frustrating. Our failure in this effort demonstrated the strength of Japan in the Australian market. Michael and I accompanied the senior staff of the Canadian company, Combustion Engineering, to Brisbane on several occasions, in attempts to beat out the Japanese on a huge power project.

I called on the state premier, Jo Bjelke Petersen, several times on behalf of the Canadians and actually got them into meet him on one occasion. We had to counter the Japanese, who were pulling every trick in the book in their attempt to win the project. I found the premier a delightful person to talk with, and we got along well, but there was a tremendous obstacle with which Canada had to contend. Japan was a very large market for Queensland raw materials, such as coal and bauxite. The Japanese never let the Queenslanders forget this and expected to be rewarded with such prizes as the power project. I am sure we were ahead insofar as price and quality were concerned, but we could not overcome the power of Japan in Queensland.

The best tour of a territory I've ever taken was one put on by the Brisbane Chamber of Commerce. Senior executives of foreign resource-based companies, financial experts, and people like myself, all who wanted a quick, first-hand course on the Australian outback, found this tour invaluable. We were about twenty and had our own plane.

From Brisbane, we flew to northern Queensland to visit sheep and cattle stations and sugar plantations before heading inland to Mount Isa. This large mining town with about twenty-four thousand people in northwestern Queensland was Australia's main source of silver, lead, zinc, and copper.

We went down one of the deepest operating mines in the world. We had to strip completely and put on white coveralls without underwear or shirts. We were given socks and heavy boots and helmets with lights. Large belts were wrapped around our waists, on which were attached an array of emergency equipment. Around our necks, they fastened emergency breathing apparatus. We couldn't recognise one another. I felt I was heading for the moon instead of descending into the bowels of the earth. True to the thinking of people who fear the devil, it was very hot down there. It was also wet. In spite of plenty of forced fresh air, it must have been a tough place to work day after day. We watched men manipulate a range of machines that dug, cut, extracted, and loaded ore onto trucks and trains on the first phase of its transportation to the surface.

I was also interested in the huge open pit mines in areas of the north. This type of mining was used extensively in the extraction of bauxite, the ore of aluminum. This ore seemed to be everywhere on the Cape York Peninsula of Queensland, which is just below Papua New Guinea, and on the Gove Peninsula in the Northern Territory. A road would descend around and around the rim as the pit became deeper. The one we were taken down required several miles of driving in ever descending circles before reaching the bottom. These were great eyesores but were generally so distant from inhabited areas that there were at first few complaints. The Aborigines eventually drew the attention of the country and the world to these great scars on the landscape. They seemed to have been well-informed by their legal advisers about land claims, particularly when it was often discovered that the mining was on sacred tribal lands.

We visited several Aboriginal reserves, including the huge Arnhem Land Reserve. This was in an area of the Northern Territory known as Arnhem Land, which occupies an area just a little less than the area of the island of Newfoundland. The settlement we entered on the reserve was a strictly run mission station. No consumption of alcohol was permitted. It seemed the consumption took place just outside the reserve boundary, for there was by the side of the road a mountain of beer cans at least fifteen feet high. In a number of these areas where mining was done on recognised Aboriginal land, the local communities were fairly wealthy from royalties. The problem was that the Aborigines had not had time to ease themselves into Western society. The Aborigines could, for example, afford to buy cars, but there were few mechanics amongst them to maintain them. We were told that some people bought cars and drove them until they needed repair, at which point they abandoned them and bought new ones. I'm not sure of the authenticity of this story since the royalties paid by the mining companies went into the Aboriginal Benefits Trust Fund.

We stayed overnight at Weipa, a town of twenty-five hundred on the northeast coast of Cape York Peninsula on the Gulf of Carpentaria. Ten million tons of bauxite ore was extracted annually from the open pit mine and conveyed by one of the longest belts in existence to ships in the bay for export around the world. Across the gulf in the Northern Territory, we visited Nhulunbuy, a similar town-site on the Gove Peninsula, east of Darwin and north of Groote Eylande. These towns boasted more social clubs per capita than anywhere else in the world. There were said to be some sixty clubs catering to every possible interest in a town of several thousand.

There were also the pubs that were going through a difficult period trying to integrate the Aborigines into the Australian beer-drinking habits. The courts had ruled that Aborigines straight out of the bush, as well as the Aboriginal stockmen, who were more integrated into rural society, had to be accommodated in the local pubs. It wasn't a pretty scene. It didn't do much for the Aboriginal cause to have drunken men and women flaked out in and around the buildings and grounds.

One early morning after a stay in one of these far-northern mining towns, I went for a walk. I was just getting used to the signs posted on the beaches, warning against swimming because of crocodiles, when I noticed a herd of strange looking cattle grazing on a football field. A local resident who passed by told me not to go close to them, for they were wild buffalo and could be quite dangerous. Not far out of town, I passed a downed World War II bomber. It was in very good shape and had been left there and turned into a memorial to the many fliers who had lost their lives and had never been found in that sparsely settled north country.

We stopped on our way south on Groote Eylande in the Gulf of Carpentaria. There were two thousand people on the island that was part of the Arnhem Land Reserve. There are large manganese deposits and some mining on the island; otherwise it was very underdeveloped and seemed to be a lonely place, cut off as it was from the mainland.

Flying south from Groote Eylande along the eastern shore of the Gulf of Carpentaria, the pilot invited me to the flight deck to sit with him. He was flying at only a few hundred feet, skimming the water and weaving in and out of the inlets and bays, giving all of his passengers a magnificent view of the Gulf of Carpentaria. I had the best seat for the show. We watched flocks of birds of every description scatter in our path. Crocodiles, buffalo, and other wildlife reacted with great uncertainty to this invasion of their territory by scurrying about in all directions. I stayed with the pilot as long as I could until the setting sun quickly turned the gulf and the surrounding country to darkness and the pilot had to take the aircraft up to normal flying altitudes.

I loved visiting this outback and far north country. Not too long after this introduction to the "unknown" country, I was invited by the commissioner of the Northern Territory (a friend of the New South Wales governor) to make an official visit to the Territory. Peggy joined me and we flew to Darwin. I called on the commissioner, and we were provided with an escort to show us around. After a tour of the growing city of Darwin, the Australian town most heavily attacked by the Japanese during the Second World War, they flew us north by a small aircraft to Bathurst Island in the Timor Sea. Bathurst Island was the closest point in Australia to Indonesia. It was the target of the first Japanese bombing attack against Australia in 1942. Indeed, on the day of our visit, Aborigines found the remains of a Japanese plane in a swamp not far from where we were. It was thought to be a Zero. The Aborigines had carried a four- or five-foot bottom section of the fuselage from the swamp, and after cleaning it with a hose, they took a picture of me holding it upright. It was peppered with bullet holes that obviously had been the reason for its disappearance into the swamp some forty years before. Bathurst Island had only a population of about one thousand and was the site of a large mission station. Ownership of the island had been passed from the Crown to the Tiwi Land Council of tribal representatives. We were received by the tribal leaders. They looked somewhat different than the Aborigines on the mainland. You could see a slight Melanesian appearance in some of the population.

We flew south along the famous highway connecting Darwin with Alice Springs. I would have liked to have driven that highway, but Peggy would never hear of it. She was much more practical, pointing out that the highway was in many places only paved in the middle, and even this space was claimed by the great truck-trains that transported cattle and sheep at tremendous speeds. They assumed that anybody coming the other way would have the good sense to clear the way.

We were met at Alice Springs by representatives of the Territory government, who installed us in comfortable quarters and showed us everything there was to see in the city. Alice Springs was a fascinating small city in the middle of the never-never, or the great outback country. There was a lot to see and experience. When it rains, there is water galore, but generally the sky is blue, and the only water available is from artesian wells.

I was really amused by the great sporting event, "Boat Races on the Todd," the river that "flowed" through Alice Springs. I visualised the splashing of paddles in cool clear water as one would see anywhere in Canada. The races actually consisted of crews manning boats that had no bottoms in them. Holding onto the sides, the crew raced by foot down the dry river bed of the Todd, for there wasn't enough water to give a suggestion of a flow.

Equally unique were the races at the local race track. It was a regular racing facility like the track in every respectable town in Australia. The great difference was that instead of jockeys mounting their horses, in Alice, the jockeys mounted camels. It was very serious racing with pari-mutuel betting, but it was so different and unusual that those of us from the outside world didn't know whether to take it seriously. The locals certainly did. Most non-Australians are surprised at the mention of camels in Australia. They were introduced during the exploration age and, like a lot of domesticated animals everywhere, were often released to fend for themselves or escaped domesticity and returned to the wilds on their own. In any event, there are many wild camels roaming the backcountry.

Ayre's Rock was not on our official schedule, but I was determined to visit the area. Peggy and I flew from Alice Springs. Those were the days before the big hotels and other tourist facilities had been built to cater to the many tourists. We stayed in the most spartan of accommodation but were comfortable enough. Indeed after all the official care and attention from our hosts in the Northern Territory government, it was good to be on our own again. We rose early with all of the other tourists just before sunrise to see the rising sun light up Ayre's Rock. This is the largest monolith, or single block of stone, on earth. The play of the morning sun changed the colour of the rock by the minute, making it a sight that would be difficult to duplicate anywhere else in the world. After the sun ended its show, we breakfasted and took a leisurely ride out to the Rock. Peggy had no interest in climbing the Rock, which all the machos considered to be the thing to do. She chose (I think wisely) to walk around the monolith. She did this, not for the sake of circumnavigating the Rock, but because she had read that some of the most interesting things to see were at the Rock's base. She found numerous caves and areas where the waters, when pouring down the Rock in the rainy season, had created water holes, around which the Aborigines from ancient times had frequented. She later insisted on taking me to one of these spots where, when it rained, the waters had for centuries poured from the rock face to form a pool. Above, at the height of man, were Aboriginal drawings.

While Peggy was exploring the base of Ayre's Rock, I felt I had to climb it. The first third of the way up was quite crowded, but not surprisingly, the climbers decreased in number the higher we got. Part of the way up, there was a chain to hold onto, for the rock at this point was not only steep but very smooth and slippery. I reached the top and signed the book to record my ascent. The view was extraordinary, with desert stretching for hundreds of miles in every direction until it disappeared into the "never-never."

Of equal interest were the Olgas, not too distant from Ayre's Rock. These were smaller, several-hundred-foot monoliths resembling huge marbles strewn on the desert floor. What made the Olgas and Ayre's Rock so spectacular was that these great masses were the only things for miles that disrupted an otherwise flat and monotonous expanse of desert. Like Ayre's Rock, the Olgas provided a favourite meeting place for the Aborigines. Around the "marbles" were water holes, and around these were Aboriginal paintings.

We didn't have to venture far from our house in Sydney to find Aboriginal rock paintings; some were no more than several hundred yards from the bottom of our garden. Across the street, a cliff dropped several hundred feet to a street below.

We were invited to a house on this street because of an article that appeared about Peggy in one of the local newspapers. Peggy was born a mile or so from our residence. The article gave a lot of background on her family.

A few days after its publication, an elderly gentleman arrived at our door and introduced himself as an acquaintance of Peggy's family. He later phoned and invited us to tea. His house was below the cliff, and the garden from his house to the cliff was wild and untended. He said he would like to show us something at the end of his garden. We walked up a path through thick bush to the cliff facade. Below an overhang was a cavelike area with magnificent rock paintings and signs of smoke from fires on the ceiling of the overhang. Clearly it had been used extensively by Aborigines. Whether it was one hundred years old or ten thousand, the old man had no idea.

He said he was reluctant to bring in experts because he feared he would be bothered by crowds of the curious. On the other hand, he feared that the new construction on the properties above the cliff with the run-off from swimming pools and fertilisers would eventually ruin the site if something was not done. We tried to persuade him to contact the museums and seek their advice. He was a very nice, but rather eccentric, old man; he had piled in one of his rooms all the daily papers going back several decades. He also had his own small "museum" of relics from around the local area that was most interesting. I was sure that other than ourselves, he was the only person to visit his museum. He was able to show Peggy many items of a historical nature relating to her family and other people who had resided in the area many years earlier.

Sydney seemed to be a drawing card for Canadian politicians, particularly during the cold Canadian winter months, which was high summer in Australia. I had many Canadian cabinet ministers, federal and provincial, visit Australia when I was there. All worked hard, but some made a greater impact on the Canadian-Australian relationship than others. One of the best provincial representatives was the deputy premier of Saskatchewan, Eric Berntson, who did much for Canada as well as for his native Saskatchewan in pushing Canadian dryland farming methods and equipment in western New South Wales. I accompanied him to a country trade fair where our companies sold millions of dollars of Canadian equipment for use in dryland farming.

I have already referred to the visit of former Trade Minister Jack Horner. His successor, Gerry Regan, appeared for the Commonwealth Games as minister responsible for sport. We enjoyed having him because, besides being a minister and former premier of Nova Scotia, he was a colleague of mine from Dalhousie University days in Halifax, Nova Scotia. He did cause us some concern when he requested, before his arrival, that we arrange a tennis match for him with Ron Laver, one of Australia's best tennis players. Gerry enjoyed tennis, but he was certainly not in the class of Laver. I was surprised when Laver agreed. I asked Art Perron who was the best player we had at the consulate general to join the minister and to try to give the Australian a decent match. Laver had his wife with him. I didn't attend, but I understood a "good time was had by all." I really didn't appreciate what Laver was up against until Peggy and I quietly watched the minister, several days later, playing an early morning game in Queensland. He loved the game, but this didn't compensate for the fact that his serve was as weak as mine; there was nothing in his game that would frighten me, let alone Laver.

A most interesting and controversial ministerial visitor during my time in Sydney was the man in the "green hat," Agriculture Minister Eugene Whelan. He was a character and a decent man but a rather difficult guest. He delighted in the fact that he could not perform well in either of Canada's two official languages.

One of the areas that I liked most in Australia was Toowoomba. This was one of the smaller cities near the Queensland and New South Wales border that had so impressed the British Shakespearean actor who performed for us in Newfoundland so many years ago. He said that the smaller towns in this area enjoyed one of the best climates and qualities of life in the world. Having seen it first hand, I had to agree. Toowoomba was a town of some eighty thousand people, set high on the edge of a plateau on the Great Dividing Range in southeastern Queensland. It was a service centre for the Darling Downs, a livestock, grain, and dairy region. It was a well-planned town with many parks.

Peggy and I were invited to Toowoomba, where I was to make a speech and lend support to Canadian artistic performers. We flew by single engine aircraft from Brisbane inland up the eastern side of the Great Dividing Range. We had a bit of a scare when attempting to land, for another aircraft came in almost on top of us. Both planes had to abort and sort themselves out for a second attempt.

We had let it be known that Peggy was a keen gardener, so the local horticultural society took us in hand. They showed great delight in guiding us around the best of their public and private gardens. These could compete with gardens anywhere. Situated on the edge of the tableland, the city was above the steamy tropical heat of coastal Queensland, yet it was well watered and well within the influence of the tropical north. Despite the altitude, the area facing the eastern seaboard never experienced frost. We were particularly struck by one property that was a kaleidoscope of colour, with a most peaceful view to the west of rolling pastures studded with sheep, disappearing very gradually into the blue mountains beyond. When you turned around to face east, you looked down a thousand feet onto the coastal plain that stretched all the way to the Pacific. For me it was the closest thing to Eden.

Chapter Thirty-eight
With the Exporters

In the summer of 1983 in Sydney, Australia, Peggy and I decided that we should take home-leave to see our children and our young grandson Derek in Canada. We flew to Vancouver and from there to Calgary, where we rented a car to visit our daughter Julie, who was working with Parks Canada in the Rockies. She was eager to take us on a hike in the mountains. I guess she recalled the many happy times we had mountain-walking when she was a child growing up in Switzerland.

We did an overnight hike with Julie that Peggy and I will never forget. It was in a most beautiful valley not too far from Banff, Alberta. Julie briefed us on the importance of not throwing anything away while on the hike. These were unnecessary instructions, for we were well-trained from our years in Switzerland not to damage the environment. However, her reason for the warning was not only because of the environment, but because of the presence of grizzly bears.

We were advised before we started that there had been a recent sighting of a grizzly family in the valley, which sort of put a damper on the outing for us. The grizzly, unlike the bears in my native Newfoundland, didn't have to be provoked to attack. It wasn't just a matter of finding yourself between an adult and her cubs. Just to surprise them on the trail could lead to unpleasantness. They were just plain dangerous. We walked up a trail for about seven hours, and for every minute of the hike, I rattled a beer can filled with pebbles. If there were bears around the corner, they certainly would know we were coming. The country was most striking, and the day perfect, but the thought of grizzlies, added to the steep path we had to climb, rather distracted us from the beautiful vistas. We reached our destination late afternoon. It was a warden's cabin close to the snow line. When we left Banff, it was a warm summer's day, but up where we were, it was cool and we had frost that night.

The warden's cabin in its setting was a picture that anyone from outside

Canada would consider their "dream cabin in the Canadian Rockies." It had everything except the Mountie standing outside the door. It was strongly built of heavy logs and was as bear-proof as man could make it. The cabin was in a little valley surrounded by lodge or flag-pole conifers, and all around there were views of the most magnificent snow-capped mountains. A fast-flowing stream rattled down the valley a hundred yards from the front door. Julie had the key to the cabin, and when we went in, we could see that it was stocked with everything one would ever need in the wilderness, including dry kindling to start our fire. Poor Peggy was so exhausted after the climb that she just flopped on one of the bunks. I always recall for her that she didn't even take off her knapsack. She denies that.

As soon as we had a good fire going and a bite to eat, I decided to try my hand at fishing. There was a rod hanging over the cabin door. It was an hour or so before dark, so I strolled down to the stream. It reminded me of the sandy and pebble-bottomed streams I had fished in as a boy in Newfoundland. Like the streams of my memory, this one had icy cold water that was so clean you would not hesitate to drink it. I walked up the stream, casting the fly rod, when suddenly my eye went to the sand around my feet, and there, on the edge of the stream, a foot away from my boots, was the imprint of a great beast. I knew enough about animal footprints from my years in the woods of central Newfoundland to know that this one was fresh. There was still water seeping into the impression, which meant the creature that made the imprint must be close enough to be watching me. As calmly as I could, I reeled in my line and made my way up the bank towards the cabin. I don't think I breathed until I was inside behind the sturdy cabin door. The only concern I had that evening was the thought of our return trip on that lonely trail next morning. Since it would be all downhill, we would at least do the trip in half the time it took us to climb our way up.

After visits with our children in Peterborough and Oakville, Ontario, we headed for Ottawa. On about our last day there, we had a luncheon at the home of our good friends, Bob and Eleanor Latimer. Bob was assistant deputy minster, Trade Policy, in External Affairs. After the lunch, Bob, rather nonchalantly and almost as an afterthought, suggested that I had better have a word before I left Ottawa with my old friend Tom Burns, who was president of the Canadian Exporters Association (CEA). I asked Bob what this was all about. He said that the CEA was considering approaching me to be a candidate for the presidency of the association.

I was dumbfounded. I was enjoying my job in Australia and knew from observing Tom that the presidency of the CEA would be a big and demanding job. If I got the position, it would most likely mean that I would have to resign from the Canadian government service. I went to see Tom Burns that afternoon. Tom was to the point. He told me that there was a CEA search committee looking for a new president to replace him because he planned to retire from the association in a matter of months. He said that the search committee had identified a number of prospects, but his guess would be that I would be invited to become the next president of the Canadian Exporters Association.

Tom suggested that before returning to Australia I drop into Toronto, where he would set up meetings with members of the search committee, such as Keith Hendrick and other senior members of the CEA. I spent the next day in Toronto speaking to a number of exporters before heading back to my post in Australia.

During the next several months, I spent a lot of time on the phone with Tom Burns, Paul Soubry, the CEA board chairman, and Ray Anderson, who was now assistant deputy minister of trade in Ottawa. The CEA was simply asking if I would accept the presidency should it be offered to me. The pay and allowances were certainly all one could ask for. It would, however, mean leaving a position that I enjoyed. As long as I could, I held off. Ideally I would have liked a secondment from the Canadian government to the CEA. The CEA made it clear that they would not entertain a secondment; the president had to be able to speak to the government for the private sector without any strings attached. Several months later, just before the 1984 CEA annual Ottawa meeting with senior bureaucrats, where they were to decide on the new president, I agreed that I would accept the position if selected. During the meeting, the search committee made their choice known, and my name was accepted by the membership and publicly announced.

My next hurdle was to extract myself from the foreign service and from Sydney in particular. Here I had no trouble. I had the full support of the Department of External Affairs, particularly Bob Johnson, the deputy minister of trade. Bob told me that the department would like to see someone in the position as president of the CEA whom they could work with, and I met that requirement. Bob and my old friend Ray Anderson were most cooperative in arranging my transfer back from Sydney to Ottawa. I resigned from the government the day I arrived and started work at the CEA the next morning.

Little did I know the pressures one could be subjected to in that position. When I returned from lunch on the first day on the job, there were three television crews in my office. As I waded through the technicians, cords, and cameras to my desk, I asked what was the big event. One of the interviewers told me that the Canadian dollar had dropped, and they wanted to know for the national news the view of exporters concerning this development. Nobody could have been less prepared to face television cameras than I was at that moment; I hadn't had a briefing on the issue. I winged it. I watched a ten-second clip later in the evening on the national news and thought it came out fairly well. From that moment on, I had to be prepared for questions from the media on the full range of developments affecting international trade.

In the government, particularly in Ottawa, I had been able to summons a briefing on a subject and have it on my desk in a matter of minutes. This was not the case in the CEA. Our resources were so thin that I had to prepare most of my own briefing. I had to write the speeches I was required to give several times a week. There was little backup to assist me in research or fact-finding. One hesitated to encroach upon the time of the few officers we had, such as Jim Moore, who was overworked and underappreciated. Jim did all the CEA's work on United States border problems, and shipping, and freight issues (he ran singlehandedly the Canadian Shippers Council). In his "spare" time he wrote the CEA weekly news bulletin, the mouthpiece of the association to the membership. There were only two other officers, and they were equally busy. I was shocked at the prospect of having to beef up the CEA secretariat to be on a footing with the other well-funded business associations in Ottawa. Yet, resources or not, whenever there were developments affecting exports, we were expected by the government and the business community to have a considered view.

On my way back from Australia to Canada, it was suggested by Tom Burns that I travel by way of Japan and meet with the Japan Machinery Exporters Association. This group and the CEA had scheduled a conference for their interested members in Calgary several months later to determine how Canada and Japan might work together on major development projects around the world. Peggy flew straight to Canada from Australia, and I went to Tokyo. My good fiend Barry Steers, who was Canada's ambassador in Japan, and his wife, Martha, invited me to stay at the residence. He kindly arranged a series of meetings for me with senior Japanese business leaders associated with the Japan Machinery Exporters Association. He accompanied me to many of the meetings. I was rather troubled that the CEA, which was an association of the full range of exporters, including exporters of machinery and equipment, but also of engineering and other services, should have a working relationship with a Japanese association restricted to machinery exporters. I feared that the Japanese focus would be on working with Canadian engineers to supply Japanese equipment on projects to the exclusion of Canadian equipment suppliers. This would be intolerable for me unless the projects were Japanese and Canadian engineering firms were being invited by the Japanese to participate.

The Calgary meetings proved that my concerns were well-based. The Japanese gave every indication that what they had in mind was supplying Japanese equipment to projects won by Canadian engineering firms, not only abroad but in Canada. I met privately with the thirty or forty Canadian exporters attending meetings and attempted to orchestrate them a little, as I was sure the Japanese had done with their participants.

It was a delicate matter because if a Canadian engineering firm and a Japanese equipment supplier felt it made good business sense for them to work together on a project in Canada, I didn't want to be seen as discouraging such cooperation; however, neither did I want to be seen by Canadian machinery and equipment suppliers to be cochairing a conference to help their Japanese competitors at their expense. I was to be always uncomfortable with the CEA's relationship with the Japanese Machinery group, although I did cochair several future meetings in Canada and Japan, and Canadian and Japanese companies did in a few instances work together to the mutual benefit of both countries.

An important objective of the CEA was to ensure that the highest levels of government were fully aware of the views of exporters. To reach consensus amongst exporters, we had committees of twenty or thirty representatives of exporting firms (self-elected) dealing with every conceivable trade subject. We had a committee on international financing that met regularly with the Export Development Corporation and other financial institutions. We had a foreign aid committee whose focus was working with the Canadian International Development Agency and the international financial and development institutions. (This committee organised annual "CIDA Days" meetings attended by several hundred exporters and government people.) There were committees on taxation, on export promotion, on trading houses, on United States market access, on issues peculiar to the high technology exporter, on government liaison (where twenty or thirty exporters would meet with senior officials in the trade related departments), on legal questions, on transportation, on agriculture, and on industries with particular problems. In short, we established in the CEA, committees or groups where exporters with any problem could meet and seek solutions by working together and with the government offices concerned.

When I arrived at the CEA, all activity was conducted out of Ottawa. Indeed, all annual conventions had for decades been held in Ottawa or in nearby Montebello, Quebec. I sought to change this, against much opposition. My first convention as president was in Toronto, with an attendance exceeding any convention held previously. Thereafter the annual conventions were held from coast to coast.

Among the great demands on my time were bilateral trade committees that had been established, not by the CEA, but by others to develop trade between Canada and a number of our trading partners. There were groups with Japan, Korea, Taiwan, Pakistan, the countries of the Middle East, and many others. Bob Latimer, the assistant deputy minister (Trade Policy), used to accuse me of setting up such joint committees. I did. When with a minister in a country where Canada had little profile, a formal bilateral committee could stimulate two-way interest in the relationship. Canadian exporters, when bidding on projects abroad, often felt that it would enhance their chances if there was a joint committee. The companies could generally gain the support of our embassy in the country concerned and of the Canadian banks that would be involved in financing the projects. The Trade Department's country desk officer in Ottawa, whose job it was to stimulate the relationship, would also be supportive. The unfortunate thing was that if the Canadian bids were unsuccessful, the instigator would often abandon the joint committee. It then could become a negative rather than positive tool of trade development.

The Canadian chamber of commerce set up a large number of such bilateral committees. Some of them were good. Most were a waste of time. I felt we had to take some of them seriously, and I was asked to do so by the chamber. I made an effort to attend meetings when they were held in Ottawa, particularly if CEA members were interested. I soon abandoned almost all, tending to confine my efforts to the Canada-Japan, the Canada-Korea, and the Canada-Taiwan committees, on which the bulk of our CEA members served. I also remained active in the Pacific Basin Economic Council, under whose umbrella the Pacific region bilateral groups met. Most important of all was the Canada-United States committee; I regularly attended their meetings, particularly when the Canada-United States Free Trade issue was the major issue of the day.

Chapter Thirty-nine
Southern Africa

One of the most interesting and certainly most challenging tasks I had as president of the Canadian Exporters Association (CEA) was to attempt to keep open trade between Canada and South Africa. It was interesting because I became directly involved not only with Canadian exporters and South African importers, but with investors, with the South African and Canadian governments, and with black and white African business groups. It was challenging because the Canadian government (under whatever political stripe) was opposed to anything that might be interpreted as being supportive of the apartheid regime in South Africa. It was, of course, argued by many that to trade with South Africa was to support the apartheid system.

I had always maintained that Canada, with a third of its income and employment coming from exports, should never adopt a policy of turning down customers for political reasons. I officially and privately opposed apartheid. At the same time I was strongly opposed to cutting off trade contacts as a means of demonstrating our opposition. I felt that Canada would merely pass business to the French and others if we were to implement sanctions unilaterally. If sanctions were to be applied multilaterally, that is, by the international community, that would be a different matter.

I had worked with South Africans for many years in Geneva, Ottawa, Capetown, and Johannesburg. As chairman of the GATT Balance of Payments Committee in Geneva, I had watched South Africa emerge from its long period of import protectionism imposed through comprehensive quantitative import restrictions. I was very much aware of their desire to do *something* to defuse the threats to their trade contacts with the rest of the Western world. Through the CEA, I made a proposal to them that had nothing to do with GATT or any other formal relationship. It was that Canadian and *black* South African businesses open a relationship.

We were faced with a situation where most, but not all, developed countries were imposing embargoes on trade with South Africa. In our case, while we imposed serious limitations on imports from South Africa of products such as wines and against Canadian exports of defence and strategic materials to South Africa, trade in peaceful goods was for the most part allowed to continue. One might ask why we bothered to pursue the relationship, given the opposition voiced by Canadian organised labour, church groups, and academics. The fact remained that South Africa was one of our better overseas markets for manufactured goods. We were exporting to them annually about one hundred million dollars' worth of such products. In addition, South Africa provided an important market for Canadian resource products.

I was invited to attend several meetings on South Africa with External Affairs minister and former prime minister Joe Clark, a person I had the highest respect for, but in the usual "fair" External Affairs manner, he invited people to these meetings who represented all the groups opposed to any Canadian relationship with South Africa and few on the other side. I was generally isolated as the only one present who would speak out against a disruption of our exports.

There were interests present supporting Canadian investment in South Africa, but they tended to keep a low profile. I was put on the defensive, because the consensus seemed to be that we should cut off all contact with the South African government. The others, without exception, were against any economic relationship with South Africa. There was Stephen Lewis, who had been the leader of the socialist New Democratic party in Ontario and, at the time, was our ambassador to the United Nations; there was Shirley Carr, then president of the Canadian Labour Congress; and there were representatives from various church groups.

Joe Clark must have felt a little sorry for me, and I know that he had some sympathy for the position of exporters. He asked to meet with me privately after one of these meetings. He pleaded that we "exporters" do something positive and public to counter the pressures not only against ourselves but against the government. Unless we moved positively, the government would find it difficult to fight off the pressures to cut all trade contact with South Africa.

Robert Noble, a trade commissioner, who had been seconded by External Affairs to the CEA, was invaluable in helping me to draw up a positive program as suggested by Minister Clark. I asked him to work on a plan in consultation with exporters, investors, External Affairs, and the Canadian International Development Agency (CIDA). What emerged was a comprehensive program for the development of a relationship between the CEA and black entrepreneurs in South Africa and with the private sectors in the neighbouring southern African states.

One of the great problems was that there were few black entrepreneurs in South Africa. The apartheid system was not conducive to black business development. Yet we felt that when the blacks took over the government as they were destined to do, unless there was a nucleus of free enterprise–minded black businessmen, the country would be under undue influence from the extreme left, which seemed to be the norm in the powerful African National Congress. The obvious thing to do, we thought, was to work to create black business. The way to do this was through the Canadian companies that had investments and facilities in South Africa. We contacted the twenty or so Canadian manufacturing and resource processing companies located there. Most indicated a readiness to work with us to help develop black entrepreneurs.

Robert Noble and I went to South Africa. In Capetown we stayed with our Ambassador Ted Lee and his charming wife, Bev. Ted and Bev were amongst the best friends Peggy and I had when we were all in Ottawa, and they had long been our neighbours. Ted arranged meetings for us at senior levels of government and accompanied us to these meetings. We explained in detail to South African ministers what we were up to, and they agreed to allow us to do what we planned. Without their blessing, we would be unable to move easily around the country and meet all those we wished to meet.

We made ourselves known to the Black Chamber of Commerce and other black business groups. They in turn cooperated to give us an inventory of black entrepreneurs. There were few. Clearly if progress was to be made in any relationship with black entrepreneurs, we would have to proceed with our original plan and create some. We called on many of the Canadian companies in the country and for the most part found them most cooperative. The proposition we put to them was that they might consider subcontracting to black entrepreneurs certain functions that they undertook themselves and that in Canada they would normally have had done under subcontract. For example, in Canada certain parts of the shoe would be manufactured by subsuppliers, but in South Africa, it was all done in-house. We persuaded a shoe company to consider giving such parts to a couple of entrepreneurs who would set themselves up to do the job. Similarly, a shirt manufacturer gave orders for parts of the shirt collar to an outside firm of blacks. Another black entrepreneur collected the soft plastic cuttings from one of the

311

Canadian textile plants and produced pillows. All of this had to be done in a way that made economic sense.

We spent a day in a large "coloured" township outside Capetown, arranged for us by the South African authorities. "Coloureds" were people of mixed race; there were several millon of them. Under the apartheid system, they were treated as a separate racial group. These people were close to the white population in language, religion, and customs, yet they were set apart. Amongst them you could find entrepreneurs galore. We were, however, by our own objectives and by the attitudes of the Canadian government and the Canadian groups that opposed South Africa, to restrict ourselves to helping the "blacks." In the coloured township we met a coloured furniture designer and manufacturer who showed us through his plant. He said that at one time, he had employed three hundred workers of all races. He now had less than a hundred. He used to have a steady flow of Afrikaner farmers visiting his plant and buying his production. Recent race riots had scared off whites, and his sales had fallen drastically causing him to lay off employees. He was convinced that if he could have a showroom in Capetown, he could substantially increase his sales and again employ three hundred, but this was not possible under the current race law.

In Johannesburg, Robert and I met with a number of black business-men. Amongst them was a brother of Winnie Mandela, the wife of the first black president of South Africa. We had lunch with the brother. Unlike his sister, he was anything but a radical. One of our most interesting contacts was the head of an Anglican group, "Get Ahead Limited." This was a high profile group; Archbishop Desmond Tutu, the head of the almost two-mil-lion-strong Anglican church in South Africa, was on their board of directors.

The man who ran it was a white lawyer who was highly considered by all the blacks I met. He had made a name for himself defending people who had run afoul of the racial laws. Indeed, he told me that if a black business-man wanted to establish himself in the white areas of Johannesburg, his group would "front" a business purchase and defend any legal challenge to the right of the black to establish a business. In recent years, the authorities often didn't legally challenge such incursions. He drove us himself by a minibus, with a few of his black assistants, into Soweto, the huge black township that had been the scene of so much racial violence during the past few decades. Soweto adjoined Johannesburg and was at one time part of the city. Its name was derived from "South Western Township." It has a population approaching three million, and most of its labour force com-

312

muted daily to Johannesburg for work. These people, for the most part, lived in terrible conditions. There were a number of areas where the homes were more acceptable; there were a few houses, such as Winnie Mandela's house, that was pointed out to us, that seemed very grand indeed! It was interesting to see the security around that particular residence. I was very positively struck by the sight of children returning home from school. They were all in school uniforms in the British tradition, and in their neatness and behaviour, they contrasted greatly with the children one often sees today returning home from North American schools.

Soweto was a living demonstration for me that the blacks were entrepreneurs. Every backyard seemed to have some type of business, even if it was only the bottling of soft drinks. Get Ahead Limited had a program under which they would make small loans in South African rand, equivalent to less than a hundred dollars, to individuals to help them get established in small businesses. At one point, we stopped at the side of the road in the centre of Soweto, where a woman had set up shop. Our friends talked to her about the state of her business. Get Ahead Limited had lent her a small sum to buy inventory. They told me that they had made hundreds of such loans and, as a matter of policy, insisted on the recipients paying a small amount of interest. This helped impress upon them good business sense and the realisation that they were not getting a handout but rather a commercial loan. We were told that there had never been a default on the loans or on the payment of the interest. Most of these businesses in Soweto, even the few manufacturing firms, were operating illegally. If the strict South African safety and sanitary codes had been enforced, virtually all businesses would have been closed.

Our friends from Get Ahead Limited took us to a migrant workers' camp near Soweto. Soweto's houses were like palaces by comparison with the long huts for the workers brought in from outside the country. There was certainly nothing in their accommodation that would entice them to stay permanently. Obviously we should not have been in the area, for our guides hustled us in and out very quickly. The huts we looked at were empty; the occupants being away at work. I felt a bit of a trespasser. I did glance through the windows, which had no frames or glass, to see but a few mats used for sleeping. There was no furniture or any of the basic things we would associate with even the poorest of homes.

Robert and I felt that we had uncovered enough possibilities in South Africa for a relationship with black business for us to put recommendations

313

to Minister Joe Clark and Canadian exporters and investors. We had a number of highly respected groups with us in both South Africa and Canada. We formed the Canadian Association for Black Business in South Africa and appointed an executive council of nine. There were two representatives from the National African Federated Chamber of Commerce and Industry (NAFCOC); two from Canadian-linked businesses in South Africa (including John Turpin, who was of tremendous help and would become executive chairman); one from Get Ahead Limited (to concentrate on the informal sector); another from Job Creation Limited, which had specific expertise in assisting small and medium-sized black enterprises; one from the Centre for Development Business at the University of the Witwatersrand; and one each from the Canadian Business Association of South Africa and the CEA.

Minister Clark supported our recommendations, and the Industrial Co-operation Division of CIDA gave some financial support. This government funding was made available to the black business organisations in South Africa to carry out their side of the undertaking. The Canadian-linked companies gave funding in money and kind. They provided office space and support services in South Africa. They made available executive services and time to ensure that black suppliers received the marketing guidance and quality control advice needed to implement a successful contractual arrangement.

What we did in South Africa was very modest when one considered the job that needed to be done. We were very much restricted to Canadian and Canadian related companies operating in South Africa. Unfortunately most Canadian investment had been pulled out as a result of the pressures from Canadian labour unions, church groups, and politicians. Indeed while we were beginning our work in South Africa, some of the most cooperative Canadian companies closed their operations.

One senior executive told me that pressures from Canada for Canadian related companies to raise wages for unskilled workers meant that many had to be laid off. He introduced me to the office "tea-lady," who for some twenty years had been on the legal basic wage. It was claimed that with gratuities she was able to make a good contribution to the family income. Canadian labour unions had objected so strenuously to the basic wages being paid that the company had decided to let her go and to replace her with coffee and tea machines (that were made in Japan). In the few areas where we were able to help, I feel we made a small contribution to the uplifting of business and industry skills amongst disadvantaged black entrepreneurs, permitting them to participate more fully in the South African economy.

The CEA never hid the fact that its efforts in South Africa had the selfish motive of keeping open our trade links with that country. We also hoped to ensure that when the black majority assumed power, there would be black entrepreneurs to counter what promised to be a very racial and far-left incoming government.

We had equally selfish motives for involving ourselves in Zimbabwe and Botswana, which were "front-line" states to the north of South Africa. Minister Joe Clark wanted to see the front-line states that were highly dependent on their links with South Africa become less dependent. He wanted Canada to play a role in diversifying their contacts. We in the CEA came up with a proposal that again the minister accepted as being helpful.

We established the Canadian Association for the Private Sector in Southern Africa (CAPSSA). The purpose of CAPSSA was to promote Canadian private sector involvement with the private sectors of the Southern African region in the pursuit of new economic relationships for these countries with Canada. The objectives were to promote industrial linkages through private sector joint ventures, investments, and transfers of technology and training. We also wished to create an awareness about Canadian industrial capabilities. There was great ignorance of Canada. The countries normally turned to Britain or other countries of Western Europe as an alternative to South Africa.

In February 1988, I led a mission of twelve exporters to Harare, Zimbabwe, to attend an international Southern African Development Co-ordination Conference (SADCC) on new opportunities for investment and trade in Southern Africa. The conference was attended by all the notables in the front-line states, such as Zimbabwe president Robert Mugabe, so we felt it would be a good time to launch our new association under which Canada would work with southern Africa. We were pleased when the international conference (SADCC) singled out the Canadian and Nordic business communities as being the most active in cooperating with southern African countries. If the Canadian government and Minister Clark needed any more convincing about our proposal, this was it.

To put "flesh on the bones" of our new association, we had to recruit the best of local businessmen to serve on its board. We concentrated first on Zimbabwe. I went to see my friend Bernie Chidzero, the internationally respected finance minister. Bernie gave us a list of six or eight of Zimbabwe's best businessmen, both black and white. We contacted most of them and they readily agreed to serve on a council to administer the association. They were senior executives from agribusiness, industry, mining, commerce, and finance. Our high commissioner (ambassador), trade commissioner, and CIDA's program manager, were appointed ex officio members of the council.

We had our first meeting of the council at the Royal Harare Golf and Country Club. This was a very beautiful golf course, and I only wished that I had had time to play it. The most shocking thing about the club (formerly the old Royal Salisbury Golf Club) was that, despite independence and a "black" government and a change of name, there were no black members in the club. I asked some of my new-found black business friends why there were no black members, and they gave the obvious response that few black businessmen who could now afford to join had ever played golf.

One of the black Zimbabwe businessmen, Lawrence Vambe, was elected chairman of the new association. Canadian Bob Gibbons was appointed the executive director of CAPPSA, residing in Zimbabwe. He was to focus his activities on ten countries in southern Africa. Some fifteen projects ranging from mining to agriculture and animal husbandry were successfully completed in the first few years.

Robert Noble, who made an extraordinary contribution to closer business relations with southern Africa, was reassigned from the CEA back to External Affairs. I hated to see him go. On our last trip together in Africa, we decided to visit one of the great attractions on the continent that we had never seen. We booked seats by air for a Sunday morning from Harare to Victoria Falls. According to my habits we were at the airport long before the flight was to depart. Following Robert's practice, we went off for a leisurely breakfast before lining up for the flight.

Robert kept insisting all during breakfast, in response to my nervousness about missing the flight, "They would never go without us; relax!" When we eventually arrived at the gate, the plane had already pulled away. Robert was speechless, but only for a moment. He then did some very fast talking to anyone who would listen. As a result of his pleading, the ground staff agreed to drive us out to the plane on the runway with a ladder for a climb to the cabin door. We boarded without problem but were advised as soon as we entered the plane that because we were late, they gave one of our two seats to a standby passenger, and there was only one seat left. I gave the seat to Robert and was assigned a jump seat with the crew forward.

However, a member of the crew had to take the seat during takeoff, so I was escorted to seats occupied by an African family with a three-year-old little girl. They kindly allowed me to sit in the child's seat as long as I held the child during takeoff and landing. So I divided my time between the kind African family and the crew. I often wonder if the experience cured Robert of the casual way he approached airport departure gates.

We spent the day at Victoria Falls. The water flow over the falls was said to be very low because of the drought situation in the surrounding country, but it still was very spectacular. What fascinated me most was the mini-climate created by the falls on the several hundred meters of shoreline exposed to the continuous spray from the tumbling water. Here the vegetation was lush. Beautiful tropical flowering plants grew in profusion, whereas several hundred metres away they would have perished in the dry conditions existing there.

We took a boat trip down the Zambesi River that forms the border between Zimbabwe and Zambia. There were the expected sightings of crocodiles and of other African wildlife on the close-by shores. The most impressive sight was when we landed on an island in the river and were shown the damage that had been done by elephants that had used the island in their crossing of the Zambesi. It was rather disconcerting, seeing huge trees uprooted and the land torn up as if a score of great bulldozers had run amuck.

Robert was replaced in the CEA by Ed Gorn. Ed was also with External Affairs and was happily located with our High Commission in London when I requested his recall. I don't know if Ed ever forgave me for asking External Affairs to pull him out of London, which he loved, but he was my one and only choice as a replacement for Robert, and External Affairs agreed to bring him home. Ed had worked with me on international trade for many years, and I considered him one of the best informed and best motivated officers in the service. The exporters liked him and were delighted to have him in the CEA.

Ed was a delight to travel with. He had only one leg, and while he would flare at any suggestion that he should be given any preference in the office because of his loss, he was not above using it to get us upgraded on flights abroad. We always travelled business class. As soon as we entered the airport lounge, he would drag out his cane (which he never used in Ottawa). In his immaculate London-tailored, dark-blue suit, he would hobble over to the lady in charge and announce in his most charming manner, but with authority, "Good evening; I am travelling tonight from Canada to South Africa with the president of the Canadian Exporters Association."

As I slid away to the other side of the lounge, Ed would very politely ask, "If by any chance there are first class seats available, I would be most grateful if we could be seated in them." Then he would mention how we always flew Air Canada, British Airways, or whatever airline the person he was speaking to represented. It invariably worked (much to the annoyance at one time of several senior colleagues from External Affairs who were travelling with us but who had to spend the night at the back of the plane while we flew in first-class comfort). Once settled, Ed would remove his artificial leg and toss it into the bin above our heads. This would not go unnoticed by the cabin crew, who would be most sympathetic and attentive to Ed's (and my) needs.

On one visit to South Africa we had a spare weekend in Johannesburg. Good friends of Ed's in Swaziland invited us and an accompanying colleague from CIDA, Pierre Charlebois, to spend the weekend at their home. One of the companies we were working with provided us with a car and a driver, so we set off for the five-hundred-kilometre drive east. I was amused to see a homemade sign in the front window of the car claiming that we were diplomatic VIPs, which the driver felt gave him the licence to exceed all speed limits. It was a superhighway, and the driver made full use of it. Fortunately, there was little traffic, for he maintained a speed of 120 to 140 kilometres all the way. We kept our minds off the driving by singing. The driver who was roughly our vintage enjoyed every song, and I was told that, for years afterwards, he told everybody he met about the wonderful sing-song he and his Canadian passengers had while driving from Johannesburg to Swaziland.

Pierre Charlebois was a frequent visitor to Africa. He fitted in well with our group. He gave us cause for great amusement when we crossed the border from South Africa to Swaziland. The Swaziland border guard who, besides his native tongue, was an Anglophile, won our hearts when, on seeing our Canadian passports, he declared, "I see every kind of passport in this job, but without doubt, Canadian passports are the best in the world." I had crossed a hundred borders and I knew that this man was sincere. While he had no trouble pronouncing the names Petrie and Gorn, he stumbled terribly over the French Canadian name Charlebois. He finally returned

Pierre's passport with a polite, "Thank you, Mr. Charlie-boy." Thereafter, Pierre was known to us, whether in Ottawa or abroad, as Charlie-boy.

Swaziland was one of the loveliest places I've visited. It was a small landlocked country surrounded by South Africa except for a short eastern border with Mozambique. Formerly a British Protectorate, it became independent in 1968. It had a population of only six hundred thousand. The climate varied from subtropical in the east to temperate in the hilly west, where we stayed. I'm sure that the pleasant company I had as travelling companions and as wonderful hosts contributed to my enjoyment of the place, but I was not prepared for the sheer beauty of the country.

We were the guests of Bill Campbell and his wife Brenda. Bill was the honorary consul of Swaziland to Canada and, clearly, highly respected in Swaziland, where for much of the year he made his home. His home, when we were there, was a sprawling bungalow on top of a mountain, overlooking the Valley of Heaven. The flora and the panoramic view from anywhere in the bungalow were something to behold. Bill was somehow involved, through investment, in the casino in the valley far below. This was a major attraction for the thousands of South Africans who visited each weekend. We visited the casino as Bill's guests, each with a pocket full of chips that Bill had forced upon us. He shepherded us like a mother hen, and after an hour or so at the tables, he took us to a restaurant on the mountainside, which belonged in the Swiss or Austrian Alps, rather than in southern Africa. A few years later, I was saddened to hear that Bill had died unexpectedly and certainly prematurely.

Chapter Forty
Giant Steps Forward

There have been a lot of harsh words written about Prime Minister Mulroney. Whether these are deserved, I have my doubts, There were certainly many things about him that would be difficult for even his greatest supporters to defend. I would say, however, that insofar as international economic affairs were concerned, he deserved far greater credit than he received. He took a direct interest in Canada's exports. He was the first and only prime minister up to his time to address the Canadian Exporters Association rather than send his minister of trade, as all his predecessors had done. I feel that in the field of international trade, he will eventually be acknowledged as having been a forward-looking leader. Against great opposition, he started a ball rolling that would in a short time be pushed by the Americans towards Western Hemisphere free trade. His initiatives were giant steps towards the eventual barrier-free flow of world commerce.

The wilful campaign of untruths unleashed against Prime Minister Mulroney and his government on the subject of free trade with the United States must go down in Canadian political history as one of the most terrible orchestrated assaults carried out in Canadian public life. The emotional and blatantly protectionist opposition by the New Democratic party and many of its supporters in the labour movement showed the political party of the left to be desperately trying to hang on to a socialist trade program that had no place in the final decades of the twentieth century. The trade policy they advocated had been discredited and cast aside almost everywhere else in the world. The leader of the Liberal party, John Turner, and most of his followers knew better but were determined to pursue for selfish political gain a vicious campaign against free trade. They threw around a red herring about the threat of free trade to Canada's social programs, old age pensions, Medicare, and the like. The passage of only a few years has shown their predictions of Canada's ruin because of free trade to be utter nonsense. Indeed, the Liberal party, when it assumed power in 1993, fully adopted and implemented the trade policies of the Mulroney government regarding free trade that they had so vigorously opposed when in opposition.

The Americans were not the instigators or the leaders in the move towards Canada-United States free trade. The Canadians were the initial "pushers and pullers." However, for the United States, with the deal with its northern neighbour and largest trading partner under its belt, it was almost natural to visualise the inclusion of their southern neighbour, Mexico. Here, the United States certainly took the lead, and Canada had little alternative but to follow. From Mexico to the inclusion of others in Latin America was to be only one more step, albeit a giant step, for the United States to take.

The General Agreement on Tariffs and Trade (GATT) had never set worldwide free trade as an objective. The preamble to GATT puts its purpose as being directed to achieving the "substantial reduction of tariffs and other barriers to trade and to the elimination of discriminatory treatment in international commerce." Complete free trade was thought of by GATT as something to be accomplished in a customs union (such as the original European Economic Community) or in a free trade area (such as the Canada-United States agreement). The GATT made provision for such limited free trade but did not envisage free trade universally. Europe, the Western Hemisphere, and the Asian countries all seem determined to have a freeing of trade in their respective areas. Surely forward-looking trade policy people will be able to visualise the day when the three major regions will move to tackle the remaining trade barriers between them.

The Canada-United States Free Trade Agreement was not a radical departure from what had gone before. Historians will almost certainly look back on this agreement and say it was inevitable. In Canada's case, it was an inevitable consequence of the trade policy that was followed for much of the twentieth century with a very high degree of success.

Canada had entered into a number of bilateral agreements with the Americans, the most notable of which was the Auto Pact. Since the Second World War, Canada pursued most of its trade objectives through the multilateral trading framework of GATT, in which the United States was the major player. Through successive rounds of negotiations in GATT, Canada aimed to, and succeeded in, gradually lowering tariffs and other barriers to its trade, particularly with the United States. As a result of negotiations between 1950 and 1975 for example, the volume of world trade expanded five times and the world economy doubled in size. Canada was a major beneficiary of these developments but realised that much remained to be done, especially in improving and securing access to its most important export market, the United States. The Canada-United States Free Trade Agreement would remove for Canada those remaining tariffs and barriers that survived the many GATT rounds of negotiations.

The membership of the Canadian Exporters Association was very supportive of efforts to free up the major United States market that took some three-quarters of Canada's exports. The polls we conducted, not surprisingly showed support of well over ninety percent. The only opposition came from exporters who had higher costs imposed upon them by Canada's trade-restrictive system of marketing boards. If a company was canning chicken, there would be no way of competing with American canned chicken if the Canadian processor was forced to purchase chicken at the high noncompetitive prices set by the Canadian marketing board.

The CEA was a member of a coalition of business organisations supporting the move to free trade. I found myself having to deliver several speeches each week supporting free trade and explaining the importance of exports for Canada's economic well-being. I also joined Canadian business leaders in regular meetings with American executives who were equally supportive of free trade. Free trade with Canada didn't have the high profile in the United States that it had in Canada. While our concern in Canada was to counter the strong opposition to the proposition from the opposition parties in government and much of organised labour, the American businessmen's problem was to stimulate interest and support among the United States public and American legislators. Trade with Canada was not very high on the public or legislative agenda in the early months of the debate. We held these Canada-United States meetings under the umbrella of the Canadian and United States Chambers of Commerce.

Important as the United States market was for Canadian exports, in the Canadian Exporters Association we could not neglect our markets overseas; a majority of CEA members relied heavily on markets offshore. The forty or fifty consulting engineering firms, in their export activity, depended almost exclusively on trade with countries overseas, as did the large number of exporters of machinery and equipment for resource-based and infrastructure projects.

The Free Trade Agreement, dealing as it did with improving and securing access to the United States, answered the needs of most exporters to that market. There was little need for political or diplomatic support for individual firms doing business in the United States, where language and ways of doing business were comparable to the situation at home. The same was not true for our exporters dealing with China, Taiwan, India, or Egypt. Most of the demands on the association, as on the government, by individual companies, were for help in markets where international financing was required or sales to government owned or controlled entities were involved or where normal Canadian political and diplomatic relations did not exist.

Chapter Forty-one
Bumps on the Trade Trail

One should not be surprised by the current and threatened strife in the trade field between the West and countries like China and those of the former Soviet Union. Much has to be done before these nations can be fully integrated into the world trading system. Western countries, in spite of being like-minded allies with comparable market economies, took years of working together before they were successful in establishing mutually acceptable trading relationships. These "friends" had almost all confronted each other many times in fierce trade battles during the last half century.

The confrontations within and between these nations on issues of trade have torn apart governments. In Western Europe where countries joined to bring about a common market and economic union, governments have risen and fallen, and their peoples have become terribly divided over the issues. This European turmoil was extended to overseas developing countries that had been their former colonies. Many of the close economic relationships that had existed between former colonisers and colonised were ended. More developed countries such as Australia and New Zealand, which had been traditional suppliers of agricultural products to Britain, saw their trade virtually come to an end. Canadians were torn by the debates over free trade with the United States. The wrath of Americans could be whipped up at any time over talk of Japanese restrictive treatment of American products.

The most serious postwar action against freer trade was taken by the United States Congress. Immediately after the Second World War, when the Allied victors were setting up the international institutions to manage the affairs of the postwar world, Congress turned thumbs down on the establishment of the International Trade Organisation. The reaction of the Western trading world was, fortunately, not to crawl away in defeat, but to create the "temporary" General Agreement on Tariffs and Trade (GATT). Congress almost destroyed at birth the early attempts of the postwar democracies to nudge the world towards a multilateral nondiscriminatory trading system.

If the relatively like-minded Western countries had such a difficult time coordinating their trade policies, we should not expect to see the accommodation of countries such as China and those of the former Soviet Union without considerable turmoil. The problems still being experienced in opening the "non-Western" Japanese market to world competition indicate the troubles that lie ahead when China and other non-Western countries are brought into the world trading club. It will be a long time before we will be able to access these markets as we do the markets of the United States and Western Europe.

In spite of some fifty years of international cooperation in the trade field and a generally recognised positive impact on virtually every citizen in the West from the liberalisation of world trade, there remain strong feelings and active opposition to any action to remove remaining impediments to the freer flow of trade. One wonders about the reasons for the almost general opposition to more open markets.

My experience while heading the Canadian Exporters Association was that the well-reasoned appeal of many hundreds of competitive companies for freeing up markets was often drowned by the clamour of a relatively few noncompetitive firms and their unions for continued protection. The closure of one plant overshadowed the increased export activity of a hundred others. The protectionist groups usually disguised their demands for continued protection as righteous cries for the safeguarding of jobs against lower paid workers elsewhere. If the protectionist line of argument was generally accepted, the Germans could insist that since their wages were half as high again as North American rates, they should have protection from lower paid American and Canadian producers.

Lobbies that claim to be "protecting our way of life" can have much greater public appeal and, consequently, political support, than those that support freer trade with their imprecise and distant promises of improved exports and eventual economic betterment. It is interesting to recall that one of the strongest pressure groups in the United States a century ago was the "buggy whip" lobby. This group was intent on stemming the movement from horse-drawn carriages to the "horseless" carriage. The general acceptance of the automobile would spell the doom of the buggy whip.

In spite of the well publicised and widely supported protests against new trade initiatives, governments, in the end, generally support most trade-expansion efforts. This is often because they are pulled along by their trading partners, particularly in negotiations within the multilateral system. They do not want to be seen as obstructionist in agreements supported by other friendly countries. Prime Minister Jean Chretien and his Liberal government, for example, reversed their positions on a number of trade agreements once elected. Gone were the Liberal threats to tear up the Canada-United States Free Trade Agreement. They quickly fell into line on that agreement, on the North American Free Trade Agreement, and on all elements of the Uruguay round of GATT. They knew that not to do so would have had Canada branded as the pariah of North America and the world trading community.

The protection of the worker against low-cost imports has generally been the rationale used by protectionists in the United States, Canada, Australia, and Western Europe, where living standards are high and unemployment bothersome. In other countries, differing political and cultural conditions are more likely to be used as the reason to stem the flow of competitive imports. The "politically different" argument has diminished since the demise of the Soviet Union and the shaking off of Communism by the countries of Eastern Europe. The swing towards the free market economy by most developing countries, many of whom were, to varying degrees, disciples of Marx and Lenin, meant that the "politically different" argument had less and less meaning. This swing, like all swings, will be back and forth many times before the world rids itself of the economic mess created over the past seventy years by communism and extreme socialism in former Communist countries and in the developing world.

In Asian countries and, to some extent in Canada and France, protectionism can hide behind the alleged need to safeguard cultural purity (which can be translated, "to keep out American influence"). France has repeatedly expressed concern about the adverse impact of American films on the country's culture. Canada has likewise expressed alarm about American magazines and television, but more out of concern for a possible American tidal wave swamping the relatively small Canadian cultural industry rather than to maintain Canadian cultural purity. Most Canadians accept that since they live alongside the American giant, little can be done to offset American cultural influence without imposing upon ourselves unacceptable restrictions that would smack of censorship.

In Asian countries, the restriction of trade for "cultural" reasons is best illustrated by Japanese policies, practices, and attitudes. We will see a lot of similar problems arise in our relationships with other countries of Asia as trade with this area expands. Every few years over the past several decades, amidst great fanfare and promises, Japan has announced "far reaching" trade liberalisation measures to address the problems that Japan's "valued" customers complain about. Each of these announcements claimed that the latest opening of doors was the most significant and comprehensive ever. Japan claimed to be an integral part of the world community, on which it depended more than most for its exports. Yet, it practised a system of "government administrative guidance" in the trade field that ensured that outside products and influences were kept to an absolute minimum. This produced an attitude, still evident in older managers, that it is a sin against the nation to import. If even half of the claims of liberalisation regularly announced by Japan were what they were said to be in form and effect, Japan would be the most open market in the industrialised world. The opposite is more the case.

In spite of more than thirty-five years of pleading, threats, and pressures on Japan by her trading partners to open her market to those who had opened their own markets for Japanese goods, Japan remains a most difficult market to penetrate. Japan, the world's second largest economy in recent years, flies in the face of the almost universally held view that in business and trade, you heed your best customers. Japan has amassed from her overseas customers previously unheard of trade surpluses of hundreds of billions of dollars annually.

It was not surprising that Japan's trading partners, having been flooded with Japanese goods, asked if Japan's policies and business culture denied them a fair chance in the Japanese market. I have asked this question of the Japanese numerous times. Their immediate response is a simplistic one; if a Canadian or other offshore company is competitive, then they should be able to do business in Japan. I have met with many competitive Canadian companies that have been very successful in competing with Japanese firms in third markets and at home but have been unable to do so in Japan.

Japan is certainly more open than it used to be. It would be surprising if thirty-five years of preaching to the Japanese by one hundred nations in GATT did not have some impact. The Japanese now claim that they have done everything possible to assist imports. They point to their import tariff on manufactured goods that has been slashed to levels comparable to the lowest in other industrialised countries. They can even point to a policy of subsidies to aid imports; Japanese companies that increase their imports of

327

an array of manufactured goods can earn a tax credit. Yet, although the official position favours imports and formal barriers are largely gone, there remains a host of impediments.

Foreign companies have found that, for example, in the high technology field, where they have through great effort found a niche in the Japanese market, their competitive advantage can disappear overnight. In the midst of their success, the Japanese bureaucracy is well capable of deciding that the newly successful foreigner requires a license. By the time the license is granted, the offshore firm could discover that a Japanese competitor has taken over the market.

Foreign companies have complained that many of the procedures they are required to go through in Japan are nontransparent. They are not open or based on criteria known to all that are affected. In this situation, Japanese companies that have a good relationship with the all-powerful Japanese bureaucracy can cause the delay of the entry of competitors into the market.

Japan must hold a record for having one of the most protectionist policies on earth in the case of its leather industry. It virtually shuts out non-Japanese leather from its market. It claims this is necessary to safeguard the jobs of *burakumin,* Japans' feudal outcasts, somewhat comparable to India's untouchables. These people traditionally work in the so-called dirty trades as butchers, grave-diggers, and tanners. A close look at the statistics shows that the need for this almost absolute protection is questionable. Of over one million burakumin, only some two thousand work in tanneries. Surely a wealthy country like Japan could, through social programs, attend to the interests of these people rather than impose a restriction on international trade in their name. In any event, one wonders why, in the late twentieth century, a sophisticated, wealthy, industrialised country should tolerate such feudal thinking towards a segment of its own people.

A serious impediment for foreign companies has been Japanese business and social culture. The main impediment in the business culture is referred to as *keiretsu.* This is a business relationship between Japanese companies under which they agree to buy and sell to one another. The companies do not necessarily have formal ties. The relationship can be very difficult to break, since it is considered by the companies concerned to be an obligation. These long-standing business relationships tend to be exclusive. Keiretsu often excludes new members, particularly foreigners. A better product at a lower price may not break the keiretsu. According to one foreign business representative in Japan, company links through keiretsu, bidding cartels, and the old-boy network still present formidable obstacles that the Japanese do not generally face in foreign markets.

The business culture that faces foreigners is difficult but not insurmountable. A more disturbing impediment to good relations, trade or otherwise, between Japan and the rest of the world is Japan's preoccupation with race. Japan possibly has the most ethnically homogeneous population of the leading countries of the world. As a people they are remarkably uniform in physical appearance. The Japanese population is also culturally homogeneous, and they take great pride in what they consider to be their distinctiveness and their differences from other people. They had had little experience with foreigners until the "barbarian" Western traders forced themselves on the country in the mid–nineteenth century. On first contact, they found the Caucasians strange and revolting with their big noses, curious colouring, blue eyes, and red or blonde hair. The Caucasians were distressingly smelly because of their heavy woollen clothing, and their diet was rich in animal fat. The Japanese attitude toward the black race is far worse. Having had almost no contacts with them until American soldiers were stationed in Japan after the Second World War, they tend to view them with wonderment and revulsion.

The Japanese have had great success through their cultural and racial "purity" in achieving a general allegiance to common national economic and trade goals. Some observers would say that they have developed a tacit national collusion against foreigners and their imports. Certainly, there is much truth in the Japanese saying, "The nail standing up gets hammered down." Conformity to social norms and standards is relentlessly enforced in the family, school, and workplace. Shame and banishment from the group are the penalties for nonconforming behaviour. The result is a society that is highly exclusive, with feelings of racial superiority.

These feelings are often demonstrated by national policies that reflect outright racial prejudice, demonstrated in particular by the measures imposed against Japan's own resident Korean community. Japan has legally treated its two-thirds of a million ethnic Korean population as second-class citizens. Most of them were born in Japan of families that have been there for many generations. Many speak only Japanese. They have faced terrible discrimination in employment. Only recently have moves been taken to have them relieved of the requirement to undergo fingerprinting and to carry identification papers.

Even more discriminated against by the Japanese are the Asian migrant workers from Pakistan and Bangladesh. The Japanese press in the early 1990s disclosed that an internal police training manual singled out Pakistanis for contempt, characterising them as "smelly people with skin diseases." Police officers were warned that it was "absolutely necessary to wash your hands after dealing with Pakistani subjects." The press noted that seventy-eight Pakistanis were arrested in 1988, compared with over sixteen hundred Chinese, yet there was no mention in the police training manual about the Chinese.

One of Canada's ambassadors to Japan told me that the Japanese, with their emphasis on hierarchy within their own society, tend to think of other countries and peoples in a hierarchical order. They rate the races of the world from top to bottom by placing themselves on top, the Chinese next, then the Caucasians, followed by other Asians, depending on the darkness of their skin, and with the black races at the bottom of their list.

He advised me that the offspring of postwar unions between black American servicemen and Japanese women left the Japanese with a problem they couldn't cope with. Orphanages founded for such children could only hold out the hope that they might in time find a life for themselves in the New World. The Brazilian government agreed to admit many of them as immigrants, and some left the country of their birth to settle in Brazil, where racial attitudes are the extreme opposite of the Japanese.

Racists attitudes are not confined only to the man-in-the-street. Ten years ago, Prime Minister Nakasone remarked that the level of intelligence in the United States had been undermined by the presence of blacks, Mexicans, and Puerto Ricans.

The Japanese have no monopoly on racism. The peoples of other Asian countries hold views that are not dissimilar. Indeed, although Japanese, Koreans, and Chinese are racially very similar, most would view marriage with one another with almost as much distaste as marriage with a Caucasian. I have had a distinguished Korean ambassador to Canada tell me that he could not visualise a son or daughter of his marrying a Caucasian. Chinese Trade Minister Pai Hsiang-Kuo told me the same thing on seeing Chinese and Caucasian couples walking hand-in-hand in Vancouver.

Yet all mention of racism throughout the Western world seems to be about white against black or white against brown. The Western media, legislatures, church groups, and academics have focused almost exclusively on the problems of white racism in southern Africa or in the southern United States and most recently on white racism in Western countries against their

330

minority nonwhite citizens. Little is ever said about Japan or other Asian countries, probably because in these countries a white or black minority is virtually an impossibility. It is all but impossible to envisage a white or black Japanese or Chinese as we would a Japanese or Chinese Canadian, American, or Brazilian.

In 1977, the UN, in New York, issued two postage stamps dedicated to the fight against racial discrimination. These stamps consist of a scribbling of the words, "Combat Racism." I am sure that any man or woman in the street or, indeed, any ambassador to the UN, if asked to explain the reasons behind the issuance of the stamps, would point to the terrible racism that existed at the time in South Africa. This was white against black, or so-called coloured. The more enlightened or more daring might have even pointed to the discrimination that existed in some of the countries of Africa against East Indians or whites. Few would point to the terrible attitudes and practices regarding race throughout Asia. On the same date of the issuing of the "Combat Racism" stamps in New York, the UN issued two "Combatons le racisme" stamps at their European headquarters in Geneva. The Geneva issues depicted the colours of the world's five main races spun into one firm rope. In general, Geneva issues tend to be exact copies of the New York stamps except for language. Why these European UN stamps differed is unknown to me. They did make it clear that racism was not restricted to black and white. I often wonder how my former colleagues in the Japanese and other Asian missions to the UN in Geneva would have viewed this appeal against racial discrimination, which reached its zenith in their countries.

An Asian country that presented a very different trade problem was Taiwan. It was discriminated against by China and, at China's insistence, by much of the world. On the other hand, Taiwan itself blatantly discriminated in its trade policy in favour of the United States. Taiwan was excluded from GATT membership as long as China insisted that it was part of China. Being outside the trade club, Taiwan showed little inclination to abide by world trade law or practices.

In Taiwan, Canadian trade efforts were continually frustrated. We had no diplomatic relations, and for years we had attempted to have the Canadian government open some sort of office in Taipei. Because of the "one China" policy insisted upon by Beijing, the Canadian government would not contemplate any form of relationship. There was always the concern that the large traditional grain trade with China might be endangered should Canada act against China's wishes.

It was eventually agreed that the private sector would put a man in Taiwan. Working with the Canadian chamber of commerce, we selected Bob Kelly, a former Canadian trade commissioner. The chamber formed a Canada-Taiwan group of businessmen dedicated to expanding two-way trade, and I was asked to serve on this group. I travelled to Taipei with representatives of the chamber of commerce and a number of Canadian businessmen for the first meetings.

Taiwan offered excellent prospects for Canadian exports. It had a fast-growing economy and a rapidly rising standard of living. Its currency and foreign reserve holdings were very strong. The major impediment for Canadian exports was the discrimination practised in favour of the United States, which would be their shield and sword if the Chinese were to carry out their threats of aggression. The Taiwanese ensured that the Americans got more than their fair share of their market.

It was difficult for Canada to raise this discrimination issue at high levels in Taiwan when, politically, "Canada's eggs were all in the Chinese basket." The CEA and the chamber could and did. I travelled to Washington several times on behalf of Canadian groups to meet with the unofficial Taiwanese "ambassador" to the United States. He was reluctant at first to meet with me. My old friend from GATT Geneva days, Constant Shih, was of great help in arranging the meetings.

The Taiwanese representative was outspoken in his annoyance with Canada's political stand but warmed when I told him that the CEA and the chamber of commerce were attempting to do something about it. I maintained that it would contribute to a normal relationship if Taiwan would follow the internationally accepted practice of nondiscrimination in its dealings with countries like Canada. He was well aware of how well Taiwan was doing in the Canadian market; he seemed to accept that it was difficult for us to oppose Canadian restrictive action against Taiwanese exports to Canada while Taiwan continued to discriminate against Canadian goods. It took months of such preaching to make any dent in Taiwan's discriminatory trade policy.

In Taipei I was disturbed to see that little heed was paid to international rules on patents and copyright. The stores were full of pirated medical and other professional books being sold for a fraction of their price in the West. Tourists had an enjoyable time buying cheap fake watches that in appearance and name were perfect copies of the best Swiss brands. Everybody knew that behind the "Swiss" exterior there was a "Mickey Mouse" interior.

It was another matter when the Taiwanese marketed automotive brake linings that were counterfeited to give the impression that they were genuine products of the North American automotive industry. They were generally inferior products, far below the safety standards imposed in North America. There was one report of a Taiwanese shipment of bagged fertiliser to a North African country, each bag marked as having been produced by one of the largest and most respected chemical companies in North America. The bags contained nothing but poor quality soil. Concerns about such counterfeit trade developing in pharmaceutical and medical products put the problem high on the international agenda. It remains an issue in a number of Asian countries.

A major exception to the swing towards the free market in the developing countries has been India, which more than most countries is a product of its past. It shuns Western capitalism as the means of extricating itself from the miserable economic bog it has been wallowing in since its independence. It is a widely held view that India still harbours a fear of the East India Company that so dominated economic life in India in the early British colonial period. Indian politicians seem to equate capitalism and the free market economy with their collective hazy recollections of India's plight long ago under the East India Company. It is also a view, perhaps a rather unfair one, that India's politicians and intellectuals prefer ideological purity and poverty rather than progress aided by capitalism. Only in the last short while has India shifted from its inept approach to economic policy, one that to most observers made less sense than the worst of Communist central planning.

I had visited India on several occasions for bilateral economic discussions and, on one occasion, was involved in meetings with Prime Minister Indira Gandhi. One could not help contrasting India's attitudes and economic approach at these meetings with that of India's neighbours in Southeast Asia. India had chained itself to a close rupee-ruble economic relationship with the Soviet Union while its Southeast Asian neighbours jumped with both feet into the world economy and achieved phenomenal growth and economic progress. One need only point to the sorry plight of the ruble and the Soviet Union that backed it to conclude that India "picked the wrong horse" in its choice of foreign economic policy.

Chapter Forty-two
The Old Order Changes

The truth of the words about the old order changing and giving place to the new has been thrown at us almost daily over the last few years. For good or bad, and sometimes for both, there has been more change in the world in the past ten or twenty years, and certainly since the Second World War, than during the preceding several centuries.

The great technological changes of recent years have affected almost every aspect of our daily lives. We only have to consider the changes in such diverse activities as our cooking, banking, transportation, communications, and office work. Like these great technological changes, we can anticipate a political world and a world economy in the next twenty or thirty years that will be radically different from ours today; in a few years, it will be as different from ours as ours is from Adam Smith's world of 1776. Smith, in the midst of all the thunder of the American Revolution, was the man who shifted the focus in economic affairs from the nation to the world.

The end of the Second World War saw the beginning of the end for the great empires of Britain, France, the Netherlands, and Portugal. These empires had embraced almost all the developing world outside of Latin America that had earlier declared independence from Spain and Portugal. Indeed only a handful of countries, notably Thailand, had escaped the embrace of the European colonial powers. The ending of colonial power resulted in an explosion in the number of independent nation states. More recently came the demise of the Soviet "empire" and the entry of an additional assortment of nation states onto the world scene.

At the time of the ending of the Western colonial empires, there was the emergence of the world's great international institutions. The United Nations, the International Monetary Fund, the World Bank, the GATT, and the host of regional and subject-specific bodies like the World Health Organisation made their entry onto the world stage.

Along with the great changes to the maps of the world, there are a number of major developments that together are nudging us towards a very different world. The rise of Islamic fundamentalism changed Iran radically and is threatening to do the same in such countries as Algeria, Egypt, Sudan, and Pakistan, and in other countries in North Africa and the Middle East. Also threatened are a number of countries where fundamentalism is for the present held brutally in check, but where the passing of the current "strongmen" could open the way for more radical change. One thinks in this regard of countries like Saudi Arabia, Libya, and Syria. The future of Saudi Arabia is of particular concern, since it is the world's largest producer of oil and is considered to be a firm friend of the West.

The great movement of peoples from the disturbed, depressed, or poorer parts of the globe to the richer urban areas and to the developed countries is another reality that is radically changing the world. Chinese immigration into Vancouver from Hong Kong, or Mexican and Cuban movements into the United States is altering the demographic makeup of what were areas populated predominately by people of European extraction. In Western Europe, there are over ten million recent legal immigrants from Africa and Asia, and one can only guess about the number of illegal newcomers. Official estimates put smuggled aliens into Western Europe from all sources including Eastern Europe at three hundred thousand annually. These flows, together with other moves such as the waves of Africans into the Republic of South Africa, make this period one with possibly the greatest movement of racially diverse peoples in history. We regularly hear predictions that, with skyrocketing immigration from the developing to the developed world and with the great differences in birth rates between the newly arrived and the already well established, that non-Europeans will be in a majority in great parts of Europe and North America in the very close future.

Predicting the future is of course most difficult. History is full of warnings against trying to do so. A hundred years ago in London, futurists warned that unless something was done about the explosion of the use of horse-drawn carriages, London would be several feet deep in horse manure in a matter of decades. To judge the impact of developments in the present decade on the probable global situation twenty or thirty years hence could cause similar ridiculous predictions. Perhaps it would be safer to take a more philosophical approach about the future, as did Chinese Premier Chou En-lai. When asked about the significance of the French Revolution, Chou En-lai was said to have responded, "It is too early to tell!"

Certainly international trade will play a crucial role in the shaping of the future. Freer trade is essential for an effective global economy. A rebound of protectionism would spell trouble for any thoughts of a global economy. The degree to which trade will play a role depends on whether the forces of consolidation between nations or the forces of fragmentation within nations win out. Over one hundred new nations have been born in recent years, and they are still being created. These have been mainly in the developing world and in the former Soviet Union.

At the same time, we have seen most of the Western democracies giving up important elements of their economic sovereignty through the negotiations in GATT or through the formation of regional groupings to bind themselves more closely economically to their neighbours. It is a great contrast to consider the breaking up of the former Soviet Union into numerous nation states and, at the same time, having the dismantling of the nation state in Western Europe. The evolution of a single market in Western Europe certainly has been a long and agonising process, but we must recognise the recent elimination of frontier controls between many partners of the European Union as being one of the most significant developments of our times in international relationships.

While the countries of Western Europe move to consolidate, Europe's former colonies, particularly in Africa, continue to fragment into more and more nation states. Eritrea is the latest product of this process. Many others would quickly follow if it were not for the continued respect in Africa for the often arbitrary and generally meaningless old colonial boundaries that the new countries inherited on gaining independence. These boundaries rarely make sense, cutting across tribal and linguistic lines as they do. The question is whether Africa will continue to fragment into smaller tribal homelands within these boundaries or modify them by forming, through regional integration, larger political unions or economic communities.

The World Bank has been favouring funding by region rather than by country for many of their projects in Africa, thus encouraging trends towards regional integration. There is also the tendency of foreign investors to favour larger markets that should have an impact on integration trends in Africa. African politicians must keep in mind the competition they face from other developing countries and the former communist world for investment. We will have to wait and see whether the forces of consolidation in Africa, which are based for the most part on economic reason, can win out against the strong forces of fragmentation. Fragmentation has its base in the emotional desire of people with a comparatively narrow and limited outlook on the world to have local autonomy. Many people in many areas of the African continent would be content to continue to tie their futures to those who share their immediate geographic location.

It has been generally accepted during the past twenty years or so that the Pacific Rim is the coming centre of the world insofar as trade and economic activities are concerned. The epicentre of international commercial life is certainly shifting from the Atlantic to the Pacific. With the populations around the Pacific increasing in number and income, it is tempting to jump to the conclusion that the twenty-first century belongs to that part of the world. Besides population and income, measures such as productivity and education are cited as accelerators that will propel the countries of East Asia to the forefront of nations. On our side of the world, there are many pessimists who warn that our Western countries are in a tailspin, and the Pacific is where the real economic action will take place.

It is true that growth rates have been slower in the Western world and that there are many causes for serious concern. It could be, however, that our pessimists are far too pessimistic. I wouldn't be too fast to write off the Western capacity to set things right. It is true that in recent years the countries of the Asian Pacific Rim have started to pull themselves out of the general poverty that permeated most of their area until the last few decades. They had nowhere to go but up. One thing is certain: the Pacific Rim could not have prospered had the Western nations not maintained fairly open markets for East Asia as they did for the rest of the world. The Western countries served as the engines of growth for the East, while the Western countries themselves were generally shut out of Eastern markets for balance-of-payments reasons or for reasons of straight protectionism. It was GATT and the other institutions launched by the Allies after the Second World War that set the stage for the tremendous positive explosion of the economies of the Pacific Rim, particularly the economies of Japan, of the countries of Southeast Asia, and of China and Taiwan. They could not have done it without Western markets.

The fact does remain that the Pacific Rim countries have produced economic wonders. The Japanese do build an automobile with one third of the labour required in North America. Yet, Japan itself is being squeezed by other countries in Asia that can produce "Japanese" cars even more economically. It is a brand new world. Unless we are determined to keep in front, we will have to watch from behind. As the saying goes, "Unless you are the lead sled dog, the view will always be the same."

The challenge for the West is to reassume the role as innovators and economic leaders. In order for Western nations to do so, they have to rid themselves of the many albatrosses they carry around their collective necks, which block them from achieving their full international potential.

One albatross is the widespread feeling that, "The government owes us a living!" Western nations have fallen away from the "work ethic," a phrase on everyone's lips until the advent of the welfare state. This is not to advocate the destruction of the many wonderful social programs that have contributed to a quality of life very different from, and superior to, that enjoyed by most of the countries of the Pacific Rim. We must, however, not allow our welfare systems to be applied and abused in a way that strangles our ability to remain competitive in the new world economy that is rushing towards us at breakneck speed. The good news is that almost all of our Western governments, of every political stripe, have awakened to the fact that welfare can be and is being abused. Even Sweden, which for years served as the welfare model internationally, has retreated. They have been forced to do so because of the exodus of capital and firms stifled in their competitiveness by Sweden's high taxes that were imposed and maintained to support the comprehensive welfare system. If Sweden had to act, Canada and other countries with their extremely costly social safety nets have also to change their ways.

There is another albatross that is rarely talked about, but which saps the energy of countries of the Western world or does not allow them to achieve their full potential. We pride ourselves in the West for having built countries where every person counts and has an opportunity to excel. We could not contemplate having a class of "untouchables," such as they have in India, or a class of burakumin to do the "dirty" chores, as they do in modern Japan. Yet we continue to tolerate in the West, particularly in parts of Western Europe, a class system where heredity rather than ability dictates one's station in life. The best people are not automatically permitted to rise to the top. While this is diminishing, it is still very widespread and all too generally accepted. Canada's system of an appointed rather than an elected senate is a continuation in the New World of this archaic and undemocratic practice of the old. The trade unions, particularly in the English-speaking Commonwealth countries, tend to perpetuate the feeling of class distinction with their clamour for the interests of the "working man," which implies

338

that management and those in the professions don't work. In the United States, it is almost impossible to sit through a news report or a presidential speech without hearing the words "middle-class America," which is an admission that America is far from a classless society.

In the United States where the Constitution makes much of "equality," there indeed exists a strong "class attitude." This was most apparent amongst some of the American Founding Fathers. President Jefferson, who was so much ahead of his time in his contributions to the drafting of the American Constitution, was determined to exclude the slaves from his great declarations of equality. To be fair to the man, he was a "good" slavekeeper (if there can be such a person) and was determined that all who belonged to him would be treated well, as if they were "children." Indeed, he maintained the view (which was probably one of the best of the times) that most born into slavery were in a sense like children: they would be completely at a loss if they were to be freed into the white society of the day.

Partially as a consequence of slavery, there is in the United States a very large "underclass" that exists on the outside of the mainstream of society and makes little contribution to America's economic betterment. This underclass is a minor contributor to the positioning of America in the modern world, and has a tremendous negative impact on America's ability to create wealth. The costs to society of the crime that permeates this large group, and the weight of welfare payments borne by the American taxpayer in the largely failed attempts to change things, is staggering. These comments about the United States are not meant to let Canada, Australia, or others off the hook. These and many other countries have their own underclass, albeit, in the case of Canada and Australia, a smaller group that includes many native peoples who have not been fully accommodated in normal economic activity. The United States, however, with its proportionally much larger underclass, has tremendous problems. Foremost is how to integrate the very large black population, which makes up a large part of the underclass, into the main channels of American life. Many blacks, despite the odds, have "made it." Most have not. This is particularly so in the South and in urban centres in the North.

Since my retirement I have been able to observe a little of this American problem first-hand. For some six years, I have spent two mornings a week during the winter months assisting in a small way in the education of the prison population in my adopted winter retreat of Vero

Beach, Florida. Florida has a very positive program, under which an inmate who graduates from the equivalent of high school while in prison can get several months off his sentence. The inmates of "my" prison who are first offenders are about eighty to ninety percent black. One can speculate about the reasons why there are more young black men in prison than there are enrolled for higher education. The reasons are many, ranging from the breakdown of family life to lack of opportunity for these ghettoised people and the widespread drug and gun culture. The fact remains that most blacks, whether on the inside or outside of prison, are largely condemned to remain outside the mainstream of American society. In a sense, because of this, they are more comparable socially to India's untouchables or Japan's burakumins than they are to the majority of white Americans.

In my years in Florida, I have yet to find more than the occasional black in any of the mainline churches or living in the suburbs or communities that accommodate the local white population and the temporary winter visitors from the North. They have their own churches and communities, for they know that for the most part they would not be welcomed in white society. Unofficial segregation is still the general practice. The only real integration, in Florida at least, seems to be in the armed forces, the schools, sports, entertainment, and the prisons.

The United States military has made a major contribution in helping to rid the country of its underclass. The elimination of discrimination in the military made the services available as a profession for blacks and for training in a host of trades. The United States must in this sort of way harness the wealth of untapped black talent in its peacetime pursuit of an expanded economy.

I strongly believe that the only way to overcome the "underclass" problem in the United States is through education. The many blacks who have "made it," particularly the multimillionaires in the sports and entertainment world, should be somehow persuaded to contribute time in the schools throughout the United States; they should work to persuade black (and other) children to accept the absolute necessity of a good education. Most of the successful black professional athletes in America were, after all, propelled into their careers through university scholarships, coaching, and training paid largely out of public funds. The recipients should be expected to pay a little back by serving as positive role models for those who have not had the opportunity to extract themselves from the ghettos.

There are many other albatrosses that are a burden to Western countries in maintaining a leading position in the world. One is the debt situation in most of our countries. We continue to be deprived of the use of a large part of tax revenue because of its use for the mandatory high interest payments on the debt. This requirement means an inability to reduce taxes and consequently there is a negative impact on our international competitiveness. This debt burden also has a great direct influence on our interest rates and borrowing capacities and on the value of our currencies. I need but mention the fall in the dollar's value in terms of the Japanese yen or the Swiss franc.

In spite of all of our problems in the Western world and all the claimed positives that are contributing to the upsurge of the countries of the Pacific Rim, there remain many questions about the ability of the Asian region to outpace the West. The political stability of much of Asia is a question that largely hinges on China and will not be answered until we can assess the future of that giant of the region. What happens in China in the next decade could affect the rest of the region and indeed the entire world for much of the next century.

China, the generally predicted "comer" of the twenty-first century, is plagued with many serious problems. These problems have tended to be downplayed in the wake of the enthusiasm of the Western world and Japan for China's more open attitude, particularly towards outside investors. The positive international publicity about the impressive growth rate, which has remained around ten percent since the middle of the 1980s, has also tended to mask a host of difficulties.

Among the major problems with which China is saddled is the future of its state industries. These leftovers from the Maoist years are most inefficient and drain off much of the life that has been pumped into China by the new private sector. They are kept afloat by China's troubled banks that extend credit that no truly commercial enterprise would ever consider. The state industries are in direct contrast to the new private sector plants that have blossomed since China began placing emphasis on foreign trade and investment.

One of the offshoots of the rise of the new entrepreneurial sector in China, which is for the most part located in the coastal provinces, has been the development of terrible regional inequalities. This can be observed when you travel from the new skyscraper cities on the coast to the inland rural areas, where living conditions have hardly changed from the pre-Revolutionary days of the Western missionaries. Peggy and I, during a visit in 1992,

341

travelled from Beijing to what used to be Inner Mongolia. We were shocked by the facilities at roadside stops. We were accustomed to substandard "loos" all over the world, but those in the Chinese countryside defied description. Regional inequalities are bound to have a tremendous unsettling effect as the deprived rural population seeks to improve itself and obtain more and more of the "better" life that they now know about in the great urban centres.

Another problem facing China is how to deal with its seriously entrenched inflation and volatile exchange rate. There is little confidence amongst the business community in the currency. Peggy and I witnessed huge truckloads of Chinese consumer goods being baled and trucked to chartered flights for shipment to Russia, where they were to be bartered for Russian raw materials. Bartered they had to be, for the entrepreneurs involved would not use either the Chinese or Russian currencies as means of exchange.

China also faces a bankrupt banking system, and its legal system is in a very sorry state. It is essential, if China is to assume the leading role it envisages for itself as an international trader, that it completely overhaul its entire ineffective legal system.

Even if China were to overcome all of these many difficulties, it will still be faced with is greatest problem of how to reconcile an undemocratic and all-powerful Communist party and government with a quickly emerging liberal market-oriented economy. The Communist party, which is corrupt and above the law, still has fairly wide support. This is understandable, given that after a decade or so of radical change and uncertainty, people worry about the alternatives to the current system. The only alternatives are felt to be a military takeover or chaos, and few would relish the thought of either.

Elsewhere in Asia, the hands to be played in the early decades of the next century have, for the most part, yet to be dealt. Taiwan's situation vis-à-vis China is still uncertain and still to be decided. For Taiwan, a lot depends on what happens in Hong Kong when it is enveloped by China in 1997.

The Philippines is still far from making its triumphal entry into the international trading world; it will be preoccupied for some time with its militant Muslim minority and with the many problems of a developing nation with which the Philippines seem to be particularly burdened.

Malaysia has economically taken off like a rocket but not without damaging relations with the West, particularly Britain. It remains to be seen how awakening Muslim awareness amongst its population will evolve and whether economic reason and good relations with Malaysia's large Chinese minority and the rest of the world will be allowed to prevail.

Singapore, for all of its publicity and noise about representing the "new way," is but a city-state and will always remain so. The only other Asian countries that can make a sizeable impact in the early twenty-first century are Indonesia, India, and Pakistan.

Indonesia, in spite of its great natural wealth, huge population and ambition to become the dominant power in Southeast Asia, has many problems, most of which are of its own making. Thousands of islands of diverse peoples stretch across thousands of kilometres of ocean. Indonesia's heartland, Java, will be engrossed for decades in trying to knit together this vast country. There appears to be little threat that Muslim fundamentalism will pose a real problem for Indonesia's economic advance. The majority Muslim population has lived in relative harmony with Indonesia's religious minorities. Much will depend on who assumes power once the restraining hand of President Suharto and his circle moves from the scene.

India and Pakistan have for years been flagged as rising stars. Both have fallen far short of expectations and have yet to emerge from the doldrums from which they set to extract themselves on their independence. It seems that one of the main things that both countries have in common is a hatred for one another and an inability to set their economic houses in order. Glaring at each other and figuring out the future of their unhappy relationships with each other and the rest of the world should occupy both for years to come. Both countries have tremendous potential and someday could become major powers in the region and the world. Given the internal problems that plague them, they cannot be considered contenders to ride the tides that will sweep much of Asia forward in the next few decades.

With all their warts and spots, it seems very likely that the Western nations will lead the world into the twenty-first century. The qualities that led to the development by the West of the world's great institutions are still there. Indeed, it would be difficult to envisage the countries of Asia, Africa, or elsewhere outside the Western world taking the leadership now, which the West took five decades ago, to establish the United Nations, the GATT, the World Health Organisation, the World Meteorological Organisation, and the host of other institutions that have done so much to push the world towards saner international policies. The West continues its thrust for economic integration, as evidenced by the major steps being taken in Western Europe towards a united Europe and in the Western Hemisphere towards hemisphere-wide free trade. In spite of the calls within Asia for moves to emulate the West with economic integration of their own, it is difficult to envisage meaningful steps being taken for many years. The economies, cultures, religions, and aspirations of China, Japan, Indonesia, the Philippines, India, and Pakistan are so varied. Any common regional moves forward will require long and difficult negotiations if more than a facade of economic integration is to be achieved.

All of these areas of the world remain a long way from the hills and bays of Newfoundland. They are certainly "farther than ever the puffin flew." Yet what happens in these areas will affect Newfoundland and every other corner of the world. It will be a major task in the twenty-first century for the world community to develop common outlooks and views about this shrinking world of ours. If the West and East and the North and South are truly to meet and together resolve the world's problems, it looks like it is going to have to be for the time being through Western leadership and Western-inspired institutions. It can only be hoped that the Western nations will be able to get their own houses in order to make them equal to the task.

Index

345

Mao Tse-tung, 131, 133–135, 140, 141, 156
Maraj, Rama, 205
Marcos (Pres. Phillipines), 222, 223
Marcos, Imelda, 223
Marshall Plan, 70
Masada (Israel), 278, 279
Matamores (Mexico), 25
Matheson, J. R., 224
Maugham, Somerset, 219, 220
Melbourne (Australia), 42, 55, 258, 272, 289
Mennonites, 260, 261
Mercer, John, 3
Mexico, 25, 27, 30, 321
Miami, 259, 260
Ming Tombs (China), 153
Montana-Crans (Switzerland), 119
Moore, Jim, 305
Morgan, Fred and Edna, 3, 60
Montevideo (Uruguay), 198
Morris, David, 177, 179
Moscow, 137, 247–250, 252
Mount Allison University (New Brunswick), 22, 205
Mugabe, Pres. (Zimbabwe), 266, 315
Mulroney, Brian (PM), 213, 320, 321

N

Nadi (Fiji), 162, 163
Nakasone (PM), 330
Naples, 59, 99
Nauru, 44, 48, 49
Newcastle (Australia), 282
Newfoundland Regiment, 14
Newfoundland, S.S., 32
Newfoundland Squadron, RAF, 14, 33
New Hampshire, 62
New South Wales, 2, 52, 54, 282, 290
Nhulunbuy (Australia), 295
Nickson, Rex, 68
Nippers Harbour (Newfoundland), 18, 19
Noble, Robert, 310–313, 316
Nodwell, Jack, 214
Norfolk Island, 44, 48, 49

Norman (Minister, Zimbabwe), 265
Northern Arm (Newfoundland), 11, 13
Northern Territory (Australia), 48, 294, 296, 297
North Sydney (Nova Scotia), 14, 21
Noumea (New Caledonia), 284
Nova Scotia, S.S., 32
Nuevo Laredo, Mexico, 29

O

Oakville (Ontario), 303
Oceania, RMS, 57–59
Ohio, 27, 29, 30
Olgas (Australia), 298
Oliver, Craig, 160
Omsk (Siberia), 250, 251
OOPS, 225, 226, 228, 234
Oronsay, RMS, 99
Orsova, RMS, 99, 100
Osbaldestein, Gordon, 225
O'Sullivan, Sean, 293

P

Pai Hsiang-kuo, 132, 149, 150
Palais des Nations (Geneva), 73–75, 114, 116, 120, 197
Panmunjom, (Korea), 271
Papua New Guinea, 44, 48–51, 294
Paquette, Roger, 259
Paraguay, 259, 260
Parrot, Tom, 260
Pattee, Sam, 201
PCO-PMO, 106–109, 112, 113, 269, 270, 273
Pearson, Mike (PM), 105, 107, 108, 111, 112, 128, 224, 268
Pearson's Peak (Newfoundland), 111, 112
Peking Univ. (Chiang Hua), 133, 135, 139
Pelletier, Marc, 236, 237
Pepin, Hon. Jean Luc, 110, 124, 129, 130, 133–142, 144, 149, 150, 172, 210
Perrault, Ray (MP), 130
Perron, Art, 221, 293, 300
Perth (Australia), 41, 42, 58
Peterborough (Ontario), 303